CRIMINAL LITIGATION

CRIMINAL LITIGATION

Editor & Co-author
Maura Butler

OXFORD
UNIVERSITY PRESS

OXFORD
UNIVERSITY PRESS

Great Clarendon Street, Oxford ox2 6DP

Oxford University Press is a department of the University of Oxford.
It furthers the University's objective of excellence in research, scholarship,
and education by publishing worldwide in

Oxford New York

Auckland Cape Town Dar es Salaam Hong Kong Karachi
Kuala Lumpur Madrid Melbourne Mexico City Nairobi
New Delhi Shanghai Taipei Toronto

With offices in

Argentina Austria Brazil Chile Czech Republic France Greece
Guatemala Hungary Italy Japan Poland Portugal Singapore
South Korea Switzerland Thailand Turkey Ukraine Vietnam

Oxford is a registered trade mark of Oxford University Press
in the UK and in certain other countries

Published in the United States
by Oxford University Press Inc., New York

Library of Congress Cataloging in Publication Data

Data available

Typeset by RefineCatch Limited, Bungay, Suffolk
Printed in Great Britain
on acid-free paper by
Ashford Colour Press, Gosport, Hampshire

ISBN 1–84–174178–7   978–1–84–174178–9

1 3 5 7 9 10 8 6 4 2

Disclaimer

While every care has been taken in the production of this book,
no legal responsibility or liability is accepted, warranted or implied by the
authors, editors publishers or the Law Society in respect of any
errors, omissions or mis-statements.

OUTLINE CONTENTS

OUTLINE CONTENTS

DETAILED CONTENTS

DETAILED CONTENTS

DETAILED CONTENTS

DETAILED CONTENTS

PREFACE

The aim of this book is to set out the main procedural areas of relevance to trainee solicitors. The academic credentials possessed by each trainee in Criminal Law principles are presumed, as a prerequisite Law Society of Ireland entrance examination qualification. As with all Law Society training at the Professional Practice Course level, the emphasis in this text is on the practical application of the law in a real world context.

The objective of this book is to emulate the real time sequential manner of the journey of an accused person from the initial investigation of crime to the determination of that case, up to and including any judicial reviews or appeals. The generic nature of the chapter contents includes both a prosecution and a defence perspective. It is thematically subdivided into five sections thereby creating a demarcation between generic practice considerations, the law of evidence, preliminary procedures, trial formats and venues and apposite areas of specialised practice.

It is hoped that the material produced herein will demystify the practicalities of representing a case in the criminal courts at all levels, as a prosecutor or defence advocate, and thereby assist the trainee in comprehending this specialised area. Furthermore the basic procedural steps outlined are now transferable to other areas of practice and must therefore be integrated as part of the expertise of those lawyers whose clients may have breached defined areas of Competition Law, Company Law, Environmental Law, and Computer Misuse offences to name some of the many areas of Corporate Crime.

Every effort has been made to ensure that the text is accurate, but the editor would be grateful to learn of any errors or omissions. Any such comments or queries should be sent to the editor at the Law Society. No decision or course of action should be taken on the basis of this text and competent professional legal advice should be sought before any decision or course of action is taken.

The editor has addressed the coincidence of the signing of the Criminal Justice Act 2006 (CJA '06) on July 16th and the final edits of this text, by making minor amendments to the following: Chapters 1, 4, 5, 6, 7, 8, 9, 10, 11, 12, 13, 14, 15 & 17. The reader should refer himself/herself to the OUP Online Resource Centre at *www.oxfordtextbooks.co.uk/orc/lsim/*, which supports this text, for a resume of the many changes included in this extensive piece of legislation and its commencement orders. The Online Resource Centre will be updated on an ongoing basis.

The editor tenders grateful thanks to the 13 co-authors and the OUP team who collaborated with the editor in the production of many drafts of this text, as the law constantly changed. In its final format it has benefited from the practical reflection on the teaching and learning needs of the trainees and tutors of the Law Society's Criminal Litigation training programme.

PREFACE

On a personal level, Declan, Shane & Daniel are thanked for their moral support.

Maura Butler, Editor
October 2006

AUTHORS

Editor and co-author

Maura Butler BA (Legal Science) LLB, Dip EL, Dip. Criminological Studies, MSc IT Education qualified as a solicitor in 1985 and practiced as a criminal defence advocate. She is the Course Manager for Criminal Litigation, Criminal Advocacy and Corporate Crime in the Law Society of Ireland.

Authors

Eamonn Barnes BA, BL is a former Director of Prosecutions for Ireland.

Caroline Butler BA qualified as a solicitor in Solicitor in 1996. She is a sole practitioner who is a defence advocate.

Francis H. Cassidy qualified as a solicitor in 1990 and his career has been with the Chief State Solicitor's office. He has recently been appointed as Legal Advisor to the Criminal Assets Bureau (CAB).

Barry Donoghue is the Deputy Director of Public Prosecutions for Ireland. He qualified as a solicitor in 1979 and his career has been with the Chief State Solicitor's Office and The Office of Public Prosecutions.

Prof. Caroline Fennell B.C.L., LL.M., B.L., Ph.D is Dean of the Faculty of Business and Law and Head of Department of Law in University College Cork (UCC). Her publications include Law of Evidence in Ireland, 2nd ed. (Lexis Nexis, 2003); Labour Law in Ireland with I. Lynch (Gill and Macmillan, 1993); Crime and Crisis in Ireland; Justice by Illusion (Cork University Press, 1993). Further publications are listed at http://www.ucc.ie/en/lawsite/staff/cfennell.

David Keane BA (Mod), LL.M having worked as a defence solicitor advocate, qualified as a barrister in 1998.

Monika Leech BCL, Dip E.L. having worked as a prosecution solicitor advocate, qualified as a barrister in 1999.

Moirin Moynihan B.Ed qualified as a solicitor in 1993. She is an associate of Garrett Sheehan & Co Solicitors.

AUTHORS

Liam J. Mulholland BCL qualified as a solicitor in 1991 and his career has been and continues to be with the Chief State Solicitor's Office as a prosecution advocate.

Attracta O'Regan BA LLB qualified as a barrister in 1995. She is a Course Leader in The Law Society of Ireland and the Author of Insurance Law in Ireland (Round Hall Sweet & Maxwell, 1999).

Dara Robinson LLB qualified as a solicitor in 1992. He is a defence advocate and a partner with Garrett Sheehan & Co Solicitors. He is one of the authors in the Law Society of Ireland Human Rights Law Manual in this OUP series.

Andrea Ryan BA BCL LLM is a Junior Lecturer in Law at the University of Limerick. Her publications list can be found at http://www.law.ul.ie/web/Andrea.Ryan/.

David Wheelahan BA (Hons), LL.B., LL.M. worked as a defence solicitor advocate from 1992–2001 and then qualified as a barrister in 2001. He is a member of the Bar of Victoria, Australia.

TABLE OF CASES

TABLE OF CASES

TABLE OF CASES

TABLE OF STATUTES

TABLE OF STATUTES

TABLE OF STATUTES

PART I

INTRODUCTION TO CRIMINAL LITIGATION AND GENERAL PRACTICE CONSIDERATIONS

CHAPTER 1

INTRODUCTION

1.1   Origins

The Criminal Law has its origins in British Common Law, which replaced the Celtic Brehon Law system. Since the independence of our State was established, we have developed inherited legislation (eg the Larceny Act 1916 is now the Criminal Law (Theft & Fraud Offences) Act 2001) and created other pieces of legislation which have an identity which is distinct from such inheritance (eg the Non-Fatal Offences against the Person Act 1997).

The regular employment of subjective rather than objective tests distinguishes us from the English system (eg our law on self-defence) and aligns us more closely with the Australian or Canadian jurisprudence in criminal law. The fact that we have a written constitution often aligns us with the American counterpart. It has been mooted that the freedoms enshrined in our constitution are superior to those espoused in the European Convention on Human Rights. We have enshrined a constitutional referendum, which ensures that the death penalty will never again be implemented in this jurisdiction. As with other jurisprudence in Ireland, the constitution of 1937 takes precedence over all other instruments of the criminal justice system, which includes the few remaining common law crimes, and primary and secondary legislation.

There is a constant stream of new legislation emanating from our legislators. Certain trends have emerged and tend to be popular or otherwise, depending on what side of our adversarial system of criminal justice one happens to find oneself. The Bail Act of 1997, for example, was introduced as a result of a referendum, which overturned the liberal decision based on constitutional precepts in *A.G. v O'Callaghan* 1966 IR 301. Certain limitations on the right of the accused to remain silent in the course of a detention have been limited by the Criminal Justice Act 1984 and offences against the State legislation. It is to be noted however, as discussed in **Chapter 6**, that the European Court of Justice may not favour the trend of some of our legislation, which seems to impinge on the accused's right against self-incrimination.

1.2   Vibrant jurisprudence

Criminal law in this jurisdiction as applied through our courts is an ever-changing and vibrant jurisprudence. The Criminal Law Act 1999, which was implemented in October 2001, introduced major changes in the procedures applicable to the disposal of indictable crimes. Most recently the Criminal Justice Act 2006, comprising 196 sections, illustrates the vibrancy described. As with all developing jurisprudence, those pieces of legislation which have been recently introduced have yet to be tested in our courts and already some of them (eg the introduction of the intoximeter offences in the context of driving a mechanically propelled vehicle whilst under the influence of an intoxicant) are constantly subject to the judicial review process.

1.2.1 CORPORATE CRIME

We have not had a tradition of pursuing what criminologists refer to as 'white collar crime' in this jurisdiction. However, the implementation of the Company Law Enforcement Act 2001 heralds a new era in this direction. The initial stimulus for this development was the McCracken tribunal report of 1997, which created a focus and a desire for change in the area of corporate malpractice. The 280 separate criminal offences which existed in the Companies Acts had rarely been subject to a state prosecution. Enforcement had largely been left in private hands, assisted by the High Court in a supervisory capacity. The DIRT inquiry propelled a movement for the prosecution of corporate crime.

The Company Law Enforcement Act 2001 established the Office of the Director of Corporate Enforcement (ODCE). The Director's role is the encouragement of compliance with company law and the investigation and enforcement of breaches of the Companies Acts.

The options opened to the Director are threefold:

(a) an invitation to the defaulter to pay an administrative fine in lieu of facing summary prosecution;

(b) summary prosecution;

(c) referral to the DPP in anticipation of trial on indictment.

Members of An Garda Síochána are assigned to the office of the Director. These Gardai are possessed of all of their pre-existing powers to facilitate the gathering of evidence and the taking of statements. Furthermore, as the penalty applicable to many offences under the Company Law Enforcement Act is for five years on indictment, the procedures under s 4 of the Criminal Justice Act 1984 will apply, as discussed in **Chapter 6**. The consequences for company law and criminal law practitioners are very far-reaching indeed.

1.2.2 THE INTERNATIONAL CRIMINAL COURT

The International Criminal Court is based in the Netherlands, at The Hague. The stated purpose of the International Criminal Court Bill of 2003 is to give effect to the provisions of the Statute of the International Criminal Court concluded at Rome on 17 July 1998, signed by Ireland on 7 October 1998 and ratified on 11 April 2002. It provides for the punishment by courts in the State and by courts-martial of genocide, crimes against humanity, war crimes and other offences within the jurisdiction of the International Criminal Court, which was established

to enable effect to be given to requests by that Court for assistance in the investigation or prosecution of those offences, including requests to arrest and surrender persons, to freeze assets and to enforce any fines or forfeitures imposed by it; to make provision in relation to any sittings of the Court that may be held in the State; and to provide for related matters.

1.2.3 EUROPEAN UNION POLICY

The Justice & Security brief of the EU, the Third Pillar of Maastricht, concerns itself, amongst other matters, with the following: Immigration, Transatlantic Relations, Transport Security, Anti-Terrorism Policy, Organized Crime, Biometrics and Travel, Economic Migration, Border Control and The Hague Programme 2005–2010 (where the Commission has put forward proposals to allow information on potential criminals to be made available across state borders).

The consequences for this jurisdiction of consequent EU directives will result in the implementing of enabling legislation in this jurisdiction as has occurred with money laundering. The Council of Europe adopted the third money laundering directive on 20 September 2005. Its stated aim is to include terrorist financing within the money laundering provisions.

Information on current trends in policy matters at this level may be viewed at <http://europa.eu.int/comm/justice_home/index_en.htm>. This website displays data on the following:

(a) asylum;

(b) immigration;

(c) organized crime;

(d) drug smuggling and addiction;

(e) judicial cooperation between national courts, both in civil and criminal matters;

(f) cooperation between national customs and police forces;

(g) fundamental rights;

(h) citizenship in the European Union;

(i) cooperation with third countries and international organizations;

(j) the justice and home affairs '*acquis*' in the enlargement process; and

(k) the external dimension of justice and home affairs.

Matters emanating from Europe which more frequently impinge currently on the Irish criminal lawyer include extradition, the European Arrest Warrant, and the European Convention on Human Rights (**Chapter 2**).

1.2.4 EXTRADITION

Where a person is detained in one jurisdiction and, subject to the fulfilment of certain qualifications and procedures, is delivered to another jurisdiction, in custody, he is referred to as extradited.

1.2.4.1 Legislation

The legislation in Ireland which governs extradition includes: the Extradition Act 1965, the Extradition (European Convention on the Suppression of Terrorism) Act 1987, the Extradition (Amendment) Act 1987, the Extradition (Amendment) Act 1994, the Extradition (European Union Convention) Act 2001, and the European Arrest Warrant Act 2003.

1.2.4.2 General qualifications

There are a number of matters which require compliance in advance of extradition, generally. They include the principle of reciprocity, wherein it is presumed that the jurisdiction requesting the extradition is acting in a bone fide manner and that, as a result, the suspect will be charged for the offence for which he is sought. The offence must be one which is punishable by imprisonment for at least 12 months. For extradition to be applicable under the Extradition Act 1965, the suspect must be required in the requesting state to answer charges relative to conduct which would constitute a criminal offence in Ireland, and the requesting state must discharge the requisite burden of proof necessary to establish that fact. This procedure establishes the dual criminality test, as discussed in *Trimbole v Governor of Mountjoy Prison* [1985] ILRM 449. It is also a requirement that the suspect must be prosecuted only for the offence for which he was extradited.

An offence regarded as extraditable must not be a political offence, an exclusively military offence or a revenue offence. The leading authority on what constitutes a political offence is *Finucane v McMahon* [1990] ILRM 505, and the constituents of what comprises a revenue offence were discussed in *Byrne v Conroy* [1998] 2 ILRM 113.

1.2.4.3 Implementation of treaties and legislation

Reciprocal arrangements exist between Ireland and the other countries through various multilateral and unilateral treaties, whereby a suspect can be extradited from one jurisdiction for prosecution in the other. Such treaties can be given force of law through the application of Part II of the Extradition Act 1965. Part III of the Extradition Act 1965 deals with procedures specific to the United Kingdom and the Channel Islands. Applicable offences must follow the dual criminality test and must be offences which are punishable summarily with a six-month sentence or are indictable offences. Offences of a political, military and revenue nature are excluded from UK extradition requests to this jurisdiction.

The European Union Conventions on Extradition of 1995 and 1996 endeavour to simplify extradition procedures between Member States of the European Community. A suspect may now consent to surrender and be processed through simpler transfer and authentication procedures. Through the Extradition (European Conventions) Act 2001 these conventions have been implemented in Ireland. Consequent upon such implementation, it has become necessary to interpret pre-existing Irish law in this area through the medium of the 2001 Act where the requesting state is a designated EU state.

1.2.4.4 The European Arrest Warrant

The Tampere European Council in 1999 expresses its objective towards the establishment of free movement of judicial decisions in criminal matters under principles of freedom, security, and justice, by approving the abolition of formal extradition procedures with regard to convicted persons, sentenced persons and the expedition of procedures applicable to those suspected of having committed an offence. The ensuing Council Framework Decision of 13 June 2002 manifested in this jurisdiction as the European Arrest Warrant Act 2003. The European Arrest Warrant is defined in s 2(1) as:

> *A warrant order or decision of a judicial authority of a Member State, issued under such laws as give effect to the Framework Decision in that Member State for the arrest and surrender by the State to that Member State of a person in respect of an offence committed or alleged to have been committed by him or her under the law of that Member State.*

The dual criminality principle manifests as s 5 of the European Arrest Warrant Act. There is an obligation, outlined in s 10 of this Act, to arrest and surrender a suspect where a judicial authority in the requesting state issues a European Arrest Warrant. This warrant is transmitted through the Minister for Justice, Equality and Law Reform, to the High Court for endorsement for execution. The format of the European Arrest Warrant is annexed to the Act.

1.3 The Law Society Criminal Litigation Course

1.3.1 PRESUMPTIONS

All trainee solicitors undertaking the Law Society of Ireland Professional Practice Course Part 1 (PPC1) will have successfully passed the Final Examination Part 1 (FE1) in Criminal

Law. It is consequently assumed that a high level of academic expertise has been achieved, with regard to the concepts which determine the mens rea of crime, the actus reus, concepts of strict liability, levels of participation and in the myriad of crime which exists, and the defences and exemptions applicable thereto.

1.3.2 FOCUS

The focus of the PPC 1 Criminal Litigation Course is to equip the trainee solicitor with the procedural knowledge and skills to ensure best practice in the task of ongoing prosecution and defence of criminal allegations.

Insofar as this basic criminal procedure text allows, all new legislation which affects the methodology of the prosecution and defence of crime has been referred to. It is impossible to give adequate exposure to all procedures and all new legislation in a criminal litigation text which is aimed at the recent undergraduate embarking on a solicitor-training course. It is, however, prudent to draw attention to some legislation which has extended the range of the criminal lawyer's practice.

1.4 Layout of Criminal Litigation Course Manual

The text as outlined in the following chapters is subdivided into five categories as follows:

Part I: Introduction to the Course and General Criminal Justice Considerations.
Part II: Law of Evidence in Criminal Courts.
Part III   Preliminary Procedures in the Prosecution of Crime.
Part IV: Selected Mode of Trial and Procedure in Trial Courts.
Part V: Specialized Procedures.

1.4.1 INTRODUCTION TO THE COURSE AND GENERAL CRIMINAL JUSTICE CONSIDERATIONS

Part I first conceptualizes the Law Society of Ireland Professional Practice Course within the current criminal justice system and then examines matters, outside of the rules of criminal procedure, which impinge on the ability of a solicitor to competently represent the client's interest in either a summary or indictable criminal court environment. The impact of human rights law, whilst a discrete area in its own right, as outlined in **Chapter 2**, has the potential to enormously influence the practice of criminal litigation. It behoves all who practise in this area to become accomplished in the applicable human rights principles. The practice of a criminal lawyer, in common with any other practitioner, requires practice management skills, as outlined in **Chapter 3**.

1.4.2 LAW OF EVIDENCE IN CRIMINAL COURTS

As an examination in the Law of Evidence is not one of the pre-requisites of the Law Society of Ireland Entrance Examination (the FE1), **Chapter 4** focuses on the fundamental principles of evidence in a Criminal Litigation context. It is crucial that any potential criminal advocate is fully conversant with the rules of the Law of Evidence, which determines issues such as the admissibility of evidence, burden of proof in criminal proceedings, competence and compatibility of witnesses, corroboration, opinion evidence and illegally obtained evidence, which are some of the topics explored in **Part II**.

This knowledge will be applied during Criminal Advocacy training, which will be presented as an independent module during the Criminal Litigation course.

1.4.3 PRELIMINARY PROCEDURES IN THE PROSECUTION OF CRIME

In **Part III** the reader will become familiarized with the powers available to the state through the Gardai, to investigate crime, together with the applicable rights and obligations which attach themselves to the state and the accused and the preliminary issues for an accused after the arrest, detention and charging process is complete. Such issues include the commencement of proceedings procedures, rights to bail and state subsidy of legal representation in the form of Free Legal Aid. Procedural rules facilitate the remand (adjournment) of cases and the commencement of proceedings, bringing the reader through the preliminary steps of the criminal justice procedure where decisions are made in relation to the method of disposal of the case.

1.4.4 SELECTION OF MODE OF TRIAL AND PROCEDURE

Having become familiarized with relevant human rights issues, practical practice considerations, the impact of the Law of Evidence, the application of evidential principles as an advocate, and preliminary procedural matters, **Part IV** then addresses the procedure applicable to the disposal of criminal cases. This disposal may be at either the District Court level (summary disposal) or 'on indictment' in the higher courts which include the Circuit Criminal Court, the Special Criminal Court and the Central Criminal Court.

Trainee solicitors will become familiar with the required procedural steps in a chronological fashion, tracing the procedure from the choice of venue selected by the Director of Public Prosecutions (the DPP) first to the disposal of crime at summary level in the District Court on either a plea of 'guilty' or 'not guilty', and secondly at indictable level, again on either a guilty plea or a not guilty plea.

Whilst the juvenile justice system shares a lot of the procedures similar to criminal procedure generally, nevertheless given its nature it warrants exclusive discussion in **Chapter 13**. Thereafter, matters which are applicable to all forms of disposal and at various stages of the criminal process are discussed in the chapters which deal with sentencing, appeal, and judicial review procedures.

1.4.5 SPECIALIZED PROCEDURE

Part V addresses road traffic offences, money laundering, and the Criminal Assets Bureau. Whilst in general the same criminal procedure applies to these areas, the strict liability nature of road traffic offences means that the proofs applicable are often very technical. It is an area of practice which has been widely litigated and is familiar to firms which may not otherwise specialize in criminal law. The EU money laundering directive has had far-reaching consequences in our jurisdiction which challenge principles of solicitor/client confidentiality. The use of civil proofs by the Criminal Assets Bureau (CAB) in confiscating assets in circumstances where no criminal conviction has occurred, as a pre-determinate of property being the proceeds of crime, has been the source of much debate.

1.4.6 APPENDICES

Part VI of the Course Manual is a compilation of some of the more widely used standard documentation in a criminal practice. It is available on the Trainee Intranet, *Moodle* database, to facilitate tutorial requirements which relate to the completion of some standard procedural documents. A diagram of the course design and criminal justice courts system is intended to visually assist the trainee solicitor's perception of the sequence of procedures and the court hierarchy.

1.5 Rules of professional conduct

1.5.1 INTRODUCTION

Rules which can be found in the Guide to Professional Conduct of Solicitors in Ireland, published by the Law Society of Ireland (The Law Society Guide) are designed to ensure the proper performance by lawyers of rules which are recognized as essential in all civilized societies.

Responsible ethical conduct by solicitors will assist public confidence in the administration of justice. This can be done through adherence to guidelines on the following issues:

(a) the protection of the client's interests;

(b) a consciousness of the need to redress a perceived imbalance of power between solicitor and client;

(c) the maintenance of high professional standards between colleagues;

(d) the administration of procedure in the courts when the solicitor is representing the client;

(e) the maintenance of an independent profession, free of coercion from any outside forces.

The Law Society Guide incorporates the International Bar Association's Code of Ethics Code of Conduct for Lawyers in the European Community adopted in Strasbourg in 1988 and a Code of Conduct by the Law Society Criminal Law Committee. The common thread in all of these regulations is a regard for general principles, which incorporate

(i) the independence of lawyers;

(ii) trust and personal integrity;

(iii) confidentiality;

(iv) respect for the rules of other Bars and Law Societies within the European Union.

1.5.2 SOME GUIDELINES FOR PROFESSIONAL CONDUCT FOR CRIMINAL LITIGATION PRACTIONERS

(a) A solicitor should not, either by him/herself or by anyone on his/her behalf, approach a person who might become a client with a view to representing that person.

(b) Before taking instructions from any person in any criminal case, a solicitor should satisfy him/herself that the person has not already engaged the services of another solicitor in that particular case or in related proceedings.

(c) In the event of disagreement between solicitors relating to the transfer of a solicitor's case from one solicitor to another in a criminal matter, the matter should be referred to the Guidance and Ethics Committee of the Law Society of Ireland for resolution.

(d) Where a solicitor requires, for consultation purposes, to visit a prisoner in custody in cells within the courthouse or in the immediate vicinity of a court, the solicitor should so inform the court and seek to have the accused's case put back to enable a consultation to take place.

(e) Where an accused is brought before a court on charges which may in normal circumstances be described as 'new charges', but such person has already retained a solicitor in related proceedings, no solicitor shall accept instructions from such person on those new charges unless he or she receives instructions in respect of all charges before the court and complies with the provision of paragraph (h) below, in discharging the retainer of the previously instructed solicitor.

(f) A solicitor may accept an instruction to act for a client in an appeal even if that solicitor did not act for the client in the original proceedings, except where another solicitor has previously been retained and is on record in respect of the appeal.

(g) A solicitor should not actively encourage or offer inducements to any person with a view to obtaining instructions from such a person.

(h) A solicitor shall not accept instructions to act for a client in a case where another solicitor has already been retained in that matter without ensuring that the other solicitor's retainer is discharged. This provision will not be applicable where a solicitor is assigned by a court to act for the accused on legal aid.

A solicitor who is in breach of any of the provisions of this part of the code of conduct will be liable to disciplinary proceedings for unprofessional conduct.

1.5.3 PRACTICAL APPLICATION OF ETHICAL PRINCIPLES

An idealist may like to presume that every solicitor and trainee solicitor will highly prize the translation of ethical philosophy into a practical set of rules based on the collective wisdom of practitioners over many years. It would be gratifying to believe that pride in oneself and the good name of the profession and common decency manifested through self-discipline would be the norm for every practitioner.

In the real world some pressures may manifest themselves which may impinge on such characteristics. There are increasing demands on our profession to provide a speedy and cost-effective service to the client. This may create the danger of compromise on some of the basic standards referred to above. Such compromise should be strenuously resisted.

1.5.4 CONSEQUENCES OF A RELAXATION OF STANDARDS

What every practitioner must remain conscious of is that, if the high standards expected are relaxed, then such ethical transgressions may have very serious consequences. A negative effect on the reputation of a practitioner will have an automatic knock-on effect on the public's ability to trust the administration of justice. Misconduct may result in being reported to the Law Society with the subsequent consequences of disciplinary action being taken, the ultimate sanction being that one is struck off the Roll, ie disbarred. Professional negligence claims result where a client has suffered loss as a direct result of the misconduct of a solicitor.

1.5.5 DISTINCTION BETWEEN MISCONDUCT AND NEGLIGENCE

There is sometimes a very thin line between misconduct and negligence. It is therefore important to understand the importance of concepts such as:

- integrity;
- confidentiality;
- conflict of interest;

- the need to maintain professional standards;
- the unique position of the solicitor as an Officer of the Court.

It is necessary to learn:

- how to relate to colleagues;
- how to interact with Counsel for the benefit of the client;
- how to relate to third parties in the course of transacting business for your clients.

1.5.6 DUTIES OF THE DEFENCE SOLICITOR

1.5.6.1 The defence solicitor

The defence solicitor has all the usual duties to act in the client's best interests but in addition has an overriding duty not to mislead the Court. Where a client admits guilt to a solicitor he/she may continue to act, even on a not guilty plea. A solicitor may permit the client to plead not guilty before the Court and thereafter may do everything possible during the prosecution case, eg cross-examine their witnesses as vigorously as possible provided this does not involve advancing any untruthful version of events. However, a solicitor may not permit the client to go into the witness box or call perjured evidence. Accordingly, if a client does admit guilt to the solicitor, it is vital to point out that one can continue to act for him even if a 'not guilty' plea is entered, on the condition that no evidence will be called which supports what is known to be untrue.

It may be appropriate to approach the prosecution to see whether they are willing to reconsider the decision to prosecute. Under s 6 of the Prosecution of Offenders Act 1974, a solicitor is entitled to make representations to the Director of Public Prosecutions (DPP) on behalf of the client. The following factors may be relevant:

    (a)   triviality of the offence;

    (b)   staleness;

    (c)   youth or old age and infirmity of the offender.

For example, one may wish to persuade the DPP to deal with a young person by way of caution rather than a prosecution.

    (d)   mental illness and stress.

1.5.6.2 The prosecution solicitor

The duties of the prosecuting solicitor reflect those of the defence solicitor in so far as he/she is an officer of the Court and must therefore not mislead it. It is not the duty of a prosecutor to 'get a conviction at all costs'. The prosecutor must not conceal evidence from the defence or the Court and must present the evidence in best practice mode in pursuit of discharging the burden of proof, which is 'beyond all reasonable doubt'.

1.5.6.3 Post conviction

Once the burden has been discharged and the judge in summary cases or the jury in indictable cases is satisfied that no reasonable doubt as to the guilt of the accused exists, a conviction will then follow, at which point the defence will address the court to persuade the judge to mitigate the sentence. A decision with regards to the appropriateness or otherwise of lodging an appeal within defined time limits will be addressed by the defence in consultation with the client. It is also open in certain circumstances for the DPP to consider the appeal of certain sentences which he considers lenient.

CHAPTER 2

THE IMPACT OF HUMAN RIGHTS LAW ON CRIMINAL LITIGATION PRACTICE

2.1 Introduction

Human rights law in Ireland derives from a number of sources, chief among them being our Constitution, and the two great post Second World War political documents, the (United Nations) International Covenant on Civil and Political Rights ('the Covenant'), and the European Convention on Human Rights and Fundamental Freedoms ('the Convention').

Irish lawyers are assumed to be familiar with the Constitution. The Covenant is relatively little used in this jurisdiction. However, the Convention has been the subject of considerable interest in recent times, as a result of Ireland's proposed incorporation of the Convention arising from our international obligations under the Good Friday Agreement.

The European Convention on Human Rights Act 2003 will not be given full force of law in Ireland, but will enjoy a status somewhere between the Constitution and enacted legislation. However, the Convention will enjoy some direct applicability in the Irish Courts for the first time, although incorporation is less whole-hearted than, say, the United Kingdom's Human Rights Act 1998.

2.2 The Convention documents

The text of the Convention, consisting of over sixty Articles and an increasing number of Protocols, is widely available and therefore is not included in this manual. The essential texts, from the point of view of criminal litigation, are Articles 1–14 and Protocols 4 and 7, the latter of which is likely shortly to be ratified by Ireland.

2.3 Relationship between Convention and Irish criminal law

Direct 'incorporation' of the Convention, regardless of how it is done, will inevitably mean greater numbers of Convention points being argued in front of Irish Courts. However, the impact of the Convention has already been felt on a number of occasions in the past.

The most recent impact manifested in both *Heaney and McGuinness v Ireland* [21 December 2000] [ECHR] (unreported) and *Quinn v Ireland*, application 36887 [1997], which were determined against Ireland on an issue arising from the use of the Offences Against the

State Act 1939, s 52 (as amended). The European Court of Human Rights sitting in Strasbourg effectively outlawed the statutory offence of failing to give an account of one's movements pursuant to a demand made under s 52 of this Act.

In the context of criminal law, the previous most significant finding against Ireland was the case brought by Senator David Norris, a Strasbourg judgment which obliged Ireland to decriminalize most forms of consensual homosexual activity (*Norris v Ireland* judgment of 26 October 1998, Series A no 142).

As will be seen from the following discussion, Ireland's system of criminal litigation suffers from various weaknesses, which may well be the genesis of Convention-based challenges in the Irish jurisdiction or in Strasbourg over the coming years.

2.4 General principles of interpretation

2.4.1 INTRODUCTION

Both the Strasbourg jurisprudence and the common law acknowledge a guiding principle of human rights law interpretation, which is suitable to give to individuals the full measure of the fundamental rights and freedoms referred to. Courts have long acknowledged that human rights legislation has a 'special character' which calls for a 'broad and purposive approach to construction' (*R v Goodwin (No 1)* [1993] 2 NZL 153). Domestic courts which are signatories to the Convention, and which are considering questions which have arisen in relation to the asserted Convention Rights, are required to take into account decisions of the European Court and the (now abolished) European Commission.

2.4.2 MAINTENANCE OF IDEALS AND VALUES OF DEMOCRACY

Among the general principles previously established by the Court and Commission are those that the Convention 'is an instrument designed to maintain and promote the ideals and values of a democratic society'. Critical features of such a society are 'pluralism, tolerance and broad mindedness' and 'respect for the rule of law' (see, for example, *Dudgeon v UK*, 1982 4 EHRR, 149).

2.4.3 FAIRNESS IN THE ADMINISTRATION OF JUSTICE

The Convention jurisprudence is constantly developing, and the Court is not bound by previous decisions. As a living instrument, which must be interpreted in the light of present day conditions, the Convention has evolved significantly, particularly as regards the principle of fairness in the administration of justice. In *Airey v Ireland* [1979] 2 EHRR 305, a case which effectively imposed a civil legal aid system on Ireland, it was said that the Convention 'is intended to guarantee not rights that are theoretical and illusory but rights that are practical and effective'. Many of the 'rights' conferred by the Convention also contain limitations (see, eg, Articles 8–11).

Any interference with rights must be justified by the State in the context of the permissible restrictions contained in each Article. The onus will be on the State to show that the restrictions were, first, appropriately prescribed by law, and secondly, necessary in a democratic society, and exceptions to the rights 'must be narrowly interpreted' (*Sunday Times v UK* [1979], 2 EHRR 245).

2.4.4   OTHER PRINCIPLES

In broad terms, the principle of proportionality, which the court considers in assessing the validity of any restriction on rights, involves balancing the demands of the community and the protection of the fundamental rights of individuals. Article 18 further prohibits States applying permissible restrictions to purposes outside those prescribed by the Convention. There is a 'margin of appreciation' allowed in terms of social and moral policy. This amounts to an acknowledgement that each State has or may have different standards that will inform how they deal with particular issues of a human rights nature.

2.5   Selected Articles of the Convention

2.5.1   ARTICLE 1

The 'High Contracting Parties' (ie the signatory States) shall secure to everyone within their jurisdiction the rights and freedoms defined in Section 1 of the Convention. This means that Convention rights are guaranteed to everyone, non-nationals and stateless persons included, and must be secured directly 'to anyone within the jurisdiction of the Contracting State', by the provision of an effective remedy. The fact that an applicant under the Convention, did not have leave to enter the jurisdiction of the relevant State, has been dismissed as an 'artificial and technical construction' (*D v UK* [1997] 24 EHRR 423).

2.5.2   ARTICLE 2—THE RIGHT TO LIFE

There is no derogation allowed from Article 2, seen as 'one of the most fundamental provisions in the Convention (which) . . . enshrines one of the basic values of the democratic societies making up the Council of Europe' (*McCann and Others v UK* (1996) 21 EHRR 97). Any deprivation of life by State agencies must be subject to the most careful scrutiny and must be fully and publicly investigated.

2.5.3   ARTICLE 3—PROHIBITION OF TORTURE

No derogation is allowed from Article 3 either, which prohibits covering torture and inhuman or degrading treatment or punishment. The court has adopted a low threshold test in respect of individuals who are assaulted in detention. It has stated, for example, that any recourse to physical force which has not been made strictly necessary by the applicant's own conduct diminishes his/her human dignity and is in principle a breach of Article 3 (*Ribitsch v Austria* [1996] 21 EHRR 573). That high standard set by the court has not always led to findings of violations against States. (See, for example, *Ireland v UK* (1978) 2 EHRR 25 on techniques used to interrogate Nationalist detainees in Northern Ireland which were held to constitute inhuman treatment but not sufficiently severe or cruel to amount to torture.)

Interestingly, Article 3 has been held to have application to potential mental suffering experienced by condemned prisoners awaiting execution in the USA, known as 'the death row phenomenon' (*Soering v UK* [1989] 11 EHRR 439). In practice, the *Soering* case has effectively brought an end to extraditions between Ireland and the USA for capital crimes allegedly committed in the USA, without an undertaking from the relevant US state or federal authority that the prisoner would not be made subject to the death penalty.

Torture is defined in s 1(1) Criminal Justice (United Nations Convention Against Torture) Act 2000, as amended by s 186 Criminal Justice Act 2006.

2.5.4 ARTICLE 5—RIGHT TO LIBERTY AND SECURITY

The aim of this most fundamental right to liberty and security, provided for in Article 5, is 'to ensure that no one should be dispossessed of his physical liberty in an arbitrary fashion' (*Engel v Netherlands (No. 1)* (1976) 1 EHRR 647). Those circumstances set out in Article 5 (1), paragraph (a)2(f) provide the only circumstances in which persons may lawfully be deprived of their liberty, and these provisions are to be given a narrow construction (*Winterp v Netherlands* (1979) 2 EHRR 387).

A recent Irish case, *Croke v Ireland*, 33267/96 ELHR, addressed the detention provisions of the Mental Treatment Act 1945 (as amended). This case was the subject of a negotiated 'friendly settlement' in Strasbourg and has resulted in a drastic change to the scheme for the involuntary detention of persons in Ireland who are allegedly mentally ill, and further underlines the contemporary significance of the Convention.

Article 5(1)(c) allows for the arrest or detention of suspected criminals and should cause little difficulty. The arrest or detention must be grounded on 'reasonable suspicion', meaning the existence of facts or information which would satisfy an objective observer that the person concerned may have committed the offence. The arrest is for the purpose of bringing the person before the 'competent legal authority' (the District Court in the case of Ireland).

Article 5(2) provides that everyone arrested must be told promptly the reasons for their detention in a language which they understand, and of any charge against them. This seemingly simple provision has of late taken on added significance in Ireland with the arrival of many non-nationals who neither speak nor adequately understand our English or Irish languages.

Article 5(3) obliges States to ensure that arrested persons are brought 'promptly' before a judge, who must be independent of both the executive and the parties, and who must have the power to order release. In this context, it may be noteworthy that judges of the District Court have no power to grant bail on charges of murder or in extradition proceedings, even in circumstances where there is, strictly, no objection to bail.

Article 5(3) entitles detained persons to trial within a reasonable time or to release pending trial, by way of bail. The permissible bail regime within the Convention is actually more restrictive than that permitted under the Irish Constitution. Acceptable objections to bail fall into four categories, of which the first two are the traditional *O'Callaghan* grounds—the risk that the accused will fail to appear at trial, or that they will interfere with the course of justice. The Convention jurisprudence also permits a denial of bail if there are good reasons to believe that the accused if released on bail would be likely to commit further offences—a ground added to *O'Callaghan* by the Bail Act 1997. The Convention further permits bail to be denied on the basis of 'the preservation of public order', where the nature of the crime alleged and the likely public reaction are such that the release of the accused may give rise to public disorder. However, this latter objection is heavily circumscribed by the case law, allowing for temporary detention nature only, and also being confined to offences of particular gravity (*Letellier v France* (1997) 14 EHRR 83).

Every detained person is entitled, under Article 5(4), to take proceedings by which a court will decide the lawfulness of his/her detention speedily and release ordered if his detention is not lawful. There is some overlap between this provision and Article 40 of the Irish Constitution. The hearing must be adversarial, involve legal representation, and enable the calling of witnesses. The burden of proving the legality of the detention falls on the State (*Hussain v UK* (1996) 22 EHRR 1).

2.5.5 ARTICLE 6—THE RIGHT TO A FAIR TRIAL

The entirety of Article 6 refers to the determination of criminal charges but Article 6(1) is also applicable to civil rights and obligations. Put simply, Article 6(1) entitles everyone to a fair and public hearing within a reasonable time by an independent and impartial tribunal established by law. The court has traditionally interpreted this Article broadly, on the grounds that it is of fundamental importance to the operation of democracy. Considering that the right to the fair administration of justice holds such a prominent place, the restrictive interpretation of Article 6(1) would not correspond to the aim and purpose of that provision (*Delcourt v Belgium* (1970) 1 EHRR 355). In considering whether any 'proceedings' are civil or criminal, the Convention takes an 'autonomous approach'. It will disregard any categorization of a matter by the State as civil if the nature of the alleged offence and the severity of any penalty imply that the matter should properly be regarded as criminal.

'Equality of arms' is the most important principle of Article 6 as developed by the case law. It postulates the idea that each party to a proceeding should have equal opportunity to present its side of the case and that neither should enjoy any substantial advantage over its opponent. Obviously, the right to legal representation in appropriate cases flows from this requirement. The Court has already held that it would be a breach of the principle where an expert witness appointed by the defence is not accorded the same facilities as one appointed by the prosecution (*Bonisch v Austria* (1987) 9 EHRR 191). Similar principles oblige prosecuting and investigating authorities to disclose any material in their possession which may assist the accused in exonerating themselves, or which may undermine the credibility of a prosecution witness (*Jespers v Belgium* [1981] 27 DR 61 E COMM HR).

2.6 Evidence and fair trial procedures

2.6.1 GENERALLY

Broadly speaking, the rules of evidence are a matter for each contracting State, although the Strasbourg Court will exceptionally examine whether the proceedings as a whole were fair, or assess the weight of the evidence before a State's court. Perhaps surprisingly, the Court has held that Article 6 does not necessarily require the exclusion of illegally obtained evidence. This contrasts with States which operate a strict 'exclusionary rule', which prima facie rule out evidence obtained in consequence of breaches of rights.

2.6.2 PREJUDICIAL PUBLICITY

Particularly if a case is to be tried by a jury, a 'virulent press campaign against the accused' (*X v Austria* 11 CD 31 [1963] is capable of violating the right to a fair trial. However, the court will take account of the fact that some press comment on a trial involving a matter of public interest is inevitable, and will also consider what steps the judge has taken to counter the effect of the prejudice in his charge to the jury.

2.6.3 REASONS FOR A DECISION

It is a basic requirement of a fair trial in both civil and criminal cases that Courts should give reasons for their judgments. Obviously this does not apply to jury trials. Where a submission to the Court in the course of a trial would, if accepted, be decisive of the outcome of the case, it must be specifically and expressly addressed in a ruling by the Court (*Hiro Bilani v Spain* (1995) 19 EHRR 566).

2.6.4   THE RIGHT TO A PUBLIC HEARING

The fundamental entitlement to a hearing in public is designed to protect litigants from 'the administration of justice in secret with no public scrutiny' (*Pretto v Italy* [1983] 6 EHRR 182 ECtHR) and to maintain public confidence in the courts and in the administration of justice. For these reasons, only in exceptional circumstances can the press be excluded.

2.6.5   THE ENTITLEMENT TO TRIAL WITHIN A REASONABLE TIME

Of particular interest in Ireland is the right to trial within a reasonable time. There are frequent complaints from litigants, the media and indeed many of the judges about the delays in getting cases on for trial, in the higher criminal courts in particular. The entitlement to trial within a reasonable time is intended to prevent a person charged from remaining 'too long in a state of uncertainty about his fate' (*Strogmuller v Austria* [1969] 155 ECtHR). The reasonable time guarantee runs from the time an individual is charged. What constitutes a 'reasonable time' is extremely flexible and there are no absolute time limits set by the Convention or its jurisprudence. A more rigorous standard theoretically applies when the defendant is in custody. The State is responsible for delays attributable either to the prosecution or the court, but understandable delays may arise from complex cases including numerous defendants or charges, or where unusually difficult legal issues arise.

2.6.6   THE PROTECTION AGAINST SELF-INCRIMINATION

This issue regarding protection against self-incrimination arose in the cases of *Quinn v Ireland* and *Heaney and McGuinness v Ireland* cases referred to above (see **2.3**). The right to a fair trial in the criminal case includes 'the right of anyone charged with a criminal offence . . . to remain silent and not to contribute to incriminating himself' (*Funke v France* [1993] 16 EHRR 297). The European Court of Human Rights found a violation of Article 6 in the case of *Saunders v UK* (1997) 23 EHRR 313 in which a senior company executive was compelled by one government authority to provide information about the business activities of the company, which incriminated himself, and the government then turned the information obtained over to prosecuting authorities to be used in criminal proceedings subsequently brought against him (*Saunders v UK* [1997] 23 EHRR 313). The European Court of Human Rights has generally considered that the rights to silence and not to incriminate oneself are universally recognized international standards lying at the heart of the idea of fair procedure. In the *Saunders* case, the Court held that the privilege against self-incrimination was 'closely linked' to the 'presumption of innocence'.

Different considerations have been held by the Court to apply to laws permitting the drawing of adverse inferences from the silence of suspects under interrogation who subsequently become accused at trial (*Murray v UK* (1996) 22 EHRR 29). This is likely to attain some significance in Irish criminal law and procedure with 'adverse inferences' provisions being included in major recent criminal statutes, including the Criminal Justice (Drug Trafficking) Act 1996, and the Offences Against the State (Amendment) Act 1998.

2.6.7   THE PRESUMPTION OF INNOCENCE

The presumption of innocence is another fundamental guarantee of Article 6. It applies only to persons who are charged, and has no application at the time of investigation into alleged offences. However, provided that the overall burden of proof of guilt remains on the prosecution, Article 6(2) does not prohibit rules which transfer aspects of the burden of proof to the accused, and presumptions of law or fact operating against the accused are permitted. However, such rules, either shifting the burden of proof or applying presumptions against the accused, must 'be confined within reasonable limits' (*Salabiaku v France* (1988) 13 EHRR 379).

2.6.8   SPECIFIC GUARANTEES TO ENSURE FAIRNESS IN CRIMINAL TRIALS

Specific guarantees to ensure fairness in criminal trials are of the utmost importance and are contained in Article 6(3) and Protocol 7. An accused person has a right to be informed of the charge against them. This principle is aimed at what the accused must be told at the time of charge, rather than the disclosure of evidence in the course of the preparation for the trial itself.

The accused must be given adequate time and facilities for the preparation of a defence. Obviously the adequacy of the time allowed will depend upon the complexity of the case. The European Court of Human Rights has seen it as fundamental that the defence lawyer must be appointed in sufficient time to allow the case to be prepared properly (*X and Y v Austria* [1978] 12 DR 160). The requirement to afford adequate facilities for the preparation of the defence case obliges the State to adopt such measures as will place the defence on an equal footing with the prosecution.

Article 6(3)(c) provides an accused with the right to represent himself or herself in person or, should they wish, through legal assistance of their own choosing. It also provides that an accused may have legal assistance provided free of charge, if the interests of justice require it and the accused does not have sufficient means to pay for a lawyer. This is part of the 'equality of arms' set of rights discussed briefly above (see **2.5.5**). States may, however, place 'reasonable restrictions' on the right of an accused to counsel of their choice, although as a general rule the accused's choice of lawyer should be respected (*Goddi v Italy* (1984) 6 EHRR 457). There must be good reason for excluding a lawyer from the court, such as a breach of professional ethics.

In order for the requirements of Article 6(3)(c) to be met, representation provided by the State must be effective. The State will not generally be responsible for the inadequacies of a legal aid lawyer, but the authorities may be required to intervene where 'the failure to provide effective representation is manifest' and it has been brought to their attention.

Denial of access to a solicitor during detention in a garda station may constitute a violation of Article 6, particularly if adverse inferences are to be subsequently drawn from a defendant's failure to answer questions in interview whilst in detention at the garda station. These requirements sit uneasily with the current state of the law in Ireland. The case of *Lavery v The Member in Charge, Carrickmacross Garda Station* [1999] 2 IR 390 expressly removed the entitlement of a solicitor to be present at the interviews.

Article 6(3)(c) has also been interpreted as requiring confidentiality of communications between detained persons and their lawyers, citing such confidentiality as 'one of the basic requirements of a fair trial in a democratic society' (*S v Switzerland* (1992) 14 EHRR 670).

2.6.9   THE RIGHT TO CONFRONT PROSECUTION WITNESSES

Controversy in this area has tended to revolve around questions of hearsay and anonymity of witnesses. Broadly, hearsay evidence is not admissible, but the European Court of Human Rights has allowed some flexibility in the admissibility of ordinarily prohibited hearsay evidence (see, eg, *Trivedi v UK* (1997) EHRLR 520). Similarly, the European Court of Human Rights has held that ordinarily, witnesses should not remain anonymous, as ignorance of their identity may deprive the defence of particulars which would enable them to demonstrate that the witness is prejudiced, hostile, or unreliable. However, in exceptional circumstances, arrangements to preserve the anonymity of a witness could in principle be justified if there was an identifiable threat to the life or physical safety of the witness. Although such evidence is admissible in restrictive circumstances, the evidence should still be treated with 'extreme care', and a conviction should not be based 'solely or to a decisive extent' on evidence given anonymously (*Doorsen v Netherlands* (1996) 22 EHRR 330).

2.6.10 THE RIGHT TO FREE INTERPRETATION

Article 6(3)(e) provides that the accused has the right to the free assistance of an interpreter if the accused cannot understand or speak the language used in court. This is part of the State's obligation to run its judicial system fairly. The right is unqualified. A charged or convicted person cannot therefore be ordered to pay the costs of an interpreter.

2.6.11 THE RIGHT TO REVIEW OF A CRIMINAL CONVICTION OR SENTENCE

The right to review of a criminal conviction or sentence is guaranteed by Article 2 of Protocol 7, subject only to exceptions in regard to offences of a minor character, as prescribed by law. These exceptions are cases in which the person concerned was:

(i)   tried in the first instance by the highest tribunal; or

(ii)   convicted following an appeal against an acquittal.

2.6.12 DOUBLE JEOPARDY

An obscure provision in Article 4(2) of Protocol 7 challenges the fundamental and seemingly immovably established principle of the common law, namely the prohibition on double jeopardy. Simply stated, a person once acquitted at trial of criminal offences can, historically, in the common law jurisdictions, never be retried. Article 4(2) permits an exception to that situation 'if there is evidence of new or newly discovered facts, or if there has been a fundamental defect in the previous proceedings which could affect the outcome of the case'. There is as yet no recorded instance of the operation of this section.

2.7   Freedom from retrospective criminal legislation

Article 7 intends to prohibit the retroactive application of criminal proceedings resulting in a conviction or the imposition of a criminal penalty. It seeks to avoid the penalization of conduct which was not criminal at the time when the relevant act occurred.

A major exception in Article 7(2) is intended to allow the application of national and international legislation enacted during and after the Second World War to punish war crimes and other lesser offences. This exception, when created, was intended to allow the application of national and international legislation enacted expressly to deal with such offences, as it became clear that such offences had occurred and that there was no specific legislation to deal with offences which had attracted universal abhorrence.

2.8 Positive rights

2.8.1 THE RIGHT TO RESPECT FOR PRIVATE AND FAMILY LIFE, HOME, AND CORRESPONDENCE

Jurisprudence under this heading is less likely to form part of the criminal lawyer's daily work than the substantive and procedural protections dealt with above. However, in the context of criminal litigation, the Court has considered issues such as lawful and unlawful surveillance, and the use of unlawfully obtained evidence in breach of Article 8 rights (*Schenk v Switzerland* (1991) 13 EHRR 242).

The Court has attached an extremely high premium to confidentiality, privacy, and privilege with respect to communications between solicitor and client. In short, letters from a lawyer should only be opened where the authorities have reason to believe that the letters contain illicit enclosures that could not be detected in any other way. In such circumstances, it should be opened in the presence of the prisoner (*Campbell v UK* (1993) 15 EHRR 137). In fact, the Irish prison practice of opening all letters, including those clearly marked as correspondence from solicitors, is manifestly in breach of the Convention, and it is only a matter of time before the appropriate case finds its way to Strasbourg. On a more general level, many Irish prison practices are likely to trouble the Courts in due course, although these would more properly fall under the head of civil litigation.

As a result of the *Norris* case, and the consequent change in Irish law, relatively few cases involving consensual sexual activity now find their way before the Irish Courts. The European Court has consistently found that offences involving consensual sexual activity in private are disproportionate to the protection of morals. However, the Court has used the 'protection of health' as a way of upholding domestic decisions outlawing unusual sexual practices which took place entirely in private and entirely with the consent of the participating adults (see *Laskey v UK* (1997) 24 EHRR 39).

2.9 Freedom of expression and freedom of assembly and association

Although not strictly connected, these rights, provided for by Articles 10 and 11 respectively, can be considered together, as they enjoy both a high degree of protection under the Convention by virtue of their tending to be the basis of political expression. The limitations on the exercise of political rights have tended to be construed narrowly by the Court, and the justification of any criminal sanction must be 'convincingly established' (*Sunday Times v UK (No 2)* (1992), 14 EHRR 229). However, prosecutions for obscenity and, increasingly commonly, race hatred, are less likely to be struck down by the Court.

2.10 Conclusion

The rights and liberties of suspects and defendants in criminal litigation have always enjoyed some measure of protection from the Irish Constitution, but it now seems likely that those entitlements will enjoy a further level of protection arising from the concepts contained in the Convention. It is, at this early stage, difficult to assess exactly how the Irish courts will deal with Convention issues, bearing in mind in particular that they will frequently arise in the District Court, which has been expressly excluded from the

Convention of Human Rights Act 2003. However, it is clear that a good working knowledge of the Convention, its rights and protections, will henceforth be an essential tool in the hands of the criminal defence lawyer.

CHAPTER 3

MANAGING A CRIMINAL LITIGATION PRACTICE

3.1   Introduction

To a greater extent than perhaps any other area of legal practice, criminal litigation (and this chapter is geared predominantly if not exclusively to criminal defence) requires a commitment of time and emotional resources that borders on a vocation.

If a solicitor is to undertake criminal defence work seriously, then he or she must be prepared to be available for urgent calls on most hours of most days, often from panicky or distressed clients or their relatives, and often in circumstances of great pressure, for financial rewards that are, by the standards of the legal profession, relatively modest. Those legal practices in our larger cities that are substantial and successful have been developed and built over many years, by dint of long hours and hard, often unacknowledged, work.

It is ironic that criminal work, which was seen by many lawyers as 'seedy' and untouchable over generations, should have acquired a superficial glamour and attractiveness in the last few years. This has come about mainly as a result of numerous novels and television series devoted to the subject. The reality of the work is not well reflected through the mirror of fiction. For every high-profile case, there are a hundred mundane ones. Even those few major cases often carry enormous, very public, pressures. But for the most part, criminal work is conducted in unpleasant surroundings, for modest reward.

This is not to say that there are no attractions. Virtually no two cases are alike, there is constant human contact, and the work is never dull or boring. The memoirs of a successful criminal solicitor would make endlessly fascinating reading. There are even times when it is possible to affect a client's entire life for the better. Substantial personal and professional satisfaction can accrue from an acquittal, or from persuading a court not to imprison an accused that has pleaded guilty. Equally, because the work undertaken will impact on the reputation and, frequently, liberty of citizens, it is of the utmost importance that an appropriate level of skill and commitment is devoted to it. It is, more than most fields of employment, an area in which one should not dabble. Balancing the demands of the clients, the prosecution and the courts, together with the daily demands of practice management requires constant vigilance and concentration. Ultimately, the greatest asset of a solicitor is his or her reputation, and the solicitor needs to be aware of the practical and ethical pitfalls that can undermine it. That reputation must be without blemish so far as concerns judges, colleagues, the Gardaí, and clients.

It follows that embarking on a career in criminal litigation is not to be undertaken lightly. Those planning on setting up in practice should have a good working knowledge of criminal law and procedure, some experience in advocacy, and a readiness to take on any case, no matter how unpleasant or trivial, with a view to establishing a client base. The reputations of the best solicitors tend to spread by word of mouth, and that will take time. Unfortunately, it seems accepted that one bad recommendation can undo many good ones.

It is recommended that new entrants to criminal practice should undertake as many courses as possible in the relevant fields, and of course commit themselves to a programme of continuing legal education. Developments in criminal law and procedure over the last 10 years have been very rapid, and look set to continue.

All of that being said, the most important attributes to be brought to criminal defence practice are the willingness to act fearlessly and independently on behalf of all clients, and to respect without exception their dignity and human rights.

3.2 Ethics

This topic is dealt with more fully in **Chapter 1**. Alluding to the subject at this stage is done solely with the intention of underlining the need to be constantly alert. No field of legal work is as likely to present ethical difficulties or conflicts of interest and nowhere are there to be found as many 'grey areas'. All practising solicitors need to exercise constant care to maintain the highest ethical standards, and need to be fully familiar with the Law Society of Ireland's guide to professional conduct. There are also helpful Codes developed and published by the International Bar Association and the Association of Criminal Lawyers.

Solicitors must not shirk difficult ethical decisions. If such a decision means losing a client or a substantial, possibly lucrative, case, then so be it. The alternative is to gain a reputation for sharp practice, and ultimately risk the loss of one's livelihood.

When ethical difficulties of any kind arise, they must be addressed at once. There is no obstacle to seeking independent advice outside the firm, if there are no colleagues of sufficient seniority within the firm. Senior peers, members of the appropriate Law Society committees, and even Counsel will all be capable of offering relevant advice. An approach can be formal or informal, as the situation requires. When in doubt, err on the side of caution.

3.3 Diary management

Absolutely rigid diary maintenance is the only acceptable standard. Missing a case in Court is visible to all, discourteous to the judge, potentially negligent, appears unprofessional and is generally bad for business. All members of staff should be inculcated with the idea that a date should go in the solicitor's diary as soon as it becomes known to them. Far better that it should go in more than once than not at all.

The diary should be reviewed regularly and available resources compared with work commitments. Where necessary, Counsel should be instructed, preferably in good time, and arrangements made to have Counsel attended. It is intelligent practice to avoid over-extending the firm, by avoiding taking on work outside the usual geographical catchment area. Such cases invariably take on a life of their own, and become a huge drain on the office's resources.

A regular review of the diary should operate in tandem with a watchful eye on the prisons. Again, a full record must always be available of persons in custody. The failure to visit clients in custody, often the most time-consuming activity, will result in the disintegration of the practice. The reverse also holds true; there are some firms who have an exceptional reputation for advising prisoners and that tends to lead to a demand for their services.

3.4   Record keeping and file management

When it comes to record keeping and file management, although it may sound morbid, the ideal to work to is to assume that you will die suddenly and a colleague will have to take over your entire workload with no knowledge of the cases except what is contained in your files. In that scenario, the incoming solicitor will have the benefit of a note or copy of every attendance, meeting, consultation, letter, or telephone call undertaken in the matter. This is a useful ideal to work to for a number of reasons, not least because it makes the job easier. In particular, in a practice with more than one fee-earner, it makes work practices considerably more flexible. It also means that any disputes are more likely than not to be resolved in your favour.

By way of a cautionary note, an increasing number of solicitors have found themselves giving evidence in court over the last few years, in a variety of circumstances. So proper dated timed attendances and notes of telephone calls are becoming increasingly important.

In the current state of affairs, most criminal defence work is dealt with by way of legal aid and hence standard fees. That in turn presents a temptation to cut corners and try to maximize profits. This temptation must be resisted. In the worst case scenario, the Law Society or courts may at some point seek to scrutinize your file or even a hostile team of lawyers in the event of an action for professional negligence. It must not be forgotten that a failure to maintain a reasonable standard of work amounts to professional misconduct for which solicitors can be sued or disciplined.

In the event that one is privately retained, a proper basis for fees should be agreed with the client, committed to writing in accordance with the statutory requirements and retained on file. If an hourly rate is agreed, then proper time recording is essential, both to enable a full and proper account to be rendered to the client and to set out your record in the event of dispute.

Many criminal cases are of relatively short duration and generate little paperwork. There is accordingly even less excuse than usual for sloppy file management. Once closed, files should be kept securely for, it is suggested, seven years. These days, it is probably acceptable to scan the papers onto disc and shred the originals, with the concomitant savings of space and expense. Different considerations may prevail in major cases.

It may be worth considering an application for approval under a quality system. Certainly the very high standard of professional practice and procedures required for, say, a 'Q' mark, will give some idea of the target to be aimed for by way of delivery of an excellent service.

3.5   Office personnel

Although the major cities now all have a number of small criminal practices operating, in effect, out of the practitioners' briefcases, the ideal to aim for is obviously a proper and fully serviced office. The staffing level required will clearly depend on the workload. As the practice develops, extra staff can be recruited. Some of the larger UK practices have a managing partner, a financial manager, an office manager, a franchise manager and so on. However in the early years of a firm, an able, computer-literate legal assistant, not necessarily qualified, can perform a number of functions, including those of secretary/receptionist, attending court and consultations with Counsel, some legal research, etc. Sensible use of resources, preferably involving advance planning, is extremely helpful.

It must always be remembered, however, that no matter how able the staff, the final responsibility for any case rests with the principal or partners of any firm. Accordingly, suitable levels of supervision must be maintained at all times. From the point of view of the client, the ideal is a single contact person in the firm who will always be aware of the situation in his or her case. In this context, it is imperative that each and every member of staff has impressed upon them the need for absolute client confidentiality. All clients of solicitors are entitled to expect that their affairs will be dealt with in complete privacy, and the clients of criminal practitioners are no exception. It is particularly important that staff joining or leaving are reminded of the requirement. Again, a failure to adhere to this standard will be the responsibility of the principal or partners.

A particular problem for smaller firms is suitable cover for annual leave and major holidays. Larger firms can obviously deal more comfortably with staff absences. For small firms, including sole practitioners, holidays can mean no effective emergency cover for a period. This is unfortunate, but some sort of contingency arrangement should be made, if necessary by an answering machine message advising callers of the position and referring them to a reputable local firm. The unpalatable alternative may be unhappy clients who were arrested and unable to contact their trusted adviser for no obvious reason, and who have decided to take their business elsewhere as a consequence.

3.6   Garda stations

There is nothing more likely to throw a carefully planned day into chaos than a sudden arrest and detention for questioning at the Garda station requiring the solicitor's attendance. Furthermore, there is often a high degree of stress attaching to attending at the station.

A telephone call received from or on behalf of a detained client should be dealt with urgently. If it cannot be attended to rapidly and competently, a decision should be made as to whether the client should be referred to a colleague.

All practising criminal defence solicitors should familiarize themselves with the powers of detention of the Gardaí, and the investigative entitlements. Although some emergency situations can be dealt with by telephone, the most desirable course is to visit the client in custody. If the client wants a visit for advice and that cannot be undertaken promptly, both client and Gardaí should be so advised, so that the client can choose another solicitor if necessary. Under no circumstances should the client or Gardaí be advised of a time for a visit that is not, in the context of existing commitments, likely to be met.

Garda station expertise is crucial to the criminal litigation practice. Solicitors should attend courses, read articles, statutes and judgments, and otherwise develop their skill and knowledge in this area. Many cases are won or lost at this stage of the investigation and experience is the only teacher. It is ironic that one's best work, if it prevents one's client being charged, will cost one the fees for a case, but such an outcome can only enhance one's reputation.

3.7   Relations with the client

As indicated above, clients should be treated with absolute respect, regardless of the allegations against them, or the difficulties they may pose for the solicitor. All office personnel should treat clients politely and courteously. It is axiomatic that staff will follow the example of the solicitor. Telephone calls should be returned promptly, and correspondence answered without delay. Clients should not be denigrated behind their backs, as this will only lessen the respect with which they should be treated.

Many clients will be reasonably familiar with the criminal justice system, but for those who are not, special consideration is required. In many ways, the most important cases will be those accused who are new to the system. All clients should be made aware of the respective roles of the solicitor and client, and the limitations on the function of the solicitor. Some clients, particularly those new to the system, assume that the solicitor will make all key decisions for them. This misapprehension must be cleared up from the start.

A course in interviewing skills is recommended and valuable materials are available from the Law Society. In terms of cost-effectiveness, for every veteran whose demands on one's time are modest there will be a client who will need careful, and sometimes repeated advising, so that things tend to even out financially over time.

The manner in which a solicitor deals with a client is a personal matter. It seems obvious that the better the client and solicitor communicate, the more they are likely to understand one another. The reality is probably subtler. The solicitor must be careful to maintain a distance from the client, as a perception that one is too close to the client will threaten one's reputation. So a careful balance is required, enabling a good solicitor–client relationship to flourish, without impinging on one's perceived independence. Experience is the key.

At a minimum, the client must always understand the advice that is being given. Without that, they are unable to make any informed choices. Lawyers have long been criticized for using pompous and verbose language. Criminal clients are statistically likely to be poorly educated. It is entirely the responsibility of the solicitor to ensure that there is appropriate communication, in good time, to enable the client to make appropriate decisions. The client should be kept informed, in straightforward language, of all material developments in the case.

Solicitors should not shrink from spelling out certain hard realities to clients. Clients may not appreciate bad news when they first hear it, but better that they should understand the position before they go to court than that they should be sentenced when they are not expecting it. Again, experience will gradually enhance both the quality of the advice and the manner of its delivery.

3.8   Use of and relations with Counsel

Judicious use of Counsel is an invaluable aid to practice. Counsel will be asked to assist in various sets of circumstances, but some ground rules remain constant. First, the solicitor will always be responsible for the fees of Counsel who is instructed in a case. It follows that the firm should secure the payment of adequate fees for the case, or be legally aided. Secondly, Counsel should be appropriately and fully instructed. The job, whatever it is, cannot be properly done unless Counsel is apprised of all the facts. Thirdly, instructing Counsel at the last minute should be avoided. This is sometimes unavoidable, such as when there is a late return from another barrister; but in general, astute practice management should enable papers to go to Counsel well in advance.

Most, if not all, of the advocacy in the higher courts will be done by Counsel. It is essential that a responsible member of staff of the firm attend them both for last-minute consultations and so that a good note of the proceedings is taken. The solicitor must also ensure the attendance of any witnesses whom it is proposed to call, and must deal with any other preparation as advised by Counsel.

Counsel can also be briefed for the District Court, but solicitors who defend regularly in court would expect to be well capable of dealing with most matters in the lower court. Very occasionally, a client will have business of such a nature as to justify retaining Counsel for a District Court matter, usually when privately retained. This would be so in a drink-driving prosecution, for example, where the technical proofs are constantly becoming more refined and complex. Again, for the same reasons as above, it is vital to attend Counsel. Occasionally, workloads demand the use of Counsel for routine District Court work, as solicitors are unable to appear. Ideally, Counsel should also be attended on these matters.

Finally, solicitors may ask Counsel to advise in consultation at an early stage of proceedings or where an unusual problem has arisen. It is worth developing good relationships with a number of junior and senior Counsel, so that informal discussions can establish whether there is a ready solution to the problem, perhaps obviating the need for formal instructions.

PART II

THE LAW OF EVIDENCE IN CRIMINAL COURTS

CHAPTER 4

FUNDAMENTAL PRINCIPLES OF THE LAW OF EVIDENCE

4.1 Introduction

The rules of evidence are essentially procedural safeguards. The nature of our criminal justice system determines in whose favour these rules operate. Both are inextricably linked. Though the rules of evidence are also relevant to civil litigation they are not as vitally so. In a civil case the parties can waive certain rules of evidence, whereas in the resolution of guilt in a criminal case no waiver of the exclusionary rules of evidence is possible. Thus when one reads newspaper blurbs of criminals *getting off scot free* because of 'technicalities' it is not strictly correct to infer that minor considerations have prevailed in the case in question to obstruct our system of justice. In fact, these 'technicalities' are an integral part of our justice system.

At the basis of our criminal justice system lies the tradition of the adversarial process and the essential premise that a person is 'innocent until proven guilty'. It might be asserted that our rules of evidence have been moulded by and for a different age. It may be valid to seek reforms in the light of modern problems and knowledge. Yet if that is so and reform should take place, it should be in the context of a complete review of our criminal justice system and should not take the form of ad hoc and ill-researched changes, causing our legal system to be changed *de facto*, while masquerading under a *de jure* regime, with which it is out of step.

The law of evidence is essentially moulded by the society it operates within, and within the common law system itself very different perspectives and value preferences are to be found. On a more pragmatic level the effective use of the law of evidence depends to a greater or lesser extent on the advocate, judge, and tribunal involved.

Recent changes implemented through the Criminal Justice Act 2006 will be uploaded onto the website supporting this text, insofar as they affect this chapter.

4.1.1 DEFINITION OF EVIDENCE

'The evidence of a fact is that which tends to prove it—something which may satisfy an inquirer of the fact's existence' (Tapper, *Cross & Tapper on Evidence* (9th edn, 1999, Butterworths).

The rules of evidence are essentially exclusionary in nature, operating to withhold from the tribunal of inquiry certain facts which are regarded as belonging to categories of evidence best excluded in order to uphold certain value principles. The basis upon which evidence is excluded are relevance and admissibility.

4.2   Relevance and admissibility

Relevance is determined according to the criteria of whether evidence is either: (a) the facts in issue; or (b) facts directly relevant to a fact in issue. If the evidence in question falls within either of these two categories it is deemed to be relevant. All relevant evidence is not, however, admissible.

Admissibility is the essential political side of the process and is determined on the basis of rules developed over the centuries, which are at the core of our criminal and civil justice systems. For example, grounds of public policy exclude evidence obtained illegally in some circumstances. Similarly, hearsay evidence is not admissible on the basis that cross examination is central to the adversarial nature of our legal system, and hearsay avoids the subjection of the maker of the statement to questioning. A further example is that reliability can be a factor as to the admissibility of confession evidence where it is found by the court that a confession was not made voluntarily. Without the examination of the overall reasons and values, which determine the rules of evidence, the law in this area appears to the student or practitioner as a large and amorphous bundle of seemingly incomprehensible rules.

'An item of evidence may be relevant for more than one reason . . . In other words, the major premise of a syllogism may be altered, although the minor premise and conclusion remain the same' (Tapper, *Cross & Tapper on Evidence* (9th edn, 1999, Butterworths).

Relevance is not primarily dependent on rules of law; admissibility is quite different. The admissibility of evidence depends first on its being relevant to a sufficiently high degree, and secondly on whether or not the evidence tendered infringes any of the exclusionary rules that may be applicable to it.

4.3   Classification of evidence

4.3.1   DIRECT AND CIRCUMSTANTIAL EVIDENCE DEFINED

Evidence can be categorized as direct, circumstantial, primary or secondary evidence.

Evidence is said to be direct when it consists of testimony concerning the perception of facts in issue in the case. Circumstantial evidence consists of evidential facts from which facts in issue must be inferred. The latter type of evidence has two major weaknesses: (a) the witness may be lying; and (b) even if the witness is speaking the truth, the inference from that fact to the fact in issue may happen to be incorrect in that particular case.

4.3.2   PRIMARY AND SECONDARY EVIDENCE DEFINED

An alternative classification of evidence is that between primary and secondary evidence. Primary evidence is that which does not by its nature suggest the existence of 'better' evidence, eg an original document. Secondary evidence is that which does suggest the existence of 'better' evidence, eg a copy of a document.

4.4   The 'best evidence' rule

The 'best evidence' rule requires the production of the best evidence which the nature of the case would admit. In the case of *Omychund v Barker* (1745) 1 Atk 21 at p 49, Lord

Hardwicke stated that 'the judges and sages of the law have laid it down that there is but one general rule of evidence, the best that the nature of the case will allow'. However, 'decisions to this effect are . . . no longer law and the best evidence rule may generally be treated as a counsel of prudence to adduce the best available evidence rather than a rule of law excluding inferior evidence when superior evidence can be adduced'. *Cross & Wilkins* (at pp 19–20) (see *R v Francis* (1874) LR. 2 CCR1 28; *Dowling v Dowling* (1860)101 CLR 236).

4.5 Burden of proof

The phrase 'burden of proof' can have two meanings:

    (a)   the legal burden of proof; and

    (b)   the evidential burden of proof.

4.5.1 THE LEGAL BURDEN OF PROOF

The legal burden of proof is essentially an obligation to persuade. The House of Lords in *DPP v Morgan* [1976] AC 182 refers to the legal burden of proof as 'the probative burden'. What the law regards as adequate proof in a criminal matter is indicated by a degree of persuasion, which is required in order to prove 'beyond a reasonable doubt' that the accused committed the crime alleged (*Woolmington v DPP* [1935] HC AC 462). In a civil action, proof on the balance of probabilities suffices. This latter standard also becomes relevant to some exceptions to the general procedure in criminal cases, as discussed in **Chapter 4**.

4.5.2 SHIFTING OF THE LEGAL BURDEN OF PROOF

A legal burden of proof cannot shift due to the mere production of evidence by the other party to the proceedings. On the other hand, as the initial placing of the legal burden of proof is determined by a rule of law, it may shift as a result of the operation of some other legal rule, such as a compelling though rebuttable presumption of law. On a more pragmatic level, however, there may come a point in the course of a trial when the legal burden regarding the issue seems to have been satisfied, in the light of the evidence so far adduced. In such circumstances considerations of prudence or good tactics, but not of law, impose an obligation upon the opponent. Where, for example, the prosecution seem to have discharged the legal burden of proof 'beyond all reasonable doubt', the defence may decide that the only tactic available is to 'go into evidence' in order to disprove or rebut the prosecution evidence. The defence is then said to bear a tactical burden of proof.

4.5.3 THE EVIDENTIAL BURDEN OF PROOF

The evidential burden of proof is an obligation to raise an issue or to adduce sufficient evidence to *prima facie* establish it, and so get the issue past the trial judge and before the 'trier of fact'. To describe the evidential burden as a 'burden of proof' is therefore something of a misnomer. Similar to the legal burden, the evidential burden relates to a particular issue and may therefore be differently placed in respect of the different issues which may arise in a case. The evidential burden is discharged by evidence sufficient to warrant, but not necessarily to require, an affirmative finding by a reasonable jury (or a judge in a summary jurisdiction). If the evidence is sufficient, the issue must be put before the jury. Whereas it is for the jury or 'trier of fact' to determine whether a legal burden has been satisfied, discharge of an evidential burden is the exclusive concern of the judge.

4.5.4   WHO BEARS THE BURDEN OF PROOF?

It is case law precedent or the construction of a statute which determines on which party to the proceedings the burden of proof lies. At common law, the evidential burden in respect of a defence may lie upon the accused, but the legal burden in respect of all issues except insanity lies upon the prosecution. Allowance must be made, however, for instance where a statute may by means of a 'reverse onus clause' expressly place the legal burden in respect of a particular issue upon the accused. The prosecution bears the legal burden of 'negativing' provocation, but the issue will not be put to the jury unless the accused discharges the evidential burden relating to it (*Mancini v DPP* [1942] AC1). It is always the duty of the prosecution to prove the guilt of the accused beyond reasonable doubt. Subject to statutory exceptions and the defence of insanity, the State must prove every ingredient in the crime establishing the golden thread principle discussed in *Woolmington v DPP* [1935] AC 462.

It is case law precedent or the construction of a statute which determines on which party to the proceedings the burden of proof lies. At common law, the evidential burden in respect of a defence may lie upon the accused, but the legal burden in respect of all issues except insanity lies upon the prosecution. Allowance must be made, however, for instances where a statute may, by means of a 'reverse onus clause', expressly place the legal burden in respect of a particular issue upon the accused.

4.5.5   EXCEPTIONS TO GENERAL RULES REGARDING WHO BEARS THE BURDEN OF PROOF

4.5.5.1   Insanity cases

In *McNaughten's Case* [1843] 10 Cl & F 200 (HL) it was held that the legal burden of establishing the common law defence of insanity rests upon the accused. This principle was followed in *AG v O'Brien* [1936] IR 263 and *Doyle v Wicklow County Council* [1974] IR 55. The relevant standard is 'proof on the balance of probabilities' (*Bratty v AG for N Ireland* [1963] AC 386). There is a burden on the accused to adduce evidence in respect of some defences, including that of sane automatism.

4.5.5.2   Peculiar knowledge principle

If on its true construction a statute prohibits the doing of an act except in specified circumstances, the defendant must (by way of exception to the fundamental rule of criminal law that the State must establish every element of the offence charged) prove the existence of the specified circumstances. This rule does not depend upon the defendant's possession of peculiar knowledge enabling them to prove the positive of a negative averment (see *Minister for Industry & Commerce v Steele* [1952] IR 304).

4.5.5.3   Statutory exceptions or 'reverse onus' provisions

The constitutional validity of statutory exceptions or 'reverse onus' provisions was accepted in *O'Leary v AG* [1991] ILRM 454 in relation to provisions relating to membership and possession of incriminating articles under the Offences Against the State Act 1939. This decision was subsequently confirmed in *Heaney and McGuinness v Ireland and AG* [1994] 3 IR 593 and *Rock v Ireland* [1998] 2 ILRM 35. Relevant 'inference from silence' provisions would include ss 18 and 19 of the Criminal Justice Act 1984, s 7 of the Criminal Drug Trafficking Act 1996, and s 5 of the Offences Against the State (Amendment) Act 1998. These provisions have been discussed in **Chapter 2**. However, it should be noted that a finding made by the European Court of Human Rights has recently criticized the offence described in s 52 Offences Against the State Act, as discussed in more detail in **Chapter 2**.

4.5.5.4   Implied statutory exception

A court should be very slow to infer from a statute that Parliament intended to impose an onerous duty on the defendant to prove their innocence in a criminal case. Traditionally, such inferences were generally limited to offences arising under statutes which prohibited the doing of an act save in specified circumstances, or by persons of specified classes, or with specified qualifications, or with the licence or permission of specified authorities.

4.5.6   DEGREES OF PERSUASION

Phrases such as 'standard of proof' and 'quantum of proof' refer to the size of the legal burden of proof. It is the duty of the 'trier of fact' to determine whether the probative force of the evidence adduced to discharge the legal burden on a particular issue adequately outweighs the probative force of the evidence tending to show the contrary. In jury trials, it is the responsibility of the judge to direct the jury as to the nature of that standard or quantum.

As previously outlined, the common law knows two standards of proof, ie persuasion on a balance of probabilities and proof beyond reasonable doubt. The latter owes its rationale to a system of justice that in criminal cases adheres to the presumption that a person is 'innocent until proven guilty' and prefers to assume a state of affairs where the possibility of an innocent man being convicted is negligible, although this may of necessity import a risk of a guilty man being acquitted. It is important to note, however, that when the legal burden regarding a particular issue is in exceptional circumstances placed upon an accused in a criminal case, it is the civil standard of persuasion 'on the balance of probabilities' which must be satisfied. Furthermore, with regard to the direction by the judge to the jury as to the standard of proof required in a particular case, it is the overall effect of that judge's 'summing up' which is important.

In *Miller v Minister of Pensions* [1947] 2 All ER 372, Denning J said:

> 'Proof beyond reasonable doubt does not mean proof beyond the shadow of doubt. The law would fail to protect the community if it admitted fanciful possibilities to deflect the course of justice. If the evidence is so strong against a man as to leave only a remote possibility in his favour which can be dismissed with the sentence "of course it is possible but not in the least probable" the case is proved beyond reasonable doubt, but nothing short of that will suffice.'

With regard to the balance of probabilities criteria, Denning J in the same case stated:

> 'If at the end of the case the evidence turns the scale definitely one way or the other, the tribunal must decide accordingly, but if the evidence is so evenly balanced that the tribunal is unable to come to a determinate conclusion one way or the other, then the man must be given the benefit of the doubt. . . . It must carry a reasonable degree of probability but not so high as is required in a criminal case. If the evidence is such that the tribunal can say: "We think it more probable than not", the burden is discharged but, if the probabilities are equal, it is not.'

In *AG v Byrne* [1974] IR 1, Kenny J held that the trial judge's use of the words 'satisfied' and 'to your satisfaction' was not correct, as one can be satisfied and still have a reasonable doubt. He pointed out that when two views are possible, the accused is entitled to the benefit of the doubt.

4.6 Presumptions

4.6.1 INTRODUCTION

Certain presumptions of fact and law are recognised by the courts. Presumptions may be rebuttable or irrebuttable. Where a presumption operates, the court may or must draw a certain conclusion. (*Phippson on Evidence* (15th edn, 2000, Sweet & Maxwell).

4.6.2 PRESUMPTIONS THAT DO AND DO NOT DEPEND ON THE PROOF OF BASIC FACTS

No facts need be proved to bring into play the presumption of innocence, the presumption of sanity, or the presumption that the accused was acting voluntarily, in a criminal case. Presumptions that do depend on proof of basic facts include a presumption of the existence of one fact (the presumed fact) which must be made, in the absence of further evidence, when another fact (the basic fact) is either proved, admitted or judicially noticed. For example, once a child has been born in wedlock there is a presumption of legitimacy; once a person has been proved unheard from by those who would be expected to hear from them for seven years, there is a presumption of death.

4.6.3 TYPES OF PRESUMPTION

There are four basic types of presumption:

(a) *Presumptions of fact* are assumptions which may be made on proof of the basic fact. The court is under no obligation to make the assumption even if no evidence to the contrary is given. Examples are: a presumption of continuance; a presumption of intent; and a presumption of guilty knowledge on a charge of receiving stolen goods.

(b) *Irrebuttable presumptions of law*, strictly speaking are rules of law. For example, in Ireland a child under seven years cannot commit a criminal offence. Similarly, in the past a boy of less than 14 years was irrebuttably presumed to be incapable of committing the offence of rape. The Criminal Law Rape (Amendment) Act 1990 removed this latter presumption.

(c) *Rebuttable presumptions of law* are assumptions which must be made in the absence of evidence to the contrary. For example: the presumption of legality; the presumption of accuracy; the presumption of legitimacy; the presumption of marriage; and the presumption of death.

(d) *Statutory presumptions* provide for assumptions with regard to particular forms of evidence. For example, the Road Traffic Act 1968, s 44(2)(a), provides that a certificate stating that a specimen of a person's blood contained a specified concentration of alcohol should be conclusive evidence that, when the specimen was taken, the concentration of alcohol in that person's blood was as specified in the certificate.

4.7 Pleas of autrefois acquit and autrefois convict

Autrefois verdicts are the nearest equivalent to cause of action estoppel in criminal cases. They are available whenever:

(a) the accused is in danger of being convicted of the same offence as one for which there has already been an acquittal or conviction; or when

(b) the accused is in danger of being convicted of an offence of which they could have been convicted at a former trial.

4.8 Judicial notice

4.8.1 NOTORIOUS FACTS

4.8.1.1 Universally notorious

There are certain matters of fact which are considered too notorious to require proof or to be susceptible to disproof. Such matters are the subject of judicial notice in its simplest form. The judge will take notice of their existence and of their nature without requiring them to be proved. Any matter that is of such common knowledge that it would be an insult to the intelligence to require its demonstration is dealt with in this way; for example, the fact that Christmas Day falls on 25 December or that the sun rises in the east.

4.8.1.2 Locally notorious facts

Facts which, although notorious, are only locally notorious are also covered by the doctrine of judicial notice; for example a fact of local geography.

4.8.2 JUDICIAL NOTICE AFTER INQUIRIES

The doctrine of judicial notice has been extended so as to apply to facts which, although not notorious, are capable of demonstration by resort to sources of virtually indisputable accuracy, readily accessible to those who are members of the court; for example the fact that 1 November 1944 was a Wednesday, the time of sunset in a particular place on a particular day or the longitude and latitude of Dublin. Judicial notice of such facts is said to be 'taken, only after inquiries'.

4.9 Competence and compellability

4.9.1 INTRODUCTION

At common law a general rule existed that if a person was capable of giving testimony that person had a duty to do so, and was often compellable to give it.

Evidence is usually taken on oath from a witness. The oath may take any form the witness wishes, and unsworn evidence is also allowed, particularly in the case of children. It is possible to make an affirmation, as opposed to an oath, in the event that the deponent is of a non-Christian faith or is an atheist or agnostic. In each case where false testimony is given the crime of perjury has been committed.

4.9.2 CATEGORIES OF COMPETENT WITNESSES

The following categories of witnesses are regarded as competent to give evidence:

(a) persons with a physical disability—if they are capable of giving evidence, by whatever means, it will be treated as admissible;

(b) persons of defective intellect—the judge must be satisfied that the deponent can understand the nature of the oath for their evidence to be treated as admissible;

(c) children—s 27 of the Criminal Evidence Act 1992 provides that in any criminal proceedings the evidence of a person under 14 years of age may be received, otherwise than on oath or affirmation, if the court is satisfied that the child is capable of giving an intelligible account of events which is relevant to those proceedings. This Act makes changes to the manner of receipt of children's evidence in the form of live TV link and video testimony.

4.9.3 THE USE OF TECHNOLOGY IN THE COURTROOM

The facility in certain criminal proceedings for live television link, video testimony and evidence through an intermediary is established in Part III of the Criminal Evidence Act 1992, and is quite radical in departing from the requirements for oral testimony to be given by witnesses in the presence of the accused, subject to the sanction of the oath or affirmation and cross-examination. However, s 14 mandates that the court operate on the basis of the 'interests of justice', and s 16(2)(b), in the context of video evidence, specifically states that the court should have regard to all the circumstances, including any risk that the admission of evidence through this medium could result in unfairness to the accused. The constitutionality of this provision was upheld in *Donnelly v AG* [1998] 1 IR 321.

4.9.4 DEFENDANT'S SPOUSE AS A PROSECUTION WITNESS

4.9.4.1 Rule at common law

There existed a general rule at common law that a spouse was not competent as a witness for the prosecution at a criminal trial. The rule extended to the joint trial situation, so that even if the evidence of a spouse was only against the co-accused, the spouse was not permitted to testify. The rationale of the rule lay in the public policy of upholding the institution of marriage. Inroads were made into this rule both at common law and by statute.

4.9.4.2 Part IV of the Criminal Evidence Act 1992

The Criminal Evidence Act 1992, Part IV, s 21, provides for the competence of the spouse of an accused as a prosecution witness in any criminal proceedings. The spouse of an accused is also rendered compellable as a witness in certain instances. Section 22 of the Act provides that the spouse of an accused shall be compellable as a prosecution witness in the case of a violent or sexual offence against the spouse, a child of the spouse or accused, or any person who at the material time was under 17 years of age.

This change in the law with regard to spousal competence and compellability was preceded, and mandated to some degree, by the Irish Court of Criminal Appeal in *DPP v TJ* (1998) 3 Frewen 141, where Walsh J found that there was a basis for rendering a spouse competent and compellable, in cases where personal violence had been perpetrated upon a member of that family by the other spouse, in the Constitution's protection of the family (Article 41), together with its vindication of personal rights (Article 40.3) and in particular the rights of individual family members.

4.9.5 THE ACCUSED AS A PROSECUTION WITNESS

The accused is not competent to give evidence as a prosecution witness, with one exception provided for in the Public Nuisance Act 1887. When there is more than one accused, they cannot give evidence against one another. However, it is possible for the prosecution to get around this prohibition by means of various technical devices. Examples of such devices are as follows:

(a) If no evidence is offered against an accused who is therefore acquitted, the defence of 'autrefois acquit' operates as a bar against possible subsequent prosecution and the individual concerned is free to testify against the other accused.

(b) The prosecution can *nolle prosequi* the charges preferred against an accused, which protects the accused de facto from the possibility of a trial on the same charges again. The accused is then free to testify against others.

(c) If the co-accused individuals are not tried together and one pleads guilty and is sentenced, the latter is then free to give evidence against the others.

4.9.6 NON-COMPELLABILITY OF DIPLOMATS

Under the Geneva Convention and the Diplomat Act 1937, a diplomat cannot be compelled to give evidence. This provision is also extended to cover the diplomat's family, provided they are not nationals of the deciding State.

4.10 Corroboration

4.10.1 INTRODUCTION

In *R v Baskerville* [1916] 2 KB 658, the Court of Criminal Appeal stated:

> 'We hold evidence in corroboration must be independent testimony which affects the accused by connecting him or tending to connect him with the crime. It must be evidence that implicates him i.e. which confirms in some material particular not only the evidence that the crime has been committed but also that the prisoner committed it.'

As a general rule, corroboration (confirmatory or supporting probative material) of otherwise admissible evidence is unnecessary. Yet there are two main instances when the court considers the issue of corroboration as being a pre-requisite where:

(a) corroboration is required as a matter of law, and

(b) corroboration is required as a matter of practice, ie:

    (i) an accomplice's evidence is uncorroborated;

    (ii) identification evidence is uncorroborated; and

    (iii) the evidence of the sexual assault complainant is uncorroborated.

4.10.2 CORROBORATION REQUIRED AS A MATTER OF LAW

4.10.2.1 Statute law

The Treason Act 1939, ss 14 and 22, provide that corroboration is required as a matter of law with regard to the charge of perpetrating the act of treason, or of aiding, abetting, or harbouring the perpetrator of same. Corroboration is also required as a matter of law with regard to certain offences under the Road Traffic Acts.

4.10.2.2 Common law

There is one instance when corroboration is required as a matter of law at common law. Corroborative evidence must be produced by the State to successfully secure a prosecution of the crime of perjury.

4.10.3 CORROBORATION OR WARNING REQUIRED AS A MATTER OF PRACTICE

Corroboration or a warning to the jury has been required as a matter of practice in the past and now has effect as a rule of law.

4.10.3.1 Accomplice evidence

The Chief Justice in *AG v Linehan* [1929] IR 19 stated:

'We do not think that a narrow or precise definition of accomplice should be or indeed can be laid down. We think however, that a person implicated either as a principal or an accessory in the crime under investigation is an accomplice within the rule, though the degree or gravity of such complicity may vary, and in as much as the extent of the effect of such complicity upon the credit of the witness or upon the weight of his uncorroborated testimony will vary accordingly so shall the degree and the gravity of the warning be measured.'

In *Davies v DPP* [1954] AC 378, Lord Simonds LC stated:

'There is in the authorities no formal definition of the term "accomplice" . . . On the cases it would appear that the following persons, if called as witnesses for the prosecution, have been treated as falling within the category:
(1) On any view persons who are *participes criminis* in respect of the actual crime charged, whether as principals or accessories before or after the fact (in felonies) or persons committing, procuring or aiding and abetting (in the case of misdemeanours) . . . surely the natural and primary meaning of the term "accomplice". But in two cases, persons falling strictly outside the ambit of this category have, in particular decisions, been held to be accomplices for the purpose of the rule: viz:
(2) Receivers have been held to be accomplices of the thieves from whom they receive goods on a trial of the latter for larceny.
(3) When X has been charged with a specific offence on a particular occasion, and evidence is admissible and has been admitted, of his having committed crimes of this identical type on other occasions, as proving system and intent and negativing accident; in such cases the court has held that in relation to such other offences, if evidence of them were given by parties to them, the evidence of such other parties should not be left to the jury without a warning that it is dangerous to accept it without corroboration.'

The court in *Davies v DPP* has stated the rationale of the corroboration requirement with regard to accomplice evidence as follows:

(a) The accomplice may wish to curry favour with the prosecution.

(b) The accomplice may also be in a position to fabricate evidence which may seem credible because of its close relation to what actually happened.

(c) The accomplice is morally culpable.

(d) Accomplice evidence may be that of a co-accused who gives evidence and drops you both in it.

In *People (DPP) v Hogan* CCA 12 January 1994 (unreported) it was held that when giving the necessary warning in relation to the dangers attendant on the evidence of an accomplice, the court should be mindful that the purpose of pointing to the need for corroboration was to find whether it implicates the accused in the crime with which they are charged and not to confirm the accomplice's account.

In the cases of *People v Ward* 27 November 1998, SCC (unreported), *DPP v Holland*, 15 June 1998, CCA (unreported), and *DPP v Meehan*, 29 July 1999 (unreported), the use of accomplice evidence through the medium of the State's witness protection programme was sanctioned. The Special Criminal Court refused to accept that any particular warning was required in relation to such participants, apart from the standard warning in relation to accomplices.

4.10.3.2   Confession evidence

An additional requirement of corroboration has now been introduced in relation to confession evidence, which would seem to fit into this category. Section 10 of the Criminal Procedure Act 1993 provides:

> *(1)   Where at a trial of a person on indictment evidence is given of a confession made by that person and that evidence is not corroborated, the judge shall advise the jury to have due regard to the absence of corroboration.*

> *(2)   It shall not be necessary for a judge to use any particular form of words under this section.*

The main distinguishing feature of this category of instances requiring corroboration or a warning to the jury as a matter of practice, as opposed to the earlier category requiring corroboration as a matter of law, is that in the former instance the jury has a right to convict despite the absence of corroborative evidence.

4.10.3.3   Identification evidence

Another situation where it is highly desirable, if not considered essential, for a judge to warn the jury of the danger of acting on a certain type of evidence, although without going to the extent of demanding corroboration, arises in cases of visual identification. In *The People (AG) v Dominic Casey (No 2)* [1963] IR 33, Kingsmill-Moore J stated:

> 'In our opinion it is desirable that in all cases where the verdict depends substantially on the correctness of an identification, the jury's attention should be called in general terms to the fact that in a number of instances such identification has proved erroneous, to the possibilities of mistake in the case before them and to the necessity of caution. Nor do we think that such warning should be confined to cases where identification is that of only one witness.'

In *R v Turnbull* [1976] 3 All ER 549, the English Court of Appeal moved away from the position taken in *Arthurs v AG for N Ireland* [1971] 55 Cr App R 161 towards one resembling that of the court in *The People (AG) v Dominic Casey (No 2)* [1963] IR 33. The court laid down that the following principles:

(a)   Where the case against the accused depends wholly or substantially on eyewitness identification, which is alleged to be mistaken, the judge should warn the jury of a special need for caution and explain the reasons for same.

(b)   The judge should direct the jury to examine closely the circumstances in which the identification came to be made (eg length of time, light, distance).

(c)   In any case, whether summary or indictment, if the prosecution believes there is a material discrepancy between the material initially and secondly given by the witness, they should supply the defendant with the initial material.

(d)   The judge should remind the jury of any special weaknesses in the identification evidence.

(e)   Where the identification evidence is good and a cautionary warning is given to the jury, the latter can then be left to act on it.

(f)   Where the identification evidence is poor, the judge would withdraw the case from the jury unless there is 'supporting evidence'.

(g)   The 'supporting evidence' may be either corroboration in a legal sense or something which convinces the jury that identification is not mistaken.

(h)   The absence of the accused from the witness box is not evidence of anything; although the jury may take into account the fact that the identification has not been contradicted.

(i)   The setting up of a false alibi or telling lies of his whereabouts is not of itself proof that the accused was where the identifying witness says he was.

(j)   Failure to follow these guidelines is likely to result in a conviction being quashed.

In *People (DPP) v Patrick O'Reilly* [1991] ILRM 10 CCA 9 July 1990 (unreported), O'Flaherty J confirmed the decision in *The People (AG) v Dominic Casey (No 2)* [1963] IR 33 in relation to visual identification evidence, and laid down further parameters as to the conduct of identification parades. O'Flaherty J acknowledged that there would be circumstances where, for reasons of the singular appearance of the accused, the witnesses' previous acquaintance with the accused, or the uncooperative attitude of the suspect, the holding of an identification parade might be impossible or redundant (although a warning would still be given in accordance with *The People (AG) v Dominic Casey (No 2)* [1963] IR 33). The court expressed concern as to the implications of an informal identification procedure, warned that the *Casey* warning should not be treated as a 'stereotyped formula'. In *The People v Duff* [1995] 3 IR 296, it was held that the optimum method of visual identification was by means of an identification parade; and in *DPP v Cooney* [1997] 3 IR 205, the Supreme Court held that 'dock identifications' were undesirable and unsatisfactory but may be admitted by the trial judge with a specific warning to the jury with regard to reliance on such procedure.

4.10.3.4   Evidence of the complainant in sexual offences

Formerly, the evidence of a complainant in a sexual offence case was deemed to require corroboration as a matter of practice, or at least a warning to the jury as to the dangers of acting on such evidence. Since the passing of the Criminal Law (Rape) (Amendment) Act 1990, this position has been altered. The trial judge in such a case now has a discretion as to whether or not to give such a warning. The warning remains the traditional one in relation to sexual complainants, although no particular form of words need be utilized.

4.10.3.5   Children's evidence

The requirement that children's evidence be corroborated is abolished by s 28 of the Criminal Evidence Act 1992. It is replaced by a judicial discretion to give a warning in relation to such evidence, and no particular form of words is necessary to do so.

4.11   Privilege

4.11.1   INTRODUCTION

The courts, although not closed, jealously guard the area of private privilege, as it interferes with the administration of justice by reducing the amount of evidence available to a court.

4.11.2 PUBLIC OR STATE PRIVILEGE

The area of public privilege, by contrast, has expanded, perhaps unsurprisingly as the courts have a discretion to weigh the conflicting interests. The privilege must be asserted before it is claimed and may also be waived. A witness must claim privilege in relation to the following:

(a) privilege against self-incrimination;

(b) marital privilege;

(c) legal professional privilege.

4.11.2.1 Privilege against self-incrimination

This privilege protects everyone from having to answer in a court of law any question or produce any document or article if, in the opinion of the judge, it would be liable to expose them to a criminal charge.

4.11.2.2 Marital privilege

Section 1(d) of the Criminal Evidence Act 1898 prevents disclosure in criminal cases of communications made to a spouse during the marriage.

4.11.2.3 Legal professional privilege

This area of privilege protects communications made to a lawyer by a client from disclosure without the client's consent, as well as communications made to the client by the lawyer (see *Smurfit Paribas Bank Ltd v AAB Export Finance Ltd* [1990] 1 IR 469). Legal professional privilege does not extend to communications to a lawyer for the purpose of obtaining legal assistance other than legal advice (*Breatnach v Ireland (No 3)* [1993] 2 IR 458 per Keane J).

4.11.2.4 Journalistic privilege

Journalistic privilege is another area where a private privilege does not exist. In *re Kevin O'Kelly* [1974] 108 ILTR 97, O'Kelly, a journalist, was a prosecution witness in the Special Criminal Court and refused to answer a question, claiming privilege. Walsh J in the Supreme Court stated: 'journalists or reporters are not any more constitutionally or legally immune than other citizens from disclosing information received in confidence. The fact that a communication was made, under terms of expressed confidence or implied confidence, does not create a privilege against disclosure'.

In *State (Magee) v O'Rourke* [1971] IR 205, O'Dalaigh CJ seems to infer that where an individual who is requested to answer questions or produce documents is refusing to do so, on the basis that he might be incriminated under foreign law if he were to do so, he bears the onus of indicating some reasonable possibility of extradition or travel to the country in question.

4.12 Evidence of disposition

4.12.1 INTRODUCTION

'Disposition' means a person's tendency to act, think or feel in a particular way. It may be proved by evidence as to conduct, such as by the presentation of evidence of character, 'similar fact evidence' (see **4.12.3** below), or evidence of previous convictions. Whatever form the evidence takes, it is affected by exclusionary rules of evidence.

The notion of 'character' covers evidence of disposition as well as evidence of good reputation. Character is also an indivisible concept in law, therefore an accused cannot credit himself with good character for chastity, without opening himself to a risk of cross-examination concerning offences involving dishonesty. However, it is not implicit in an accusation of dishonesty that the accused himself is an honest man.

4.12.2   EVIDENCE OF CHARACTER

Evidence of character refers to the statements of witnesses in answer to questions concerning a party's character. Such statements are couched in general terms and hence are easily distinguishable from evidence of specific acts, which is considered under the heading of similar fact evidence (*AG v O'Leary* [1926] IR 445). An example of when an accused might introduce evidence of good character would be reference to previous acts of honesty, such as returning lost property when the charge is theft (*R v Samuel* [1956] 40 Cr App Rep 8.)

4.12.3   SIMILAR FACT EVIDENCE

As a general rule evidence of conduct, which is of no particular relevance apart from its tendency to show a bad disposition, is inadmissible. Lord Herschell in *Makin v AG of New South Wales* [1894] AC 57, at p 65, stated:

> 'It is undoubtedly not competent for the prosecution to adduce evidence tending to show that the accused has been guilty of criminal acts other than those covered by the indictment for the purposes of leading to the conclusion that the accused is a person likely from his criminal conduct of character to have committed the offence for which he is being tried.'

Similar fact evidence is admissible in the following situations:

(a)   evidence of conduct on other occasions exists which is of particular relevance in spite of its tendency to show bad disposition (*R v Armstrong* [1922] 2 KB 555);

(b)   there is State evidence which forms part of the same transaction to such an extent that the acts are so inextricably bound up that it is impossible to differentiate between them;

(c)   the evidence shows 'system';

(d)   evidence exists which may rebut a defence (*R v Dempsey* [1961] IR 268); or

(e)   similar fact evidence exists to rebut the defence that the acts performed were totally innocent and involved no guilty intent (*R v Bond* [1906] 2 KB 389).

4.12.4   ABANDONMENT OF THE 'HUDSON' DOCTRINE

Interpretation of the Criminal Evidence Act 1924 in accordance with the 'Hudson' doctrine of giving the words their 'ordinary and natural meaning' meant that attacks on prosecution witnesses by the accused came within s 1(f)(ii) of the Act and resulted in the loss of the 'shield' even where such attacks were necessary for the establishment of the accused's defence. This position unduly disadvantaged those accused persons whose defence consisted, for example, of an allegation that the police had fabricated the evidence in the case. Although a judicial discretion existed to disallow an accused's record to go in in certain cases, this was an uncertain and unsatisfactory remedy.

In a decision of the Irish Court of Criminal Appeal, in the case of *DPP v McGrail* [1990] 2 IR 38, the position of such accused persons has been ameliorated and the harshness of the

'Hudson' doctrine mitigated. The case concerned the issue of the admissibility of the accused's record (under s 1(f)(ii) of the Act) in a situation where the defence had made allegations to the effect that prosecution witnesses had fabricated evidence of verbal admissions. The trial judge had admitted evidence of the record. On appeal, Hederman J stated that such evidence should not have been admitted, and that every criminal trial involved an imputation as to the character of somebody. In this particular case, the case against the accused was based on confessions which he denied making to the police. The inescapable inference was that the police were not telling the truth. It would be intolerable, Hederman J said, if an accused were confined to suggesting a mistake or other innocent explanation rather than dishonesty, merely to avoid any risk of subjecting his own character to cross-examination. It would be otherwise, however, if the defence case was that this was the usual practice of the police in respect of any person they prosecuted. It would similarly be otherwise if an imputation of bad character were introduced relating to matters unconnected with the proofs of the material case. It is interesting to note that the court justified this departure from the previous position, established by English case law, by reference to the necessity of compliance with the principles of fair procedure.

4.12.5   IMPUTATIONS

Imputations need not involve allegations that prosecution witnesses committed crimes. In *R v Bishop* [1974] 2 All ER 1206, a man aged over 21 who was charged with burglary sought to explain the presence of his fingerprints on articles in the room of the prosecutor by alleging that they had had a consensual homosexual relationship. The Court of Appeal allowed his resultant cross-examination regarding previous convictions for offences involving dishonesty.

In *Selvey v DPP* [1970] AC 304, Selvey was charged with buggery. Indecent photographs were found in his room and medical evidence proved that someone had sexually assaulted the prosecutor on the day in question. Selvey's defence involved the allegation that the prosecutor had told him that he had already 'been on the bed' with a man for £1 and would do the same for him for £1. According to Selvey, it was annoyance at rejection that prompted the 'dumping' of photos on him by the prosecutor. This involved imputations on the character of the prosecutor, which it was alleged were necessary for the development of Selvey's defence. The trial judge allowed the cross-examination of Selvey with regard to previous homosexual offences. The Court of Appeal and House of Lords dismissed appeals. Lord Dilhorne stated that case law had established that:

(a)   the words of the statute must be given their natural meaning;

(b)   the section permits cross-examination of someone when the imputations are necessary for the accused's defence;

(c)   in rape cases the accused can allege 'consent', without placing himself in peril of cross-examination; and

(d)   denials in emphatic language do not come within the section.

The existence of a general rule that judicial discretion should be exercised in favour of an accused when imputations were necessary for the proper development of a defence was thus denied.

The test for determining whether one of two accused people has 'given evidence against' the other is to ask whether their testimony tends to undermine the other's defence. Accordingly, if two people are jointly charged with stealing an article in circumstances where the theft must have been effected by one or other or both of them, the mere denial of one that they had anything to do with taking the article will expose him to cross-examination.

An accused against whom evidence is given by a co-accused has a right to cross-examine their co-accused. The court has no discretion to prevent this as, from the perspective of the accused, the co-accused is a witness for the prosecution.

4.12.6   EVIDENCE IN REBUTTAL

If an accused were to deny a previous conviction in cross-examination, it could be proved against him in rebuttal; similarly with evidence of good character. If in cross-examination as to the issue, the accused were to deny previous misconduct of which no evidence in chief had been given, it is possible that the judge would allow evidence in rebuttal to be given; however, if the cross-examination were merely as to credit, the accused's answers would be final.

4.13   Opinion evidence

4.13.1   INTRODUCTION

Yet another exclusionary rule of the law of evidence is that concerning opinion evidence. The general rule is that witnesses must speak only facts which they have observed, and not of inferences which they draw from such facts. In part, the justification for this rule can be found in the fact that for the witness in question to draw conclusions and form opinions in regard to proved facts would constitute an usurpation of the function of the jury as trier of fact.

4.13.2   EXCEPTIONS TO THE GENERAL RULE

Exceptions to the general rule do exist. For example, experts can give opinion evidence. Generally, expert witnesses are called in relation to what are termed matters of 'science and art'.

Non-experts can also, in certain instances, give what may be regarded as opinion evidence. This type of opinion evidence is mostly received because it would be virtually impossible for the witness to confine themselves to the observed facts, and so leave the inference to the jury. Examples of this occurring include testimony as to whether the accused had been drinking; the identity of persons, things, and handwriting; the speed of a vehicle; the age of a person; and the state of the weather.

In *AG (Ruddy) v Kenny* [1960] 94 ILTR 185, the defendant was charged with drunken driving. The prosecution proposed to ask a Garda witness whether in his opinion the defendant 'was drunk and incapable of driving the vehicle'. Davitt P in the High Court held that: 'Drunkenness, unfortunately, is a condition which is not so exceptional or so much outside the experience of the ordinary individual, that it should require an expert to diagnose it. In my opinion a Garda witness, or an ordinary witness, may give evidence of his opinion as to whether a person is drunk or not.'

With regard to whether a non-expert witness may express their opinion as to whether a defendant is drunk to such an extent that they are incapable of exercising proper control over a mechanically propelled vehicle, Davitt P continued: 'It seems to me that if it is admissible for an ordinary witness to express his opinion as to whether a defendant is drunk or not it should be admissible for him to express an opinion as to how drunk he was.'

In the Supreme Court, however, although the majority concurred with the President of the High Court, Kingsmill-Moore J's dissenting is significant. Kingsmill-Moore J's objection to admitting evidence of opinion that a person was drunk was founded on the vagueness of that term, which can incorporate anything from 'stone cold sober' to 'dead drunk'. All is dependent on what the particular witness understands as drunkenness. With regard to the expression of a further opinion as to whether the defendant is incapable of driving a motor vehicle, Kingsmill-Moore J further objected, on the grounds that opinion evidence by a non-expert is 'either otiose or dangerous', particularly when the expression of opinion is as to the exact question at issue. He stated: 'I am of the opinion that the interests of justice can be adequately served by getting a witness to describe the appearance, movements, demeanour, action and words of a person whose condition is in question and leaving it to the District Justice to draw his own conclusions.'

In *DPP v A and BC Chewing Gum Ltd* [1968] 1 QB 159, where the accused was charged with obscenity, a psychiatrist was allowed to testify as to whether material was likely to corrupt or deprave, this being the test for obscenity.

In *Lowrie v R* [1974] AC 85, a clinical psychologist was permitted to give evidence on behalf of one of two accused people to establish that that accused's version of the facts was more probable than the version put forward by the other.

In *R v Anderson and Neville* [1971] 3 All ER 1152, involving the trial of *Oz* magazine for obscenity, a witness for the defence testified to show that the article in question was not obscene as it did not have a tendency to corrupt and deprave. Widgery J excluded the evidence on the grounds that whether 'an article is obscene or not is a question exclusively for the jury and expert evidence should not be admitted as to whether it is obscene or not. The courts must relate the facts of the case to the standard.'

In *DPP v Kehoe* [1992] ILRM 481, O'Flaherty J held that a psychiatrist overstepped the mark by testifying as to whether the accused had an intention to kill and whether they should be believed, saying that these were matters 'four-square within the jury's function'.

4.13.3   THE RULE IN *HOLLINGTON V HEWTHORN*

The rule in *Hollington v Hewthorn* [1943] 1 KB 587 states that a judicial finding is inadmissible as evidence of facts found in relation to different proceedings. For example, if an accused runs his car up onto a footpath and hits someone, and is charged and convicted with careless driving, on a subsequent action in the High Court for negligence the claimant shall not be able to introduce evidence of the conviction as proof of the defendant's negligence. This rule has been abolished in England and Northern Ireland, yet continues to apply in Ireland.

4.13.4   DNA FINGERPRINTING

The discovery that each of us has a unique genetic 'fingerprint' or make-up has immense potential in the legal context, because of its ability to link individuals with other persons or events. Originally used in family law and immigration issues, DNA forensics has been found to have considerable utility in the criminal law context also.

The Criminal Justice (Forensic Evidence) Act 1990 provides for the obtaining of samples for purposes of DNA testing, from individuals who are 'in custody' under the Offences Against the State Act 1939, s 30 or of the Criminal Justice Act 1984, s 4.

Some samples (eg intimate body swabs, urine, blood) can only be taken with the written consent of the individual concerned. Where such consent is refused, the court can draw inferences from such refusal. Provision is made for destruction of samples and records should charges not be proceeded or an acquittal ensues.

Given current controversy in other jurisdictions, most notably the USA, with regard to safeguarding procedure and interpretation of DNA data, caution should be exercised when faced with apparently immutable expert testimony with regard to such data.

4.14   Illegally obtained evidence

Any evidence obtained as a result of a conscious and deliberate violation of the defendant's constitutional rights must be excluded, unless there are extraordinary, excusing circumstances. An example would be evidence obtained on foot of an illegal search of the defendant's dwelling, or a statement of admission made by the defendant when in illegal custody. If the evidence is illegally obtained but none of the defendant's constitutional rights has been infringed, the judge has a discretion to allow the evidence. An example of this would be an illegal search of premises other than a dwelling house.

Any confession made by the defendant must be excluded unless the court is satisfied that the statement was made voluntarily, without any inducement or threat. The interviewing of suspects by the Gardaí is governed by the nine Judges' Rules (see **6.4.3**). However, even if the rules are breached, the judge has a discretion to rule that the evidence is admissible.

4.14.1   SEARCHING THE PERSON

Consent of the person concerned can be lawful justification for a search by a police officer. Statutory authority may provide a power of search (eg Misuse of Drugs Act 1977, s 26(3), which permits persons to be searched. In *O'Callaghan v Ireland* [1994] 1 IR 555 such a statutory power, short of arrest, under s 23 of the Misuse of Drugs Act 1977 (as amended by s 12 of the Misuse of Drugs Act 1984) was upheld under a constitutional challenge. The Supreme Court held that such persons did have all rights accruing on arrest.

4.14.2   POWER OF ARREST AND SEARCH

DPP v Fagan (1993) 2 IR 95 seems to indicate a possible 'implied' statutory power or common law power short of arrest. Carney J held that the Garda Síochána had both an implied statutory power under the Road Traffic Acts and a common law power to operate random road traffic checks involving the stopping of vehicles, even where the Gardaí did not suspect the drivers of any criminal offence. The Supreme Court confirmed on appeal (Denham J dissenting) that such a power existed at common law. On arrest a person can be searched for the protection of the arresting officer. His/her immediate environment may also be searched (*Dillon v O'Brien & Davis* vol 20 LR (Ireland) 300). Mr Justice O'Keeffe outlined in *Jennings v Quinn* (1968) IR 305, HC the parameters of police powers of search and seizure of material in the aftermath of a lawful arrest as follows:

(1)   They can take evidence in support of the crime charged on which the arrest is made;

(2)   Evidence in support of any crime charged or then in contemplation against the person; and

(3)   Evidence reasonably believed to be stolen property or to be property unlawfully in possession of that person.

Access to evidence in police possession by the accused was discussed in *Robert Murphy v DPP* (1989) (ILRM) 1971.

4.14.3   SEARCH WARRANTS

Search warrants traditionally are very specific and limited exceptions which have been made to the historically important principle of the common law that 'a man's home is his castle'. In general a search warrant is 'spent' when used once, and cannot be used again with the exception of the powers conferred under s 26 (2) Misuse of Drugs Act 1977, which allows the execution of a warrant 'at any time or times within one month from the date of issue of the warrant'. With regard to the use of a premises for the purposes of prostitution and living on the earnings of prostitution s 10(2) of the Criminal Law (Sexual Offences) Act 1993 provides that a District Court can issue a warrant authorizing a search of such premises 'at any time or times within one month from the date of issue of the warrant'.

Recent provision has involved a number of changes to provisions regarding the issue of search warrants including provision for warrants to 'live' for a period of time, and in some cases for a Garda issuance of a warrant. The more significant of these recent provisions is the issue of a warrant regarding the commission of a serious offences under s 10 of the Criminal Justice (Miscellaneous) Provisions Act 1997 and the warrant provisions under the Criminal Justice (Drug Trafficking) Act 1996.

4.14.4   APPROACH OF JUDICIARY TO ILLEGALLY OBTAINED EVIDENCE

Recently, English Courts indicate a change of approach, with regard to the admissibility of illegally obtained evidence, although the change may be more apparent than real. In *R v Mason* (1987) 3 All ER 481 the Court of Appeal commented that although the Courts' role was not to discipline the police, the 'hoodwinking' of the client and his solicitor in this case necessitated the exclusion of the evidence thereby obtained. The basis for exclusion in *Mason* and other recent English decisions is grounded in the Police and Criminal Evidence Act 1984, s 78, which the Courts state now encapsulates their previous discretion at common law. The English Courts may further change their approach in light of the Human Rights Act 1998.

The exclusionary rule in relation to illegally obtained evidence in the United States was developed initially in *Boyd v US* 116 US 616 (1866) in relation to forfeiture proceedings. *Weeks v US* 232 US 383 (1914) extended the doctrine to federal criminal trials, and *Mapp v Ohio* 367 US 643 (1961) to State criminal trials.

Furthermore the doctrine of the 'fruit of the poisoned tree' in the United States operated to exclude evidence obtained indirectly in consequence of a constitutional violation. The police base the rationale for the exclusionary rule firmly in the notion of deterrence of unacceptable violation of constitutional rights:

> 'Only by exclusion can we impress upon the zealous prosecutor that violation of the constitution will do him no good. And only when that point is driven home can the prosecutor be expected to emphasise the importance of observing constitutional demands in his instructions to the police.' (Murphy J (dissenting) in *Wolfe v Colorado* 338 US 25 (1949) at p 41.)

More recently, however, the US Supreme Court has proven less enamoured of the exclusionary rule, and in a number of decisions, has somewhat reduced its monolithic effect. For example, if the Court determines that the rationale of the rule—deterrence— will not be effected in a given case, the evidence will be admitted, notwithstanding the breach of constitutional rights involved (eg *US v Leon* 468 US 879).

The Irish judicial position is best exemplified by tracing the development of the relevant case law. The search warrants in *People (AG) v O'Brien & O'Brien* SC 1964 (1965) IR 142 contained an error in relation to the name of the street. The action was deemed illegal, thereby incorporating discretion on the part of the trial judge to exclude the evidence.

Kingsmill Moore J asked: 'Was the illegal action intentional or unintentional, and if intentional was it the result of an ad hoc decision or does it represent a settled or deliberate policy? Was it illegality of a trivial and technical nature or was it a serious invasion of important rights, the recurrence of which would involve a real danger to necessary freedom? Were there circumstances of urgency or emergency which provide some excuse for the action?' In *People v Shaw* (1982) IRL Griffin J suggested that the *O'Brien* ratio was confined to real evidence. In *People v Christopher Lynch* (1982) IR 64 Higgins CJ, however, castigated this suggestion and re-asserted that in fact the *O'Brien* ratio covered both real and confession evidence.

In *Robert Trimbole v Governor of Mountjoy Prison* (1985) 1 LRM 465 Egan J (HC) stated at p 479:

> 'the only rational explanation for the S. 30 arrest on 25th October, 1984 was to ensure that the applicant would be available for arrest and detention when Part 11 of the 1965 Act would apply to the Commonwealth of Australia. There was a gross misuse of S. 30 which amounted to a conscious and deliberate violation of constitutional rights. There were no extraordinary excusing circumstances.'

Finlay CJ (Henchy, Griffin, Henderman concurring) said at p 484: 'I am satisfied that from those decisions *State (Quinn) v Ryan* (1965) IR 70; *People (AG) v O'Brien* (1965) IR 342; *People v Madden* (1977) IR 336; *People v Lynch* (1982) IR 64 certain principles can be deduced. They are:

The Courts have not only an inherent jurisdiction but also a positive duty:

(i)   To protect persons against the invasion of their constitutional rights.

(ii)   If invasion has occurred, to restore as far as possible the person so damaged to the position in which he would be if his rights had not been invaded; and

(iii)   To ensure as far as possible that persons acting on behalf of the Executive who consciously and deliberately violate the constitutional right of citizens do not for themselves or their superiors obtain the planned results of that invasion.

> 'I am satisfied that this principle of our law is of wider application than merely to either the question of the admissibility of evidence or to the question of the punishment of persons for contempt of Court by unconstitutional action.'

In the context of the Irish Courts' approach to illegally obtained evidence, an increased willingness to admit evidence under the *O'Brien* formula is evident on occasion, which leads to a certain inconsistency among the decisions. Some recent decisions are interesting in this regard.

DPP v Lawless McCarthy, Keane and O'Hanlon JJ (delivered 28 November 1985) where the accused was convicted of an offence under the Misuse of Drugs Act 1977 it was held that as warrant defective, entry and search of premises unlawful. However, as the accused was not a tenant of the flat, there was no breach of his constitutional rights. Even if there was a breach of his constitutional rights, it was not a conscious violation. There was no evidence of deliberate deceit or illegality, no policy to disregard provisions of constitution or to conduct searches without a warrant. Even if there was a deliberate and conscious violation there were 'extraordinary excusing circumstances' and the need to prevent the imminent destruction of vital evidence. The decision in *DPP v McMahon, McMeel and Wright* (1987) ILRM 86 SC delivered 20 June 1986 (Finlay CJ) established that in balancing the public interest that crime should be detected against the undesirability of using improper methods, particular importance may attach to the fact that the Gardaí, in entering the public houses to view the machines, were trespassers only; not involved in any criminal or opprobrious conduct and that the offence of permitting gaming on licensed premises may be considered as one with grave social consequences. In *DPP v Gaffney* SC 23 February 1987, the guards were trespassers and their entry in violation of Art 40.5 (inviolability of the dwelling); and the arrest of the accused unlawful. In *DPP v McCreesh* a similar factual situation arose but this time the accused was arrested on the driveway leading into his house. Nonetheless the Court held the same constitutional protection applied and being without authority the Garda invasion of the property tainted the evidence obtained after the arrest (SC 7 March 1991).

This situation has now been the subject of attention in the Road Traffic Act 1994. Sections 10 and 11 provide for a power on the part of the Gardaí to arrest without warrant in relation to 'drink-driving' offences. Section 39 provides for a power to enter a dwelling in relation to 'hit and run' offences (s 106(3)(a) also gives a power to arrest without warrant in relation to it). A power to enter the curtilage of a dwelling is also provided for in this section. This applies to 'drink-driving' offences, as does the power to enter a hospital to obtain a specimen. In *DPP v Forbes* [1994] 2 IR 542 the Supreme Court held that there is an implied permission on the part of every householder with regard to entry onto the forecourt of the premises. This may be rebutted but was not here, so that the arrest of the defendant for drunk driving on a third party's property (driveway of a private house) was valid. The Court of Criminal Appeal certified a point of law of exceptional public importance for the Supreme Court in *People (DPP) v Mark Kenny* (1990) ILRM 569 viz, whether the forcible entry of the accused's home by the Gardaí on foot of an invalid search warrant constituted a deliberate and conscious violation of the accused's constitutional rights such as to render any evidence obtained thereby inadmissible at the trial of the accused. The Supreme Court held that the warrant was invalid and so breached Article 40.5 of the Constitution. Further, the breach was deliberate and conscious, as it was immaterial whether the person carrying out the breach was aware it was illegal or it amounted to a breach of constitutional rights. There were no extraordinary excusing circumstances. Hence, the evidence was inadmissible at the trial. *DPP v Yamanoha* [1994] 1 IR 565 followed Kenny where a warrant issued in relation to a hotel room under s 26 Misuse of Drugs Act 1977 (as amended s 13 Misuse of Drugs Act 1984). The warrant was challenged on the basis that the information on oath was confined to reciting the Detective Sergeant's reasonable grounds was not sufficient. The DPP contended that oral evidence was given as well. However, as that was unsworn, the warrant was invalid. In *DPP v Dunne* [1994] 2 IR 537, a warrant under s 26 was again deemed invalid as the words 'is on the premises' were deleted from it. Carney J held that if the inviolability of the dwelling is to be set aside by a printed form, it should be clear. *Freeman v DPP* [1996] 3 IR 565 held: that the initial arrest was invalid as although it was in a public place, the appellant's presence there induced by Garda. The exclusionary rule did not entitle Garda to breach constitutional rights in extraordinary excusing circumstances. Given that the Gardaí came upon the appellant in flagrante delicto and that his dwelling was being employed in the commission of an offence, the District Justice could exercise his discretion to admit the evidence. There was ample evidence grounding the search warrant independent from that perceived upon the unconstitutional entry.

The High Court held in *DPP v Delaney Kelly Lawless & Crowley* [1997] 3 IR 453 and the Supreme Court confirmed on appeal that the safeguarding of life and limb was more important than the inviolability of the dwelling. *People v Veronica Balfe* (CCA 15 May 1997) [1998] 4 IR 50 held that a search warrant which innocently describes premises incorrectly is not without operative effect. Property seized in innocent reliance thereon may be admissible. Kenny was distinguished on the grounds that the warrant gave no indication on its face of inherent flaw and the defendant could have refused Garda access. In *Hanahoe v Hussey* [1998] 3 IR 69 a search warrant was issued regarding the applicants' office premises. Damages were awarded, as although publicity did not of itself invalidate the warrant, there was a duty of care on the part of the Gardaí to the citizen regarding information which was being made public. The accused in *People v McCann* [1998] 4 IR 397 was convicted of the murder of his wife and foster-child at the family home. He unsuccessfully argued that forensic evidence gathered from the burnt dwelling was inadmissible as it was gathered without his consent. The extraordinary excusing circumstance of this case prevented the destruction of vital evidence.

The 'Fruit of the Poisoned Tree' principle was discussed in *People (DPP) v O'Donnell* [1995] 3 IR 551. The accused was a suspected IRA member. The Court of Criminal Appeal affirmed conviction holding that evidence obtained following a deliberate and conscious breach was only excluded if obtained as result of that breach and where a causative link existed between the breaches and obtaining that evidence. Even if it were conceded that the search of the right hand side pocket was unlawful, there were no casual connections between that search and the later search of the pocket containing explosives.

Admissibility of illegally obtained evidence, in the context of the use or abuse of the pre-trial process, has been the subject of changing judicial attitude in the United States (formerly exclusionary, now a more inclusive approach); Britain (formerly inclusive now rather more exclusionary); and in the Irish Courts the *O'Brien* formula, although still an applicable criterion to determine admissibility (*Kenny*), has been seen to demonstrate a facility for inclusion or exclusion of evidence, dependent on the interpretation not only of 'extraordinary excusing circumstances' but also the phrase 'deliberate and conscious'. It may be the most recent *Kenny* decision has resolved the position at least in relation to the latter criterion. Overall, however, certain fluidity in terms of approach is evident from the case law in this area.

4.15 The rule against hearsay

4.15.1 INTRODUCTION

'A statement other than one made by a person while giving oral evidence in the proceedings is inadmissible as evidence of any fact or opinion stated.' The rule against hearsay applies not only to spoken but also to written assertions. It also applies to non-verbal assertions, at least if intended to be assertive, such as deliberate gestures.

It is important to note that the hearsay rule is concerned only with assertions, whether express or implied, which are tendered as evidence of their truth. The rule does not apply, therefore, in the case of evidence tendered to show that a statement, true or false, was made. Again, words, the utterance of which tends to show that a particular state of mind was induced in another, do not offend the rule against hearsay if what is asserted is not their truth, but rather the fact that they may reasonably have been believed by the other. Furthermore, evidence of the previous statements of a witness, if admitted in order to bolster credibility, do not contravene the rule against hearsay. Neither is the rule offended against when a witness is allowed to use a document for the purposes of refreshing his/her memory. There are, therefore, many exceptions to the hearsay rule. These exceptions were summarized by Kingsmill-Moore J in *Cullen v Clarke* [1963] IR 368:

> 'there is no general rule of evidence to the effect that a witness may not testify as to the words spoken by a person who is not produced as a witness. There is a general rule, subject to many exceptions, that evidence of the speaking of such words is inadmissible to prove the truth of the facts which they assert; the reasons being that the truth of the words cannot be tested by cross-examination and had not the sanctity of an oath. This is the rule known as the rule against hearsay. . . . I may perhaps call attention to some of the cases in which evidence may properly be given of words uttered by persons who are not called as witnesses.
>
> First: the utterance of the words may itself be a relevant fact, quite apart from the truth or falsity of anything asserted by the words spoken. To prove, by the evidence of a witness who heard the words, that they were spoken, is direct evidence, and in no way encroaches on the general rule against hearsay.
>
> Second: where a fact or transaction is an issue, declarations which accompany or explain the fact of transaction are generally admitted under the somewhat vague principle that they form part of the *res gestae*.
>
> Third: the statements accompanying the act may be offered as showing the mind of the actor at the time of the doing of the act. Here there is a breach of the hearsay rule, in so far as reliance is

placed on the truth of the words uttered, a truth, which is not sanctified by an oath or capable of being tested by cross-examination.

Fourth: as to the admissibility of declarations as to states of mind, where such declarations are made prior to or subsequent to an act and unconnected therewith, the authorities are not uniform, but the modern tendency is to admit such declarations.'

In *People (DPP and Kelly) v McGinley* [1998] 2 ILRM 233, hearsay evidence tendered by the Gardaí in a bail application with regard to threats to the victim's family was objected to on the basis of its being inadmissible hearsay. This objection was upheld on the basis of natural justice.

4.15.2   EXCEPTIONS TO THE RULE

4.15.2.1   Confession evidence

One of the major common law exceptions to the rule against hearsay in criminal cases is the rule that permits the prosecution to adduce in evidence admissions and confessions made by the accused person. This is an exception to the hearsay rule because it amounts to the offering in evidence by the prosecution of a confession or admission which they assert to state the truth of facts of which they have no personal knowledge. Confession evidence has, however, proven contentious. Judicial attitudes with regard to its probity and value as evidence have varied down through the years. In *R v Thompson* [1893] 2 QB 12, at p 18, Cave J expressed the following sentiments with regard to confession evidence:

'I always suspect these confessions which are supposed to be the offspring of penitence and remorse, and which nevertheless are repudiated by the prisoner at the trial. It is remarkable that it is of very rare occurrence for evidence of a confession to be given when the proof of the prisoner's guilt is otherwise clear and satisfactory; but when it is not clear and satisfactory, the prisoner is not infrequently alleged to have been seized with the desire to supplement it with a confession; a desire which varies as soon as he appears in a court of justice.'

4.15.2.1.1   *Public policy considerations*

Public policy considerations have also entered the realm of judicial reasoning, with regard to the exception permitted to the hearsay rule by the admission of confession evidence. It is felt particularly by a judiciary who have to uphold constitutional guarantees that the admissibility of such evidence should be strictly controlled, born as it is of the direct confrontation between the State and the individual, and tinged as it always will be with potential dangers of undue and exclusive reliance by the agents of the State on such methods of investigation and conviction.

Given the development of a mature constitutional jurisprudence by the Irish Supreme Court in particular, Irish case law in this area tends to resemble more that of the United States than our more geographically proximate common law neighbours. The distinction in attitude can be easily illustrated by contrasting the traditional position of the English court in *Kuruma v R* [1955] AC 197: 'The test to be applied in considering whether evidence is admissible is whether it is relevant to the matters in issue. If it is, it is admissible and the Court is not concerned with how the evidence is obtained.' The attitude of the Scottish courts which starts from the opposite premise that practically all illegally obtained evidence, including confessions, is admissible.

The Irish courts have stated that both with regard to real and confession evidence, the position is such that if illegally obtained, the judge has a discretion to exclude it, but if it is obtained as a result of the infringement of constitutionally guaranteed rights, such evidence is, subject to limited exceptions, automatically excluded. Kennedy CJ in *AG v McCabe* [1927] IR 129 stated: 'However desirable it is to have the *ipsisimma verba* of a deponent, it is not the law that the statement of an accused person must as a matter of law be rejected if it is not in his *ipsissima verba*.' In *People (AG) v Cummins* [1972] IR 312, Walsh

J emphasised the fact that a trial judge has no discretion to admit a confession which is not voluntary.

4.15.2.1.2 *The voluntary nature of a confession*

In *AG v McCabe* [1927] IR 129 at p 134, Kennedy CJ adopted and endorsed the rather technical and limited definition of the criterion of voluntariness laid down by Lord Summer in *Ibrahim v R* [1914] AC 599, which stated:

> 'It is a positive rule of law that such a statement shall not be admitted in evidence against the prisoner unless it is a voluntary statement in the sense that it has not been obtained from him either by fear of prejudice or hope of advantage exercised or held out by a person in authority and the onus is on the prosecution tendering the statement to show that it is voluntary in that sense.'

Where an inducement was held out by someone not being a person in authority, if in fact it was made in the presence of a person in authority, the position is the same as if that person in authority had themselves held out the inducement, unless they indicated dissent from it (*The People v Murphy* [1947] IR 236).

In the Supreme Court decision of *People (AG) v O'Brien* [1965] IR 142, Walsh J at p 170 said:

> 'The courts in exercising the judicial powers of government of the state must recognise the paramount position of constitutional rights and must uphold the objection of an accused person to the admissibility at his trial of evidence obtained or procured by the state or its servants or agents as a result of a deliberate and conscious violation of the constitutional rights of the accused person where no extraordinary excusing circumstances exist, such as the imminent destruction of vital evidence or the need to rescue a victim in peril. . . . I would also place in the excusable category evidence obtained by a search incidental to and contemporaneous with a lawful arrest although made without a valid search warrant. . . . In my view evidence obtained in deliberate conscious breach of the constitutional rights of an accused person should, save in the excusable circumstances outlined above, be absolutely inadmissible.'

In *People v Christopher Lynch* [1982] IR 64, O'Higgins CJ applied the criteria laid down with regard to real evidence in the case of *People v O'Brien*. The confession evidence presented in the former case. The requirement is that the evidence be obtained without 'deliberate and conscious' breach of the constitutional rights of the accused and if obtained illegally although not automatically excluded, the trial judge retains discretion to exclude it. Hence this case puts paid to the suggestion of Griffith J in *People v Shaw* [1982] 1 IR 1 that the *O'Brien* ratio applied only to real evidence.

In *R v Prager* [1972] 1 WLR 260, Esmond Davies LJ adopted the statement of Sachs J in *R v Priestley* (1966) 50 Cr App R 183, in referring to what constituted 'oppression' in the context of the Judges' Rules, in the following manner:

> 'to my mind, this word, in the context of the principles under consideration imports something which tends to sap and has sapped, that free will which must exist before a confession is voluntary. . . . They include such things as the length of time of any individual period of questioning, the length of time intervening between periods of questioning, whether the accused person had been given proper refreshment or not, and the characteristics of the person who makes the statement. What may be oppressive as regards a child, an invalid, or an old man, or somebody inexperienced in the ways of this world may turn out not to be oppressive when one finds that the accused person is of a tough character and an experienced man of the world.'

4.16 Application of the principles of the 'judges' rules'

In *People (AG) v Cummins* [1972] IR 312, Walsh J enumerated the Judges' Rules as they applied in Ireland (see **Chapter 6**). It is important to remember that these rules are purely discretionary in effect, and breach of them does not automatically lead to the exclusion of evidence.

In *Travers v Ryan* [1985] ILRM 343, Finlay P stated that in relation to a person under 14 years of age it is most desirable in the interests of justice that, unless there are practical impossibilities, if they are suspected of crime they should not be questioned except in the presence of a parent or some person of 'an adult kind' in the position of guardian. Kennedy CJ said in *AG v Bridget Cleary* (1983) 72 ILTR 84 that a caution must not be a mere parrot-like recital.

It was held in *People (AG) v Stephen Murphy* [1947] IR 236 that a confession is not inadmissible merely because it was obtained as a result of questioning by the police, nor is it necessarily voluntary whenever it is preceded by a caution. In *McCarrick v Leavy* [1964] IR 225, Davitt P of the High Court stated that it was never intended by the Judges' Rules that a police officer should caution every person of whom he proposed to ask a question. In the Supreme Court, however, Walsh J stated as follows:

> 'A failure to comply with the provisions of the Judges' Rules gives a discretion to the trial judge to refuse to admit the evidence in question, but the exercise of that discretion is not governed by whether or not the statement is voluntary. A statement obtained in breach of the provisions of the Judges' Rules is admissible provided it is a voluntary one. But the fact that it is a voluntary one does not take away the trial judge's discretion to refuse to admit the evidence if it has been obtained in violation of the Judges' Rules.'

In *DPP v Anthony Hoey*, 16 December 1987, SC (unreported), a statement by a detective, which was held to be an inducement, was adjudged on the basis of what effect it was calculated to produce upon the person to whom it was made and not the subjective test of what was intended or even hoped for by the person who made it.

It should be remembered here that the Criminal Procedure Act 1993, s 10, requires a judge to advise a jury to have due regard to the absence of corroboration of a confession.

In the course of his detention under the Offences Against the State Act 1939, s 30, the accused in *People v Ward*, 23 October 1998, SCC (unreported), in the absence of a request from Ward, had his girlfriend and 74-year-old mother taken in to see him. The court described this procedure as 'a deliberate ploy' designed by the police to cause Ward to incriminate himself and consequently regarded it as a conscious and deliberate disregard of the accused's basic right to fair procedure. All admissions which occurred as a result of this 'ploy' were ruled inadmissible.

Admissions other than formal admissions, made by a party for the purposes of a particular trial, made by a party or one privy to him, may be proved against him, as an exception to the rule against hearsay. Such admissions may be expressed or implied by conduct.

4.17   Statements forming part of the *res gestae*

4.17.1   GENERALLY

The doctrine of *res gestae* is an inclusionary one, unlike most of the rules of evidence. There are four exceptions to the hearsay rule associated with the doctrine of *res gestae* in criminal cases.

4.17.2   EXCEPTIONS TO THE HEARSAY RULE ASSOCIATED WITH THE DOCTRINE OF *RES GESTAE*

These exceptions are:

    (a)   statements accompanying and explaining a relevant act;

    (b)   spontaneous statements relating to an event in issue;

(c)   a person's statements concerning his contemporaneous state of mind or emotion;

(d)   a person's statements concerning his contemporaneous physical sensation.

Wilberforce LJ in *Ratten v R* [1972] AC 378 at p 389 stated: 'it must be for the Judge, by preliminary ruling to satisfy himself that the statement was so clearly made in circumstances of spontaneity or involvement in the event that the possibility of concoction can be disregarded.' Lord Tomlin was not so complimentary to the doctrine of *res gestae* in *Holmes v Newman* where he stated that it was merely 'a phrase adopted to provide a respectable legal cloak for a variety of cases to which no formulae of precision can be applied'.

4.17.2.1   Statements accompanying and explaining a relevant act

The vital issue in any instance of evidence claiming to come within the ambit of the *res gestae* doctrine is that it is a statement which accompanies and explains a relevant act. The vital prerequisites are that the statement is contemporaneous with the act in question; that the statement is made in relation to the act; and that the person performing the act makes it.

4.17.2.2   Spontaneous statements relating to an event in issue

On the whole the case law in this area concerns emergency situations. In *Edward's case* (1872) 12 Cox CC 230 where the wife of the accused handed a knife to a neighbour saying that she would feel safer if it was out of the way the statement was held admissible as evidence to prove that previous threats had been made.

In *R v Foster* (1834) 6 C&P 325, the deceased had been knocked down on the road, and a statement on his part at the time of the accident was admitted in evidence as was the statement on the part of the accused at the same time 'that he shouldn't have done it'.

4.17.2.3   Statements concerning the maker's contemporaneous state of mind or emotion

Statements concerning the maker's contemporaneous state of mind or emotion are admissible under the doctrine of *res gestae* as evidence of the said state of mind or emotion. In *R v Vincent Frost & Edwards* (1840) 9 C&P 275, it was alleged that general alarm had been caused at a public meeting. Statements of what people attending the public meeting felt, namely that they were frightened, were admitted.

4.17.2.4   Statements concerning the maker's contemporaneous physical condition

In *People (AG) v Crosbie and Meehan* [1966] IR 490, prosecution evidence to show that within a minute or so of receiving a fatal wound the deceased had said 'he has a knife, he stabbed me', was admitted in evidence against the two accused charged with the murder who were at the time of the statement standing beside the deceased.

The House of Lords in *R v Andrews* [1987] 1 All ER 513 held that hearsay evidence made to a witness by the victim of an attack describing how he got his injuries is admissible as part of the *res gestae*, if the statement is made in conditions sufficiently spontaneous and sufficiently contemporaneous with the event to preclude the possibility of concoction or distortion. The victim's statement had to be so closely associated with the event which excited the statement that the victim's mind was still dominated by the event and that the circumstances were such that there was no possibility of concoction or distortion.

4.18 Dying declarations of the deceased in charges of homicide

'The oral or written declaration of the deceased is admissible evidence of the cause of his death at a trial for his murder or manslaughter, provided he was under a settled hopeless expectation of death when the statement was made, and provided he would have been a competent witness if called to give evidence at that time' (*Cross & Wilkins on Evidence* at p 171). The underlying rationale of this rule is the presumption that a person is unlikely to die with a 'lie on his lips'.

The declaration in *The Crown v Mooney Dublin City Commission* (1851) 5 Cox CC 318 was held inadmissible, as the deceased had not been told expressly that she was dying, though the doctor had told her she was dangerously ill and the clergyman warned her to prepare for death. In *R v Fitzpatrick* (1912) 46 ILTR 173, Palles CB stated that neither upon principle nor upon authority could it be held that a dying declaration was inadmissible only because it was cast in narrative form. He had always regarded it as a settled rule of practice that the fact that a declaration was based on answers to questions went to the weight but never to the admissibility of the evidence. On a claim for compensation, which was a quasi-criminal matter, a dying declaration was not admissible, as the rule applies only to cases of homicide (*Eliza Smith v Cavan County Council* (1927) 58 ILTR 107).

4.19 Statements proven as original evidence

Statements other than those made by a witness while testifying in the proceedings may be proved as original evidence when the fact that they were made, as distinct from their truth: is an issue; is relevant to an issue; or affects the credit of a witness. It is important to distinguish clearly between hearsay and original evidence in this area (see *Subramariam v Public Prosecutor* [1956] 1 WLR 965 at p 969).

Evidence of a statement made to a witness by a person who is not called as a witness may or may not be hearsay. It is hearsay and inadmissible when the object of the evidence is to establish the truth of what is contained in a statement. It is not hearsay and is inadmissible when it is proposed to establish by the evidence not the truth of the statement but the fact that it was made. Another example in this area is a previous statement made by a witness which is inconsistent with subsequent evidence given by the said witness in court.

4.20 Other declarations

Other declarations which may form part of the *res gestae* are those made by deceased persons in the course of duty, declarations as to pedigree matters and declarations as to public rights.

4.21 Admissibility of documentary evidence

4.21.1 PART II OF THE CRIMINAL EVIDENCE ACT 1992

The Criminal Evidence Act 1992 ('the Act') makes provision in Part II for the admissibility of documentary evidence in criminal proceedings as evidence of any fact therein of which direct oral evidence would be admissible. A person who had or may reasonably be supposed to have had knowledge of the matters dealt with therein must have compiled such documents in the 'ordinary course of a business'. In the case of information in non-legible form (eg information on microfilm, microfiche, magnetic tape or disk) that has been reproduced in permanent legible form, it must have been reproduced in the course of the normal operation of the reproduction system concerned (s 5). 'Business' under s 4 of the Act includes any trade, profession or other occupation carried on for reward or other-wise, either within or outside the State, and includes any government-funded person or body, EU institution, national or local authority in any jurisdiction outside the State, or international organization.

Privileged information or information supplied by someone who would not be com-pellable is not rendered admissible by the section; nor is information compiled for the purpose of a criminal investigation or disciplinary proceedings (s 5(3)(c)). Exception is made, however, for the admission of documents containing a map, plan, drawing, or photograph; a record of a direction given by a member of the Gardaí pursuant to any enactment; a record of the receipt, handling, transmission, examination, or analysis of anything by a person acting on behalf of any party to the proceedings; or record of a registered medical practitioner's examination of a living or dead person (s 5(4)(b)). A birth certificate naming a person as father or mother of the person to whose birth the certificate relates is admissible as evidence of said relationship (s 5(5)).

4.21.2 ADMISSIBILITY OF EVIDENCE UNDER THE CRIMINAL EVIDENCE ACT 1992

Provision is made under the Criminal Evidence Act 1992 ('the Act'), s 5(6), for the interpretation of information which shall be given either orally or in a document, when that evidence is not intelligible to the average person. Notice of the fact that such docu-mentary evidence is to be produced at trial must be given to other parties to the proceed-ings under s 7 of the Act. The party who wishes to tender such documentary evidence must also produce evidence of its admissibility by virtue of s 5, in the form of a certificate stating the information was compiled in the ordinary course of business and that it is signed by a person 'who occupies a position in relation to the management of the business in the course of which the information was compiled or who is otherwise in a position to give the certificate'.

4.21.3 WEIGHT OF DOCUMENTARY EVIDENCE PRODUCED UNDER THE CRIMINAL EVIDENCE ACT 1992

The Criminal Evidence Act 1992 ('the Act'), although making major changes to the operation of the rule against hearsay insofar as it concerns documentary evidence and its admissibility in criminal proceedings, provides in s 8(1) that such evidence shall not be admitted if the court is of the opinion that in 'the interests of justice' such evidence should not be admitted. Section 8(2) provides that the court should have regard to all the circumstances, including whether the information is reliable (s 8(2)(9)), authentic (s 8(2)(b)), and whether its admission or exclusion will result in unfairness to the accused (s 8(2)(c)).

The latter subsection is perhaps the most interesting, and will require a judicial assessment of the extent to which the rationale of the hearsay rule, which of itself is not confined exclusively to trustworthiness, is rooted in a belief that oral evidence, cross-examination and confrontation are elements or prerequisites to 'fairness' from the perspective of the accused. The interpretation and application of this provision by the judiciary, therefore, have considerable implications for the effect of the Act.

Finally, s 8(3) of the instant Act provides that, in estimating the weight to be attached to information, regard shall be had to the circumstances from which any inference can reasonably be drawn as to its accuracy or otherwise. Evidence as to the credibility of the supplier of information is admissible by virtue of s 9.

4.21.4 PRODUCTION OF COPIES OF DOCUMENTS UNDER THE CRIMINAL EVIDENCE ACT 1992

Section 30 of the Criminal Evidence Act 1992 ('the Act') provides that copies of a document may be produced in evidence whether or not the original is in existence, if they are authenticated in such manner as the court may approve and it is immaterial how many removes there are between copy and original or how (including facsimile) the copy was produced. The term 'document' in this section includes film, sound recording or video recording. The extent to which videos or computer-generated information can be interfered with is undoubtedly a factor, as is the question of how it can be safeguarded or secured against such interference so as to ensure that it is admissible.

CHAPTER 5

THE SKILLS OF THE CRIMINAL ADVOCATE

5.1 Introduction

Advocacy is regularly presented as both an art and a science. Consequently, it has been accorded an aura that can appear daunting to the trainee and the newly qualified practitioner, and it is helpful therefore to demystify it and place it in context. This concept encompasses interaction within society generally, as ideas, opinions, and arguments are discussed.

Advocacy within the law, of necessity, builds on these general skills within society. Coupled with an understanding of the principles of a given area of law and the manner in which it is procedurally applied, each newly qualified solicitor has the potential to become an advocate in any area of law.

Applied in legal practice, this general conceptualization of advocacy would occur as a solicitor advises a client as to the varied legal options available in relation to a specific problem or set of problems between lawyers discussing a case over the phone or engaged in the negotiation process.

5.2 Advocacy in the criminal practice

A solicitor has a right of audience in all of the courts in our criminal justice system. There is little room for negotiation in the criminal justice process, although there are unofficial custom and practice overtures in existence with regard to plea-bargaining. Other legal skills are also employed, eg client interviewing and counselling legal and factual investigation and drafting skills.

5.2.1 THE DISTRICT COURT ENVIRONMENT

Solicitor advocacy exists throughout the criminal defence and prosecution practice, in the context of the District Court system, including the attendance on the client who has been detained at the Garda station. The solicitor will interact as an advocate in the following ways:

(a) The initial visit to the client in custody.

(b) Interacting with the member in charge of the Garda station.

(c) Presiding and representing the client's interests at an identification parade.

(d) Presenting the initial applications for legal aid and bail.

(e)   Taking the client's instructions.

(f)   Advising the client with regard to the plea options which are open to him.

(g)   Remanding cases.

(h)   Presenting pleas in mitigation.

(i)   Running a trial.

(j)   During the presentation of probation and community services reports.

The solicitor who represents the DPP will have consultations with the prosecuting Gardaí, advise them on proofs, and assist in the presentation of the facts on behalf of the state when the accused pleads guilty or not guilty.

5.2.2   THE SUPERIOR COURTS ENVIRONMENT

In the context of the superior courts, the solicitor interacts as advocate in the following ways:

(a)   High Court bail applications.

(b)   Appeals to the High Court against a District Court refusal to grant bail.

(c)   Appeals to the High Court against bail terms which were fixed by the District Court which the accused believes are excessive.

(d)   Judicial reviews at a High Court level.

(e)   Arraignments of accused client sent forward for trial to the Circuit Criminal Court, Special Criminal Court and the Central Criminal Court.

(f)   Empanelling of juries (where seven challenges can be made 'without cause' and seven 'with cause shown').

(g)   Application to the trial court for a dismissal where the defence are of the view that the prosecution have not established 'a prima facie' case.

5.3   Collaboration between the solicitor and the criminal bar

As a busy criminal practitioner cannot appear for every client on a given day, in practice a lot of the pre-trial procedures are delegated to our colleagues at the criminal bar, both at District Court and Superior Court level. Invariably, those colleagues will also be instructed in relation to the trial itself and will collaborate with the instructing solicitor with regard to advice on proofs in preparation for trial.

It is crucial that best practice be followed with regard to the early introduction of the barrister to the client. Whilst the seminal relationship is between the solicitor and the client, an accused whose liberty is at stake must have a fiduciary relationship with instructed counsel. Further guidance with regard to the correct management of a criminal practice can be gleaned from **Chapter 3** of this text.

5.4 Sensitivity to client needs

5.4.1 THE DEFENCE SOLICITOR

As implied in **Chapter 3** on practice management, sometimes one's clients in a criminal practice may emanate from a less privileged background than the practitioner. By analogy, the death of literacy skills may prejudice the client's ability to comprehend the content of the charge sheet, witness statements, reports from expert witnesses retained and the contents of the book of evidence, where applicable. It is important to be mindful of such impediments and to incorporate a sensitive method to facilitate the reading of materials and the dictation by the client of relevant statements and instructions.

Some clients will be suffering the consequences of substance abuse due to their addiction to alcohol, glue or drugs. Others may present with psychological or psychiatric disabilities.

Clients who face criminal prosecution are usually tense and worried. Those who have knowledge of the criminal justice system may present as nonchalant, but nevertheless are acutely aware that their continued liberty may be at stake if the prosecution prove the case beyond reasonable doubt. Many are not familiar with the criminal justice system at any level and are therefore terrified to find themselves in what they consider an alien environment: eg juveniles, a first-time alleged offender and those who are accused of road traffic offences or corporate crime. Consequently sensitivity to a client's needs yields an ability to put the client at ease culminating in the solicitor's enhanced ability to obtain clear instructions and to render salient advice.

5.4.2 THE PROSECUTING SOLICITOR

As a prosecutor, similar client-focused skills are required to ensure that full and relevant instructions are received through the members of the Gardaí from the alleged victims of crime, witnesses to crime, and forensic experts.

The fact that the victim is just another witness as the DPP prosecutes on behalf of the people of Ireland can leave that victim with a sense of being marginalized. Our adversarial criminal justice system also tends to exacerbate the victim's anxiousness. Due to some lobbying by our Rape Crisis Centres, a level of access to legal advice has been given to victims of sexual offences to ensure that they are aware of court procedure. However the victim's legal adviser does not partake in the processes of the criminal trial. Victim impact reports apply to the sentencing of perpetrators of violent crime. This procedure is discussed in detail in **Chapter 14**, which deals with sentencing matters in general. The sensitivity of the prosecution team to the concerns of the victim will result in an improved composure of that witness at trial.

The prosecuting solicitor will have received the file through the office of the Director of Public Prosecution (DPP), who in turn has been briefed by the investigating Gardaí. Mindful of the burden of proof which applies to the prosecution of a criminal matter, as outlined in **Chapter 4**, the State must ensure that there is no break in the chain of evidence presented at trial. Consequently, the evidence must be scrutinized and extra statements of evidence must be obtained, where necessary and possible, to ensure that a prima facie case is presented in court.

5.5   Preparation of a criminal case

5.5.1   DUTIES OF DEFENCE AND PROSECUTION SOLICITORS

Every advocate in court is only as good as the instructions obtained from the client and the research undertaken. It is the defence solicitor's duty to ensure that:

   (a)   the instructions taken are detailed;

   (b)   all appropriate witnesses have been interviewed;

   (c)   subpoenas have been issued where necessary; and

   (d)   all the necessary expert witnesses have been approached, have produced the necessary reports, and are available or 'on stand-by' for the trial date.

It is the prosecuting solicitor's duty to ensure that:

   (a)   all statements have been obtained legally, as outlined in **Chapter 4** of this text;

   (b)   statements have been accurately recorded;

   (c)   all witnesses are notified of the date on which they are required to attend at court, having received subpoenas where necessary; and

   (d)   the defence solicitor is notified of all relevant dates.

A prosecutor has a duty to ensure that all relevant facts and law are before the court.

5.5.2   RESEARCH

It is incumbent on both prosecution and defence criminal lawyers to ensure that they are up to date with all recent developments in criminal law. It is reckless and negligent in the extreme for a defence lawyer to consider appearing in a criminal case without diligent preparation through proper research of the applicable statute and case law. In criminal cases, the right to liberty of a citizen is at stake, or some other penalty (other than the loss of liberty) will apply on conviction, or indeed the accused may run the risk of a conviction in the first place which in itself can have serious consequences for his lifetime.

Similarly, the victim of the alleged crime has a right to expect best practice from the organs of the State. When the DPP, at the suit of a named Garda member, is prosecuting on behalf of the people of Ireland through the chief prosecuting solicitor and his/her colleagues, the appointed State advocate must ensure that there has been meticulous preparation of the prosecution's case.

5.5.3   TAKING INSTRUCTIONS FROM A CLIENT

The same best-practice rules which apply to all areas of practice apply to this specialized area of taking instructions. The matters averted to in **Chapter 3**, 'Managing a Criminal Practice', are taken as a minimum standard to ensure the provision of a good service to one's client. Having that infrastructure in place will facilitate the solicitor taking initial instructions, which will require at least an hour to facilitate the interview of and advice to the client.

Attendance on the accused whilst in detention, presence in the court when the client is brought there in custody, or receipt of a certificate of legal aid, will put the solicitor on notice of the offence alleged and of the necessary research required in advance of the first consultation. This level of preparation will assist the advice on proofs process, the ascertaining of gaps which appear in relation to those proofs on receipt of the client's instructions, and decisions regarding the best strategy in court. The relationship between solicitor and client which is forged at this first consultation will permeate the duration of the case. Care should be taken, before embarking on any case, that the solicitor is acting in compliance with the accepted applicable codes of conduct as outlined in **Chapters 1** and **3**.

5.5.3.1 Initial instructions and the use of a checklist method

It is always a good idea to have a checklist available to you, which will ensure that you get all relevant personal details from your client, including the following:

- name;
- address;
- contact numbers;
- nationality (where applicable);
- special needs and disabilities;
- substance addiction history (if any);
- medical history (where relevant, eg substance addiction);
- responsibilities to dependants (if any);
- educational achievements;
- practical training courses attended, eg FAS courses;
- acquired skills;
- history of involvement with the criminal justice system, particularly any previous convictions (if any);
- any other pending charges, appeals or judicial review matters or outstanding bench warrants for breach of bail conditions;
- any temporary release (parole) conditions which are in operation;
- details of any potential bails persons (if necessary);
- details of any medical condition during the detention period which warranted being attended on by a doctor.

The very personal nature of some of the questions which arise in these circumstances warrant that it is incumbent on the practitioner to explain to the client in advance why it is necessary to obtain such information for the following reasons, some of which will warrant diplomatic explanation:

(a) If the accused is in custody or in custody with consent to bail, it will be necessary to ascertain that a proposed bails person is acceptable to the courts under the terms of the Bail Act 1997, as outlined in **Chapter 8**.

(b) If the accused is a non-national, it may be necessary to apply to the court for the services of an interpreter.

(c) It may sometimes be necessary to assess the possibility of psychological or psychiatric difficulties that could influence a client's 'fitness to plead', and the consequent presence of the mens rea necessary for the crime alleged, and the ability to comprehend the difficulty that presents with the allegation.

(d) Particular skills and educational background, as well as the court's recognition of dependant responsibilities, could favour the imposition of non-custodial sentences of a community service nature, in the event of the court handing down a conviction.

(e) The risk of incarceration and other forms of sentencing, in the event of a conviction, warrants the advance preparation of pleas in mitigation.

(f) Previous convictions, applicable temporary release conditions and the fact that there may be other pending litigation against the client, has a direct bearing on the advice given by the solicitor on the risk of incarceration and sentencing generally.

(g) Addiction difficulties may require that the case be disposed of in what are colloquially referred to as 'the Drugs Courts', where the focus is on rehabilitation rather than retribution.

(h) The administering of any drugs by the duty medical practitioner during the detention period may adversely affect the admissibility of any statement of admission allegedly made.

(i) The attendance of a doctor on the detainee may occasionally corroborate an account of the accused alleging the statement was not voluntary and was acquired under duress.

(j) Attendance by a medical practitioner in the context of a charge of driving whilst intoxicated as outlined in **Chapter 16**.

5.5.3.2   **Initial documentation requirements**

The initial consultation may be at the solicitor's office if the accused is released on bail to the next remand date. Alternatively, the first consultation may occur in a place of detention or imprisonment as the accused may be on bail on the instant charge but in custody on another matter. It is also possible that bail was refused, resulting in a remand in custody, or that the status quo is one of a remand in custody with consent to bail. If either of the latter two situations prevails, the issue of having one's client released on bail will take precedence during the first consultation.

The client will have been handed a charge sheet after being arrested, detained, and cautioned. Alternatively, the client may have received a summons some time after the Gardaí made their initial inquiries. The prosecution may have commenced the investigation as a result of confidential information that resulted in the issue of a search warrant. The solicitor may or may not have been in attendance at the Garda station when the accused was detained and may or may not have had sight of the custody record. There may have been an identification parade, at which the assigned solicitor may or may not have been present. The accused may or may not have made a voluntary statement of admission to the police. The provisions of certain legislation, as discussed in **Chapter 6**, which limits the right of the detainee to remain silent during interrogation may or may not apply (eg the Offences Against the State Act, 1939, as amended by the amending legislation of 1998 which shares the same title; the Criminal Justice Act 1984; and the Criminal Justice (Drug Trafficking) Act 1996).

It is usual that one is in receipt of the certificate of legal aid at the time of the first consultation. If an application has yet to be made, the accused should complete one, or be facilitated in so doing if literacy difficulties prevail. The ramifications of false declarations by the accused with regard to his disposable income or employment circumstances should be carefully explained to them.

5.5.3.3   **Initial documentation checklist**

A checklist outlining all of these permutations is useful discipline to aid the recording of initial instructions:

- statement of means;
- legal aid certificate;

- copy of the custody record (if relevant);

- charge sheet or summons;

- search warrant;

- copy of sworn information grounding the warrant;

- details of identification parade;

- copies of all statements made by witnesses, including any voluntary statement made by the accused;

- the criminal record of any prosecution witness;

- if a client has been video-taped, one should also ask for a copy of the tape;

- copies of or access to any relevant exhibits.

5.5.3.4 The '*Doyle* letter procedure'

The defence are entitled to a copy of any alleged voluntary statement of admission made by the accused and should always seek it from the prosecuting Garda. If the Garda does not comply with one's request, one should apply to the judge for a direction of compliance with the request, followed by a letter of request to the Garda or the assigned State prosecutor. The disclosure of documentation is governed by the *The DPP v Gary Doyle* [1994] 1 ILRM 529, as variously referred to in this text. Essentially, this case decided that a District Judge at his discretion may order that statements be handed over to the defence if this is deemed necessary in the interests of justice. The criteria which determine a judge's consideration of disclosure include:

(a) the seriousness of the charge;

(b) the importance of the statements or documents;

(c) the fact that the accused had been adequately informed of the nature and substance of the accusation; and

(d) the likelihood of risk of injustice in failing to furnish the statements or documents to the accused.

5.5.3.5 The penultimate preparatory steps

All charge sheets, statements, books of evidence, additional evidence and depositions should be read by the solicitor to the client whilst recording the client's responses to their content. On completion of instructions from the client, they should also be read over and the client should be invited to sign them. Occasionally, a manipulative client who wishes to delay the inevitable conclusion of a case that runs the risk of conviction may endeavour to disagree with the manner in which the solicitor is handling a case. A signed set of instructions will militate against protracted discussions and/or argument on the issue. Instructions that have been methodically recorded in a logical sequence can be of enormous benefit when the instructed solicitor is involved in the examination, cross-examination and re-examination of witnesses in the case.

The client should be given an initial indication with regard to the procedure which will apply at each stage of the proceedings in court. Lack of such clarification often results in confusion and uncertainty on the client's part, sometimes resulting in the irritation of the bench as the client tries to address the court in the presence of and to the embarrassment of the instructed solicitor.

A client should be advised that if he recalls any salient details which were omitted at the first consultation, another appointment should be arranged immediately. Similarly, the solicitor should contact the client for further consultation upon receipt of documentation pertinent to the trial.

It is always necessary to have a final consultation with the client on the day before the trial. Some time may have passed since the trial date was originally fixed and the client will need to be advised with regard to the application of the rules of the law of evidence, and in particular what to expect from the examination, cross-examination and re-examination process.

5.5.3.6 Consultations with other witnesses

It is necessary on a case to ascertain whether or not it is necessary to secure expert evidence on behalf of the client. If one needs to engage an expert witness for a client who is on legal aid, the Department of Justice Equality and Law Reform will discharge the relevant fee on receipt of their completed form 'LA5'. The client's instructions may reveal the necessity to interview and access the potential probative value of independent witnesses or alibi witnesses. Once notified that the accused has alibi witnesses in relation to matters being tried on indictment, the state prosecutor's office will interview these witnesses to determine the veracity of such statements and the consequent effect on the continued prosecution of the matter.

Witness summonses should be obtained where necessary to secure the presence of witnesses. Any witness who does not attend in answer to a summons is deemed to be in contempt of court and the trial judge may issue a warrant for the arrest of that errant witness.

5.6 The trial date

Having researched the law, taken full instructions, obtained necessary reports and arranged agreed presence of all necessary witnesses, including expert witnesses where appropriate, it is necessary thereafter to concentrate on the skills necessary for the prosecution and defence of the evidence presented. In the exercise of these skills, one must be prepared, have a goal, a clear strategy, have audible voice projection and finally act confidently.

5.6.1 COMPETING GOALS OF ADVOCATES

In a criminal prosecution in an adversarial criminal justice system, the basic goal is to win. This goal will obviously be linked to whether one is a prosecutor or defence solicitor. The prosecutor will be endeavouring to establish the presence of all the ingredients of the offence, whereas the defence solicitor will endeavour to create a 'reasonable doubt' as to the presence of one or more of those ingredients. Where a number of charges have been made against a particular accused, a defence goal may be an acquittal on one of the more serious charges coupled with an acceptance of the likelihood of a conviction on one of the lesser charges.

5.6.2 ADVOCATES' RULES OF ENGAGEMENT

5.6.2.1 The skills armoury

The methodology engaged by both prosecutors and defence solicitors is to analyse the facts of the case through the medium of:

(a) examination in chief (direct examination) of one's own witnesses;

(b) cross-examination of witnesses for the 'other side'; and

(c) re-examination where permitted.

Rules exist which assist the advocate in:

(i) eliciting the relevant information from one's witness;

(ii) achieving familiarity with the permissible use of leading questions;

(iii) identifying of the objectives of cross-examination;

(iv) prioritizing the sequence and types of questions (eg open questions and closed questions);

(v) knowledge regarding when one should press an advantage; and

(vi) developing an intuition regarding when it is prudent not to question further.

It is necessary that an advocate, in direct examination, can guide the witness when giving salient evidence under oath, and then in cross-examination discredit the opponent's witnesses' testimony thereby supporting one's own client's side of the story.

If one has an intention to refer to case law or a textbook at District Court level, one should photocopy the relevant pages twice, thereby providing a copy for the prosecution and oneself whilst giving the original to the presiding judge.

5.6.2.2 The strategy of opposing advocates

On completion of case preparation a clear strategy is needed, which will be dependent on whether one is a prosecutor or a defence solicitor. A prosecutor will introduce the allegation to the court and will endeavour to establish a chain of evidence which links the accused to the wrong committed. If any single ingredient of an offence is not established, there will be a link missing in that chain and the case for the prosecution will fail.

If one is acting on the defence side, the strategy will be to look for that missing link in the prosecution chain of evidence. A chain is only as strong as its weakest link; therefore, in deciding strategy the defence solicitor will seek the weakest link in the chain of evidence and capitalize on it with the intention of establishing a reasonable doubt with regard to the reliability of the evidence against the accused. If submissions to this effect are successfully submitted, the presiding judge will be persuaded that one's client is entitled to an acquittal.

5.6.2.3 Audible advocacy

It is essential that one project one's voice sufficiently whereby the judge, witnesses, and opposing advocate can hear everything that is said. The witness who is being examined must hear questions asked and answers given, as must the judge and other participants. In particular, the accused must be aware of everything that occurs. He must be in a position to instruct his advocate to rebut any evidence given or allegations made against him by witnesses or, if he chooses to give sworn testimony, to rebut that evidence or those allegations in his direct evidence.

5.6.2.4 The confident profile

Confidence is an important element in good advocacy and has a positive effect on one's client and an audible presence will serve to create and enhance the necessary confidence. The trainee advocate should build confidence during the in-office training period, by assisting senior colleagues in the advisory and preparatory stages of pre-trial procedure.

An appropriate example of the armoury available to advocates can be observed in bail applications, pleas in mitigation, trials and sentencing procedures. Such observation will inform the nervous beginner.

With regard to appropriate advocacy skills, the competent examination of witnesses, the recognition of the duties of one's position as an officer of the court and the proffering of courtesy towards the judiciary, all witnesses and colleagues, can initially acquire skills by advocating in simple adjournments. Such modest beginnings will yield dividends in the creation of an environment which is amenable to the advocate, culminating in a positive self-image.

The judge determines matters of law and fact in a court of summary trial. Maintaining eye contact will variously strengthen the impact of one's advocacy or alert one to the necessity of not pursuing a line of argument that does not appear to gain favour. It is stating the obvious to say that appropriate professional attire also serves to project a confident profile.

5.6.2.5 Witness management

One should never engage in arguments with witnesses, badger or ridicule them. The clever use of closed questions can control the most aggressive hostile witness. Having a flexible list of the logical sequence of the facts of the case can lead the advocate to their goal. Dexterity in the use of open questions may endear one's witness to the court, if one has deduced a capacity in that witness for brevity and ability to be logical and succinct. The fatal attraction of becoming carried away with one's own exuberance can lead to asking one question too many. One must acquire the discipline to cease examination when the set goal has been achieved.

The prosecution gets to put their case first and the defence then cross-examines the State's witnesses. It is important for the defence advocate to remember to put the defence case to the witness for the other side during such cross-examination, as such evidence cannot be raised *de novo* in direct evidence by the defence, which may follow in rebuttal, if the defence choose to present evidence. It is not necessary to present sworn evidence on behalf of the accused, as the burden of proof lies squarely with the prosecution. However, it may be prudent to do so if there is available evidence to rebut the prosecution case. Some accused are their own worst enemies and have poor self-assessment skills. They should be advised not to give evidence. If they are truculent in insisting on presiding in the witness box, a full attendance of advice given should be recorded on file. It is always the province of an advocate to resign from a case where the client insists on deciding strategy. The court is willing to discharge legal aid certificates in such circumstances.

5.6.2.6 Court etiquette

When the District Court Clerk calls the case, the State and defence solicitors identify themselves to the judge. Usually, at District Court level, the expression 'I appear in this case, Judge, on behalf of the State/the Director' or 'I appear in this case, Judge, on behalf of the accused' will suffice. Regularly, the prosecuting Garda member rather than a prosecuting solicitor will represent the State.

The prosecutor may briefly outline the case to the judge although the defence advocate would prefer that this advantage does not fall to the prosecutor, who is the first to present his case. The prosecutor then calls his witnesses to give their evidence orally and under oath. The oath states as follows: 'I swear by Almighty God that my evidence to the court in this case shall be the truth, the whole truth and nothing but the truth.' Non-Christians who do not wish to swear an oath on the Bible can affirm that they will tell the truth. Any false evidence given on oath or on affirmation will result in charges of perjury.

5.7 Rules pertaining to the examination of witnesses

The examination of a witness can be divided into three categories as outlined above: examination in chief, cross-examination, and re-examination. The principles outlined in **Chapter 4** are applied in the courtroom. In brief, it should be noted that hearsay evidence is not permitted, except as part of *res gestae* or the evidence that the advocate seeks to admit was spoken in the presence of either party to the proceedings. No expressions of opinion will be tolerated, with the notable exception of evidence proffered by expert witnesses. Restrictions also apply to admissibility and relevance of evidence; illegally obtained evidence; direct and circumstantial evidence; primary and secondary evidence; shifting of the legal burden; formal admissions; competence and compellability; corroboration; identification evidence; evidence of character; similar fact evidence; DNA fingerprinting; confession evidence; public policy considerations; application of the principles of the Judges' Rules; and admissibility of documentary evidence; as outlined in the aforementioned chapters.

5.7.1 CHARACTERISTICS OF EXAMINATION IN CHIEF

Examination in chief, sometimes referred to as 'direct evidence', by the party calling a witness must not include leading questions. A leading question is one which is effectively rhetorical in character. However, if the matter which is being elicited is not in dispute, then a leading question may be permissible in the context of an examination in chief, eg the name, address, and occupation of the accused, or a statement that the accused was present at the scene of an assault where the defence is one of self-defence and therefore the accused is not contesting his own presence at the scene of the alleged crime. The witness should give the evidence; it is not for the advocate to proffer the evidence on the witness's behalf. Leading questions cannot be asked with regard to a matter in issue. Many practitioners have found it beneficial to prefix their questions in a direct examination context with words such as 'What?', 'Why?', 'When?', 'How?', 'Where?', and 'Who?'

It is important to use simple, clear language and to frame the questions asked in a chronologically logical fashion to ensure that the events unfold in the manner outlined in one's instructions. There is little disclosure of the evidence in advance of a summary trial, and what disclosure does occur takes place through the *'Gary Doyle* procedure', which is between the advocates on each side of the case, on behalf of their respective clients. The judge therefore is hearing this evidence for the first time and consequently a methodical, logical unfolding of the alleged events will greatly facilitate the bench's understanding of one's client's case.

The position differs somewhat with regard to the trial on indictment, insofar as the facts of the case are disclosed to the judge through the medium of the book of evidence. However, at this level (with the exception of the Special Criminal Court), the decision of the discharge of the burden of proof on the facts as presented rests with the jury, who do not have any prior disclosure.

It is necessary to control one's witness during the examination in chief process. On occasion it may prove useful to ask an open-ended question like 'What happened next?' If, however, the witness starts to wander, warbling irrelevancies, it may be necessary to have the ability to bring the witness back to the issue at hand, eg stating 'If I might stop you there for a moment'; and then asking a closed question by either referring to something previously stated by the witness, or some fact already accepted by both sides of the case.

Evidence which has been satisfactorily established by a witness in answer to a question in direct examination should not be sought by repetition of the question as a matter of emphasis. It is unwise and may be unethical for an advocate to prepare a list of questions for rehearsal with one's witness before the commencement of the trial. It is unethical to coach a witness. The potential witness needs only a short, general summary of the matters on which one is likely to examine. The witness should be advised to maintain eye contact with the judge at summary trial, or judges in the Special Criminal Court, and the jury in the Circuit and Central Criminal Courts.

5.7.2 CHARACTERISTICS OF CROSS-EXAMINATION

Leading questions are allowed, even advised in the cross-examination process. One should not copper-fasten the opponent's case by giving their witness an opportunity to restate their version of the facts. A short cross-examination is much more effective than a long one. A comprehensive note of the evidence given in direct examination should be recorded, particularly any evidence which contradicts one's client's instructions.

It is imperative that one should not ask a question in cross-examination to which the answer is unknown, as exploratory questions are dangerous. It is necessary to be flexible in one's approach and be ready to change tactics, a process colloquially referred to as 'thinking on one's feet'.

It is generally unwise to accuse a witness of 'being economical with the truth' when a suggestion that the witness 'may be mistaken' will suffice without creating the same level of hostility. Experienced judges will be quick to notice inconsistencies and contradictions in the evidence. In a jury setting, the advocate will ensure, when summing up the evidence in the submission to the jury, to alert them to any such conflicts in the evidence proffered. Where a witness in cross-examination gives evidence which clearly contradicts evidence which one's client or the client's witness will give, one must, in cross-examination of that witness, put to that witness the evidence which such client or witness will give, to allow the testifying witness the opportunity to rebut it.

One is bound by the answers given by a witness in cross-examination. It is important to know when to stop questioning the witness. If one gets an admission from a witness in cross-examination which benefits one's own client, it is not clever to press the advantage, as it may prompt an unhelpful elaboration or, indeed, a retraction.

5.7.3 CHARACTERISTICS OF RE-EXAMINATION

New evidence, which may have been elicited out of the cross-examination, may be re-examined for the purpose of clarification.

5.8 Objections

A solicitor acting for a party in court should object in the course of a trial to:

(a) any leading questions being put by the opposing advocate in the direct examination of a witness;

(b) any question which is irrelevant; and

(c) any attempt to adduce hearsay evidence.

One must state the grounds on which the objection is based. The objection should not be frivolous and should be made clearly and distinctly. When making legal submissions at the conclusion of a trial, it is imperative that they are logically and coherently presented and that one is cautious of not patronizing the bench.

5.9 Determination of guilt or innocence

After the prosecutor informs the court that there is no further evidence to be called on behalf of the State, at this point the prosecution case is closed. At the conclusion of the prosecution's case, the defence may apply for a direction or an acquittal if the evidence adduced does not establish the facts alleged against the accused. If there is a material defect in the summons or charge sheet, and/or there has been a failure to adduce certain essential proofs, a similar application may be made. If appropriate, case law or other legal authority may be submitted to show that the prosecution has failed to discharge the burden imposed on it.

5.10 Pleas in mitigation of sentence

Once there has been a finding of 'guilty as charged', the defence advocate endeavours to minimize the impact of the punishment which the court is entitled to impose. **Chapter 14** addresses the issue of sentencing in detail. The persuasive powers of the advocate must be at their peak during this procedure. Particular attention should rest on professional conduct standards, which determine that the court must not be misled in one's zeal to minimize the punishment which is imminent.

One should check the facts of the case beforehand with the prosecution. Such facts should not be disputed if one's client is pleading guilty. One can, of course, clarify any point and, in particular, elicit evidence from the prosecuting Garda that is advantageous to your client, eg recovery of stolen goods, no previous convictions, client was cooperative and/or apologetic, compensation has been proffered to the injured party, client has prospects of employment, and client supports spouse/partner and young family, if applicable, can be mentioned in mitigation of punishment.

The defence lawyer decides whether or not it is appropriate to call the defendant to give sworn evidence on his or her own behalf where a guilty plea has been entered. It is never appropriate to ask the judge if he or she would like to hear the client. One should never suggest or propose or even hint to the judge the order that he or she should make. The judge has a number of options open to include adjournment of the case for the purpose of ascertaining suitability for supervision of a probation officer, community service officer, or to determine whether a fine, compensation or incarceration are the appropriate options.

5.11 Composition of the courts

5.11.1 ESTABLISHMENT

The jurisdiction of the Criminal Courts derives from Article 34.1 of the Constitution. The enabling legislation includes the Courts (Establishment and Constitutional) Act 1961, the Courts (Supplemental Jurisdiction) Act 1961, the Offences Against the State Act 1939, and the Defence Act 1954.

The latter two Acts refer respectively to the Special Criminal Court and Courts-Martial. What are referred to as the ordinary courts with criminal jurisdiction include: the District Court, the Circuit Court, the High Court, the Court of Criminal Appeal, and the Supreme Court.

5.11.2 THE COURTS SERVICE

The day-to-day central administration of all courts has been vested in the Courts Service, an independent body set up under the Courts Service Act 1998 <www.courts.ie>. Its functions include the management of the courts, the provision, management and maintenance of court buildings, the provision of support services to members of the judiciary, dissemination of information on the courts system to the public and provision of facilities for those who use the courts.

5.11.3 THE DISTRICT COURT

The District Court system comprises the Dublin Metropolitan District and twenty-three District Court Districts, which are presided over by the President of the District Court and fifty-two District Court Judges. The Districts are divided into District Court Areas. The geographical jurisdiction of each area is limited to those before the court who are from its area and those who are accused of criminal matters arising within the Court Area.

5.11.3.1 Jurisdiction of the District Court

The District Court is referred to as a court of summary jurisdiction, which correctly implies that it can deal with offences referred to as summary or minor offences. It can also deal with what are described as 'hybrid offences', which are indictable offences of a minor nature, where the accused chooses to 'plead guilty as charged' with the consent of the Director of Public Prosecution (DPP), before the District Court.

The vast majority of criminal offences, both summary and indictable, commence procedurally in the District Court. In exceptional circumstances the Special Criminal Court will be the accused's first port of call in the courts system.

The administration of the courts often permits specialization insofar as a court may deal exclusively with road traffic offences or where the District Court sits as the Children Court in Smithfield in Dublin. A pilot 'Drug Court' project has been established since 2001.

The District Court can exercise a constitutional jurisdiction with regard to the exclusion of any illegally obtained evidence which confronts the constitutional rights of the accused. **Chapter 4** deals with instances which could give rise to the existence of such evidence. A District Court Judge may refer a 'case stated' to the High Court where it seeks clarification and direction with regard to the correct interpretation of the law as it arises in a case before the District Court. This type of procedure is discussed later in **Chapter 15**.

5.11.3.2 Children's Court

The Children Act 1908 was amended by the Children Act 2001, which is being implemented in piecemeal fashion. Those who appear before the District Court as juveniles are entitled to have their cases heard 'in camera' and to have their cases segregated from the usual District Court list for adults, if a separate building is not available. The Juvenile Justice system is dealt with in **Chapter 13**.

5.12 The Constitution Courts of trial on indictment and their jurisdiction

When an accused is charged with an offence which is too serious a matter for disposal in the District Court, that accused is sent for trial to the higher courts, being the Circuit

Criminal Court, the Central Criminal Court, or the Special Criminal Court. The Circuit Criminal Court and the Central Criminal Court are constituted to sit with a Circuit Court Judge in the former venue and a High Court Judge in the latter. A jury of twelve citizens sits in both venues. The Circuit Criminal Court deals with all indictable offences except murder, rape and other offences scheduled in the OASA 1939 where the DPP has not intervened under s 45(2) OASA 1939.

The Central Criminal Court has jurisdiction to deal with all indictable offences returnable to it, but specifically murder and rape offences. Theoretically, the Central Criminal Court may deal with any criminal allegation, even without any return, since it has full original jurisdiction under the Constitution.

The Special Criminal Court ('the Special') is a judge-only court, ie it sits without the assistance of a jury. Typically, there will be a sitting of three judges simultaneously, one District Court Judge, one Circuit Court Judge, and one High Court Judge. The Special may deal with all offences, summary and indictable. There are specific areas of jurisdiction which are confined to the Special:

(a) scheduled offences (OASA 1939) which arrive before the Special:

    (i) by valid return from District Court where the DPP has not intervened under s 45(2) of the Act;

    (ii) by reason of an accused having been charged before the Special bypassing the District Court and the DPP has so directed;

(b) non-scheduled offences (s 46 OASA 1939) which arrive before the Special:

    (i) by virtue of an accused having been charged before the Special, on DPP's direction coupled with DPP's Certificate that ordinary Courts are inadequate to secure effective administration of justice;

    (ii) transfer from ordinary Courts by DPP's direction and Certificate;

    (iii) by virtue of a valid return to the trial court coupled with a Certificate from the DPP that the ordinary Courts are inadequate to secure the effective administration of justice.

5.13 Functions of a judge in the indictable courts

The judges in the Circuit Criminal Court and the Central Criminal Court have many functions as follows:

(a) To preside over Court and exercise his or her inherent jurisdiction to ensure its process is not abused.

(b) To ensure a fair trial and vindication of rights of parties before it.

(c) To rule on procedure to be adopted in the court of trial.

(d) To rule on all questions of law, eg admissibility of evidence, publicity of trial.

(e) To rule on the adequacy of the prosecution case on receipt of an application from the defence for an acquittal on the basis that they have 'no case to answer' at the conclusion of the prosecution's evidence.

(f) To instruct the jury on the law which applies to the instant case.

(g) To review the evidence for the jury.

(h) To charge the jury.

(i)   To instruct the jury on questions of fact for their consideration in deciding guilt or innocence.

(j)   To instruct the jury on alternative verdicts or special verdicts.

(k)   To consider evidence and/or submissions deemed relevant prior to sentence where there has been a finding of 'guilty' against the accused.

(l)   To impose sentence.

5.14   The jury

The function of a jury in the Circuit Criminal Court and the Central Criminal Court is to decide the issues of fact having being advised by the trial judge in relation to the legal burden of proof. Thereafter they must, through their foreperson, announce their verdict of guilt or innocence to the trial court.

5.14.1   COMPOSITION OF THE JURY

A jury consists of twelve men or women selected at random from a jury panel. The jury may in the course of the trial fall to a minimum of ten through excusal (eg sickness) or possibly through ineligibility or disqualification not discovered prior to commencement of the trial.

The jury are asked in the first instance to seek to arrive at a unanimous verdict. If a jury have not been able to reach such a unanimous verdict in such period as to the judge seems reasonable (and never less than two hours) a majority verdict of not less than 10/2 or 11/1 shall be accepted (Criminal Justice Act 1984, s 25 (1)). A 'hung jury' is a jury which is unable to reach a verdict. In such circumstances they are discharged and the accused is free to leave the court. There is the possibility that the State will charge the accused again and look for a re-trial date.

5.14.2   JURY EMPANELMENT

Jury summonses are served on persons whose names appear on the Electoral Register for Dáil Éireann. They are delivered by post or served by hand. The entire panel is generally required to attend on the first day of a sitting. In Dublin, the panel is sub-divided and called on certain days (usually Mondays) in the course of the sittings as is thought appropriate.

If a summonsed jury panellist does not attend an empanelment, an offence has been committed which is triable summarily. The Registrar of the trial court calls out the names of those summonsed. As each potential juror answers he/she is called towards the bench and asked:

(a)   to affirm his/her identity;

(b)   to outline any reason why he/she should not serve as a juror.

The judge will outline to the jurors circumstances which would deem them disqualified or ineligible and furthermore warn them with regard to the penalty applicable to participating as jurors in such circumstances. It is possible to object to a juror by reason of his disqualification/ineligibility.

5.14.2.1   Challenges under the Juries Act 1976

A list of the panel of available jurors is available for inspection by the defence and prosecution lawyers. This list outlines the names, addresses and occupations of the potential jurors. The prosecution, defence or the accused may challenge or object on seven occasions in the course of an empanelment 'without showing cause' (giving a reason). It is provided that any further challenge must be for cause shown, ie that 'cause must be demonstrated upon objection being made'. There is no right to question a potential juror in advance of showing challenge for cause, but having challenged for cause questioning is permitted to demonstrate the cause. As the jury panel discloses little information, it is not usually possible to base an objection on it, unless the accused knows the person to whom he wishes to object or knows of some reason which might manifest as prejudice towards the accused. Objections without cause are usually on the basis of subjective assessment based on the visual inspection of jurors, their demeanour and occasionally their occupation.

5.14.2.2   Eligibility to become juror

Eligibility has been widened considerably since the original qualification of being a property owner was dispensed with (*De Búrca v AG* [1976] IR 38). Each county constitutes a Jury District and juries are summonsed to sittings of the Court within the Jury District (the Juries Act 1976, s 5(4)). Otherwise, every citizen aged 18–70 years and whose name appears on the Dáil Electoral Register is eligible. Persons involved in the administration of justice, ie solicitors, barristers, court personnel, Gardaí, prison officers, defence forces, or the President of Ireland are not eligible for jury service.

5.14.2.3   Circumstances which disqualify a potential juror

The following categories of persons are disqualified from jury service:

(a)   Persons convicted of an offence in any part of Ireland and sentenced to five years' imprisonment/detention are disqualified for life.

(b)   Persons convicted of an offence in any part of Ireland and sentenced to three months' imprisonment or detention are disqualified for ten years.

5.14.2.4   Circumstances which excuse a potential juror

The following categories of persons are excused from service as of right, if exercised:

(a)   Members of the Oireachtas.

(b)   Religious.

(c)   Doctors/nurses.

(d)   Chemists.

(e)   Persons who have served on a jury in the three years before.

(f)   Those excused for life by a court.

The following reasons may excuse a potential juror from service at the discretion of the Registrar or court of trial:

(a)   Illness.

(b)   Any other reason which is acceptable.

PART III
PRELIMINARY PROCEDURES IN THE PROSECUTION OF CRIME

CHAPTER 6

THE CRIMINAL INVESTIGATION

6.1   Introduction

In recent years, a wide range of new statutory powers has been conferred on the Gardaí as the investigators of crime in the State. The exercise of these powers, in conjunction with the pre-existing ones, necessarily encroaches upon the rights of any individual upon whom suspicion may fall. The role of the solicitor in this regard is to provide advice concerning the powers of the investigator and the rights of the suspect.

6.2   Forensic science

6.2.1   GENERALLY

The establishment in this jurisdiction of the Forensic Science Laboratory in 1975 has assisted in crime investigation throughout Ireland. It is understood by those involved in crime investigation that the criminal law requires the establishment of guilt beyond reasonable doubt. Forensic scientists hold that fundamental principles of science provide a basis for a reliable means by which this standard of proof can be attained. Science can confirm that a crime has been committed or indeed the innocence of a suspect or a person charged with an alleged offence.

6.2.2   FUNCTIONS OF THE FORENSIC SCIENCE LABORATORY

The Forensic Science Laboratory is an office of the Department of Justice, staffed by civil servants who, through their training and experience, provide scientific and technical expertise to the Garda Síochána and the courts. Their work includes examination of samples submitted in criminal cases, issuing reports of findings and giving evidence in court.

The laboratory is utilized in many circumstances which include:

    (a)   helping the investigation of a crime;

    (b)   providing statements for a file on which a decision on prosecution may be based;

    (c)   providing statements for the court which may be used to help determine the guilt or innocence of an accused person.

Whereas some of the laboratory's help in the investigation of crime focuses on the identification of substances such as illicit drugs or suspected explosives, most of its efforts are focused on the area of 'trace evidence', where it attempts to establish whether or not there are links between persons, places, or objects. The forensic scientist searches for physical evidence (such as blood, body fluids, paint, glass, and fibres of hair) and compares it with appropriate control samples from potential sources. All items submitted to the laboratory must be properly handled to ensure that their evidential value is not affected.

Physical evidence transfers readily and may not be visible to the naked eye. Samples from individuals must be taken at the earliest opportunity, as a matter of a few hours' delay can greatly diminish the chances of finding evidence. The recommended practice of crime investigators is therefore to take samples immediately and, if necessary, a decision is taken later on whether or not they should be sent to the laboratory for analysis. Static samples at a crime scene are less likely to be prejudiced by a less urgent approach.

6.2.3   CASE SUBMISSION

Preferably someone involved in the case, as this ensures direct contact between the scientist and the investigating unit, usually submits items by hand for laboratory examination. Some items may be sent by registered post and should be addressed to the relevant section head or, if in doubt, the director. It should be noted, however, that the chain of custody may be challenged if items are sent by registered post. The defence can seize upon any such break in the chain of evidence in an effort to create a reasonable doubt in favour of an accused. A case submission form is completed, either in the station or in the laboratory, which outlines briefly the circumstances of the case and the member in charge, and lists the items submitted.

6.2.4   RETURN OF EXHIBITS

When work is completed, statements are dispatched to the relevant Gardaí. The items which have been submitted are returned via the Forensic Liaison Office to the relevant Garda station. In major cases, where an exhibit officer has been appointed, an arrangement is made for this officer to collect the items directly from the scientist concerned. Samples such as blood are generally destroyed after examination, as they constitute a health hazard.

6.2.5   PACKAGING

Items or samples must be packed to avoid material being lost and to prevent the item picking up extraneous material. Items should be packed, sealed (using Sellotape) and labelled at the time and place of seizure rather than being transported to the Garda station for packing.

Clothing and other samples taken in the station should be packed, sealed and labelled in the room in which they are taken and by the member who takes them. Shoes should be packed in a separate bag from clothes. Bags should not be re-opened until the items are examined in the laboratory.

6.2.6   LABELLING

The label on each item should contain sufficient detail to enable the item to be identified without difficulty and to facilitate the composition of an exhibit list, eg 'denim jeans of Tom White taken 10/10/05 at Athlone Garda Station by Garda John Smith'. A very detailed description of the item or the incident under investigation is unnecessary. Ideally items should also be labelled with an identification number normally using the Garda's initials and sequential numbers for each sample (eg Garda John Smith's samples may use JS1, JS2, JS3 etc. as an identification code).

6.2.7   CONTAMINATION

In forensic science terms, 'contamination' is any transfer of evidence which occurs after a crime. It can occur via a third party not involved with the crime, because of there being a common place of contact, eg the victim and suspect being transported in the same patrol car, or different sets of exhibits being exposed to each other in the same room. Contamination is probably the greatest problem that exists in the area of trace evidence, and the possibility of its occurring exists from the first moment of contact between the scene, suspect or victim and the Gardaí. Primary transfer of evidence can occur from direct contact between items, and secondary transfer by, for example, the same officer handling items from different aspects of a case or packing items from different persons or crime scenes in the same room.

Failure to follow the standard procedure recommended by the laboratory and the required safeguards may result in non-acceptance of material into the laboratory or render evidence found completely meaningless.

The following recommendations should be followed in order to avoid contamination of evidence:

(a)   The same Garda patrol car should not be used to convey, for example, a victim to hospital and a suspect to the station.

(b)   If it is necessary to link a suspect to a scene, any officer who has been to the scene or who plans to visit or examine the scene should have no dealings with the suspect. In this respect, dealing with the suspect includes arrest, taking clothes or fingerprints and visiting places to which the suspect has legitimate access. Depending on the circumstances, the same precautions apply to dealing with a victim. A suspect or victim should not be brought to a crime scene wearing the same clothing which may have been worn during the crime.

(c)   In the station, suspects and victims should not be interviewed in the same room or sit on the same seat.

(d)   Clothing and other samples from victims and suspects should be taken, packed and sealed by different officers in separate rooms. Bags should be sealed with Sellotape.

(e)   Bags should be labelled immediately after sealing to eliminate any need for reopening.

(f)   Sealed bags should not be opened *for any reason* before submission to the laboratory. This means that an exhibits officer may at this stage need to rely on the information on the label.

(g)   An officer who handles firearms should not examine suspects for traces of firearm residue.

(h)   Persons handling bulk samples of drugs or explosives should not handle items which may subsequently be examined for traces of these materials.

(i)   Samples of liquid accelerants should be packed and stored separately from samples of fire debris.

(j)   A new blade should be used for each new sample of paint in paint transfer cases.

(k)   Packaging must be adequate and appropriate to the sample type.

(l)   A 'history' of the handling and packing of an exhibit must be made available to the forensic scientist.

6.3   Powers to stop and search

6.3.1   STOP AND MAKE INQUIRIES

A member of the Gardaí has a broad range of statutory and common law powers to call upon in the detection of crime and the bringing of offenders to justice. It has been held that the Gardaí could not carry out their duties unless they had the power to make reasonable inquiries of members of the public. Accordingly, it is well established that a Garda member may approach any member of the public in order to make such inquiries. Moreover, it has recently been held that the Gardaí have the additional power at common law, in the exercise of their duty to prevent and detect crime, to require motorists to stop their vehicles in order to make inquiries to ascertain whether an offence under that Act has been committed, even in the absence of a reasonable suspicion that the motorist in question has committed an offence. This was the decision of the Supreme Court in *DPP (Stratford) v Fagan* [1994] 3 IR 265. The decision has been criticized on the grounds that police powers should be strictly and narrowly construed since they necessarily encroach on personal rights under the Constitution. However, it is clear that there is no common law power to stop persons generally, simply in order to put questions to them.

6.3.2   STOP AND SEARCH

There are a number of different statutory provisions that empower the Gardaí to stop persons for the purpose of conducting a search. These powers have been progressively conferred in a piecemeal fashion over the last two centuries, with the result that they do not form a logical or coherent scheme. For example, there is a power to stop and search on reasonable suspicion of possession of stolen property under s 29 of the Dublin Police Act 1842, yet no such power exists outside the Dublin Metropolitan Area. Various powers have been conferred to stop and search under customs and excise, wildlife and road traffic legislation. More significantly, the Misuse of Drugs Acts 1977 and 1984, s 23 allows a Garda member to stop and search any person reasonably believed to be in possession of a controlled drug. Persons may be stopped and searched under the Offences Against the State Act, 1939, s 30, and vehicles and their occupants may be stopped and searched under the Criminal Law Act, 1976, s 8. *The DPP v Rooney* [1993] ILRM 61 established that a person stopped under any statutory power must be told of the reason for the action and the nature and description of the power invoked.

6.3.3   SEARCH AND SEIZE

At common law, members of the Gardaí can search suspects, upon arrest, for the purpose of taking into custody any dangerous weapon or other item which may be of evidentiary value found on that person. They may also seize anything found at the place of arrest which is in the custody of the person detained and reasonably believed to be either evidence in support of a criminal charge, or property that is unlawfully in the person's possession. This may be done in order to prevent the subsequent removal or destruction of the item or items in question. In addition to these common law powers, there are certain statutes, most notably the Misuse of Drugs Acts 1977–84 and the Offences Against the State Act 1939, that allow Gardaí to arrest persons found on the premises that are the subject of a search warrant.

6.3.4 ENTER AND SEARCH OF PREMISES

The entry onto premises to effect an arrest or to conduct a search must take place within the parameters of a properly issued warrant or pursuant to a statutory or common law power of entry without warrant, in order to be lawful.

A search warrant is a written legal authority, given to the person or persons named therein, empowering entry onto specified property and seizure of specified property thereon. Its scope and the circumstances of its issue are governed by a variety of rules set out in a number of different statutes. A warrant may allow the search of a person only, the search of premises only or both. A District Judge or a Peace Commissioner, on consideration of sworn information (colloquially referred to as 'an information'), may issue most warrants. In such cases, the granting authority is obliged to act judicially and to satisfy itself that facts exist which constitute reasonable grounds, rather than simply acting on the statement of reasonable belief of the applicant. Other warrants may be issued by senior officers of the Garda Síochána, with or without the necessity for the laying of 'an information'.

Section 9 of the Criminal Law Act 1976 refers to searches carried out under that Act or pursuant to any other power. It allows a Garda member who finds or comes into possession of anything that he believes to be evidence of an offence or suspected offence to seize and retain it for a reasonable period for use as evidence. This power is subject to an exception in respect of documents covered by legal professional privilege.

Where a warrant to search relates to a person's home, particular regard must be had to Article 40.5 of the Constitution of Ireland which states: 'The dwelling of every citizen is inviolable and shall not be forcibly entered save in accordance with law.' This in turn prompts consideration of the well-established principle that evidence obtained by a violation of the constitutional personal rights of a citizen must be excluded, unless a court is satisfied either that the act constituting the breach of constitutional rights was committed unintentionally or accidentally, or that there are extraordinary excusing circumstances which justify the admission of evidence at the court's discretion. This is the clear import of the Supreme Court decision of *The People (DPP) v Kenny* [1990] 2 IR 110. As a result of the Supreme Court's decision in *The DPP v Delaney & (Ors)* [1997] 3 IR 453, it has been established that the inviolability of the dwelling must yield to a bona fide belief on the part of a Garda member (or, presumably, other person) that it is necessary to enter in order to safeguard life and limb.

Where a search warrant has been executed and the person to whom it was addressed seeks legal advice, it is essential that they request a copy of the warrant and any information sworn to obtain it from the investigating authorities. The warrant and, where applicable, the sworn information on the basis of which it was issued should be carefully scrutinized for authorization by, and strict compliance with, the statutory power under which they were made.

6.4 Powers of arrest, detention, and interrogation

6.4.1 ARREST

Article 40.4.1 of the Constitution provides that: 'No citizen shall be deprived of his personal liberty save in accordance with law.' A person may be arrested for the purpose of charge either pursuant to a validly issued warrant or without warrant in the case of a person suspected, with reasonable cause, of committing an 'arrestable offence'. Only a member of the Gardaí may arrest a suspect where the commission of an arrestable offence is merely, albeit with reasonable cause, suspected. Any person may effect an arrest where an arrestable offence is being or has been committed, but only where that person suspects, with reasonable cause, that the suspect is trying to avoid or would otherwise attempt to avoid arrest by a Garda member. Persons so arrested must be transferred into the custody of the Gardaí as soon as is practicable.

An arrestable offence is defined by the Criminal Law Act 1997 ('the 1997 Act') as one for which a person of full capacity and who has not previously been convicted may, under or by virtue of any enactment, be punished by imprisonment for a term of five years or by a more severe penalty, and includes an attempt to commit any such offence. Consequently, offences which are summary only in nature and thereby subject to a maximum of 12 months' imprisonment do not fall within the definition of 'arrestable offence'. Section 8 of the Criminal Justice Act 2006 includes common law offences punishable by five years or more. Section 4(6) of the 1997 Act confirms the validity of a motley collection of pre-existing statutory and common law arrest powers (eg the common law power to arrest in order to prevent personal injury or a breach of the peace).

Persons arrested without warrant are entitled to be told the grounds upon which they are being detained, in ordinary language and general terms, unless the circumstances are such that this must be apparent to them, or unless they themselves render this impracticable, such as by running away, resisting arrest or otherwise causing a commotion. The Supreme Court has thus adopted with approval, in *The People v Walsh* [1980] IR 294, the test laid down by Viscount Simon in *Christie and Morris v Leachinsky* [1947] AC 573.

A warrant to arrest may be issued by a District Court judge exercising judicial discretion on the basis of the sworn information of a member of the Gardaí. In any case where a warrant to arrest has been issued, it is good practice for a defence solicitor to request in writing from the prosecution a copy of the sworn information grounding the issue of the warrant and a copy of the warrant itself. If the warrant was wrongly issued, or discloses some defect on its face, or if the member executing the warrant exceeded the authority conferred by it, then the arrest may have been unlawful.

It should be borne in mind that it is proper to argue for the exclusion of any evidence obtained as a result of an unlawful arrest, and it may also be possible to question the validity of any subsequent legal proceedings in such circumstances. While the use of reasonable force to resist an unlawful arrest is permissible, the more prudent course of action must always be for the suspect to acquiesce, thus eliminating the risk of committing the further offences of assault, assault of a Garda member or obstruction of a Garda in the course of his duty.

As outlined above, one can be arrested for the purpose of being charged with a criminal offence and being brought before the court. One can also be arrested for the purposes of detention for questioning. Depending on the legislation under which they are detained they can be held for questioning in a Garda station for up to 12 hours (s 4 Criminal Justice Act 1984) or in other instances for 48 hours (s 30 Offences Against the State Act 1939 as amended by the Offences Against the State (Amendment) Act 1998) or under drug trafficking legislation for up to seven days (s 2 Misuse of Drugs Act 1999).

6.4.2   DETENTION

Until 1984, detention for questioning outside the context of State security was unknown to Irish law. Section 30 of the Offences Against the State Act 1939 allowed for the detention of suspects for up to 48 hours. Otherwise the position was as summarized by the Supreme Court in *The People (DPP) v Shaw* [1982] IR 1. In that case, Walsh J stated that 'no person may be arrested with or without a warrant for the purpose of interrogation or the securing of evidence from that person'. The sole purpose of arrest, whether under statute or common law, was to make the person arrested amenable to the judicial process. In what was probably the single most significant transformation of the Irish criminal process since the inception of the State, that position has now been profoundly altered.

Section 4 of the Criminal Justice Act 1984 introduced a power to detain for questioning a person reasonably suspected of having committed or having attempted to commit an 'arrestable offence' being an offence punishable by five years' imprisonment or more. A person so suspected can be arrested by a member of the Garda Síochána without warrant and conveyed to a Garda station where detention will follow if the member in charge has reasonable grounds for believing that detention is necessary for the proper investigation of the offence. Detention may be for a period of up to six hours initially, but can be extended at the direction of an officer not below the rank of Superintendent for a further period of up to six hours. Such officer must have reasonable grounds for believing that an extension is necessary for the proper investigation of the offence. Section 9 of the Criminal Justice Act 2006 permits a further extension on similar grounds for 12 hours on the direction of a Chief Superintendent. The possible interposition of an eight-hour rest period between midnight and 8 am means that a person may be detained in a Garda station under s 4 for a maximum period of 32 hours.

Section 2 of the Criminal Justice (Drug Trafficking) Act 1996 ('the 1996 Act') allows for the detention of a person arrested without warrant on reasonable suspicion that the person in question has committed a drug trafficking offence as defined by the Criminal Justice Act 1994, s 3(1). An initial six-hour detention period is allowed, subject to the Garda member in charge believing, on reasonable grounds, that the detention is necessary for the proper investigation of the offence. Thereafter an extension of up to 18 hours and a further extension of 24 hours are possible, based on the same belief of an officer not below the rank of Chief Superintendent on the same grounds, bringing the aggregate total up to two days. A further extension of up to a further three days may be granted on application to a judge of the District or Circuit Court, if the court considers such extension necessary for the proper investigation of the offence concerned, and if the court is satisfied that the investigation is being conducted diligently and expeditiously. A final possible extension of yet a further 48 hours may be granted on the basis of a similar application, bringing to seven days the total cumulative detention period permissible under the 1996 Act.

Finally, the Offences Against the State Act 1939 ('the 1939 Act') s 30, the State security provision which provided the inspiration for the detention powers just described, must also be considered. Section 30 of the Act allows a member of the Garda Síochána to stop, search, interrogate, and arrest any person suspected of involvement in the commission or attempted commission of any scheduled offence, and for that person to be detained for up to 24 hours. That period may be extended by a further 24 hours from the time of arrest if so directed by an officer not below the rank of Chief Superintendent. The Offences Against the State (Amendment) Act 1998 amended s 30 to allow for a still further 24-hour extension of detention, on application to a judge of the District Court by an officer not below the rank of Superintendent who has reasonable grounds for believing it necessary for the proper investigation of the offence. Before granting it, the District Judge concerned must be satisfied that the extension sought is necessary for the proper investigation of the offence, and that the investigation is being conducted diligently and expeditiously.

For the purposes of s 30, a 'scheduled offence' is one the government has so declared by Order. In *The People (DPP) v Quilligan* [1987] ILRM 606, the Supreme Court approved the use of s 30 detention in the investigation of non-subversive cases involving scheduled offences. In *The People (DPP) v Howley* 3 Frewen 130 [1989] ILRM 629, the Supreme Court upheld the practice of questioning detainees about non-scheduled offences. These decisions serve to confirm the very broad range of non-subversive cases to which s 30 may be applied.

6.4.3 INTERROGATION

The Supreme Court has set out the Judges' Rules as they apply in Ireland. Walsh J in *The People (AG) v Cummins* [1972] IR 312 stated at p 323: 'The Judges's [sic] Rules which are in force in this country are the ones mentioned in *McCarrick v Leavy* [1964] IR 225; they are sometimes called "the Judges' Rules of 1922" though they first appeared in 1912 when the judges in England, at the request of the Home Secretary, drew up four rules as a guide for police officers in respect of communications with prisoners or persons suspected of crime. The Rules were signed by Lord Chief Justice Alverstone and were then four in number; they were printed at the end of the report of *R v Voisin* [1918] 1 KB 531. In the judgment of the Court of Criminal Appeal given in that case, the following statement appears at p 539 of the report: 'These Rules have not the force of law; they are administrative directions the observance of which the police authorities should enforce upon their subordinates as tending to the fair administration of justice. It is important that they should do so, for statements obtained from prisoners, contrary to the spirit of these rules, may be rejected as evidence by the judge presiding at the trial.' The origin of the Rules is again mentioned in *R v Cook* (1918) 34 TLR 515. By 1922 the rules mentioned in those cases had increased to a total of nine. 'These nine rules (set out in the head note of the judgment) are the ones which have been followed in this State since that date. The first four of them are the ones which were originally formulated in 1912 and they are mentioned in the cases decided in 1918. The fact that the Judges' Rules which are now in force in Great Britain are different from the one in force here has been noted. . . .' Walsh J adopted the rules as follows:

i.   When a police officer is endeavouring to discover the author of a crime, there is no objection to his putting questions in respect thereof to any person or persons, whether suspected or not, from whom he thinks useful information may be obtained.

ii. When a police officer has made up his/her mind to charge a person with a crime, they should first caution the person before asking them any questions or any further questions, as the case may be.

iii. Persons in custody should not be questioned without the usual caution first being administered.

iv. If a prisoner wishes to volunteer any statement, the usual caution should first be administered. It is preferable that the last two words of such caution be omitted and that the caution end with the words 'be given in evidence'.

v.   The caution administered to a prisoner when he is formally charged should therefore be in the following words: 'Do you wish to say anything in answer to the charge? You are not obliged to say anything unless you wish to do so, but whatever you say will be taken down in writing and may be given in evidence.' Care should be taken to avoid the suggestion that the prisoner's answers can only be used in evidence against them, as this may prevent an innocent person making a statement which might assist in clearing them of the charge.

vi. A statement made by a prisoner before there is time to caution them is not rendered inadmissible in evidence merely because no caution has been given, but in such a case the prisoner should be cautioned as soon as possible.

vii. A prisoner making a voluntary statement must not be cross-examined and no questions should be put to them about it except for the purpose of removing ambiguity in what has actually been said. For instance, if they have mentioned an hour without saying whether it was morning or evening, or have not made it clear to what individual or place they intended to refer in some part of the statement, they may be questioned sufficiently to clear up the point.

viii. When two or more persons are charged with the same offence and their statements are taken separately, the police should not read these statements to the other persons charged. Rather, each of such persons should be given by the police a copy of such statements and nothing should be said or done to invite a reply. If the person charged desires to make a statement in reply, the usual caution first should be administered.

ix. Any statement made in accordance with the above rules should, whenever possible, be taken down in writing and signed by the person making it after it has been read to them and they have been invited to make any corrections they may wish to make.

In *The People (DPP) v Farrell* [1978] IR 13, the Court of Criminal Appeal emphasized that, while they are not rules of law, the Judges' Rules have stood the test of time and will be departed from at peril. While statements obtained in breach of the rules have in very rare cases been admitted in evidence, a court will only allow this in exceptional circumstances.

To be admissible in evidence against an accused person, a statement of admission or confession must be voluntary. It must not have been made either through fear of prejudice or hope of advantage held out by a person in authority. That is to say, any person or persons associated with the investigation must not have brought about any inculpatory statement through the use of threats or inducements.

A further requirement for the introduction into evidence of an alleged admission is that it should not have been obtained by means of oppression. Lord McDermott postulated the following definition of oppression, which has since been accepted by the Court of Criminal Appeal in cases such as *The People (DPP) v McNally and Breathnach* [1981] 2 Frewen 43: 'Questioning which by its nature, duration or other attendant circumstances (including defective custody) excites hopes (such as the hope of release) or fears, or so affects the mind of the subject that his will crumbles and he speaks when otherwise he would have remained silent.'

Beyond the requirements of voluntariness and lack of oppression, in Ireland there is a further imperative that there should be a fundamental fairness of procedures in any criminal investigation. In this regard, the most frequently cited statement of the law is the following made by Griffin J in *The People (DPP) v Shaw* [1982] IR 1: 'The judge presiding at a criminal trial should be astute to see that, although a statement may be technically voluntary, it should nevertheless be excluded if, by reason of the manner or circumstances in which it was obtained, it falls below the standard of fairness. The reason for the exclusion is not so much the risk of an erroneous conviction as the recognition that the minimum or essential standard must be observed in the administration of justice.'

6.5 Coercion of information and material

6.5.1 OBLIGATION TO FURNISH INFORMATION

There exists a steadily increasing range of statutory provisions that oblige a suspect to furnish information or material to the Gardaí. One of the first of these to be introduced was the Offences Against the State Act 1939, s 52, which requires a person detained under s 30 of that Act to give an account of his or her movements during a specified period. Failure to do so when properly cautioned constitutes an offence under the section.

The Criminal Justice Act 1984 ('the 1984 Act') introduced a number of measures designed to coerce the provision of information. Section 15 of that Act obliges a person to account for the origin of any firearm in their possession, while under s 16 a person must account for possession of certain property. Again, failure to furnish such an account in either case is deemed an offence, although information furnished under constraint of either section cannot be given in evidence against the person furnishing it or the spouse of such person.

A different method of coercion is employed by ss 18 and 19 of the 1984 Act. The first of these seeks to oblige a person to account for any object, substance or mark on them, in their possession or at the place where they are arrested. The second is designed to compel a person to explain their presence at a particular location in certain circumstances. Failure to comply with either demand, properly made, may give rise to the drawing of inferences by a judge or jury at either the preliminary examination stage or at trial.

Section 7 of the Criminal Justice (Drug Trafficking) Act 1997 allows the drawing of similar inferences in respect of drug trafficking offences. However, the information sought to be compelled under the threat of this sanction extends to any fact relied upon in defence of any prosecution ultimately instituted. All that is necessary for an inference to be drawn is a failure to respond to questioning by disclosing such a fact, if the suspect could reasonably have been expected to mention it when questioned. This is therefore a very far-ranging provision indeed.

The most recent of these measures for coercing the provision of information are those created by the Offences Against the State (Amendment) Act 1998. Sections 2 and 5 of that Act allow inferences to be drawn from the failure of a suspect to mention facts later relied on in his defence when being questioned by members of the Gardaí. Section 9 makes it an offence for a person to stay silent without a reasonable excuse, when they have information that they know or believe might be of material assistance to the Gardaí.

How these statutory encroachments on the privilege against self-incrimination are to be reconciled with the Judges' Rules is as yet unclear, beyond the fact that the latter must yield to the former, save insofar as the requirements of the Constitution mandate otherwise.

6.5.2   OBLIGATION TO FURNISH MATERIAL

Beyond the requirement to provide certain information in the circumstances described above, there is an obligation on all persons detained under the Criminal Justice Act 1984, s 4, to furnish their name and address, submit to a search, allow themselves to be photographed and fingerprinted, allow skin swabs and hair samples to be taken, and to submit to the seizure for testing of anything they have in their possession, all under pain of criminal sanction under the 1984 Act, s 6, for obstruction in the event of failure to cooperate. Section 7 of the Criminal Law Act 1976 imposes similar requirements on persons detained under the 1939 Act, s 30.

Section 2 of the Criminal Justice (Forensic Evidence) Act 1990 as amended by s 14 Criminal Justice Act 2006 obliges persons detained for questioning to submit to the taking of a number of different samples for forensic testing, when properly requested to do so, with failure amounting to obstruction under the Act. While the detained person's consent is required for the performance of the more invasive kinds of sampling procedures, inferences may be drawn in subsequent criminal proceedings from any failure to furnish such samples. Forensic Science methodology is generally discussed in previous paragraphs of this chapter.

Before leaving this topic, it is worth noting that there also exists a statutory miscellany of other coercive evidence-gathering procedures. For example, there is an obligation under the Misuse of Drugs Acts 1977 and 1984, s 23, to submit to a search by a member of the Gardaí who reasonably suspects the person in question to be in possession of a controlled drug. A refusal to accompany the requesting member to a Garda station for this purpose where so directed amounts to an offence under the section. Other coercive powers vested in the Gardaí include s 13 (provision of breath, blood, or urine sample), s 14 (production of driving licence on demand) and s 107 (provision of information concerning the driving of a vehicle) of the Road Traffic Act 1961, as amended. A more recently created power of coercive interrogation is that vested in an inspector appointed under the Companies Act 1990 to require answers to questions asked. In each of these instances, it is an offence not to furnish the information sought.

6.6 Identification procedures

6.6.1 THE RISK OF MISIDENTIFICATION

Misidentification has historically been the single most pervasive cause of wrongful conviction in the common law world and there is no reason to believe the Irish criminal process is any different in this respect. Thereby a heavy responsibility is placed on the advising solicitor to protect the client, as far as is professionally possible, from the risk of mistaken identification.

6.6.2 IDENTIFICATION PARADES

In Ireland, an unsatisfactory situation currently exists whereby the conduct of identification parades is not governed by a statutory code of practice. The *Garda Síochána Criminal Investigation Manual* ('the manual') contains a 23-point procedural plan for the conduct of a formal identification parade, together with an explanatory prologue, which reads like a 1969 UK Home Office circular. A parade is described in the prologue as the placing of a suspect among at least eight persons similar to him (or, presumably, her) in height, age, general appearance, dress and class in life. Its purpose is twofold: to exclude any suspicion of unfairness of the risk of error and to test the ability of the witness to identify the suspect adequately and independently.

6.6.3 PROCEDURAL RULES

The twenty-three procedural rules set out in the manual are as follows:

(a) A member of the Gardaí other than the member in charge of the investigation should conduct the identification parade.

(b) The member in charge of the investigation may be present at the parade but should take no active part.

(c) The conducting member should see the suspect before the parade, explain the arrangements to him and ask him if he has any objection. If he objects to participating in the parade, it should not be held.

(d) The conducting member should inform the suspect that he may have a solicitor or friend present at the parade.

(e) The conducting member should have the names, addresses and descriptions of the witnesses and be familiar with the facts of the case.

(f) The suspect should be placed among at least eight persons (known as 'volunteers') who are, as far as possible, roughly the same as the suspect in:

   (i)   age;

   (ii) height;

   (iii) general appearance;

   (iv) dress; and

   (v)   class in life.

(g) No witness should be given an opportunity of seeing the suspect before he is placed on the parade or of seeing a photograph of the suspect before the parade.

(h) Volunteers taking part in the parade must not be known to any of the witnesses and no witness should be given an opportunity of seeing the volunteers, their descriptions or photographs before the parade.

(i) All unauthorized persons, including members of the Gardaí, should be excluded from the parade.

(j) The parade should be formed in a line and those present should remain in front of the parade.

(k) If the parade is held indoors, a well-lit room is essential and, if possible, it should have entry and exit doors to facilitate the witnesses. If the parade is held outdoors, similar facilities should, where possible, be available, but the parade ground should not be overlooked from windows. In a situation where a witness has seen the person he is trying to identify outdoors in daylight on the occasion of the crime under investigation, it is desirable that the parade be held outdoors, if possible.

(l) The suspect should be asked if he has any objection to any of the volunteers forming the parade. He should be asked to give reasons for any objections and any reasonable objections should be met.

(m) The suspect should be told that he may select his own position in the parade and that he may change his position after each witness has left the parade.

(n) Once the identification parade has been formed, everything thereafter in respect of it should take place in the presence and hearing of the suspect.

(o) The witnesses should be isolated in a room as far as possible away from the room or place where the parade is being held. A member should be available to ensure that there is no communication between witnesses waiting to view the parade and any witness who has viewed the parade.

(p) The conducting officer should address each witness in the presence and hearing of the suspect as follows: 'This is an identification parade. I want you to look very carefully at this line of men and see if you recognize the person you have come to identify (or the person who assaulted you; the person you saw at [place], at [time], on [dates]). Do not say anything until I ask you a question.'

(q) When the witness has scrutinized the parade, the conducting member should ask him if he has identified any person.

(r) If the witness indicates that he has 'made an identification', the conducting member should ask him to place his hand on the identified person's shoulder. When a witness has made an identification, the person identified (if he is the suspect) should be cautioned and his reply, if any, noted.

(s) A witness, for example a child or a nervous person, might be reluctant to touch the suspect, in which case identification by pointing out may be permitted.

(t) Any reasonable request made by a witness should be granted, for example to see the parade walk, have them remove headgear, hear them speak, or to see the parade from the rear. In the last-mentioned case all present should remain in front of the parade.

(u) When all the witnesses have been called, the suspect should be asked whether he has any comments to make concerning the manner in which the parade has been conducted.

(v) Where there are two suspects of similar appearance, they may be paraded together with at least twelve other persons. If the suspects are not similar in appearance, or if there are more than two suspects, separate parades should be held using different volunteers on each parade.

(w) There is no objection to having a parade made up entirely of suspects. This would only apply where there are not more than two culprits sought and all of the suspects are of roughly similar appearance. Two suspects of obviously dissimilar appearance should not be included in the same parade.

It should be noted that identification parade ('ID parade') procedure in England was addressed by the Devlin Report on 'Evidence of Identification in Criminal Cases' HC 338 1976, which made a number of suggestions for reform. The report contains too many recommendations to mention them all here, but perhaps the most significant in practical terms is the suggestion that a witness should only be allowed to see a participant in the parade walk or hear them talk if that witness has already picked the person out and merely wishes to confirm the identification.

Many of these suggested reforms were incorporated in the subsequent *British Home Office Guidelines* 1978 and the conduct of identification parades is now governed in the UK by Annex A of the *Identification Code* promulgated under s 66 of the Police and Criminal Evidence Act 1984. In Ireland the only stricture, albeit a potentially very significant one, governing pre-trial identification procedures is the constitutional requirement of fairness, fair procedure, and due regard to the dignity of the individual. This requirement was identified by the Supreme Court in *The State (Healy) v Donoghue* [1976] IR 325.

6.6.4   SIGNIFICANCE OF ID PARADES

In evidential terms, the significance of an identification parade is as follows. Where identification is in issue an identification parade should be conducted, if possible, as stipulated by the Court of Criminal Appeal in *AG v Costello*, 18 December 1928 CCA (unreported). But this is not an absolute rule. Evidence that results from the improper conduct of an identification parade or by way of an arranged confrontation between a witness and suspect may be admitted. In *The People (AG) v Martin* [1956] IR 22, the Supreme Court stated, per Lavery J, that 'each case must be considered and ruled on the evidence and on all the circumstances'.

From *The People (DPP) v McDermott* [1991] 1 IR 350, two propositions emerge. First, that an identification made from an ID parade is potentially admissible in evidence and does not necessarily require corroboration. Secondly, that in such circumstances a warning should be given as to the difference in opportunity, control, and credibility between an informal identification and a properly conducted identification parade. On the authority of *The DPP v Cooney* [1997] 3 IR 205, a dock identification in court may constitute admissible evidence, albeit evidence to which very little weight should attach. *The People (DPP) v O'Reilly* [1990] 2 IR 415 was a case in which a conviction was quashed due to the failure to hold an identification parade. In that case, O'Flaherty J pointed out that an identification parade might be impractical and therefore unnecessary, where the suspect is of singular appearance or where the case involves recognition rather than identification. Most significantly, the court added that if a suspect refuses to take part in an identification parade or seeks to frustrate it once assembled, they would have to live with the consequences. Generally, the consequence will be identification by confrontation at the door of the holding cell or dock identification in court.

6.6.5   THE ROLE OF THE SOLICITOR AT AN ID PARADE

The solicitor has a number of important functions to fulfil while attending an identity parade. They must ensure as far as is possible that the parade is conducted in a fair manner. This means compliance with the procedural rules and the observance of fair procedures in general. To this end the solicitor should check with the Gardaí that none of the witnesses will see either the suspect or any members of the line-up beforehand. Ideally, there should not even be contact between witnesses. Certainly any witness who has viewed the parade must have no contact with those who have not.

The solicitor must ensure that the parade as constituted is a fair one. This means being satisfied that the other people on the parade are similar in age, height, appearance, and status to the suspect. This is sometimes more difficult than it sounds. Frequently, the Gardaí have problems in getting people to partake in the first place, and pressure may well be put on a solicitor to accept a particular line-up. It is important therefore to be aware of these pressures and to be patient and firm while awaiting suitable people to be found.

When the Gardaí are assembling the identification parade, the solicitor should note down the names, addresses, ages, general appearance, and distinctive physical characteristics of the people on the parade. The parade should then be viewed and objection should be made to any people on the parade with whom the solicitor is not satisfied. The Garda member in charge of the parade may or may not accede to the solicitor's request. However, it is vitally important for the solicitor to record at that point the objections made and to make these clear to the officer in charge of the parade.

When considering a line-up a solicitor should be on the lookout for beards, moustaches, tattoos, scars, glasses, and any other distinguishing features. It may well be that the suspect has been in Garda custody for some time and may not have had the opportunity to shave or clean up. The solicitor should insist that their client be allowed to shave, clean up and otherwise regain their composure as far as possible. The solicitor should ensure that if the suspect is not wearing a jacket or coat, all other persons on the line-up remove their jackets and coats to ensure, so far as is possible, similarity of appearance. Solicitors should also check to see that all jewellery worn by persons who are to make up the parade is removed prior to the parade. Where the suspect has a prominent mark on face or hands, consideration should be given to having each person on the parade, the suspect included, wear a sticking plaster in the appropriate place. The solicitor should not be reluctant to employ this sort of ingenuity on a client's behalf. Absolute fairness is the goal.

The suspect should be told that any position on the parade may be taken up. One of the features of ID parades is that while the suspect is invariably nervous, the other people on the parade as volunteers tend to be in a jovial mood and happy to chat to each other. It is good practice for a solicitor to speak to the people on the parade once the line-up is ready, and to inform them that they are taking part in a very serious exercise. The solicitor should then ask all of them to stand straight, look out in front of them, and remain quiet and still while the witnesses are viewing the parade.

As the witnesses are brought into the parade room the solicitor should observe them closely. A witness may, for instance, walk up and down the parade or look at it for a long time. He may make an identification such as 'I think it is him', or he may ask the suspect or another member of the parade to turn around. All of these facts should be noted down and a record kept of the time elapsed where possible. If the suspect is identified they will be cautioned as to whether or not they have anything to say. If there is such identification a solicitor will normally have advised their client to say nothing in reply.

When the parade has been completed it is good practice for the solicitor to indicate to the Garda member in charge what he has noted down. For example, a witness may have said words when making an identification such as 'I am fairly sure', or 'I think', or may have taken a long time to make the identification. Matters such as these should be clarified immediately and agreed on, thus avoiding any difficulties in this regard at a subsequent trial that may be as much as two years away and avoiding any necessity for the solicitor to give evidence at trial stage.

6.6.6   IDENTIFICATION FROM PHOTOGRAPHS

The position in law in this regard has been summarized by Sandes in *Criminal Law and Procedure in the Republic of Ireland* (3rd edn, Dublin: Sweet & Maxwell, 1951), pp 186–7, as follows:

'It is not improper for the police where no arrest has been made and they are in doubt as to the culprit, or where an arrest is under consideration, to put a number of photographs of different individuals before a prosecutor or potential witness in order that they might be assisted in their efforts to find out who the culprit was. That is quite another thing to first showing him a photograph of the suspect and then taking him to an identification parade, for he is then in effect identifying a photograph when purporting to identify a man.'

In Ryan and Magee, *The Irish Criminal Process* (Mercier Press, 1983) p 137, it is suggested that a potential witness should be presented with a series of at least 12 photographs and then asked whether any of the persons depicted was the perpetrator. This approach is a reflection of the current UK statutory procedure. It is also the procedure approved by the High Court in *People v Mills* [1957] IR 106. Section 12 of the Criminal Justice Act 2006 has empowered the Gardaí to take or cause the taking of photographs for identification purposes.

6.6.7 PRE-TRIAL IDENTIFICATION IN EVIDENCE

There are, broadly speaking, three options open to the courts when confronted with dubious evidence of identification. Such evidence could simply be excluded. Secondly, it could be allowed to go to the jury but with a warning in respect of the dangers attached to it. Thirdly, it might be stipulated that such evidence should only be accepted with corroboration. In practice, the first option has been adopted as a discretionary course (and consequently one that is rarely followed). The Supreme Court has adopted the second option (thus rendering a minimum warning mandatory) whereas the third option has been firmly rejected by the same court.

Unfortunately, in the absence of legislation, there are several identification-related issues in respect of which the practitioner has only the occasional judicial pronouncement for guidance. These issues include the procedures governing the use of photographs for identification purposes, the admissibility of videotape evidence and the consequences of a breach of the rules governing identification parades.

In *The People v Casey (No 2)* [1963] IR 33, the Supreme Court, through Kingsmill Moore J, established a mandatory warning to the jury in the following terms:

'In our opinion, it is desirable that in all cases where the verdict depends substantially on the correctness of an identification, their attention should be called in general terms to the fact that in a number of instances such identification has proved erroneous, to the possibilities of mistake in the case before them and to the necessity of caution. Nor do we think that such warning should be confined to cases where the identification is that of only one witness. Experience has shown that mistakes can occur where two or more witnesses have made positive identifications. We consider juries in cases where the correctness of an identification is challenged should be directed on the following lines, namely, that if their verdict as to the guilt of the prisoner is to depend wholly or substantially on the correctness of such identification, they should bear in mind that there have been a number of instances where responsible witnesses, whose honesty was not in question and whose opportunities for observation had been adequate, made positive identifications on a parade or otherwise, which subsequently proved to be erroneous; and accordingly that they should be especially cautious before accepting such evidence of identification as correct; but that if after careful examination of such evidence in the light of all of the circumstances and with due regard to the other evidence in the case, they feel satisfied beyond reasonable doubt of the correctness of the identification they are at liberty to act upon it.'

The People (AG) v O'Driscoll 1 Frewen 351 establishes that there is no difference between identification and recognition cases for the purposes of the above warning.

6.6.8 SAFEGUARDS FOR THE SUSPECT IN DETENTION

6.6.8.1 The introduction of safeguards

As discussed previously at **6.4.2** above, the Criminal Justice Act 1984 ('the 1984 Act') introduced for the first time outside the State security context a power to detain for questioning. Experience suggests that detention for questioning is now more the norm than the exception during the investigation of all but the most trivial offences. Certain safeguards for the detainee were introduced by the 1984 Act, intended to counterbalance the new police powers it created. Whether they have done so is very much open to question.

6.6.9 THE CUSTODY REGULATIONS

The most comprehensive set of safeguards for the suspect being detained for questioning are those set out in the Criminal Justice Act 1984 (Treatment of Prisoners in Custody in Garda Síochána Stations) Regulations 1987 (SI 119/1987) ('the 1987 Regulations'). They apply to all persons detained in a Garda station and not just those held under s 4 of the Criminal Justice Act 1984. They provide for the nomination of a Garda member as 'member in charge' of detention facilities at all times, with responsibility for ensuring the application of the regulations to persons detained. The member in charge is responsible for the maintenance of custody records in which details of arrest and detention must be recorded. The detainee must be given information (set out in a printed form) listing their rights while in detention and must also be furnished with details of any charge intended to be preferred.

The 1987 Regulations contain provisions concerning notification of the detention to the suspect's family members and solicitor; provisions about the way in which inquiries concerning the detention must be handled; provisions concerning the detention of juveniles, foreign nationals and mentally handicapped persons; and provisions governing the conditions of detention and the administration of medical treatment where required. Regarding the investigation itself, there are provisions governing the conduct of interviews, searches and the taking of fingerprints.

The 1987 Regulations make mandatory extensive record-keeping concerning persons detained. The custody record, mentioned above, must contain, in addition to details of arrest and detention: details of any direction extending detention; details of the time and circumstances in which the suspect was informed of their rights; details of any request for a solicitor and the action taken in response. Other details that must be recorded include: the notification of the detention to District Headquarters; the suspect's waiver of an offer of suspension of questioning between midnight and 8 am, where made; the times of all interviews conducted and the persons present; decisions made concerning the detention of juveniles and steps taken as a result; the notification of certain rights to detained foreign nationals, requests made by them and actions taken; any searches of the person that are conducted; any fingerprints, photographs and/or swabs taken; any complaints made; medical examinations conducted and steps taken as a consequence; visits to the detainee; communications by or with the detainee; meals supplied; and the time of eventual release.

6.6.9.1 Shortcomings of record keeping system

There are a number of identifiable shortcomings associated with the record-keeping regime described above, which can be summarized as follows:

(a) It represents the creation of a welter of secondary, rather than primary, evidence. A trial court will not know what the accused said or did, but will rather be asked to rely on the documented record of what was allegedly said and done. The interrogator often composes statements of admission by reducing answers, but not questions, to writing, so as to suggest a seamless first person narrative of admission, which the suspect is then invited to sign.

(b) There is no contemporaneous judicial oversight. In civil law jurisdictions, where detention for questioning is not novel, a judge contemporaneously supervises the detention and interrogation process. In Ireland, as a result of the non-existence of such supervision, trials increasingly tend to centre on disputes concerning events in the Garda station rather than on the event or events alleged to constitute the crime itself.

(c) Most importantly, the procedural control provided by the 1987 Regulations is not rigid, since a breach of the regulations does not, of itself, affect the lawfulness of the custody or the admissibility of evidence obtained.

6.6.10 ELECTRONIC RECORDING OF INTERROGATION

The *Report of the Committee to Recommend Certain Safeguards for Persons in Custody and for Members of An Garda Síochána*, Prl 7158, Dublin, 1978, para 67, recommended that 'feasibility studies should be instituted at once to establish whether videotaping of interrogations in the investigation of serious crime is a viable proposition'.

Section 27 of the Criminal Justice Act 1984 enabled rather than obliged regulations to be introduced providing for the electronic recording of interviews. The 1987 Regulations (see **6.6.9**) did not address the issue.

The Report of the Committee to Enquire into Certain Aspects of Criminal Procedure (Dublin, 1990) strongly recommended 'as a safeguard towards ensuring that inculpatory admissions to the Garda Síochána are properly obtained and recorded, that the questioning of suspects take place before an audio-visual recording device'. A steering committee and a pilot study were subsequently set up. Ultimately, there arrived the Criminal Justice Act 1984 (Electronic Recording of Interviews) Regulations 1997 (SI 74/1997). Unfortunately, as a safeguard, the measure introduced by the Act is ineffectual. It makes it necessary to record only where proper equipment has been provided and installed and, even then, it need not take place 'if it is not practicable'.

6.6.11 THE DETAINED PERSON'S RIGHT OF ACCESS TO A SOLICITOR

Under the 1987 Regulations (see **6.6.9**), detained persons are required to be notified, both orally and in writing, of their entitlement to consult a solicitor and to have the solicitor of their choice requested to attend. In the event that the chosen solicitor cannot be contacted within a reasonable time or is unable or unwilling to attend at the station, the person shall be given another opportunity to nominate a solicitor. Where an arrested person asks for a solicitor, the Gardaí may not ask that person to make a written statement in relation to an offence until a reasonable time for the attendance of the solicitor has elapsed.

A suspect is entitled to have access to their solicitor immediately upon the arrival of the latter at the Garda station. This was established as a constitutional entitlement by the Supreme Court in *The People (DPP) v Healy* [1990] 2 IR 73. The 1987 Regulations dictate that solicitor and client are entitled to confer privately, out of earshot of other persons, although the Gardaí are entitled to have any such consultation held within sight. The Supreme Court has recently held, however, that a solicitor is not entitled to be present at the interviews held with the suspect. This unqualified statement was made by O'Flaherty J in the case of *Lavery v The Member in Charge, Carrickmacross Garda Station* [1999] 2 IR 390. It should be noted that criminal Legal Aid is not available in respect of attendances by solicitors on indigent suspects detained in Garda stations.

6.6.12 ADVISING THE CLIENT IN CUSTODY

6.6.12.1 Prompt attendance at the Garda station

As has already been noted, the 1987 Regulations preclude interrogators from asking a detained person to make a statement until a reasonable time for the attendance of a requested solicitor has elapsed see **6.6.11**. A solicitor should indicate a willingness to advise a person in custody if they are unable to attend within a 'reasonable time'. Remember that if a requested solicitor is unavailable or unwilling to attend, the detained person is entitled to ask for another solicitor. The important thing, from a responsible practitioner's perspective, is to ensure that the detained person has access to professional advice before being asked to make a statement.

6.6.12.2 Procedure on arrival at the station

There are no absolute or inflexible rules with regard to the procedure to be followed by a solicitor on arrival at the Garda station. They should first ask to speak to the member in charge. It is important to be polite but firm in seeking immediate access to the detainee. The detainee has a right of immediate access to their solicitor's advice. Any delay in this regard should be carefully noted and, if necessary, should form the subject of a formal complaint.

The custody record should be consulted in order to establish the statutory detention power invoked and the suspicion grounding its exercise. The solicitor is entitled to consult with their client privately, out of earshot of any other person, and should insist upon this. The Gardaí are entitled to keep the detainee within sight if they wish.

A criminal solicitor should be familiar with the 1987 Regulations concerning the detention of juveniles, foreign nationals and mentally handicapped persons and should be in a position to advise such persons accordingly.

It is prudent practice for the solicitor to take a careful written note of the instructions that they receive from their client and the advice provided. A fundamental question that has to be addressed regarding any detention is whether the detainee is in a fit condition, mentally and physically, to cope with interrogation. The member in charge is under an obligation to summon a doctor if the detainee is injured, intoxicated to the degree of unconsciousness, unable to respond to questions or conversation, apparently mentally ill, or otherwise appearing to be in need of medical attention. The advising solicitor should bring any such circumstance to the attention of the member in charge immediately. Drug addiction is obviously a case in point. The member in charge must also seek medical advice if the detained person claims to require medication for any serious condition and the solicitor should also be alert to this possibility. A detainee is entitled to be examined by a doctor of their own choice at their own expense where 'practicable'.

6.6.12.3 Advice on the privilege against self-incrimination

The invariably stressful and upsetting experience of detention in a Garda station is hardly the best circumstance in which to mount a reasoned defence of one's conduct in relation to any allegation. From the advising solicitor's point of view, it is very difficult to advise a client 'on the spot' whether or not to make a statement, based on a single attendance with that client in the charged atmosphere of a detention cell or interview room. After all, if given the opportunity to conduct a painstaking and unhurried attendance with a client at liberty, the solicitor would inevitably explain the desirability of either composing a careful and comprehensive statement of rebuttal or of invoking the privilege against self-incrimination, at the client's election. Accordingly, it is difficult to imagine the circumstances in which a client in custody could be counselled to provide a cautioned written statement, or any statement, then and there.

However, such advice may be given due to the situation having become increasingly complex over the last couple of decades for reasons considered earlier. The last 20 years have seen the enactment of a number of statutory provisions (see **6.4.2**) either allowing for the drawing of inferences by a judge or jury from silence in the face of questioning, or rendering silence in such circumstances a separate criminal offence in itself. It is important that the client in custody should be advised of the implication of any such possible encroachment upon their right to remain silent (the privilege against self-incrimination).

Two recent decisions must be specifically flagged in this regard. The first is that of the Supreme Court in *Re: National Irish Bank* [1999] 3 IR 145. In that case, it was held that a statement compelled under the statutory power of a Company Inspector would not generally be admissible at a subsequent criminal trial of the person concerned, unless the trial judge was satisfied that the confession was voluntary. The question then arises as to what is voluntary. At p 180, Barrington J stated: 'The fact that Inspectors are armed with statutory powers or may even have invoked them does not necessarily mean that a statement in reply to their questions is not voluntary.' If the question of whether a compelled statement is a voluntary statement must be deferred until a possible future criminal trial, then, from the point of view of a practitioner called upon to advise at the point or moment of coercion, this approach offers no guidance.

The second decision that must be noted is that of the European Court of Human Rights in *Heaney & McGuinness v Ireland* (unreported) 21 December 2000, ECHR. In that case, s 52 of the Offences Against the State Act 1939 was held to be in violation of Article 6 of the European Convention on Human Rights. The Court noted that, while they were not expressly mentioned in Article 6, the right to silence and the right not to incriminate oneself were generally recognized international standards that lie at the heart of fair procedure under that Article. The Court identified the applicants' dilemma as that of having to choose between remaining silent at risk of a criminal conviction (and six months' imprisonment), or forfeiting their right to remain silent at a time when it was unclear whether any statement made might be used against them in a future criminal trial. Pending the repeal of the offending provision, the present unsatisfactory situation is that a statement that is compelled at pain of criminal conviction and that may be used in a subsequent criminal trial is obtained in breach of the European Convention on Human Rights but in compliance with the domestic law of the State.

CHAPTER 7

COMMENCEMENT OF PROCEEDINGS

7.1   Who may prosecute?

A prosecutor is a person who initiates criminal legal proceedings against another person. In Ireland, most criminal prosecutions are brought by the Director of Public Prosecutions ('DPP') on behalf of the people of Ireland. Jurisdiction to prosecute criminal offences was conferred on the DPP by the Prosecution of Offences Act 1974. Previous to this, all prosecutions were brought by the Attorney General, who was the sole person vested with powers to prosecute criminal matters, pursuant to the terms of Article 34 of the Constitution.

The Attorney General, however, has retained power to prosecute certain offences, most notably extradition matters and those pursuant to s 18(2) of the Fisheries Acts. The consent of the Attorney General is also required in relation to the commencement of proceedings concerning certain offences related to the Official Secrets Act 1963 and the Genocide Act 1973.

In certain other criminal offences, powers are conferred by statute on specified persons other than the DPP to prosecute criminal offences of a summary nature in the District Court. For example, the Minister for Social, Community and Family Affairs retains the power to prosecute under the Social Welfare Consolidation Acts 1993 in respect of alleged social welfare offences. The Commissioner for Public Works is authorized to prosecute summary offences under the National Monuments (Amendment) Act 1987. Dublin City Council is authorized to prosecute in respect of certain offences under the Litter Pollution Act 1997. The Competition Authority has power to initiate criminal prosecutions for offences contrary to the provisions of the Competition (Amendment) Act 1996 and Dublin Bus regularly prosecutes individuals evading payment of bus fares.

Any private citizen may bring a criminal prosecution before the courts in his capacity as a 'common informer'. This is a term used by the courts to describe a member of the public who is willing to give evidence in respect of the commission of an offence. To commence a prosecution, the person must make a complaint to a District Judge who, if satisfied that a valid complaint exists, may then issue and sign the summons. If the offence is indictable and is ultimately to be disposed of in the Circuit Court, the common informer may only conduct the prosecution up to the return for trial of the accused person to the Circuit Court. Carriage of the proceedings to the DPP must then be handed over to the DPP.

As a general principle, a company or body corporate cannot prosecute a criminal offence as a common informer without express statutory authorization, as a company is regarded as a legal entity distinct from its members.

There are two methods of bringing a person before a District Court to answer a charge. The first is by way of summons served on a defendant by the Garda Síochána, which could be described as an invitation to attend court. It is a method devised to compel the attendance of the accused person before the District Court on a certain date to answer the complaint alleged against them. If the person attends court on the specified date and answers when the summons is called, it is then generally acknowledged that the summons has served its purpose and the defendant has been properly summonsed.

The second method of securing the attendance of a person before a court is by way of arrest and charge. The purpose of an arrest is to apprehend a person lawfully so that they can be brought before a court to answer the charge alleged against them. Once a person has been arrested, they will generally be taken to a Garda station for either a period of detention, if the offence so warrants, or will be charged 'as soon as reasonably practicable' with the offence for which they have been arrested.

7.2   Charge sheet procedure and station bail

Where a person is charged with a criminal offence at a Garda station, the District Court (charge sheet) Rules 1971 provide that he must be given a document setting out the charge and setting out the facts that are alleged against them. This document, which is referred to as a 'charge sheet', should also refer to the statute that it is alleged the person has contravened. The prosecuting Garda member will note on the charge sheet the remarks, if any, made by the accused person upon the charge being read out to them.

Once charged, the accused may be released on 'station bail' where the member in charge believes it prudent, and providing that there are no outstanding warrants for their arrest. Section 31 of the Criminal Procedure Act 1967 as amended by s 3 of the Criminal Justice (Miscellaneous Provisions) Act 1997 provides that the accused may be released on bail subject to their entering a recognisance that they will attend at the District Court at the next sitting or within 30 days of the next sitting. If they fail to do so, the District Judge at their discretion may issue a 'bench warrant' for the arrest of the accused. Failure to answer bail is also a criminal offence under the provisions of s 13 of the Criminal Justice Act 1993, punishable by a maximum of 12 months' imprisonment.

Certain offences are not eligible for station bail. Section 29 of the Criminal Procedure Act 1967 provides that the High Court is the only venue where a bail application can be entertained in respect of specified serious offences such as murder, piracy, treason, genocide, and breaches of the Geneva Convention. In addition, bail applications for certain offences contrary to the Offences Against the State Act may only be made to the Special Criminal Court.

Where a person is refused station bail, the only other option is to make an application to the District Court Judge. Bail is discussed in detail in **Chapter 8**.

Once the accused is before the court, a prosecutor present on behalf of the DPP will give evidence to the District Court Judge of the arrest, charge and caution of the accused, and the reply made by the accused person to the charge after caution, if any. The charge sheet will then be lodged with the court registrar.

7.3   Summons procedure

A summons is a document served on an accused person directing their attendance before a District Court to answer a complaint. The accused is not required to enter a bail bond but, similar to the charge sheet procedure, a District Court Judge may at their discretion issue a warrant for the accused's arrest if they fail to turn up in court.

The issue of the majority of summonses is governed by the Courts (No 3) Act 1986, which provides that District Court proceedings in respect of criminal offences may be commenced by the issuing of a summons by the relevant District Court Clerk following an application by the prosecutor in question. This procedure is referred to as 'making of a complaint'.

7.3.1 REQUIREMENTS FOR A VALID SUMMONS

A valid summons must state in ordinary language the particulars of the offence alleged and the name and address of the accused person. It must also clearly state the time, date and location of the proposed sitting of the District Court where the accused is requested to attend. The identity of the District Court Clerk must also feature on the face of the summons.

In certain other cases, a District Court Judge has competence to hear a complaint and to issue summonses. In a case where the defendant is a member of the Garda Síochána or a member of the judiciary, a complaint should be made by way of sworn information to a judge of the District Court who, upon being satisfied that a genuine complaint exists, may then sign and issue a summons. These summonses issue pursuant to the Petty Sessions Act 1851, s 10, and this provision should be disclosed on the face of the summons. The procedure governing the issue of summonses by a District Court Judge is set out in the District Court Rules 1997. The same procedure applies when an application is made either by a private citizen or the Gardaí to have a person bound over to keep the peace. A district Judge can make an order to bind any person over to keep the peace if a reasonable apprehension exists that a breach of the peace might occur.

7.3.2 SERVICE OF SUMMONS

Once a summons has issued, it must be served on the accused by a member of the Gardaí (other than the member who made the complaint) or by a summons server assigned to a particular court area. The service of summonses for summary offences is governed by the Courts Act, 1991, s 22, which provides that a summons may be served by either registered or recorded delivery post or by hand. Service may be proven by way of statutory declaration. Service must be executed at least seven clear days in advance of the court hearing date. Once the summons has been served, the server must endorse the declaration of service on the reverse of the original summons and enter the summons with the District Court Clerk at least four clear days before the appointed date for hearing.

7.3.3 RENEWAL OF SUMMONS

On occasion, a summons may lapse through not having been dealt with on the specified court date. Rule 64 of the District Court Rules provides that a fresh summons may be issued in respect of the same charge, provided that the complaint has been made within the six-month limitation period (see paragraph **7.4** below on time limits). This means that if the summons is struck out on the original date without prejudice, providing that the District Judge has heard no evidence the prosecutor may simply reapply to the District Court Clerk for a new summons based on the original complaint. It is essential that the new summons makes reference to the same complaint as the first summons.

This procedure would also be relevant where a summons was applied for but through inadvertence was never served. In the case of *DPP v McKillen* [1991] 2 IR, the High Court (Lavan J) held that proceedings instituted pursuant to the Petty Sessions Act 1851, s 10, permitted the reissue of a summons. The first summons had not been served and it was held that the reissued summons remained grounded upon the making of the original complaint.

7.3.4 DEFECTIVE SUMMONS

A fundamental defect on the face of a summons, such as the omission of the location of the District Court or the identity of the District Court Clerk to whom the complaint was made, will be fatal to the success of the proceedings. A District Court Judge, who is given wide powers of amendment by Rule 88 of the District Court Rules, may remedy superficial defects. Amendment of a summons is a matter for judicial discretion and in exercising this discretion a judge must take into account any prejudice that would accrue to the accused person arising from an amendment.

7.4 Time limits in criminal proceedings

Section 10(4) of the Petty Sessions (Ireland) Act 1851 as amended by s 177 Criminal Justice Act 2006 provides that in summary proceedings a complaint must be made within six months of the time the alleged offence is committed. This is the statutory framework for the time limits regarding the majority of summary offences. Special time limits apply in respect of some summary offences and are governed by other statutes. Such statutes and time limits include the following:

- National Monuments Acts—three months from the date the offence came to the attention of the Commissioners for Public Works as provided for in s 19 of the National Monuments Act 1954.

- Consumer Information Act 1978—12 months.

- Child Care Act 1991—12 months.

- Housing (Miscellaneous Provisions) Act 1992—two years.

- Excise offences—one year as provided for in the Finance Act 1985, s 39.

- Revenue offences—10 years as provided for in the Finance Act 1983, s 94(7).

- Wireless Telegraphy Acts—12 months.

7.5 Statute barred

Non-compliance with a time limit arising under statute for the making of a complaint can be a defence to a charge but is generally held not to be a condition precedent to the exercise by the District Court of its jurisdiction to hear criminal proceedings. If raised as a point of defence, it is up to the prosecutor to show that the time limits were complied with.

In this context 'month' means a calendar month (Interpretation Act 1937, s 13), and when computing days, the day of the alleged offence is taken to be included in the period within which the complaint ought to be made. The crucial date when time can be said to stop running is the date of the making of the complaint either to the District Court Clerk or the District Court Judge, and not the date of issue of the summons.

A court has no power whatever to abridge or extend a limitation period fixed by statute and, accordingly, the judicial discretion granted by rule 88 of the District Court Rules cannot be used to remedy such a crucial defect.

7.5.1   TIME LIMITS IN INDICTABLE OFFENCES

As previously outlined, the normal time limit for the commencement of summary prosecutions is six months from the date of the alleged offence. There is in general no time limit within which a case prosecuted on indictment must be commenced. Many indictable offences, however, are prosecuted in the District Court with the consent of the Director of Public Prosecutions (DPP) as discussed in detail in **Chapter 10**. Section 7 of the Criminal Justice Act 1951 provides that the six-month time limit does not apply to 'indictable' offences. The 1951 Act contains a schedule of offences which can be tried in the District Court. Scheduled offences are also listed in SI 142/72 and SI 282/72 and the offences created by the Offences against the State (Amendment) Act 1998. As new indictable offences are created by statute, they are generally not included in the schedule of the 1951 Act, but rather the method by which they can be tried in the District Court is set out in the new statute. An example of this is the Criminal Justice (Theft and Fraud Offences) Act 2001.

If an indictable offence under this Act is dealt with summarily in the District Court, the High Court has ruled that the six-month time limit did not apply to such an offence as it was an indictable offence by creation, and just because such an offence could be disposed of summarily in the District Court with the consent of the DPP did not render the offence summary in nature (*Director of Public Prosecutions v Timmons* (unreported) 21 December 2004). Section 177 of the Criminal Justice Act 2006 has now restricted the application of s 10(A) of the Petty Sessions (Ireland) Act 1851 stating that the six-month time limit does not apply to a scheduled offence or an offence which is triable at the election of the prosecution either on indictment or summarily (s 76(i) as substituted) or an offence which is triable either on indictment or, subject to certain conditions including the consent of the prosecution, summarily.

7.5.2   DELAY

While there may be no defined time limits in respect of the initiation of indictable offences, it goes without saying that severe delay in bringing certain matters before the court could result in substantial prejudice to the accused in the conduct of their defence. In such circumstances, natural justice may demand that the summons be dismissed. In the case of both summary and indictable proceedings, an order of prohibition may be sought by way of judicial review proceedings in the High Court to halt the proceedings.

The courts have examined the issue of delay in several cases and a substantial body of jurisprudence on the subject has developed in recent times. In the Supreme Court decision of *State (O'Connell) v Fawsitt & DPP* (unreported) 30 July 1986 Finlay CJ held that where a person's trial on indictment had been delayed excessively so as to prejudice their chances of a fair trial, then the appropriate remedy by which their constitutional rights could be protected and defended is by order of prohibition to stop the trial. An equal and alternative remedy would be available in summary cases by way of application to the District Court Judge to dismiss the summons on the grounds of delay.

In the later case of *DPP v Carlton* [1993] 1 IR 81, Morris J in the High Court concluded there were grounds upon which excessive delay in criminal proceedings pleaded by the defendant, namely delay which results in prejudice to the accused in the conduct of his defence and, secondly, delay alone by its very nature is unfair and unjust. Where prejudice is alleged, it is for the defendant to show how they are prejudiced. In the latter case, it is for the State to justify delay.

In the case of *DPP v Barry Byrne* (unreported) 2 March 1994, the Supreme Court held that where delay is alleged, it is for the defendant to raise the issue of delay. A time lapse between the offence and the date for hearing of nine or ten months, in the absence of specific evidence of prejudice to the accused, was not considered to be such a delay as to infringe any constitutional right of the accused in that case. It should be noted that this case was decided on its own facts and that the relevant time frame should not be held out as a yardstick. The court also held that where the delay is excessive, a court may infer prejudice without proof of specific prejudice and dismiss the prosecution or prohibit the trial. The court stated that the determination of when delay is excessive will depend on the circumstances of each case.

In the most important Supreme Court decision on delay, *DPP v Coman McNeill* [1999] 1 IE 91 (unreported), O'Flaherty J emphasized that while there is no express declaration in our Constitution requiring a speedy trial, there is provision for trial 'within due course of law' in Article 38.1, which he took to mean that a trial should come on with reasonable expedition. Referring to the decision in *DPP v Byrne*, O'Flaherty J restated the position set out in that case, namely that 'Where there is unreasonable delay, it is possible to infer prejudice.' He went on to say that what constitutes unreasonable delay must be a matter for resolution in each individual case. O'Flaherty J concluded that from a reading of the *Byrne* decision, the onus is on a defendant asserting delay to show that they have been prejudiced, which in the present case the accused failed to do.

CHAPTER 8

BAIL, ADJOURNMENTS, AND REMANDS

8.1 Introduction

Where a person is arrested and not released from the Garda station on 'station bail', an application for bail may usually be made on the person's appearance before the District Court. Section 28(1) of the Criminal Procedure Act 1967 provides that:

> *A justice of the District Court shall admit to bail a person charged before him with an offence, other than an offence to which section 29 applies, if it appears to him to be a case in which bail ought to be allowed.*

Section 29 provides that a person charged with certain offences such as murder, piracy, genocide, and treason shall not be admitted to bail except by order of the High Court.

8.2 O'Callaghan's Case

The seminal authority on bail in Ireland is the decision of the Supreme Court in *The People (AG) v O'Callaghan* [1966] IR 501. The following passage from the judgment of Walsh J (at p 513) is worthy of quotation at length:

> 'In bail applications generally it has been laid down from the earliest times that the object of bail is to secure the appearance of the accused person at his trial by a reasonable amount of bail. The object of bail is neither punitive nor preventative. From the earliest times it was appreciated that detention in custody pending trial could be a cause of great hardship and it is as true now as it was in ancient times that it is desirable to release on bail as large a number of accused persons as possible who may safely be released pending trial. From time to time necessity demands that some unconvicted persons should be held in custody pending trial to secure their attendance at the trial but in such cases necessity is the operative test. The presumption of innocence until conviction is a very real thing and is not simply a procedural rule taking effect only at the trial. In the modern complex society in which we live the effect of imprisonment upon the private life of the accused and of his family may be disastrous in its severe economic consequences to him and his family dependent upon his earnings from day to day or even hour to hour. It must also be recognized that imprisonment before trial will usually have an adverse effect upon the prisoner's prospects of acquittal because of the difficulty, if not the impossibility in many cases, of adequately investigating the case and preparing the defence.'

In *O'Callaghan* the Supreme Court critically considered the following list of matters (at pp 503–4) which Murnaghan J in the High Court had held should be taken into account when considering whether or not it is likely that the prisoner may attempt to evade justice:

(1) The nature of the accusation or in other words the seriousness of the charge. It stands to reason that the more serious the charge is the greater is the likelihood that the prisoner would not appear to answer it.

(2) The nature of the evidence in support of the charge. The more cogent the evidence, the greater the likelihood of conviction, and consequently the greater the likelihood of the prisoner attempting to evade justice.

(3) The likely sentence to be imposed on conviction. The greater the sentence is likely to be, the greater the likelihood of the prisoner trying to avoid it. The prisoner's previous record has a bearing on the probable sentence and consequently must be before the Court.

(4) The likelihood of the commission of further offences while on bail. In this connection a prisoner facing a heavy sentence has little to lose if he commits further offences. A prisoner may consider that he has to go to prison in any event and in an effort to get money to support his family may commit further offences.

(5) The possibility of the disposal of illegally acquired property. Stolen property may be stored or cached away.

(6) The possibility of interference with prospective witnesses and jurors.

(7) The prisoner's failure to answer to bail on a previous occasion.

(8) The fact that the prisoner was caught red-handed.

(9) The objection of the Attorney General or of the police authorities.

(10) The substance and reliability of the bails person offered (this is primarily a matter for the District Justice).

(11) The possibility of a speedy trial.

The Supreme Court accepted the validity and relevance of most of these criteria, subject to sufficient evidence of the matters being adduced. The onus always being on the prosecution to show that it is likely that the accused may attempt to evade justice, but the Court completely rejected proposition no 4 as:

> 'a form of preventative justice which has no place in our legal system and is quite alien to the true purposes of bail. . . . In this country it would be quite contrary to the concept of personal liberty enshrined in the Constitution that any person should be punished in respect of any matter upon which he has not been convicted or that in any circumstances he should be deprived of his liberty upon only the belief that he will commit offences if left at liberty . . . (per Walsh J at pp 516–17).'

Since this ruling, however, the Constitution has been amended following the bail referendum in November 1996, so that Article 40.4.7 now allows for provision to be made by law for the refusal of bail by a court to a person charged with a serious offence where it is reasonably considered necessary to prevent the commission of a serious offence by that person.

8.3   The Bail Act 1997

8.3.1   PREVENTATIVE DETENTION

The Bail Act 1997 came into operation fully on 15 May 2000, shortly after the new remand prison at Cloverhill in Dublin began accepting remand prisoners. Before then, it had been thought that there would be insufficient places to accommodate the extra numbers of remand prisoners at the already grossly overcrowded Mountjoy Prison.

Section 2 of the Bail Act 1997 provides as follows:

> *(1)*   *Where an application for bail is made by a person charged with a serious offence, a court may refuse the application if the court is satisfied that such refusal is reasonably considered necessary to prevent the commission of a serious offence by that person.*

(2)   *In exercising its jurisdiction under subsection (1), a court shall take into account and may, where necessary, receive evidence or submissions concerning—*

    (a)   *The nature and degree of seriousness of the offence with which the accused person is charged and the sentence likely to be imposed on conviction.*

    (b)   *The nature and degree of seriousness of the offence apprehended and the sentence likely to be imposed on conviction.*

    (c)   *The nature and strength of the evidence in support of the charge.*

    (d)   *Any conviction of the accused person for an offence committed while he or she was on bail.*

    (e)   *Any previous convictions of the accused person including any conviction the subject of an appeal (which has neither been determined nor withdrawn) to a court.*

    (f)   *Any other offence in respect of which the accused person is charged and is awaiting trial.*

    And, where it has taken account of one or more of the foregoing, it may also take into account the fact that the accused person is addicted to a controlled drug within the meaning of the Misuse of Drugs Act 1977.

(3)   *In determining whether the refusal of an application for bail is reasonably considered necessary to prevent the commission of a serious offence by a person, it shall not be necessary for a court to be satisfied that the commission of a specific offence by that person is apprehended.*

8.3.2   DEFINITION OF 'SERIOUS OFFENCE'

Section 1 defines 'serious offence' as an offence specified in the Schedule that is punishable by at least five years' imprisonment. The Schedule lists a large number of offences ranging broadly from murder to certain road traffic and public order offences and including any offence under the provisions of the Criminal Justice Theft and Fraud Act 2001, which would cover shoplifting and other relatively minor theft offences.

Section 4 of the Act provides that the previous criminal record of the person applying for bail shall not be referred to in a manner which may prejudice the person's right to a fair trial, and prohibits publication and broadcasting of information relating to the criminal record of the applicant.

8.4   Application procedure

If a member, after giving evidence of arrest, charge, and caution in respect of an accused person who is in custody makes application for a week's remand in custody, the member should be asked to give reasons for the opposition to bail. The Garda may give evidence of not being satisfied as to the identity or address of the accused. If an accused is alleged to have provided different names, dates of birth or addresses to the Gardaí, there may well be difficulty in obtaining bail. It should be noted that homelessness of itself is not a ground for refusing bail; nor is the fact that an applicant is a non-national or ordinarily resident outside the jurisdiction, for example in Northern Ireland.

If a Garda member is seeking a remand in custody to verify information in relation to the accused, it should be asked whether a week's remand is necessary for this purpose, as these types of inquiries often need take no more than a few minutes. If the objection to bail is based on an alleged threat to a witness, the witness should be in court to give evidence of such threats.

If a solicitor has not been given notice of objections to bail, a second calling of the case should be requested to enable the solicitor to take instructions from the client on the objections raised. The Supreme Court ruled in *McDonagh v Governor of Cloverhill Prison* [2005] 1 ILRM 340 that it would seem essential as a matter of natural and constitutional justice that an accused person should be made aware that an objection to bail of so serious a nature as an objection under s 2 of the Bail Act 1997 is to be brought forward by the prosecution and that the accused should be given a proper opportunity either by means of evidence or through submissions to challenge such an objection. The Garda member and any prosecution witnesses should be cross-examined, and the defence can call the accused and any other evidence to rebut the objections. It is more common in the District Court, however, for the solicitor for the accused to respond to any objections and make submissions supporting the bail application, such as suggesting terms and conditions that might be imposed to address any concerns about the accused being released. It is always advisable, if possible, for the solicitor to talk to the prosecuting Garda member before the case is called, to establish what objections are being raised and to try to negotiate bail.

Sometimes, a judge will refuse bail even when there is no prosecution objection, particularly where an accused has previously failed to appear.

8.5   Conditions of bail

The principal and essential condition of bail has always been that the accused will appear before the court when required to do so. The Bail Act 1997 prescribes two other mandatory conditions and suggests a number of other possible conditions, as set out below. The conditions imposed in a particular case are set out in a 'recognisance', which is an acknowledgement of the bail contract (ie an acknowledgement of the obligation on the accused, in consideration of being released, to comply with the conditions of bail). The recognisance is in writing and is signed by the accused, any sureties, and the judge, who will first ask the other parties to acknowledge their signatures. If an accused (or surety) refuses to sign the recognisance, the accused will not be released. Section 6(1) of the Bail Act provides:

> Where an accused person is admitted to bail on his or her entering into a recognisance
> (a)   The recognisance shall, in addition to the condition requiring his or her appearance before the court at the end of the period of the remand of the accused person, be subject to the following conditions—
> (i)   That the accused person shall not commit any offence, and
> (ii)   That the accused person shall otherwise be of good behaviour,
> And
> (b)   The recognisance may be subject to such conditions as the court considers appropriate having regard to the circumstances of the case, including but without prejudice to the generality of the foregoing, any one or more of the following conditions:
> (i)   That the accused person resides or remains in a particular district or place in the State,
> (ii)   That the accused person reports to a specific Garda Síochána station at specified intervals,
> (iii)   That the accused person surrenders any passport or travel document in his or her possession or, if he or she is not in possession of a passport or travel document, that he or she refrains from applying for a passport or travel document,
> (iv)   that the accused person refrains from having any contact with such person or persons as the court may specify,
> (v)   That the accused person refrains from having any contact with such person or persons as the court may specify.

Section 6(2) provides that a copy of the recognisance containing the conditions is to be given to the accused and any surety or sureties. Sections 6(3) and 6(4) provide for application to be made by an accused, on notice being given to the prosecutor to vary the conditions of bail imposed under s 6(1)(b), whether by altering, adding, or revoking a condition. It is common, for example, for application to be made to reduce Garda station reporting or 'signing on' conditions. An accused will often be granted bail initially with a condition of reporting at a local Garda station daily, sometimes even twice daily. As the proceedings progress, if the accused turns up at court when required to do so, it may be that the court can be persuaded to relax such a condition down to thrice-weekly reporting or less, or perhaps even to revoke the reporting condition altogether, particularly if some special reason can be advanced as to why the accused is finding the reporting condition onerous.

8.6   Amount of bail

Recognisance is fixed with a specific debt due in default of the conditions of bail. The accused will always be required to enter a recognisance and the court may also require one or two 'sureties' to enter recognisance(s), or may make provision for the lodgement of cash in lieu of sureties. A 'surety' or 'bails person' is a third party who enters a recognisance to ensure compliance by the accused with the conditions of bail.

Whether an accused is released on his or her 'own recognisance' ('own bond' or 'own bail') only or sureties are required ('independent bail') is at the discretion of the court, as is the amount of any recognisance fixed. However, 'Bail must not be fixed at a figure so large as would in effect amount to a denial of bail and in consequence lead to inevitable imprisonment' (per Walsh J in *O'Callaghan*). Section 5(1) of the Bail Act 1997, as amended by s 33 of the Courts and Court Officers Act 2002, provides as follows:

> *Where a court admits a person who is in custody to bail the court may, having regard to the circumstance of the case, including the means of the person and the nature of the offence in relation to which the person is in custody order than the person shall not be released until:*
> *(a)   An amount equal to one third of, or*
> *(b)   Such greater amount as the court may determine of,*
> *any recognisance entered into by a person in connection therewith has been paid into court by the person.*

When surety bail is fixed, it is often worth asking the court if it would consider making provision for a cash lodgement in lieu of the surety, as it will generally be much easier for an accused to come up with cash than to find a suitable bails person and have them approved by the court. However, a court may have more confidence that an accused will comply with the conditions of bail, if there is someone else prepared to go bail for him.

8.7   Sureties

If a court fixes bail at an accused's own bond of, say, €300 with an independent surety of €3,000, then, for the accused to secure release on bail, he will have to have a surety approved by the court. Section 7 of the Bail Act 1997 deals with matters to be considered by the court when deciding whether or not to approve a proposed bails person.

> *(1)   A court shall in every case satisfy itself as to the sufficiency and suitability of any person proposed, to be accepted as a surety for the purpose of bail.*
>
> *(2)   In determining the sufficiency and suitability of a person proposed to be accepted as a surety, a court shall have regard to and may, where necessary, receive evidence or submissions concerning:*
>
> *(a)   The financial resources of the person,*
>
> *(b)   The character and antecedents of the person,*

(c)   *Any previous convictions of the person, and*

(d)   *The relationship of the person to the accused person.*

The usual practice is for the defence solicitor to call the proposed surety to give sworn evidence as to these matters. This can be done immediately after bail is fixed if the court allows it and the surety is present with the necessary documentation. It is therefore always a good idea for the defence to have at least one suitable potential bails person in court, if possible, in cases where it can be foreseen that independent bail may be required. It is also advisable to have any proposed bails person bring proof of identity to court and provide it and proof of financial resources to the appropriate Garda member in advance of any bail application, so that the prosecution may make its own inquiries into the person's suitability.

If it is not possible to have a surety approved at the time bail is fixed, application may be made in the absence of the accused at a later time on due notice being given to the court and Gardaí. If money is not available to be paid into court, either by the accused or a surety, it may be lodged at whichever prison the accused is remanded to, as prison governors also have the power to acknowledge the terms of a recognisance.

A surety should be present in the District Court when an accused is sent forward for trial, as a fresh recognisance is fixed and application must again be made to the court for the approval of the surety.

8.8   Renewal of bail applications

In theory, an accused may generally apply for the granting of bail to be granted, reduced or varied on each appearance before the court (see s 28(2) of the Criminal Procedure Act 1967). In practice, however, many judges will refuse to consider fresh applications, particularly in cases where another judge has previously dealt with the question of bail. Most judges would require there to have been a change in circumstances before considering a renewed application not to be *res judicata*. If an accused has been remanded in custody for a week, there will have been an opportunity for the defence solicitor to take full instructions and the solicitor may be in a position to convey information to the court which could not be conveyed on the first occasion, and which may strengthen an application for bail. If an accused has not been able to take up bail in circumstances where it had been thought that it would be able to be taken up, the court may be persuaded to reduce the amount of bail to a figure more manageable for the accused, particularly if there is no opposition from the Gardaí.

Section 3(1) of the Bail Act 1997 provides that where an application for bail has been refused by a court under s 2, that is to prevent the commission of a serious offence, and the trial of the accused has not commenced within four months from the date of such refusal, then the accused may renew their application for bail on the ground of delay by the prosecutor in proceeding with their trial. The court shall, if satisfied that the interests of justice so require, release the person on bail.

8.9   High Court bail applications

If an accused has been remanded in custody without bail, or cannot raise the amount of bail fixed, or seeks to vary the conditions of the bail fixed, application can be made to the High Court by way of Notice of Motion to the Prosecution Solicitor grounded on the affidavit of the applicant (Order 84, rule 15(1), Rules of the Superior Court). The High Court bail list is generally on Mondays at Cloverhill Courthouse in Dublin, and the Notice of Motion and grounding Affidavit should be filed with the court and served on the

Chief Prosecution Solicitor's office in Abbey Street, Dublin by the preceding Wednesday, although orders allowing short service can sometimes be obtained from the court if, for example, an accused is before the District Court for the first time on a Thursday and is remanded in custody. Orders for the production of prisoners at Cloverhill Courthouse for the following Monday should generally be sought at the Four Courts at 12.45 pm on the preceding Thursday.

It is usually sufficient for the solicitor for the accused to swear the Affidavit grounding the Notice of Motion. The title of the Affidavit should state which court the proceedings are presently pending in. Order 84, Rule 15(1) of the Rules of the Superior Courts has been amended by SI No 811 of 2004, which came into operation on 29 December 2004. This SI provides that the applicant's affidavit shall set forth fully the basis upon which the application is made to the High Court and in particular:

(a) shall give particulars of whether and, if so, in what other court bail has been refused to the applicant;

(b) shall specify where the applicant is being detained;

(c) shall specify the usual place of abode or address where the applicant normally resides;

(d) shall specify the address at which it is proposed the applicant would reside if granted bail;

(e) shall provide full particulars of the offence or offences with which the applicant is charged;

(f) shall include the identity, address and occupation of any proposed independent surety and of the amount that such surety may offer;

(g) the terms of bail which were previously fixed in relation to the offences (if any);

(h) whether there had been any previous High Court applications for bail in respect of the offences;

(i) whether any warrants for failure to appear have been issued in relation to the applicant;

(j) what surety and/or other conditions relating to bail (if any) the applicant is proposing;

(k) the personal circumstances of the applicant and in particular whether the applicant was legally aided in relation to the charges in any other court;

(l) any other relevant circumstances.

The affidavit should also set out when and where the applicant last appeared and was remanded to. Copies of all charge sheets, if available, and any other relevant documentation should be exhibited. The SI should be consulted whenever an affidavit for High Court bail is being drafted.

The Attorney General's scheme is available for an indigent applicant for bail in the High Court. The scheme generally covers the costs of a solicitor and one counsel, and it is therefore very rare to see a solicitor appearing in the High Court to move an application for bail. The High Court bail list is usually extremely busy with dozens of applications listed before it every week, and some judges have been known to sit until close to midnight to finish the list. Sometimes the list is adjourned until later in the week, often until Thursday in the Four Courts. The Monday High Court bail list can be viewed in the Legal Diary at <www.courts.ie>. A copy of any High Court bail order, if available, should be handed to the District Judge on the next occasion the matter is before the District Court. The District Court cannot vary the terms or conditions of any High Court bail order—any such application would have to be made back in the High Court.

8.10 Failing to appear on bail

Section 9 of the Bail Act 1997 provides for the estreatment of recognisance (the process of enforcing payment of the amount of the recognisance) and the forfeiture of money paid into court where an accused person fails to appear 'before a specified court on a specified date and at a specified time and place', or where the accused contravenes any other condition of the recognisance and is arrested on warrant for such contravention.

If an accused person fails to appear on bail, a judge will generally issue a bench warrant for the person's arrest and certify breach of the bond. If the person is arrested on foot of the warrant within six months of the failure to appear, they may be charged with failing to appear on bail, which is a summary offence contrary to the Criminal Justice Act 1984, s 13 and punishable by 12 months' imprisonment.

A solicitor in the District Court will often be called upon to make an application for bail in circumstances where a client has been brought before the court on one or more bench warrants. The judge will probably want to know why the accused did not turn up to court previously. More often than not the reasons offered will be more mundane than a deliberate attempt to evade justice. Clients may claim to have forgotten or 'mixed up' their court dates, to have gone to the wrong court by mistake or to the right court, but late. They may insist that their solicitor wrote their next court date down wrongly on a business card given to them. They may claim to have been in a prison, hospital or Garda station, and explanations such as these can obviously be checked out. They may instruct that they were ill or had suffered bereavement. Whatever the reason, if there were subsequent attempts to arrange to attend at court for cancellation of the warrant and re-entry of the matter, then the prospects of bail being granted again are much better. It is advisable to write to a client who has taken a bench warrant at the last known address, advising that the warrant has issued and encouraging contact to be made with the solicitor to arrange re-entry. If such correspondence is responded to appropriately, the relevant Garda station should be contacted, and letters should be sent confirming the desire of the client to surrender at court on a convenient date. Copies of such letters can be produced when re-applying for bail. It is not uncommon for accused persons to 'take' several bench warrants during the course of the same proceedings and subsequently be the recipient of terms of bail on each occasion. If the bench warrant issues on a hearing date, however, then bail is less likely to be fixed again, depending on the explanation offered by the accused with regard to the non-appearance.

8.11 Adjournments and remands

8.11.1 GENERALLY

An adjournment is a court order postponing a case until a later time or date. A remand is the order that the court makes when adjourning a criminal case where the person before it is in custody or on bail.

A person who is being prosecuted by way of summons is described as the defendant, if the summons is issued under the Petty Sessions (Ireland) Act 1851, and as 'the accused' if the summons is issued under the Courts (No 3) Act 1986. A person who appears in answer to a summons will ordinarily be allowed to go at large without any remand during the period of any adjournment of the prosecution, although if the person fails to appear to answer the summons, either on its first return date or any adjourned date, a bench warrant may issue for the person's arrest and they may be remanded either in custody or on bail following execution of the summons warrant.

A person who is being prosecuted by way of a charge sheet is generally referred to as 'the accused' if charged with an indictable offence, and as 'the defendant' if charged with a summary offence. Such a person will be remanded until a later date if the prosecution is adjourned for any reason. The primary condition of a bail recognisance to appear at court is that the accused will appear before a particular court at a particular venue, date and time and any adjournment thereof until his presence is no longer required.

8.11.2   REASONS FOR ADJOURNMENTS

A criminal prosecution will usually not be disposed of on the first occasion it comes before the court, although this is more common in summons matters than charge sheet matters. Summonses for road traffic offences and public order offences, for example, are often disposed of on their return date (first date in court), even on a not guilty plea, as the prosecuting Garda member is often the only prosecution witness and will be ready to proceed with the case. A defendant or accused will sometimes have taken the opportunity to retain a solicitor before the first day in court and, if not, the judge may decide to deal with the case anyway, if the Garda member is present and ready to proceed, particularly if a term of imprisonment is unlikely to be imposed in the case of a conviction. If a defendant, or an accused, seeks an adjournment to consult a solicitor, the court will usually grant such an adjournment, although questions may be asked as to why this was not done beforehand. Some judges will offer defendants and accused persons adjournments to enable them to seek legal advice; some may even encourage them to obtain it. If free legal aid is granted at the outset of proceedings, an adjournment will usually be given, even if the assigned solicitor is present in court, to enable full instructions to be taken.

The prosecution may seek to adjourn a summons or charge sheet matter because the prosecuting Garda is not present; another member may stand in and claim that the prosecuting member is 'on a course', sick, or unable to attend for some other reason. Depending on the circumstances and who the presiding judge is, such an application may be successful, or else the summons or charge may be struck out, or dismissed for want of prosecution.

An adjournment is always more likely to be granted on application of one of the parties if notice has been given to the other side that the application is to be made and the reasons for the application stated. If a solicitor is on record as acting for a client in criminal proceedings, then notice of any intention to apply for an adjournment by the State should be given to the solicitor rather than directly to the client.

An adjournment, if granted, is often marked 'peremptory' by the judge as against the party applying for it. This means that, for example, if an adjournment is granted peremptorily against the State when a Garda member does not appear to prosecute, and there is again no appearance by the Garda on the adjourned date, at that point the proceedings are likely to be struck out or dismissed. Similarly, if a peremptory adjournment of a hearing is granted to the defence to enable a witness to attend on the next date, and the witness does not attend, the hearing will probably proceed in any event. If a case is adjourned for directions from the Director of Public Prosecutions ('DPP') or service of a book of evidence, and the adjournment is peremptory against the State, then if the directions are not available on the adjourned date or the book is not ready to be served, the proceedings may be struck out.

The prosecution may seek a remand in a case because they are awaiting directions from the Director of Public Prosecutions as to possible further charges, the mode of trial of an indictable offence, etc. Lengthy remands may be sought by the State in drugs cases to enable analysis of substances seized.

If the DPP directs summary disposal and the accused has a right of election, the defence may apply for an adjournment to obtain disclosure of statements in possession of the prosecution, especially any cautioned statement or memorandum of interview of the accused, before being placed on their election or required to enter a plea. If the accused eventually elects for the District Court and pleads not guilty, the case will be adjourned for hearing and the hearing date will usually be several months later. If the DPP directs trial on indictment, or a judge refuses jurisdiction, or an accused elects for trial before a judge and jury, there will usually be at least one remand for service of a book of evidence, which is supposed to be served within 42 days of the accused's first appearance in court, although this period can be extended by the District Court on application of the prosecutor under s 4B(3) of the Criminal Procedure Act 1967, as inserted by s 9 of the Criminal Justice Act 1999, if the court is satisfied that there is good reason for doing so, and it would be in the interests of justice to do so. The number of remands sought by the State will usually be fewer if the accused has been arrested on warrant and charged following the submission of a file to the DPP. In those circumstances the DPP's directions will generally be available at the time of charging and the book of evidence, if required, will generally be at an advanced stage of preparation, if not complete.

A case listed for hearing may have to be adjourned to a new date for hearing, or for mention to fix a new date for hearing, because of problems with the availability of witnesses, or problems with the availability of court time to hear the matter. Even after a person is found guilty of an offence, following either a plea of guilty or a trial, there may be adjournments before sentence is passed and the case is finally disposed of. Rather than immediately imposing a penalty, such as a fine or a term of imprisonment, the court may adjourn the proceedings for the preparation of probation and community service order reports. The authors of these reports often recommend further adjournments to supervise and monitor offenders. Cases may also be adjourned for payment by the accused or defendant or compensation to the injured party or so that they can go back before a judge who heard the facts of a particular case.

8.11.3   NON-APPEARANCE OF ACCUSED

If a person, whether in custody or on bail, is unable by reason of illness or accident to appear before the court, then the person may be remanded in their absence for as long as the court considers reasonable (but not exceeding 30 days, if the person is in custody). In the case of a person in custody, such an order is sometimes called a 'sick warrant'. Before making such an order, the court will often require the prison or hospital where the accused is being held to provide a letter to the court stating the condition of the accused. Similarly, if an accused is on bail, the court will often require a medical report to be handed up before agreeing to a remand on continuing bail in the absence of the accused. It is not unknown for a solicitor to receive a call from a client, or someone ringing on the client's behalf, on the morning of the day the client is due in court, claiming that the client is too sick to attend court, and perhaps even too sick to have attended a doctor! If a court is not prepared to grant an adjournment in such circumstances, it may be persuaded to grant a stay on the issuing of any bench warrant and/or to recommend that the warrant be executed with discretion.

If a person who is on bail or summons is not able to appear because they are in custody on another matter, the court may issue a 'body warrant', which is an order to the prison where the person is detained to produce the person before the court on a particular date, usually within a week of the issuing of the body warrant.

8.11.4   TIME LIMITS IN REMAND CASES

Section 24 of the Criminal Procedure Act 1967, as substituted by s 4 of the Criminal Justice (Miscellaneous Provisions) Act 1997 ('the 1997 Act') provides for remand time limits in custody and bail cases. If an accused is remanded in custody on the occasion of first appearing before the court, the longest possible remand is eight days, inclusive of the day of the first appearance. Therefore, if evidence of arrest, charge and caution is given in respect of an accused on a Wednesday and the accused is remanded in custody, the longest possible remand is an eight-day remand until the following Wednesday. If the accused is remanded on bail, the first remand and any subsequent remand may be for more than eight days if both the accused and the prosecutor consent. If the accused has already been granted bail, any remand is described as 'on continuing bail' and any conditions of bail, unless varied, will continue to apply. If an accused is granted bail but is unable to take up bail there and then, the accused will be remanded in custody 'with consent to bail', and the time limits will be the same as for a remand in custody.

On the second or subsequent appearance of an accused who is in custody, the longest possible further remand in custody without the consent of the accused is 15 days. If the accused and the prosecutor consent, a further remand in custody of up to 30 days is permissible.

If an accused is in custody with no prospect of bail, and is pleading not guilty to charges to be dealt with in the District Court, it is unlikely that a contested hearing of the charges will be able to take place within these custody times. In these circumstances, it is usual for a hearing date to be reserved several months into the future, and for the accused to be remanded in custody from time to time pending this reserved date, with fortnightly appearances if there is no consent to longer, or monthly appearances if there is consent to this.

If an accused is found guilty and a term of imprisonment is imposed, the court should always be asked to exercise its discretion to backdate the sentence to take account of any time spent in custody prior to the sentence being imposed.

CHAPTER 9

LEGAL AID

9.1   Introduction

Most people charged with criminal offences are unable to afford to pay for their own legal representation. Private fee-paying clients are in the minority at most criminal law practices. When a client is paying privately, it is generally prudent to insist on payment of fees in advance of work being done.

In Ireland, there are no 'public defenders' employed by the State to represent indigent people charged with criminal offences. Private practitioners who indicate their willingness to so act by entering their names on the legal aid panel undertake such representation.

9.2   The Criminal Justice (Legal Aid) Act

The Criminal Justice (Legal Aid) Act 1962 ('the 1962 Act') was enacted according to its long title 'to make provision for the grant by the State of free legal aid to poor persons in certain criminal cases'. Section 2 of the Act sets out the criteria for eligibility for free legal aid in the District Court:

> *(1)   If it appears to the District Court*
> > *(a)   That the means of a person charged before it with an offence are insufficient to enable him to obtain legal aid, and*
> > *(b)   That by reason of the gravity of the charge or of exceptional circumstances it is essential in the interests of justice that he should have legal aid in the preparation and conduct of his defence before it, the Court shall, on application being made to it in that behalf, grant in respect of him a certificate for free legal aid . . .*

The Criminal Legal Aid Scheme has been in operation since 1965, when legislation implementing the 1962 Act was introduced. Judges have a fairly wide discretion whether or not to grant legal aid, and some of them are far less liberal than others in the exercise of this discretion.

9.3   The means test

On the first appearance of an accused person, if the court is considering granting free legal aid, the judge will generally conduct an inquiry into the person's means. 'Are you working?' will often be the first and perhaps only question asked. If the answer is 'no', the person may be asked whether they are collecting social welfare, and if so, where. If an accused is unemployed but not 'signing on', ie collecting payments from the Social Welfare System, the court may want to know how the person is being supported, when they last worked, why they ceased work and how much they earned. In the case of accused persons under the age of 21, the court may inquire as to the ability and willingness of their parents to assist in paying for legal representation. Even unemployed recipients of social welfare may be asked whether they have any other income, savings or assets that could be used for obtaining legal aid at their own expense.

If accused persons are employed, they will be asked how much they earn and perhaps their occupation. Judicial attitudes to the threshold wage levels for eligibility for free legal aid vary, but most judges would probably consider that a person taking home €400 or less per week would satisfy the requisite means test. A person earning significantly more might still qualify if supporting several dependants. Judges are sometimes sceptical of claims of unemployment or low wages, especially in the case of tradespeople.

The Gardaí may express an attitude, either of their own volition or upon being asked by the judge or the defence, which is contrary to the granting of legal aid to an accused. If a defence solicitor has ascertained from the Gardaí that there is no opposition to an application for free legal aid, the solicitor may invite them to confirm that fact to the judge. In other cases, the Gardaí may contradict a claim by the accused that he is unemployed or earning a low wage. They may allege that the accused owns properties, cars or other assets, or that significant quantities of cash and/or drugs have been seized from the accused. If such property has been seized, it is of little use to an accused in terms of paying for legal representation. Nevertheless, legal aid is often refused on this basis, at least in the initial stages of a prosecution, the inference being that the accused person has access to other resources.

Section 9 of the 1962 Act provides that before being granted a legal aid certificate, a person may be required by the court to furnish a prescribed Statement of Means form, which is available from the District Court clerk. Such a statement may be required where the court is dissatisfied with the oral statements of an accused as to his means, or where the Gardaí have raised objections to the granting of legal aid. It is also available on the website of the Courts Service <www.courts.ie>. Information such as the applicant's marital status, occupation, average weekly income from all sources, dependants and assets must be set out on the form and a declaration signed at the end of this document that the particulars are true to best of the applicant's knowledge and belief.

Section 11 of the 1962 Act provides:

> (1)   *A person who, for the purpose of obtaining free legal aid under this Act, whether for himself or some other person, knowingly makes a false statement or false representation either verbally or in writing or knowingly conceals any material fact shall be guilty of an offence and shall be liable on summary conviction to a fine not exceeding one hundred pounds or to imprisonment for a term not exceeding six months or to both the fine and the imprisonment.*

Some judges will require a written statement of means to be provided to the prosecuting Garda before being furnished to the court. Some require evidence of means to be furnished such, as recent wage slips or proof of receipt of social welfare.

Section 10 (as amended by s 21 of the Criminal Justice Act 2006) empowers the Minister for Justice, Equality and Law Reform to make regulations regarding the form, rates and manner of assignment of lawyers.

9.4   Gravity of the charge

The fact that an indigent accused person is charged with an offence punishable by imprisonment does not necessarily mean that free legal aid will be granted. For example, although breaches of ss 6 and 8 of the Criminal Justice (Public Order) Act 1994 (breach of the peace and failure to comply with a Garda direction respectively) are punishable by three months' and six months' imprisonment respectively, it is quite common for indigent people charged with these public order offences not to be granted free legal aid. This is because although these summary offences are punishable by imprisonment, a judge may consider that imprisonment is unlikely on conviction.

Many judges take the view when considering the gravity of the charge that it is 'essential in the interests of justice' that an accused should have free legal aid (within the meaning of s 2 of the 1962 Act) only where a term of imprisonment is likely on conviction. Sometimes a judge will enquire of the prosecuting Garda member if the accused is 'in jeopardy' or 'at risk', ie whether, if convicted, a term of imprisonment is likely to be imposed by reason of any previous convictions of the accused. The result of judges taking this approach can be that an indigent person may be forced to face charges without legal representation and may therefore be more likely to receive a conviction than an accused who can afford private legal representation.

Legal aid is usually available for most indictable offences, even when being disposed of summarily, although in *Costigan v Brady* (unreported), 6 February 2004, the High Court refused to quash a District Judge's refusal to grant legal aid on a charge of alleged theft of food items valued at €6.44.

9.5   Exceptional circumstances

Although an offence may not be punishable by imprisonment, the consequences for the accused of a conviction may still be very onerous, such as loss of livelihood and reputation, and frustration of international travel plans. Even convictions for relatively minor road traffic offences may have serious consequences such as disqualification from driving and substantially increased insurance costs. Judges may or may not be persuaded that such considerations constitute 'exceptional circumstances' warranting grants of legal aid in individual cases; although, as far as driving offences are concerned, it should be noted that some judges are of the view that ownership of, or even access to, a car is incompatible with satisfaction of the means test.

Other exceptional circumstances may be that the accused would be incapable of adequate self-representation by reason of intellectual disability, mental illness, or lack of familiarity with the English language. Such factors might, in the words of Gannon J in *The State (Healy) v Donoghue* [1976] IR 325, at 339, 'render him unable to know and understand the nature of the charge, to appreciate its gravity, to understand the directions of the Court as to procedure and rights of the accused, to follow and test the evidence against him or to speak on his own behalf'.

If a case is likely to involve a substantial question of law or a significant number of defence witnesses, these considerations may constitute exceptional circumstances warranting a grant of legal aid for an indigent accused who would not otherwise qualify.

9.6   Application procedure

Although s 2 of the Criminal Justice (Legal Aid) Act 1962 speaks of the court granting a certificate for free legal aid 'on application being made to it', it is clear that even if application is not made by or on behalf of the accused, the court should inform an accused person who qualifies of the right to legal aid under the Act of his entitlement to make such an application. An accused person who is fully aware of this right can elect to waive it and not make application for legal aid: *The State (Healy) v Donoghue* [1976] IR 325.

It is common for solicitors to make applications for legal aid on behalf of accused persons. The accused may have attended the solicitor's office or simply approached the solicitor at court. If the accused is in custody, the solicitor may have attended at the Garda station or have been contacted by a friend or relative of the accused, requesting representation. An appearance will often be announced in these circumstances by saying, 'I have been asked to appear for the accused', rather than, 'I appear for the accused'. The solicitor can then address the judge as to the person's financial circumstances and the existence of any exceptional circumstances, such as those mentioned above, which may not otherwise be apparent to a busy District Court judge conducting an often fairly cursory inquiry for the purposes of considering the question of legal aid. Some judges will address the accused directly to ascertain the nomination of a solicitor, rather than have the solicitor nominate him/herself on the accused's behalf.

An application for legal aid may be deferred pending the furnishing of a statement of means or the possibility of further charges being laid. Even if an application is refused, it may be renewed if there is a change of circumstances such as the laying of a more serious charge, or loss of employment (which often occurs after an accused first appears in court, particularly if the person has been held in custody). After a finding of guilt, following either a plea of guilty or a trial, before passing sentence the court may see fit to grant legal aid to an indigent accused who has not previously had the benefit of being legally represented, if, for example, previous convictions or exceptional circumstances have come to light in the course of the proceedings.

Section 2(2) of the 1962 Act provides that a decision of the District Court in relation to an application for legal aid shall be final and shall not be appealed. Nevertheless, judicial review proceedings may lie if legal aid has been refused because of a miscarriage of the exercise of judicial discretion.

A fresh inquiry is conducted, at the return for trial stage, into the eligibility for legal aid of an accused who is being sent forward for trial, from the District Court to the Circuit, Special, or Central Criminal Court. A legal aid (trial on indictment) certificate may be granted under the 1962 Act, s 3. It is common for accused persons of some means to pay privately for their representation up until they are sent forward for trial from the District Court but to be granted legal aid for their trial on indictment because their means would be insufficient to enable them to pay privately at that level, where legal costs are considerably greater (covering costs of solicitor and counsel and generally of two counsel in the Central and Special Criminal Courts). If legal aid is refused in the District Court on being sent forward for trial, a fresh application may be made in the court of trial.

The 1962 Act also provides for appeal, case stated, and Supreme Court legal aid certificates. The Criminal Legal Aid Scheme does not cover extradition proceedings, High Court bail applications or judicial review proceedings, but indigent persons may avail themselves of a non-statutory scheme known as the Attorney General's Scheme in these matters.

9.7 Legal aid assignments

Where a judge finds that an accused person is entitled to a certificate for free legal aid, the person will be asked to choose a solicitor. A solicitor must be on the legal aid panel for the relevant court prior to receiving an assignment. Inclusion on the panel necessitates that a solicitor notifies the county registrar in writing of his/her willingness to act in legal aid cases and specifies in which courts legal aid assignments will be taken. If an accused does not nominate a particular solicitor, the judge will select one from the panel. This is known as an 'assignment from the bench' and it is usually of a solicitor who is in the court at the time, 'a dock brief' to facilitate immediate contact between solicitor and client. Sometimes a case will be put to a second calling so that the accused can consult with the newly appointed solicitor if, for example, there is opposition to bail or a prospect of the case being disposed of that day. If a solicitor is not in court when assigned, the receipt of the legal aid certificate will provide notification of the assignment and the next court date.

An accused will sometimes select or be assigned different solicitors on separate charge sheets or summonses on different dates. If these matters are subsequently disposed of on the same day, such as after the execution on the accused of a number of bench warrants, then the accused may be in the position of being represented by several solicitors together in court at the same time. An accused may apply to discharge a solicitor assigned on legal aid and have another appointed.

9.8   Fees

Solicitors are paid on a fixed and published scale of fees in respect of legal aid cases dealt with in the District Court. They are paid an initial 'instruction fee' plus VAT for the first appearance in court and a refresher fee plus VAT for each subsequent day in court. The fees are somewhat reduced if the solicitor represents more than one accused in the same matter or more than four legally aided clients in court on the same day. Fees are also payable for solicitors' prison visits to legally aided clients. The Garda Station Legal Advice Service covers solicitors visits to, and telephone consultations on, Garda stations to give advice to people in custody (current rates of fees payable are available on <www.justice.ie>).

A special claim form must be completed at the conclusion of a legally aided matter and forwarded to the Department of Justice for payment. Retention tax at a rate of 33.5 per cent applies at source. The legal aid claim forms and the most recent statutory instrument amending fees payable SI No 389 of 2005 can be viewed on <www.justice.ie> or via the Criminal Law Committee page of <www.lawsociety.ie>.

PART IV
SELECTED MODE OF TRIAL AND PROCEDURES IN TRIAL COURTS

CHAPTER 10

CHOICE OF TRIAL VENUE

10.1　Introduction

10.1.1　PROCEDURAL OPTIONS FOR CRIMINAL CASES IN THE ORDINARY COURTS

As in most discourses on law and procedure in Ireland, a good starting point, or perhaps more accurately a good anchoring point, is provided by our Constitution. The most immediately relevant constitutional provisions are to be found in Article 38. In referring to choice of venue the focus in this chapter is the choice as a trial court of one or other of the courts established by or under the Constitution, and not with the determination of the geographical location of the court chosen.

10.1.2　THE TRIAL COURTS—GEOGRAPHICAL LOCATION

There is only one District Court, which is divided for the orderly and convenient exercise of its jurisdiction into 'areas' and 'districts', and one Circuit Court, which for similar reasons is divided into circuits. The determination of the particular area, district or circuit in which a criminal trial in the District Court or the Circuit Court will be held is largely a mechanical one, which depends on where the offence is alleged to have been committed or where the accused person was arrested or resides. While within those parameters there remains some scope for discretion or choice, eg where any difference between the locations of offence, arrest or residence occurs, it is a matter that is governed by the relevant statute law and does not in practice give rise to any great difficulty or controversy. The legislative framework for such decisions are outlined in the Courts of Justice Acts 1924 and 1936, the numerous Criminal Justice Acts and Criminal Law Acts outlined in the Table of Statutes which prefaces this text, most recently ss 178, 179, and 180 of the Criminal Justice Act 2006, and the Criminal Procedure Acts of 1865, 1967, 1993, and 1999 which govern this and related matters.

10.2　Article 38 of Bunreacht na hEireann

Article 38 of the 1937 Constitution provides in section 1 for what our American colleagues call 'due process'. Section 2 of the same Article permits the summary trial of what are therein referred to as 'minor offences'. Section 3 permits the establishment by law of special courts for the trial of offences in the circumstances therein referred to, and s 4 permits the establishment of military tribunals for the trial of offences in the circumstances therein referred to.

123

Article 38.5 goes on to ordain that, save in the case of the trial of offences under ss 2, 3, or 4, 'no person shall be tried on any criminal charge without a jury'. The directly prohibitive nature of this provision should be noted. It does not merely confer a right to trial by jury, though such a right would seem clearly to be implicit in it. Mere rights can be waived whereas constitutional requirements cannot. Article 38.5 mandates or requires trial by jury in all cases not covered by ss 2, 3, or 4. This constitutional fact is of very great importance when one is considering questions of choice of venue, and especially the choice between summary trial and trial on indictment.

10.3 Summary trial

There are two main categories of criminal offence—summary offences and indictable offences. It is important to keep this seemingly simple and basic fact in mind when dealing with choice of venue, because procedural law in relation to that matter has become somewhat complicated, with the result that it is not always immediately clear what is meant by the terms 'summary' and 'indictable'.

10.3.1 SUMMARY OFFENCES

A summary offence is a criminal offence for which the law provides, with one exception that is referred to later, only one mode of trial, namely disposal by way of summary procedure as opposed to the more elaborate pre-trial and trial procedures appropriate to a trial on indictment. Scots law refers to this procedural dichotomy as 'summary procedure' and 'solemn procedure', and that phraseology is helpful in highlighting the importance of the distinction between the two.

As summary procedure is usually equated simply with the absence of a jury at the trial, and that is indeed its most obvious distinguishing feature, it is not its only distinguishing feature. Strenuous attempts were made in several cases over recent years to apply to summary cases many of the pre-trial procedures associated with trials on indictment. Those attempts were not entirely without success, culminating in *The DPP v Gary Doyle* [1994] 2 IR 286 (henceforth 'the *Gary Doyle* case'). The preliminaries to a summary trial and the trial itself remain simple, speedy and informal when compared with the procedure on indictment.

Such simple, fast informality is the essence and purpose of summary procedure. Without it the criminal justice system could scarcely survive. If, however, recourse has to be had to a system of summary justice as a means of disposal of the vast majority of criminal cases, which is the case in the Irish and most other jurisdictions, then it is of the utmost importance that such a system is just and is seen to be just.

One change effected by the recent case law went a considerable distance towards achieving that objective. That was the recognition in the *Gary Doyle* case of the legal obligation of the prosecutor to furnish to the defendant statements or other details of the evidence to be led by the prosecution, whenever the interests of justice so required. Prior to this case, no such legal obligation had been recognised, although as a matter of custom and practice, a defendant's solicitor, on request, would normally be afforded full access, in advance of deliberations on the case for the accused, to the detail of the case evidence. The prosecuting authorities supported the principle established in the *Gary Doyle* case, but resisted the suggestion that what would in effect be a book of evidence must be furnished in every case, whether or not the interests of justice required it. To do so would have largely abolished the concept of summary justice which is, it has to be remembered, specifically sanctioned by Article 38.2, and might well have caused the collapse of a large part of the criminal justice system. That said, very great benefits for justice and for the efficiency of the criminal justice system stem from the decision in the *Gary Doyle* case and the subsequent elaborations on it.

The preliminaries to a summary trial and the trial itself remain simple, speedy and informal when compared with the procedure on indictment. Such simple, fast informality is the essence and purpose of summary procedure. Without it the criminal justice system could scarcely survive. If, however, recourse has to be had to a system of summary justice as a means of disposal of the vast majority of criminal cases, which is the case in the Irish and most other jurisdictions, then it is of the utmost importance that such a system is just and is seen to be just. The *Gary Doyle* case went a considerable distance towards achieving that objective.

10.4 The impact of the *Gary Doyle* case

The decision in *Doyle* undoubtedly minimizes the danger of miscarriages of justice in the summary system, although nobody would claim that it eliminates it. It promotes the full disclosure of all relevant material and thereby reduces the danger of suppression of evidence by the prosecutor, whether intentional or accidental. To the surprise of many, it has also encouraged pleas of guilty which might not have been forthcoming had not the defendant or, more often, the defendant's legal advisers been made aware of the nature of the evidence available to the prosecution, and has thereby contributed to the efficient disposal of criminal business in the courts of summary jurisdiction. This development, together with the almost exponential expansion of recourse to judicial review in the past quarter-century, has had a most beneficial effect both on standards of legal precision and on commitment to constitutional principles of justice in the courts exercising summary jurisdiction.

While trial by jury is a constitutional norm, and in cases falling within Article 38.5 a constitutional imperative, with the very small number of exceptions which human nature will always throw up, the standard of summary justice in Ireland compares favourably with that of any other country. Nevertheless, choice of venue remains a very important aspect of our criminal justice system which attracts insufficient consideration and debate.

10.5 Minor offences

In addition to the mode of trial as a distinguishing feature, a summary offence is, by constitutional definition, a minor offence. The Constitution offers, however, no definition of this concept, which has been the subject of much litigation over the years. It is not appropriate in this chapter to engage in a dissertation on that rather difficult topic, in relation to which the case law has not always been as consistent as one might have wished. The principal criterion applied in the superior courts and in the legislature has been the maximum punishment prescribed by the relevant statutory provision (summary offences being invariably created by statute). Legislators, keeping one eye firmly on Article 38.2, have adhered to the punishment limits set by the Criminal Justice Act 1951 for sentences on summary conviction, namely 12 months' imprisonment and a fine of £100 or euro equivalent as amended by the Courts and Justice Act 2006. Inflation has not been relevant to imprisonment, although the District Court can impose up to two years' imprisonment cumulatively as consecutive sentences for separate offences. However, inflation has been relevant to monetary penalties, and fines of up to at least £2,000 (now in its euro equivalent) on summary convictions would now be generally regarded as being safe from constitutional challenge, as £100 in 1951 was probably worth more than £2,000 (or its euro equivalent) is today.

Apart from the penalty aspect of the matter, a common-sense approach is required in considering whether or not, objectively, a particular offence is minor and whether or not, subjectively, what would otherwise be a minor offence is a major one for a particular defendant. Such matters are relevant to the summary disposal of indictable offences, which are discussed later. They are irrelevant to the prosecution of purely summary offences, except in the rare case where a defendant might wish to challenge the constitutionality of the statute creating a summary offence.

One final matter must be mentioned before passing to indictable offences. Under the Criminal Justice Act 1951, s 6, a summary charge can in certain circumstances be tried on indictment, ie if the summary charge has been preferred in the District Court and arises from the same set of facts which ground at least one of the indictable charges in the indictment. However, while the verdict on the summary charge will in those circumstances be rendered by a jury, the procedure in relation to it is more 'summary' than 'solemn' as a Scots lawyer would say, in that there has been no procedure required before a defendant can be arraigned on an indictable charge.

10.6　Indictable offences

10.6.1　CATEGORIES OF INDICTABLE OFFENCES

With the single exception noted in the preceding paragraph, a summary offence is legally incapable of being tried on indictment. An indictable offence is one which is *capable* of being tried on indictment, although the great majority of them are not in practice so tried. They fall into the following categories:

(a)　Offences which must always be tried on indictment, ie cannot be tried or otherwise disposed of in the District Court, eg murder or rape.

(b)　Offences which may be tried summarily in the District Court:

(i)　they are created by statute where the penalty is applicable to summary conviction only;

(ii)　offences which, although indictable, may be tried summarily on the DPP indicating acceptance of a plea of not guilty in the District Court (scheduled offences);

(iii)　offences in which a written plea of guilty may be entered in the District Court with a view to the defendant being sent forward for sentence to a higher court.

(c)　Offences which, although indictable, may be tried either summarily or on indictment at the option of the prosecutor, subject to the concurrence of the court in the case of an option for summary trial (each-way offences or hybrid offences).

Sub-categories (b)(i) and (b)(iii) are not really separate categories of offence, as the offences covered by them are the same, and they are governed by the same statutory provision—the Criminal Procedure Act 1967, s 13 (as amended by the Criminal Justice Act 1999, s 10(3) and 10(4)). This section provides two very different procedures, which reflect the fact that two offences carrying the same designation may vary greatly in gravity and may therefore require different sanctions and procedures. Also, it is self-evident that if a person is being tried for an indictable offence and he is not being dealt with summarily (category (b)(i)(ii)(iii) or category (c) above) that person must be dealt with on indictment.

10.7 Features of the categories of indictable offences

10.7.1 OFFENCES, WHICH MUST ALWAYS BE TRIED ON INDICTMENT

Offences which must always be tried on indictment will be referred to as 'category (a) offences' in this chapter. There is a considerable degree of overlap between the sub-categories (hereinafter referred to simply as categories). It is, however, easy enough to compartmentalize them, despite that overlap.

Category (a) consists of all indictable offences which do not fit into categories (b) and (c). While numerically small, it includes, as one would expect, some of the most serious offences known to the law. They are listed in the Criminal Procedure Act 1967, s 13(1).

10.7.2 SCHEDULED OFFENCES

Scheduled offences (hereinafter referred to as 'category (b)(ii) offences') are listed in the First Schedule as amended to the Criminal Justice Act 1951 (hereinafter referred to as 'the 1951 Act'). That Act was not, of course, the first Irish legislation providing for the summary disposal of indictable offences. The Courts of Justice Act 1924 contained a somewhat similar provision.

Historically, the 1951 Schedule included many of the most frequently committed offences. As reform of the substantive criminal law proceeds, and as most of the new offences being created are placed in category (c), the importance of the procedure provided for by the 1951 Act, s 2, and its First Schedule is gradually diminishing. Nevertheless, very many indictable offences are still tried under it, notably in the areas of theft and dishonesty.

10.7.2.1 Conditions that apply to category (b)(ii) scheduled offences

Section 2 permits the summary trial in the District Court of a scheduled offence if three conditions are met:

(i) the court is of the opinion that the facts proved or alleged constitute a minor offence;

(ii) the accused does not object, after being informed of his or her right to trial by jury; and

(iii) the DPP consents.

10.7.3 CATEGORY (C), ie HYBRID OFFENCES

Hybrid offences (hereinafter referred to as 'category (c) offences') are often referred to as 'either-way' or 'each-way' offences. They are created or re-created by statute and typically are stated therein to be punishable: (i) on summary conviction, by a specified penalty which would be appropriate to a summary or minor offence; or (ii) on conviction on indictment, by a much greater penalty which would reflect the gravity of the particular offence before the court. The term 'hybrid offences' reflects the view that these offences are indictable offences only if the determination of venue is against summary disposal. While hybrid offences represent what would appear to have been the preferred matrix for venue determination over the past two decades, they have in fact been around for a long time, such as in the Dangerous Drugs Act 1934. These offences were considered by the superior courts in a number of cases starting in modern times with *AG (O'Connor) v O'Reilly*, 29 November 1976, High Court Finlay P, 29 November 1976 (unreported) and *State (McEvitt) v Delap* [1981] 1 IR 125.

10.7.3.1   Procedure applicable for hybrid offences

The following procedure for this category of offences is now well settled. The initial decision or election as to venue lies with the prosecutor. If the DPP elects for procedure on indictment, the matter of venue is settled, unless of course some malpractice warranting intervention by way of judicial review occurs. If the election is for summary disposal, however, different considerations apply. Unlike the procedure under the 1951 Act, the defendant has no absolute right to trial by jury. The court, however, has an obligation, mandated by Article 38.5 of the Constitution, to ensure that the offence is a minor one before proceeding to summary disposal and, if not so satisfied, to embark on a preliminary examination. In undertaking that obligation, the court must pay due regard to any relevant submissions by the defendant.

10.7.3.2   Conformity with Article 38

In theory at least, the procedure applicable to hybrid offences, in determining that the offence is a minor one, above appears to be in perfect conformity with Article 38. In practice, there is a growing tendency by District Judges to decline summary jurisdiction in 'either-way' cases. In the absence of a scientifically conducted survey, it is difficult to form any conclusion as to why this occurs. One theory advanced is that the situation obtaining in 1951 and before then, has been reversed, and that it is now the courts of summary jurisdiction which are in grave danger of being swamped by the volume of cases coming before them. It is difficult to subscribe to this theory as a reason for the tendency. In any event, the 'either-way' procedure appears likely to be the criminal procedure of the future for all but the most serious crimes such as murder, and if adequate resources are provided at both prosecutorial and judicial levels it should prove an efficient system for the disposal of the criminal business of the courts.

10.7.4   OFFENCES WHICH MAY BE TRIED SUMMARILY ON A PLEA OF GUILTY

The procedure in relation to this category of offences which may be tried summarily on a plea of guilty (hereinafter referred to as 'category (b)(iv) offences') is governed by the Criminal Procedure Act 1967 s 13, as amended, which applies to all indictable offences other than those which must always be tried on indictment, ie category (a) offences referred to above.

10.7.4.1   Applicable procedure

Offences which may be tried summarily on the DPP indicating acceptance of a plea of guilty in the District Court are provided for in s 13 of the Criminal Procedure Act 1967 as amended by s 13(2), which states:

> *If at any time the District Court ascertains that a person charged with an offence to which the section applies wishes to plead guilty and the court is satisfied that he understands the nature of the offence and the facts alleged, the Court*
>> *(a) may, with the consent of the prosecutor, deal with the offence summarily, in which case the accused shall be liable to the penalties provided for in subsection (3), or Section 13(3)(a) and (b) outline the appropriate penalties as follows:*
>
> *Section 13 (3)(a)*
>
>> *On condition by the District Court for an offence dealt with summarily under subsection 2(a) the accused shall be liable for a fine not exceeding £100 or, at the discretion of the Court, to imprisonment for a term not exceeding twelve months, or to both such fine and imprisonment.*

Section 13 (3)(b) states, however, that

> *in the case of an offence under section 11 of the Wireless Telegraphy Act 1926, the District Court shall not impose a find exceeding £10 or a term of imprisonment exceeding one month.*

The court can therefore convict the person summarily and apply a sanction or sanctions appropriate as in the case of category (b)(ii) scheduled offences to summary jurisdiction, eg not more that 12 months' imprisonment for a single offence or two years cumulatively. Apart from the necessity for a plea of guilty, the essential difference between this procedure and that under the 1951 Act (category (b)(ii)), is that the category (b)(iv) offence is not required by the Criminal Procedure Act 1967 to be a minor one.

10.7.5 PLEAS OF GUILTY SIGNED IN THE DISTRICT COURT WITH SENTENCE IN HIGHER COURTS

Section 13(2)(b) and s 13(2A) of the 1967 Act also prescribe the procedure applicable to offences in which a written plea of guilty may be entered into in the District Court with a view to the defendant being sent forward to a higher court for sentence, referred to above as category (b)(iii) offences. As already stated, this category covers exactly the same offences as those covered by category (b)(iv).

10.7.5.1 Characteristics of the signed written plea procedure

If the accused signs a plea of guilty, the District Court may, subject to s 13(2A) of the Criminal Procedure Act 1967, send him forward for sentence with that plea to that court to which, but for that plea, he would have been sent forward for trial. The accused shall not be sent forward under this section without the consent of the prosecutor. This procedure clearly envisaged offences too serious to be dealt with under the category (b)(iv) procedure and it is somewhat more solemn in that it requires the plea of guilty to be in writing.

Like the category (b)(iv) procedure, the court must ascertain that the accused wishes to plead guilty and understands the nature of the offence and the facts alleged and the consent of the prosecutor is required. Otherwise the two procedures differ.

The accused may withdraw his plea of guilty in the court to which he has been sent forward, in which case he will be dealt with as if he had been sent forward for trial and the State will prepare a book of evidence and serve it in the usual manner.

In the event that the accused does not withdraw the signed plea, the accused may be sentenced as if he had been tried and convicted on indictment, ie without the limitations which would operate under a summary procedure.

10.8 Implications of the categorization of offences

It will be noted that the 1951 Act recognized a right of the accused not conferred by Article 38.5—a right to trial by jury, in the (b) category, for a minor indictable offence. The s 2 formula (ie the 1951 Act, s 2, which permits the summary trial of a scheduled offence in the District Court) was, in the late 1970s and very early 1980s, utilized in a small number of statutes (such as the Criminal Law (Rape) Act 1981, s 12) without, however, inserting the offence in question in the 1951 Schedule. This further confused an already complex situation regarding the appropriate venue for the disposal of offences and underlines the ever-growing need to reform, consolidate and codify our system of criminal procedure.

More recent legislation referred to under category (c) ('hybrid' offences) reflected, *inter alia*, a wish to align criminal procedure on choice of venue more closely with the Constitution. In defining scheduled offences (category (b)(ii) above), it was stated that they might be tried on a plea of not guilty. This was to distinguish them from and avoid confusion with offences which can be dealt with summarily on a plea of guilty, ie category (b)(iv).

It is imperative to convey that the jurisdiction of the court to try the case summarily under the 1951 Act, s 2, is not in any way dependent on the plea made by the defendant. Once that jurisdiction is assumed in accordance with the conditions set out above, the verdict can properly be rendered on the basis of a plea of guilty, if offered, as could be done in any other court of competent jurisdiction. The jurisdiction of the District Court under the 1951 Act, s 2, once established, does not, simply because of the offer of a plea of guilty by the accused, shift to the legislative provisions forming the basis of category (b)(iv) above.

10.9 Conformity of the 1951 Act with Article 38.5 provisions

10.9.1 CATEGORY (A), (B), AND (C) OFFENCES

Obviously no constitutional problem arises under Article 38.5 in relation to category (a) offences, which must always be tried on indictment. A judicial determination as to whether or not the offence in question is a minor one is required before a category (b)(ii) scheduled offence is dealt with summarily and, in addition, the consent of the defendant and of the DPP is required, so no such problem is ever likely to arise there either. While the consent of the defendant is unnecessary for the summary disposal of category (c) hybrid offences, a judicial determination regarding the gravity of the offence is necessary and challenges to a determination for summary disposal have been relatively rare.

10.9.2 ARTICLE 38.5 AND SIGNED PLEAS SENT FORWARD AND OFFENCES TRIED SUMMARILY ON A PLEA OF GUILTY

Category (b)(iii) and (b)(iv) procedures, being those applicable to offences which may be tried summarily on a plea of guilty and signed pleas sent forward for sentencing, respectively, do not require any judicial determination that the offence is minor and the question has been raised more than once as to whether or not those procedures are fully in conformity with Article 38.5.

The answer to this serious question lies in the construction of the word 'tried' in that section. There is little doubt that a conviction on a plea of guilty involves a trial, ie a judicial determination of the issue of guilt or innocence, if for no other reason than the court in question can refuse to accept a plea of guilty if it considers it to be unreliable but also because a person can appeal against both conviction and sentence after pleading guilty whether in an indictment court or a court of summary jurisdiction. This view has been judicially upheld on many occasions.

However, the procedure of pleading guilty and the procedure whereby the court and the defendant dispensed with a jury hearing were established for many years before 1937 and Article 38.5, and in particular the word 'tried', must be construed in the light of that fact. The category (b)(iii) and (b)(iv) procedures are in conformity with Article 38.5 as so construed. Obviously, given the desire of the accused to plead guilty in each of these categories, they are in any event most unlikely to be challenged by either party to a relevant case.

10.9.3 SUMMARY OFFENCES

As to purely summary offences, neither the defendant nor the prosecutor, nor indeed the summary court itself, has any control over the assumption by the court of summary jurisdiction in accordance with the relevant statute and the only remedy is recourse to the superior courts to challenge its constitutionality. The track record for this challenge has not on the whole been very encouraging for anyone going down that road. In *People (AG) v Conroy* [1989] ILRM 139, the constitutionality of the Road Traffic Act 1961, s 49, under which a summary conviction involved mandatory disqualification from driving for one year, was considered. This case proved a very considerable discouragement to other challenges to legislation creating summary offences.

10.10   Choice of venue under Offences against the State Acts

The law relating to offences against the State has been considered and clarified by the High and Supreme Courts on several occasions, particularly since the early 1970s. The main legislative provisions are in the Offences against the State Act 1939 ('the 1939 Act') ss 45–8, which sections deal with the mechanics for the transfer or diversion of cases from the ordinary courts to a special criminal court. As there is and has been for a long time only one Special Criminal Court, which will be discussed in some detail in the next chapter, it should be borne in mind that both Article 38.3 and the 1939 Act make provision for several special criminal courts.

The circumstances in which the powers conferred by ss 45–8 can be exercised by the DPP are on their face very wide and limited only by the requirement for the DPP to make a judgment as to the inadequacy of the ordinary courts to secure the effective administration of justice and the preservation of public peace and order (Article 38.3 and the 1939 Act, ss 45–8). However, it was thought that the intent of the 1939 Act was that it should be used only to combat what was referred to as 'subversive crime' representing the public policy of the State. The short and long titles of the 1939 Act were regarded as being relevant in this regard. The practice both before and after the establishment of the office of DPP was in accordance with that view.

From a very early stage the superior courts had put the decisions of the DPP in this area effectively beyond the reach of judicial review, ie in the absence of *mala fides*. Perhaps the most significant of those was the judgment of Lynch J in the 1989 case of *People (DPP) v Foley* [1995] 1 IR 267. The first sign that this view of the proper reach of the 1939 Act might have been incorrect came with the decision of the Supreme Court in the *People (DPP) v Quilligan* [1986] IR 495, which overruled a High Court decision that the powers of arrest and detention in the 1939 Act, s 30, were available only in relation to subversive crime.

It was ruled in several later cases that the powers of diversion contained in ss 45–8 were not restricted to subversive crime either, the most significant perhaps of these, and certainly the most strenuously contended, being that of *Kavanagh v Government of Ireland* [1996] 1 IR 321; [1996] 1 ILRM 135 (HC); [1997] 1 ILRM 321 (SC).

While these cases did not reflect and were not influenced by it, they coincided with a change in the pattern of serious crime which had been taking place gradually over the previous two decades. A very considerable blurring of the lines of demarcation between 'ordinary' and 'subversive' crime and criminals had evolved, to the extent that very many apparently ordinary crimes were being committed by subversives or by gangs composed jointly of 'subversive' and 'ordinary' criminals, a development which was exacerbated by the explosion of the criminal drug epidemic.

Consequently, even before the *Kavanagh* decision, it had become more and more difficult to adhere rigidly to the old practice of having only subversive criminals tried in the Special Criminal Court. After *Kavanagh* it not only became more difficult still but arguably it would have been improper to have so adhered. The debate on the suitability of trial in the Special Criminal Court was re-ignited during trials subsequent upon the murder of a prominent crime journalist, Veronica Guerin. It must still be remembered, however, that the decision to divert a case to the Special Criminal Court cannot be arbitrary but must be founded on a clear and *bona fide* judgment as to the inadequacy of the ordinary courts.

Some relevant decisions in this area include:

- *Savage v DPP* [1982] ILRM 385;

- *O'Reilly v DPP* [1984] ILRM 224;

- *The People (DPP) v Walsh* [1986] IR 722;

- *The People (DPP) v Quilligan and O'Reilly* [1992] IT 2/11/92;

- *Kavanagh v Government of Ireland* [1996] 1 IR 321; [1996] 1 ILRM 135 (HC); [1997] 1 LRM 321 (SC);

- *DPP v Ward* Supreme Court 1997.

10.11   Reasons for decisions as to venue

Some principles are common to both choice of venue as between summary and solemn procedures and as between the ordinary courts and the Special Criminal Courts. A similar objectivity about choice of venue prevails. The Office of the DPP does not of course have total control over that choice, even in relation to matters which fall for decision by the prosecutor, as the majority of prosecutions, even for indictable offences, are initiated and processed by the Gardaí.

Where the DPP has control, it is exercised on legal criteria and on the basis of other proper considerations, some of which would not always be obvious. For instance judges might occasionally query why the DPP objected to summary disposal in one case and consented in another apparently identical one. The answer, which the representative of the DPP in court could not disclose, even for obvious reasons to the judge, would often be that one defendant had a clean record and the other an exceedingly bad one which would render a summary penalty wholly inadequate.

Sparing victims the ordeal of giving evidence is sometimes a motive for consenting to summary disposal on a plea of guilty. The plea itself might constitute a mitigating factor, especially in a first-time offender, which would cause the DPP to consent to summary disposal, where otherwise the option would be for full jury trial and the possibility of a greater penalty.

The gravity or otherwise of the particular offence is of course the central driving factor in our decisions on venue and the public perception of even-handed justice being seen to be done in a serious case could be an important factor in opting for trial on indictment where the safer option might be summary disposal, particularly if a plea of guilty was on offer. It is impossible, at least without major research, to enumerate all the very many factors which might have to be taken into consideration from case to case.

The circumstances of individual cases vary greatly and each must be treated on its own merits. In taking decisions, however, it must be kept in mind that the fundamental 'raison d'être' of the criminal justice system is the discouragement of criminal activity and that anything which militates against that objective is wrong.

The general reasons for decisions on venue as stated above apply in relation to the Offences Against the State Acts as between the ordinary courts and the Special Criminal Courts. A clear distinction is maintained between the issue of the adequacy of the ordinary courts, which is a relevant and proper consideration, and the question of whether there is a greater prospect of a conviction in the Special Criminal Court than in the ordinary courts, which is not. Few, if any, of the investigative or the prosecution services of the State, in the legal profession or in the judiciary, consider that special criminal courts are a desirable concept, necessary though they may be in certain circumstances.

CHAPTER 11

THE CONDUCT OF SUMMARY TRIALS

11.1   Introduction

As previously outlined, Article 38.2 of the Constitution provides that courts of summary jurisdiction may try minor offences. Article 38.5 provides that with this exception and that of the trial of offences in special courts and military tribunals, no person shall be tried on any criminal charge without a jury.

Having determined that an offence lends itself to summary disposal or, where appropriate, directions have been received from the DPP which consent to summary disposal, the matter will then be dealt with summarily. On occasion an accused will be 'put on election' and on other occasions the offence does not permit a procedural choice for the accused between summary and indictable disposal.

With periodic adjournments as necessary, disposal will manifest itself either by way of a District Court trial, where the accused is denying the allegations made and a contested hearing after a plea of not guilty will follow, or by way of a 'plea of guilty', where such allegations are admitted. The District Court is presided over by a District Judge sitting alone.

11.2   Minor offences

When a court is determining whether or not an alleged offence is a minor one fit to be tried summarily, it may simply rely on the content of the charge sheet or summons, or it may ask the prosecutor to give an outline of the alleged facts, or to state whether there is anything 'unusual' about the allegations, if, on the face of it, it appears an appropriate case for summary trial. The value of property allegedly stolen is obviously a factor in a theft case, for example, but judicial interpretations of what constitutes a minor offence vary widely, and while one judge might unhesitatingly certify as minor an alleged theft of a computer worth €2,000, another will immediately refuse jurisdiction. Each offence is to be considered individually. An accused may be charged with a number of 'minor' thefts or forgeries totalling several thousand euros, and still be dealt with summarily. In a theft from the person case, the age of the alleged injured party may be a relevant consideration for a judge when determining jurisdiction. In a robbery case, the judge may want to know whether it will be alleged that a weapon was produced or any actual violence used. In a residential burglary case, the judge may ask whether it is alleged that the offence took place at night or that the occupants of the dwelling were at home.

11.3   Summary offences

A summary offence can only be dealt with in the District Court, unless it is added to an indictment containing a related indictable offence or where the DPP certifies that the ordinary courts are insufficient and the Special Criminal Court procedure applies. If the penalty provision of an offence refers to liability to a particular penalty on summary conviction and contains no reference to any penalty on conviction on indictment, then the offence is a purely summary offence. Common examples are careless driving under s 52 of the Road Traffic Act 1961, breach of the peace under s 6 of the Criminal Justice (Public Order) Act 1994, and assault contrary to s 2 of the Non-Fatal Offences Against the Person Act 1997.

Sometimes clients charged with these types of offences may instruct that they 'want to go for judge and jury', and it must be explained to them that there is no possibility of a trial on indictment for a purely summary offence.

An offence need not be a summary one to qualify as a minor offence fit for summary trial. Indictable offences may also be tried summarily in certain circumstances.

11.4   Summary trial of indictable offences

11.4.1   SCHEDULED INDICTABLE OFFENCES

Section 2 of the Criminal Justice Act 1951, as amended by s 8 of the Criminal Justice (Miscellaneous Provisions) Act 1997, provides as follows:

> (2)   *The District Court may try summarily a person charged with a scheduled offence if—*
> (a)   *The Court is of the opinion that the facts proved or alleged constitute a minor offence fit to be tried summarily,*
> (b)   *The accused, on being informed by the Court of his right to be tried with a jury, does not object to being tried summarily, and*
> (c)   *The Director of Public Prosecutions consents to the accused being tried summarily for such offence.*

The list of scheduled offences, which includes forgery, larceny, burglary and robbery, is set out in Woods, JV, *District Court Practice and Procedure in Criminal Cases* (Limerick, 1994) at pp 273–4. When considering Woods's notes to the schedule, however, it should be noted that since the publication of this text, the above-mentioned paragraph (c) of s 13(2) has been enacted; therefore, the consent of the DPP is now required before any scheduled offence can be tried summarily.

11.4.2   OFFENCES WHERE THE ACCUSED HAS A RIGHT OF ELECTION

There are two categories of offences triable summarily where the accused has a right of election: scheduled offences under the Criminal Justice Act 1951, as amended, and indictable offences under the Criminal Justice (Theft and Fraud Offences) Act 2001.

Section 2 of the Criminal Justice Act 1951, as substituted by s 8 of the Criminal Justice (Miscellaneous Provisions) Act 1997, provides as follows:

> (2)   *The District Court may try summarily a person charged with a scheduled offence if—*
> (a)   *the Court is of opinion that the facts proved or alleged constitute a minor offence fit to be tried summarily,*
> (b)   *the accused, on being informed by the Court of his right to be tried with a jury, does not object to being tried summarily, and*

(c)   the Director of Public Prosecutions consents to the accused being tried summarily for such offence.

David Goldberg's *Consolidated Criminal Legislation* has an up-to-date version of the Schedule to the Criminal Justice Act 1951. Many of the offences listed in the original Schedule to the 1951 Act have been repealed and prosecutions for many of the remaining scheduled offences are rare. However, s 53(1) of the Criminal Justice (Theft and Fraud Offences) Act 2001 is in very similar terms to s 2 of the 1951 Act, providing that the District Court may try summarily a person charged with an indictable offence under the 2001 Act if—

(a)   the Court is of opinion that the facts proved or alleged constitute a minor offence fit to be tried summarily,

(b)   the accused, on being informed by the Court of his or her right to be tried with a jury, does not object to being tried summarily, and

(c)   the Director of Public Prosecutions consents to the accused being tried summarily for the offence.

Indictable offences under the Criminal Justice (Theft and Fraud Offences) Act, 2001 are the most common type of offence where the accused has a right of election, and are very frequently tried summarily.

11.5   The DPP's directions

In practice, the court will usually inquire as to whether the DPP consents (*'Are there DPP's directions?'* or, *'What does the Director say?'*) before considering the question of jurisdiction itself or placing the accused 'on his or her election'. The DPP does not give reasons for any of the decisions, but in deciding whether or not to consent to summary disposal for a particular offence will presumably consider not only the nature and seriousness of the offence itself, but also any previous convictions of the accused, as well as the recommendation of the Gardaí.

Sometimes the DPP will direct summary disposal on a plea of guilty only, which can create a dilemma for an accused who was intending to plead not guilty, as the penalties available on conviction on indictment are much heavier than those in the District Court. In such circumstances, a remand should be sought for an accused to consider the position, and disclosure of the prosecution case should be sought, if it has not been obtained already, so that the defence can make an assessment of the strength of the evidence against the accused.

11.6   The accused's right of election considerations

11.6.1   ACCUSED'S CHOICE OF TRIAL BY JURY

11.6.1.1   Scheduled offences

If the DPP has directed summary disposal of a scheduled offence, or of an indictable offence under the Criminal Justice (Theft and Fraud Offences) Act 2001, and the court has accepted jurisdiction, then the accused will be informed by the court of their right to be tried with a jury and asked to exercise their right of election. The solicitor should already have advised the client of the right and discussed the alternatives. Apart from sentencing considerations, other factors should be borne in mind. An accused convicted in the District Court has a full right of appeal to the Circuit Court by way of a fresh hearing, whereas an appeal from the Circuit Court to the Court of Criminal Appeal is on a point of law only.

Full disclosure of the prosecution case is available before a Circuit Court trial, but may not be before a District Court hearing. A trial on indictment will involve a longer delay, which may be an advantage or a disadvantage to a particular accused. A private paying client needs to be advised that the costs of a Circuit Court trial are likely to be considerably higher than in the District Court. The acquittal rate is higher in the Circuit Court, where there is a judge to filter out inadmissible evidence from the jury, which is the tribunal of fact, such as an improperly obtained confession, and a jury is probably more likely to disbelieve a Garda witness than a District Court judge. Nevertheless, it is relatively unusual to advise a client to elect for trial on indictment, although some clients, particularly those with more experience of the criminal justice system, may have very strong views of their own on this subject. They may feel they have no prospect whatsoever of receiving a fair hearing before a particular District Court judge, particularly if that judge has previously convicted them.

11.6.1.2 Hybrid offences

The right to trial by jury has been significantly eroded in recent years in that the venue or mode of trial of a number of hybrid offences (ie offences which may be prosecuted either summarily or on indictment) is now solely at the option of the prosecution, subject always to the right of the District Court to refuse summary jurisdiction in a matter it does not consider to be minor. The accused does not have a right of election, for example, if charged with an offence contrary to s 15(1) of the Misuse of Drugs Act 1977 (possession of a controlled drug for the purposes of unlawful sale or supply), s 3 of the Non-Fatal Offences Against the Person Act 1997 (assault causing harm), s 112(1) of the Road Traffic Act 1961, as amended (unlawful use, taking of, or carriage in, a vehicle) or s 2(1) of the Criminal Damage Act 1991 (criminal damage). If the DPP directs summary disposal of these offences, then it does not matter that the accused would prefer to be tried by a jury, the accused has no input into the determination of the mode of trial, and this can be difficult to explain to a client. Again, the judge does have a role, and, in the examples given, may want to know such information as what type of drug and how much was allegedly seized and the estimated street value; what type of harm was allegedly suffered, the place and time of day of the alleged assault, whether the alleged injured party lost consciousness or was hospitalized, or whether kicks were allegedly inflicted; whether a car chase was allegedly involved; and how much damage was allegedly caused. It needs to be reiterated that there is no consistency of judicial approach, and that attitudes to whether particular sets of allegations constitute minor offences are quite disparate, as are many other matters within the discretion of District Court judges.

11.7 Pre-trial disclosure

If a matter proceeds on indictment a book of evidence is served on the accused. This contains the evidence that is to be presented at the trial. Historically an accused in the District Court was denied this advantage and he only became aware of the case against him when the District Court hearing took place. As outlined in the previous chapter, the position has now changed following the leading Supreme Court decision on pre-trial disclosure in the District Court, *DPP v Gary Doyle* [1994] 2 IR 286; [1994] ILRM 529. The first question posed in that case was as follows:

> 'Where an indictable charge is being disposed of by way of summary trial in the District Court, is there a general obligation on the prosecution to furnish, on request, the statements of the proposed prosecution witnesses.'

The answer to that question was that there is no general obligation to furnish statements but 'in any such instance the District Court may direct, having regard to the interest of justice, as set out in this judgment, the furnishing of such statements'. Denham J stated that the procedure adopted in the *Gary Doyle* case would appear to be the appropriate procedure, ie that the solicitors for the accused should write to the prosecution, requisition the statements and if these were not forthcoming, the District Court judge should determine the issue. In practice the prosecution will generally furnish statements, except in the most straightforward cases.

In the case of *James (Jim Bob) O'Driscoll and Patrick Williamson v District Court Jude Brendan Wallace and the DPP* [1995] 1 IR 237 the issue was whether an accused was entitled to statements to help him to decide whether or not to elect for summary trial. The High Court held that in a case where disclosure was appropriate the accused was entitled to disclosure prior to election.

11.8 The conduct of the District Court trial

11.8.1 OPENING STAGES

In the opening stages of the hearing:

(a) the case is called by the court clerk;

(b) prosecution and defence solicitors identify themselves to the court; and

(c) preliminary applications may be made by defence or prosecution; eg the prosecution may apply to amend the charge sheet/summons or the defence may ask the judge to dismiss/strike out the matter on a particular ground, eg delay. If the judge accedes to a defence application to dismiss, obviously that is the end of the matter.

11.8.2 RULES OF EVIDENCE

11.8.2.1 The hearsay rule

These are rules of evidence (see **Chapter 4**) that prevent certain types of evidence being given in court. Perhaps the most important rule of evidence is the rule against hearsay. This rule is to the effect that statements by a person who is not giving evidence in court are inadmissible as evidence of any fact stated, eg a Garda in a dangerous driving prosecution cannot give evidence that a pedestrian told him that a car was being driven at high speed on the wrong side of the road. That pedestrian could obviously give that evidence himself in court but no one else can do it on his behalf. There are good reasons for the rule. The Rule Against Hearsay (The Law Reform Commission Working Paper No 9 1980) states:

> *A hearsay statement is by definition not made before the court and, if the maker does not testify, he cannot be cross-examined nor can his demeanour be observed or his credibility tested. Where the hearsay statement narrated is oral there is a chance that it may be altered in the telling. Where it is made formally there is the danger that it may be tailored to the requirements of the party making it.*

11.8.3 REFRESHING THE MEMORY

A witness may refresh his memory by referring to a document compiled at the time of the occurrence of the events about which the witness is testifying. Any such document should be made available to the other side and they may cross-examine on it.

11.8.4 THE PROSECUTION CASE

The prosecution lawyer calls his witnesses to establish the elements of the offence alleged against the accused in order to discharge the legal burden of proof which requires proof 'beyond reasonable doubt'. The prosecution cannot ask leading questions from prosecution witnesses when examining them in direct evidence.

When the prosecution has finished the direct examination (examination-in-chief), that witness's evidence is cross-examined by the defence lawyer. The defence lawyer puts the defence case to the prosecution witness. When the defence has finished cross-examination, the witness may be re-examined by the prosecution on matters arising out of the cross-examination.

The prosecution case is closed when all State witnesses have been called, directly examined, cross-examined and on occasion as necessary, re-examined by the prosecution.

11.8.5 THE DEFENCE CASE

At the close of the prosecution case the defence may apply for a direction, ie that the case should be dismissed at this stage because the State has not discharged its legal burden of proof, eg a vital proof has not been made out or there is a 'break in the chain of evidence'. The prosecution is entitled to challenge this assertion by the defence by indicating, with reference to proofs placed before the court, that the accused has 'a case to answer'. The judge will then determine the matter by indicating whether a dismissal is the appropriate court order.

Once it has been held by the judge that the accused has a case to answer the judge must proceed to convict the accused if the defence decide not to go into evidence.

If the defence decide to go into evidence, defence witnesses are called and examined-in-chief by the defence lawyer and cross-examined by the prosecution lawyer. If appropriate, the defence may re-examine their witnesses.

11.8.6 DECISION OF THE COURT

Having placed all the evidence from the prosecution and defence before the judge, the defence are entitled to make 'submissions' that the case against the accused has not been made out, ie that the legal burden of proof has not been discharged and the prosecution is entitled to reply to such submissions. The judge of the District Court then determines the guilt or innocence of the accused. If there is a finding of 'not guilty' the case is said to be 'dismissed'.

Where the judge decides to convict the accused the defence address the court in the form of a 'plea in mitigation' on behalf of the accused (see **Chapter 14** on Sentencing in general). The court will hear evidence of previous convictions (if any) of the accused from the prosecution prior to considering the sentence. The judge may either impose a penalty there and then or may adjourn the matter for probation or community service reports, to consider them prior to imposing sentence.

11.9 Conduct of a plea

11.9.1 POST DISTRICT COURT TRIAL CONVICTION

One of the most important aspects of conducting a plea in mitigation of sentence is knowledge of the judge's views. One judge may impose a very stiff penalty for a particular

138

offence whereas another may apply the provisions of the Probation Act for the same offence. Similarly, some judges like to hear a very detailed background history of an accused whereas others like a concise version. The importance of knowing the judge's views cannot be overemphasized.

It is crucial that the defence lawyer has taken full instructions regarding the client's background, ie the client's family history, work history, state of health, whether or not he has a drink/drug addiction problem, the history of his previous convictions (if any) and the circumstances in which these were imposed. If, for example, your client spent time in custody prior to the disposal of the case the defence lawyer should inform the court and the salutary effect this has had on the client (presuming this is the case!). This lawyer should also let the court know if the client has suffered any 'external' hardship as a result of the criminal charge, eg loss of employment. Conversely, if the client's employer is willing to re-employ the now convicted person, this should be brought to the court's attention. If possible the employer should be brought to court, both to establish his willingness to re-employ the convicted person and to proffer character evidence as appropriate.

A lawyer should inquire as to the client's ability to pay compensation to the injured party. While the District Court does not see itself as a debt-collecting agency, an amount of money in court to partly compensate the injured party for the wrong committed can be seen as a token of the client's regret and will often impress the judge and could thereby mitigate the punishment/sentence.

Legal practitioners should be aware of the maximum penalties that can be imposed, both in monetary terms and/or term of detention/imprisonment. They should also be aware of alternative penalties such as the application of the Probation of Offenders Act 1907, or the making of an order pursuant to the Criminal Justice (Community Service) Act 1993.

11.9.2 PLEAS OF GUILTY TO NON-MINOR OFFENCES

If there is a plea of guilty to an indictable offence, the offence need not be classified as minor to be disposed of by the District Court, as there is no contested hearing or 'trial'. Section 13 of the Criminal Procedure Act 1967, as amended by s 17 of the Criminal Justice Act 1984 and by s 10 of the Criminal Justice Act 1999, provides, *inter alia*:

(1)   This section applies to all indictable offences except the following—an offence under the Treason Act, 1939, murder, attempt to murder, conspiracy to murder, piracy, genocide or a grave breach such as is referred to in s 3(1)(i) of the Geneva Convention Act 1962, including an offence by an accessory before or after the fact.

(2)   If at any time the District Court ascertains that a person charged with an offence to which this section applies wishes to plead guilty and the Court is satisfied that he understands the nature or the offence and the facts alleged, the Court—

(a)   may, with the consent of the prosecutor, deal with the offence summarily, in which case the accused shall be liable to the penalties provided for in subsection (3) . . .

(b)   On conviction by the District Court for an offence dealt with summarily under subsection (2)(a), the accused shall be liable to a fine not exceeding £1,000, or, at the discretion of the Court, to imprisonment for a term not exceeding twelve months, or to both such fine and imprisonment.

A court may not be minded to exercise its discretion to deal with offences under this wider jurisdiction unless satisfied that the penalties provided for in s 13 are sufficient to meet the seriousness of the offence charged, although some judges are more content than others generally to accept jurisdiction if the DPP consents.

11.10   Non-attendance by either party

11.10.1   NON-ATTENDANCE OF THE PROSECUTOR

Where the accused (or his representative) is present at the required time and place for a District Court hearing and the prosecutor is not present, the court may strike out/dismiss without prejudice or adjourn the hearing of the complaint (District Court Rules 1997, Order 23, rule 3).

11.10.2   NON-ATTENDANCE OF THE ACCUSED

When an accused is not present in court to answer a complaint the court will issue a bench warrant for the arrest of an accused who has breached the terms of the bail bond (see **Chapter 8**). The court may also, in particular circumstances, proceed with the case in the absence of the accused, eg a parking offence summons. An accused has a fundamental right to be present at proceedings against him but if the trial judge is satisfied that he has consciously decided to absent himself from the trial, the case can be dealt with without the physical presence of the accused (*Lawler v Hogan DJ* [1993] ILRM 606).

11.11   Appeal

A person convicted in the District Court has a statutory right of appeal to the Circuit Court as delineated by s 18 (1) of the Courts of Justice Act 1928 (see **Chapter 15**). A person can appeal to the Circuit Court whether he has been sentenced on a plea of guilty or after conviction on a 'not guilty plea' and may appeal conviction and sentence or just the sentence.

The procedure to be followed is that a notice of appeal is lodged with the courts and served on the prosecuting Gardaí. The District Court then fixes recognisance that must be entered into by the accused and an independent surety, if applicable. The notice of appeal must be lodged and served within 14 days of the date of the decision. The appeal operates as a stay of execution.

CHAPTER 12

PROCEEDINGS RELATING TO INDICTABLE OFFENCES

12.1 Introduction

Indictable offences are initially prosecuted in the same manner as all other offences, in the District Court save for a few exceptions. As has been outlined in **Chapter 10**, the DPP then makes various decisions with regard to the venue of trial, based on the application of very specific criteria as therein outlined.

This chapter will build on the procedural information contained in preceding chapters. Procedures in relation to arraignment, functions of judge and jury and pre-trial proceedings will be examined and there will be a brief reference to avenues of appeal. The chapter will conclude with a separate section on the Special Criminal Court, which warrants individual attention given its non-jury status and the consequences of such status in the context of its historical origins.

12.2 Development of jurisprudence

12.2.1 THE BOOK OF EVIDENCE

Historically all witnesses gave their evidence before the District Court on deposition, which said evidence was taken down in longhand, and it was from this evidence that the judge conducted a preliminary examination (s 14 Petty Sessions Ireland Act 1851). However, nowadays the documents as outlined in the Criminal Procedure Act 1967 as amended by the Criminal Justice Act 1999 Part III (CPA 1967 (as amended)) are served on the accused by way of notice of the evidence which it is proposed to adduce at the trial. These documents have become known as the 'Book of Evidence'.

The expression 'Book of Evidence' has no statutory warrant [*People (AG) v Cummins* [1971] IR 312 and accordingly there is no statutory requirement that these documents be served in the form of a book or, for that matter, at any one time. However, they should be set out in the forms as prescribed by the District Court (Criminal Procedure Act 1967) Rules 1967 as amended. Furthermore they should be served within 42 days of the first appearance in court of the accused.

Prior to the introduction of the CPA 1967 (as amended) the District Judge was presumed to have the power to extend the time for service of such documents whenever the State failed to produce the book after a period of 30 days had elapsed from the first appearance date. There was, however, no statutory basis for this 30-day period. Given the insertion of a statutory limitation of 42 days in the CPA 1967 (as amended), the accumulated wisdom of some criminal litigation practitioners, supported by some members of the judiciary, is that the State is no longer entitled to an extension of time to serve the book.

Such service of the Book of Evidence (the Book) usually occurs when the matter comes back before the District Court on remand. During the preparatory stage of the compilation of the book, the prosecution, having had a chance to examine the Garda file in detail, may wish to amend the existing charges or prefer new charges. Should the prosecution wish to do so, such charges must be amended or preferred prior to the service of the Book.

In practical terms the case is called, new charges preferred, amendments made to the existing charges, and only then will the Book be personally served on the accused. The defence solicitor usually takes immediate custody of it. A statutory declaration as to service of the book is then sworn by the Garda who served the book and usually taken by the judge.

It should be noted that while there is no requirement to provide a copy of any exhibits listed photocopies are invariably provided and regardless, the accused has a right to inspect all such exhibits (CPA 1967 (as amended) s 4D).

Section 6 of the 1967 Act previously dealt with the inspection of exhibits. Strict compliance with the provisions of s 6 was deemed non-essential and 'substantial compliance' sufficed to leave the District Judge in a position to make a 'valid decision' (*State (Williams) v Kelleher* [1983] IR 112). It has been held that there was no breach of the 1967 Act, s 6(3) when a good explanation was given as to the absence of an exhibit (*State (Pletzer) v McGee* [1986] ILRM 441, at 443). This jurisprudence is now arguably referable to the 'right to inspect all exhibits' conferred on the accused in s 4D of the CPA 1967 (as amended).

12.2.2   DEPOSITIONS

The taking of evidence under deposition in the District Court was a procedure which was the right of either the defence or the prosecution under the old legislation. Since the introduction of s 4F CPA 1967 (as amended), the taking of such evidence is a matter of application to the trial court under s 4E as amended by s 20 of the Criminal Justice Act 2006, which has the discretion to make an order either granting or refusing the application. The trial court will have to be 'satisfied in the interests of justice' (s 4F(2)) before granting the application.

Any witness may be called including witnesses who are not in the Book. The defence, to test the veracity of the proposed evidence, has traditionally, on occasion, called prosecution witnesses on deposition. Interestingly, and despite the fact that such witnesses will be prosecution witnesses at the trial, when so called they were deemed defence witnesses, who accordingly cannot be cross-examined by the defence but can be cross-examined by the prosecutor (*State (Sherry) v Wine* [1985] ILRM 196). However, a judge, in conducting any examination, has a substantial discretion as to how the proceedings are conducted. It has been held a valid exercise of such discretion under the 1967 Act before the introduction of the CPA 1967 (as amended) to refuse to allow the accused to call further witnesses on deposition when he had already called a number of such witnesses and the judge was of the view that the accused was attempting to abuse the process by endeavouring to delay the trial (*State (Daly) v Ruane* [1988] ILRM 117).

Under s 4G of the CPA 1967 (as amended), a deposition under s 4F may be considered by the trial court on an application under s 4E(1).

Under s 4G (2): a deposition may be admitted in evidence at the trial if it is proved that:

> (a)   *the witness*
> > (i)   *is dead*
> > (ii)   *unable to attend to give evidence at the trial*
> > (iii)   *prevented from so attending*
> > (iv)   *does not give evidence at the trial through fear or intimidation*

(b)   the accused was present at the taking of the evidence, and

(c)   opportunity was given to cross-examine and re-examine the witness unless the Court is of the opinion that to do so would not be in the interests of justice.

12.2.3   ADDITIONAL COUNTS ON THE INDICTMENT

The prosecutor is entitled under s 4(C) of the CPA 1967 (as amended) to add further counts to the indictment. A challenge to the constitutional validity of a similar procedure under the old legislative system failed on the basis that it is an administrative and executive function to ensure that every defendant in criminal proceedings answers the most appropriate charges. A submission that such action was contrary to a previous exercise of a judicial function was rejected (*O'Shea v DPP* [1988] IR 655).

12.3   Trial on indictment

12.3.1   DEFINITION OF INDICTMENT

An indictment is a document which formally sets out the offence which is alleged and the particulars of the alleged offence in detail, which is sufficient to give the accused reasonable information as to the charge which must be defended. The indictment will be given to the jury in the event that they are asked to consider the question of the guilt or innocence of the accused. It is arguable that such notice is not of huge significance where a Book has already been served on the accused, thereby putting the recipient of the Book on notice of all the charges which must be 'met' and all the evidence which the State has available to it to substantiate the allegations. However, the indictment contains the essential elements of the offence and proofs must be led by the prosecution to establish everything on the indictment beyond a reasonable doubt.

12.3.2   ARRAIGNMENT

Having been 'cautioned', usually by the prosecuting Garda, to attend on the day appointed by the court, the arraignment is the accused person's first appearance before the court of trial on indictment. It serves several purposes:

(a)   Accused, having been served with an indictment, is asked to plead to the charge(s).

(b)   The accused's appearance must be secured by personal notification.

(c)   It is a convenient 'first stop' in evaluating the probable length of a trial, if the accused has determined to plead not guilty.

(d)   The prosecution's stance can be established. There is always the possibility of an application by the State for a *nolle prosequi* order, which records a decision by the prosecutor to withdraw the charge at trial stage. Where a *nolle* is entered, the accused is not in jeopardy and a discharge is not an acquittal (*State (Walshe) v Lennon* [1942] IR 112). Consequently, the State may re-enter the allegation against the accused; however, the possibility of a successful judicial review by the accused with regard to delay in pursuing the prosecution of the matter may militate against such a re-entry.

(e)   The accused is remanded to a trial date.

12.4 Establishing a prima facie case

Independent judicial review of the evidential basis of a decision to prosecute has long been recognized as necessary, and has thus been an integral part of the criminal process. Since October 2001, the judges of the superior criminal courts are now retained as 'gate keepers' of the criminal justice system, prior to committal for trial. This procedure, which hitherto existed at District Court level, acted as a type of sieve, the function of which was not to determine guilt or innocence, but simply to ensure that the prosecution had put forward some reasonable basis in evidence for the offence charged and as a safeguard to protect an accused person from having to embark on the defence of a full trial before a jury without there being at least a prima facie case to answer. The concept of 'preliminary examination' is retained, but at the discretion of the court of trial, if the defence make an Application for Dismissal under s 4E of the CPA 1967 (as amended).

There does not appear to be a large amount of judicial interpretation on what exactly constitutes 'a sufficient case' but the accepted test is whether a reasonable jury, properly directed in law, could convict on the basis of the evidence before the judge. It is clear, however, that it is not the function of a judge who hears an accused's application to dismiss under s 4(E) of the CPA 1967 (as amended), in conducting a preliminary examination, to embark on issues which are the prerogative of the court of trial, thus usurping the function of that court. It is not for instance its function under s 4E to consider the likely credibility of statements before it (*R v Norfolk Quarter Sessions, ex p. Brunson* [1953] 1 QB 503) or for that matter to the admissibility of evidence (*DPP v Windle J. and Graham Walsh* [2001] ILRM 75) or the issue of delay, all of which are clearly matters reserved either for the court of trial or the High Court on an application for judicial review.

The onus to apply for a dismissal under s 4E of the Criminal Procedure Act 1967 is on the accused, who initiates any form of review of the evidence served. Any dismissal of charges which may result from such a review, may be appealed by the State.

12.5 Procedures regarding trial on indictment

In general terms the procedure under the CPA 1967 (as amended) operates as follows:

(a) A book of evidence (to include information under Part II of the Criminal Evidence Act 1992) should be served within 42 days of the accused's first appearance in court. The phraseology of the CPA 1967 (as amended) leads to the conclusion that the District Court is likely to adhere to this time limit and would probably be loath to 'extend time for the service of the book' without good cause or reason being proffered by the prosecution.

(b) Following service of the book of evidence the accused is then sent forward for trial, with the consent of the Director of Public Prosecutions (DPP) to the court before which he is to stand trial.

(c) The prosecution can serve additional evidence up to the date of trial.

(d) At any time after the accused is sent forward for trial he may apply to the trial court to dismiss one or more of the charges and if it appears to that court that there is not sufficient case to put him on trial, the court shall dismiss the charge.

(e) The trial court can also direct the taking of evidence before a judge in the District Court by a sworn deposition but an order will only be made if the trial court is satisfied that it would be in the interest of justice to do so.

(f) Extensive powers are available to the trial court in the course of such an application to examine the book of evidence, any oral testimony on oath, any sworn deposition, or any document it thinks relevant, and to ensure that it is before the court.

(g)   There are limitations placed on publication of the proceedings.

12.5.1 AMENDMENTS TO THE CRIMINAL PROCEDURE ACTS OF 1967 AND 1973 BY THE CRIMINAL JUSTICE ACT 1999—CPA 1967 (as amended)

The Criminal Justice Act 1999 Part III (CJA 1999) s 9 inserts Part 1A of the Criminal Procedure Act 1967 ss 4A–4Q inclusive [CPA 1967 (as amended)], which outlines procedure relating to the following:

(a)   s 4A Sending the accused forward for trial;

(b)   s 4B Service of documents on the accused;

(c)   s 4C Service of additional documents;

(d)   s 4D Examination by the accused of exhibits;

(e)   s 4E Application by accused for dismissal (as amended);

(f)   s 4F Taking of evidence by the District Court;

(g)   s 4G Admissibility of deposition and video recording;

(h)   s 4H Legal Aid;

(i)   s 4I Power to exclude members of the public;

(j)   s 4J Publication and broadcast of proceedings;

(k)   s 4K Witness orders;

(l)   s 4L Witness summonses;

(m)   s 4M Amendment of charges against the accused;

(n)   s 4N Joinder of unrelated charges;

(o)   s 4O Correction of defect in charge;

(p)   s 4P Transfer of proceedings from Circuit Court to Central Criminal Court;

(q)   s 4Q Jurisdiction of Circuit Court to remand the accused to 'alternative court' and jurisdiction to hear applications.

Section 8 of the 1999 Act amends the definition of 'prosecutor' in s 4 of the 1967 Act by the substitution of the following:

4.—(1) In this Act 'the prosecutor' means in relation to an offence—in Part 1A and section 13, The Director of Public Prosecutions, and in Parts II and III, other than section 13—
(i)   the Director of Public Prosecutions,
(ii)   a person prosecuting the offence at the suit of the Director of Public Prosecutions, or
(iii)   a person authorised by law to prosecute the offence
(2)   Notwithstanding subsection (1), references to the prosecutor in Parts IA, II and III shall be construed, in relation to offences for which proceedings may not be instituted or continued except by, or on behalf or with the consent of, the Attorney General, as references to the Attorney General.

12.6 Pre-trial proceedings

12.6.1 JUDICIAL REVIEW

Judicial review proceedings are sometimes taken in the High Court in advance of trial seeking a discretionary remedy. Judicial review is discussed in detail in **Chapter 15** of this text but in general terms one should note that an accused may seek an Order of Prohibition, which endeavours to prohibit the trial, eg by reason of delay in the prosecution of the matter. An accused may have grounds to obtain an Order of Certiorari, which quashes an order previously made in the proceedings, where a judge may have acted in excess of the applicable jurisdiction. An Order of Mandamus may issue, which compels that a particular is taken, eg the naming of an informant, the granting of a certificate of free legal aid or the disclosure of some specified documents.

The importance of a 'Stay Order' in the event of the commencement of any of the above proceedings is to estop the trial until judicial review proceedings are determined.

12.6.2 A 'TRIAL WITHIN A TRIAL'

Legal argument in the absence of the jury will often occur before evidence has been heard by that jury or during the course of the trial. Such argument will often concern such issues as the admissibility or acceptance of evidence, eg validity of warrants, compliance with the Judges' Rules, failure to afford entitlements under Criminal Justice Act Treatment of Persons in Custody Regulations 1987 (SI 119 of 1987). Such proceedings are described as a trial within a trial or a *'voir dire'*.

A trial within a trial may be defined as the settling of a justiciable controversy arising in the course of a trial and heard in the absence of a jury. Invariably since the jury cannot be aware of the issue causing such controversy, publicity by the media is not permitted on penalty of a finding of contempt of court. In the course of the trial within a trial evidence touching on the issue will be heard by the judge alone, without prejudice to the trial, which remains in abeyance until the issue raised has been ruled on by the trial judge.

12.6.2.1 Typical issues argued in the absence of the jury

Evidence will be deemed admissible on the basis of the analysis of the following criteria:

    (a)   its probative value versus its prejudicial value;

    (b)   its relevance;

    (c)   the receivability of evidence, eg evidence with tainted origin;

    (d)   the application of the 'hearsay rule';

    (e)   documentary evidence presented without its author;

    (f)   illegally obtained evidence, eg searches and confessions;

    (g)   unconstitutionally obtained evidence;

    (h)   s 7(3), of the Criminal Justice Act, which contains a saving for evidence gathered notwithstanding a failure to comply with the 1987 Regulations; and

    (i)   *'causal nexus'* requirements, ie there must be a causal connection between the evidence gathered and the right infringed (*State v Paul Healy* [1990] ILRM 313).

The breach of a legal right and the invasion of constitutional rights are distinctly treated where admissibility of evidence is concerned (*McMeel Mahon v AG* [1986] IR 393 and *People (DPP) v Kenny* [1990] ILRM 569).

Evidence which has been given in the course of the trial may warrant an application to discharge the jury, for example:

(a)   irrelevant, prejudicial or inadmissible evidence which has been led deliberately;

(b)   remarks of counsel for the prosecution which may prejudice a fair trial;

(c)   remarks of the judge in charging the jury or otherwise during the trial; and

(d)   evidence which has been given or led that goes beyond the prosecution case as set out in the book of evidence.

Matters outside of the court or trial may warrant an application to discharge the jury, such as:

(a)   publicity prejudicial to a fair trial; or

(b)   behaviour inside or outside the court which could prejudice the accused, e.g. the accused remains handcuffed in sight of the jury.

12.7   Special Criminal Court

12.7.1   INTRODUCTION

The Special Criminal Court is unlike the other courts which try offences on indictment. Article 38.3 of the Constitution permits the establishment of a Special Criminal Court in circumstances where the ordinary courts are not considered adequate to secure the effective administration of justice and the preservation of public peace and order. This is a non-jury court. The present court was established in 1972. It can try both summary and indictable offences under procedures set out in the Offences Against the State Acts of 1939 and 1972. Article 38.3.1 of the Constitution reads as follows:

> *Special Courts may be established by law, for the trial of offences in cases where it may be determined in accordance with such law that the ordinary courts are inadequate to secure the effective administration of justice and the preservation of public peace and order.*

The Offences Against the State Act 1939 (the 1939 Act) Part V provides for the establishment of a Special Criminal Court. Section 35 sets out the procedure required to bring Part V into operation. The government must make and publish a declaration that it is satisfied that the ordinary courts are inadequate to secure the effective administration of justice and the preservation of public peace and order and that it is accordingly necessary to bring Part V into force. It will be seen that this format is based on the words of Article 38.3.1 of the Constitution and appears elsewhere in the Offences Against the State Acts.

Section 38 of the 1939 Act states that a court called a Special Criminal Court shall be established as soon as possible after Part V has been brought into force. While s 38 provides for the establishment of more than one court, the court that came into existence on 30 May 1972 is the only court established under Part V.

12.7.1.2   The composition of the court

Article 35 of the Constitution guarantees the independence and non-removal from office of the judiciary. Article 38.6 states that these guarantees do not apply to a Special Criminal Court. The Offences Against the State Act 1939, s 39(2), provides that each member of a Special Criminal Court shall be appointed and be removable at will by the government. Section 39(4) states that the Minister for Finance shall pay to a member of the court such (if any) remuneration and allowances as the Minister may think proper.

These references in s 39 were the subject of legal challenge in *Eccles v Ireland* [1985] IR 545. The Supreme Court ruled that, notwithstanding the words of s 39, a Special Criminal Court was entitled to judicial independence under the Constitution and that any attempt by the executive to interfere with the judicial independence of a Special Criminal Court would be prevented and corrected by the courts. It should be noted that the government, without the judge's consent, has not removed any judge appointed to a Special Criminal Court since 1972.

Section 39(3) permits the appointment to the court of serving members of the judiciary, members of the legal profession of seven years' standing and officers of the defence forces. In fact, only serving or retired members of the judiciary have been appointed to the court established in 1972 and the practice since 1986 has been to appoint only serving judges of the High Court, Circuit Court, and District Court. In practice, the court sits for the trial of offences as a chamber of three judges, usually consisting of a judge of each of the three courts.

12.7.2 COMMENCEMENT OF PROCEEDINGS

12.7.2.1 Scheduled offences

Section 36 of the 1939 Act permits the government to declare offences of a particular class or kind or under a particular enactment to be scheduled.

Making an offence a scheduled offence has two consequences.

(a) It provides an easier mechanism for the case to be sent to a Special Criminal Court for trial.

(b) It permits a member of the Gardaí to arrest and detain a person for the offence under the provisions of s 30 of the Offences Against the State Act 1939.

The scheduled offences are those listed in SI 142/72 and SI 282/72 and the offences created by the Offences Against the State (Amendment) Act 1998.

12.7.2.2 Procedure to bring accused before the Special Criminal Court

Sections 45–8 of the 1939 Act set out the procedures by which an accused may be brought before a Special Criminal Court. The provisions are complicated and a distinction is drawn between offences which are scheduled and non-scheduled. It is proposed to concentrate on the more usual methods used.

(a) Section 47 procedure: This is the most common method to bring an accused directly to a sitting of a Special Criminal Court, usually at the end of a 's 30 detention' so that the court may charge the person. The s 47 procedure is invoked:

- if the DPP directs that in lieu of being brought before the District Court, it is proper to bring the accused before a Special Criminal Court for the purpose of being charged;

- if the offence to be charged is not a scheduled offence;

- if the Director must in addition certify in writing that, in his opinion, 'the ordinary courts are inadequate to secure the effective administration of justice and the preservation of public peace and order' in relation to the trial of such person for such offence;

- if the court has power to issue a warrant to secure the attendance of an accused before the court (s 47(3));

- if it should be noted that, unlike the procedure in the District Court, an accused is not charged by a member of the Gardaí before his appearance under s 47 at a sitting of a Special Criminal Court, although he will be handed a copy of the charge sheet. The formal charging takes place in the court after evidence of arrest has been given.

When a person is charged directly in a Special Criminal Court, the matter will be remanded for service of the book of evidence and then for trial.

(b) Sections 45(2) and 46(2) of the 1939 Act govern the second most common method to secure the attendance of an accused at a sitting of a Special Criminal Court, which is for an accused to be returned for a trial to a sitting of a Special Criminal Court by the District Court after the service of the book of evidence.

- Section 45(2) states that if the offence is a scheduled offence, the accused must be returned for trial a Special Criminal Court unless the Director directs otherwise. In other words, it requires the positive intervention of the Director to ensure that an accused charged with a scheduled offence is returned for trial to the ordinary courts. This is of some practical significance because of the range of scheduled offences. For example, all offences under the Firearms Acts are scheduled offences and the vast majority of such cases are suitable for trial by jury.

- Section 46(2), on the other hand, states that if the offence is a non-scheduled offence, the District Court may return for trial to a Special Criminal Court only if the Director applies for such return and certifies in writing as to the inadequacy of the ordinary courts.

When the District Court has sent a person for trial after service of the book, the case will be remanded for trial.

(c) Section 48 permits the DPP by way of *ex parte* application to the High Court to transfer a case that has been properly returned for trial to the ordinary courts to a Special Criminal Court.

- No distinction is drawn in the section between scheduled and non-scheduled offences and the application must in all cases be grounded on the certificate of the Director as to the inadequacy of the ordinary courts.

(d) Finally, purely summary offences which are before the District Court may be sent to a Special Criminal Court under ss 45(1) and 46(1). These provisions are rarely invoked.

- A distinction is drawn between scheduled and non-scheduled offences:
  — in the former category the accused is sent for trial at the request of the Director; whereas
  — in the latter category the Director must in addition certify in writing as to the inadequacy of the ordinary courts.

In all cases where an accused is brought before a Special Criminal Court, an indictment will be drafted and filed in the ordinary way (reg 10 of the Special Criminal Court Rules 1975 (SI 234/75).

12.7.3 LEGAL CHALLENGE

It will be seen from the above that the decision as to whether a person is tried before the ordinary courts or a Special Criminal Court is one for the Director of Public Prosecutions. There have been many legal challenges to decisions of the Director to refer particular cases to a Special Criminal Court. These include:

(a) Is the Director obliged to explain why a particular case has been referred to a Special Criminal Court?

(b) In considering whether to refer a case to a Special Criminal Court, is he confined to an examination of whether the case has a subversive element or can he refer cases with alleged organized crime involvement?

(c) To what extent are the courts entitled to review the decisions of the Director to refer cases to a Special Criminal Court?

In a long line of cases, the courts have confirmed that cases with no obvious subversive element can properly be referred to a Special Criminal Court. The courts have also ruled that the decision of the Director to refer a case to a Special Criminal Court will not be reviewed by the courts unless there is evidence that the decision was arrived at *mala fides* or by the application of an improper policy (*Kavanagh v Government of Ireland* [1996] 1 IR 321) and the relevant case law cited in that decision.

The plaintiff in the latter case subsequently complained to the UN Human Rights Committee that the procedures used in referring his case for trial to a Special Criminal Court violated his rights under the International Covenant on Civil and Political Rights. The UN Committee upheld his complaint on 4 April 2001. The Committee in its view on the case laid emphasis on the fact that reasons for a case being referred to a Special Criminal Court are not given and the decision to refer is reviewable by the courts only in the most exceptional of cases. It remains to be seen what legislative proposals the government will bring forward in the light of the views of the UN Committee.

12.7.4   PROCEDURES

Notwithstanding the use of the term 'special', the court operates in almost all respects as an ordinary court. Those provisions which mark it as very different from the ordinary courts, such as the appointment of officers of the defence forces as judges, have fallen into disuse. In relation to indictable cases, the principal difference is of course that the judges and not a jury decide the question of guilt or innocence. However, the practice and procedure and rules of evidence applicable to the trial of a person on indictment in the Central Criminal Court apply to every trial by a Special Criminal Court as delineated in s 41(4) of the 1939 Act.

The People (DPP) v Yates SC 12/11/1975 (unreported) decided that the rule that permitted a jury to bring in a verdict of guilty to a different charge than that alleged on the indictment could not be applied to a Special Criminal Court as the authority to bring in any such verdict went beyond matters of practice and procedure. This lacuna was filled by the Criminal Justice (Verdicts) Act 1976, which had the effect of placing a non-jury court in the same position as a jury court, in terms of the verdicts that it could reach.

12.7.5   DECISION

The court decides every question before it, including its final verdict, by majority decision as delineated in s 40(1) of the 1939 Act. Under regulation 6(2) of the Special Criminal Court Rules, the presiding member pronounces the decision.

No member or officer of the court may disclose whether a decision was arrived at unanimously or by majority verdict. Where the decision was not unanimous, the opinion of any individual member may not be disclosed. In relation to interim decisions of the court or its final verdict, it is the practice of the court to give a written decision setting out the reasoning of the court. Accordingly, where the court convicts an accused it will deliver a detailed decision as to how it reached its verdict. This contrasts with trial by jury where the jury gives a simple verdict of guilty or not guilty.

The Special Criminal Court has the same sentencing powers as any court trying a case on indictment. A person sentenced or remanded in custody by the court will be detained in Portlaoise Prison, as that is the designated prison for the court.

Section 44(1) of the 1939 Act empowers a person convicted by a Special Criminal Court to exercise the same right of appeal to the Court of Criminal Appeal as a person convicted in the Central Criminal Court or the Circuit Criminal Court.

CHAPTER 13

JUVENILES IN THE CRIMINAL PROCESS

13.1 Introduction

Previous chapters have outlined the procedures for dealing with adult suspects and adult offenders (persons aged 18 or over) in the criminal process. This chapter reviews the law and procedures relating to offenders aged 17 and younger.

It may come as a surprise to many to realize that up until recently the primary legislation governing juvenile justice in Ireland was the Children Act 1908. There had been a number of minor amendments to the Act during the last century but the main body of the Act remained unchanged and juvenile justice in Ireland has been governed primarily by legislation enacted over 90 years ago.

On 8 July 2001 the Children Act 2001, a piece of legislation containing some 271 sections, was signed into law. The repeal section provided for the repeal of the whole of the 1908 Act. However, it was not until April 2002 that the Minister for Justice signed a commencement order implementing certain provisions of the new act from 1 May and allowing for the repeal of certain sections of the old act. Currently the law relating to young people is to be found by holding the 1908 Children Act in one hand, the 2001 Children Act in the other hand and balancing the Children Act Commencement Orders of 2002 (*SI 151 of 2002*), 2003 (*SI 527 of 2003*) and 2004 (*SI 468, SI 548, and SI 549 of 2004*) in between those Acts. This balancing has now been added to by the introduction of in excess of 50 new sections into the Criminal Justice Act 2006. A perusal of them will be uploaded onto the OUP website which supports this text.

13.2 Criminal responsibility

The age of criminal responsibility in Ireland is seven. Section 4(5) of the Summary Jurisdiction over Children (Ireland) Act 1884 declared that a child under seven is not of sufficient capacity to commit a crime. A child under seven is deemed *doli incapax* (incapable of crime).

Between the ages of seven and 14 a child was presumed to be incapable of crime. In order for a successful prosecution of a child to be effected this presumption of *doli incapax* must be rebutted in court.

> A child.... cannot be convicted unless it is proved not only that the child did the act in circumstances which would involve an adult in criminal liability but also that he knew that he was doing wrong. That knowledge is not to be presumed from the mere fact of the commission of the act, but must be proved by the circumstances attending the act, the manner in which it was done, and evidence as to the nature and disposition of the child concerned, e.g. by evidence of design, concealment, or exceptional ferocity (Halsbury (4th edn) vol 11).

Rebutting the presumption is a matter for the prosecution. See *Monagle v Donegal County Council* (HC) (1961), Ir Jur Rep 37.

However, this position is now altered by s 52 of the Children Act 2001 as amended by s 129 of the Criminal Justice Act 2006. A practitioner representing a client in this age group formerly had to be satisfied that the prosecution had in fact rebutted the presumption of *doli incapax* before a conviction could be recorded. Section 52(3) of the Children Act (as amended) has abolished the presumption. The fact that a client is not yet 15 is a major factor to take into consideration.

As outlined above, the age of criminal responsibility in this jurisdiction remains seven years under the Children Act 1908. Statutory provision to alter this age limitation is proposed at s 52 of the Children Act 2001. The proposals include the presumption of the doctrine of *doli incapax* for those under 14 years and also the raising of the age of criminal responsibility to 12 years.

> 52.—(1) Subject to subsection (2), a child under 12 years of age shall not be charged with an offence.
> (2) Subsection (1) does not apply to a child aged 10 or 11 years who is charged with murder, manslaughter, rape, rape under section 4 of the Criminal Law (Rape) (Amendment) Act 1990 or aggravated sexual assault.
> (3) The rebuttable presumption under any rule of law, namely, that a child who is not less than 7 but under 14 years of age is incapable of committing an offence because the child did not have the capacity to know that the act or omission concerned was wrong, is abolished.
> (4) Where a child under 14 years of age is charged with an offence, no further proceedings in the matter (other than any remand in custody or on bail) shall be taken except by or with the consent of the Director of Public Prosecutions.

The Interpretation section defines a 'child' as a person under 18 years. As a result 17 year-olds are now dealt with in the Juvenile Court and not in the adult courts as heretofore.

It is obvious, therefore, that one of the most important facts to be established by a practitioner dealing with juveniles is the age of their client. It is certainly one of the first questions that will be asked by the judge when the case is brought to court.

13.3   Arrest and detention

Children and young persons are subject to the general legislative powers of arrest and detention. They can be arrested for the purpose of being charged with a criminal offence and being brought before the court. They can also be arrested for the purposes of detention for questioning. Depending on the legislation under which they are detained they can be held for questioning in a Garda station for up to 24 hours (s 4 Criminal Justice Act 1984 (as amended) or in other instances for 48 hours (s 30 Offences Against the State Act 1939 (as amended)) or under drug trafficking legislation for up to seven days (s 2 Misuse of Drugs Act 1999 (as amended)).

Up until the implementation of Part 6 of the 2001 Children Act, the Criminal Justice Act 1984 and the regulations made under this act (SI No 119/87) contained specific provisions for the detention in Garda stations of persons under the age 17. These provisions related to the right of access to a solicitor, the right to have a parent or other responsible adult notified and present during questioning, and to the treatment of young persons in custody in a Garda station. Part 6 of the new Act is headed *Treatment of Child Suspects in Garda Siochana Stations* and contains the above provisions. The first section of Part 6 sets out the general obligations of the Garda Síochána in relation to the treatment of juveniles in Garda stations:

> *Section 55 states: In any investigation relating to the commission or possible commission of an offence by children, members of the Garda Síochána shall act with due respect for the personal rights of the children and their dignity as human persons, for their vulnerability owing to their age and level of maturity and for the special needs of any of them who may be under a physical or mental disability, while complying with the*

obligation to prevent escapes from custody and continuing to act with diligence and determination in the investigation of crime and the protection and vindication of the personal rights of other persons.

This part of the Act obliges the member in charge of the Garda Síochána station:

(i)   To keep detained children in cells separate from adults being detained.

(ii) To notify the child of reason for arrest.

(iii) To notify parent/guardian and to request their attendance at the station.

(iv) To ensure that no questioning is commenced or statement taken in absence of parent/guardian.

In the absence of parent/guardian the member in charge may nominate 'another adult'. A solicitor should enquire from the client as to the role played by the 'nominated adult' in relation to the interview.

Practitioners attending a minor at a Garda station often may find that proffered professional advice is in direct conflict with the advice of a parent. It is important to take full instructions where a child has made a cautioned statement in relation to this aspect of the detention. Sections 53, 59, and 76 have been amended by ss 130–134 of the Criminal Justice Act 2006.

Following a detention period, if a juvenile is then charged, he or she may be released on bail to appear in the Children's Court on a specified date. Alternatively, they are taken in custody to the Children's Court where the presiding judge will decide the issue of bail, having heard the Garda objections during the bail application (see Parts 7, 8, and 9 of the Children Act 2001, as amended).

Prior to the implementation of Part 4 of the 2001 Act a non-statutory scheme existed, known as the JLO (Junior Liaison Officer) scheme. The Gardaí, rather than charging a child or young person who had admitted a minor offence, sought to divert the person from entering the criminal justice system by administering a series of cautions.

Part 4 of the Act introduces a Diversion Programme:

> Section 19: (1) *The objective of the Programme is to divert from committing further offences any child who accepts responsibility for his or her criminal behaviour.*
> (2) *The objective shall be achieved primarily by administering a caution to such child and, where appropriate, by placing him or her under the supervision of a juvenile liaison officer and by convening a conference to be attended by the child, family members and other concerned persons.*

This effectively places the former JLO system on a statutory basis. Section 19 has been amended by s 124 of the Criminal Justice Act 2006.

Where a first-time offender appears in court on a minor charge a practitioner should always be mindful of the possibility of the suitability of the Diversion Programme scheme for such an offender. If, having taken instructions, it would appear that the client would be suitable for the programme the practitioner should raise the issue with the prosecuting Garda or make an application to the judge to have the matter remanded for consideration by the Diversion Programme.

13.4   Children Court

The 1908 Act provided for the setting up of a separate court to deal with criminal cases involving young persons aged 16 years and under. The Courts of Justice Act 1924 provided for a special weekly sitting of the District Court in the cities of Cork, Limerick, and Waterford entitled 'the Children Court'. In Dublin the Children Court, situated in Smithfield, is known as the 'Metropolitan Children Court' and sits on a full-time basis.

Despite the fact that this building won an architectural award for its design the facilities for family members who accompany a juvenile are almost non-existent. Detained juveniles can spend hours locked in the sparse cells, at one time painted black, while waiting for their cases to be called. Part 7 of the 2001 Act entitled 'Children Court' makes little change except that the court shall deal with 17 year-olds. Section 111 of the 1908 Act as amended by s 26 of the Children Act 1941 provided for separate sittings of the District Court when hearing cases involving young persons and for separation of young persons from adults pending the disposal of the matters in court. It further specified that only officers of the court, parties directly concerned with the case and *bona fide* press representatives are allowed to attend at proceedings in the Children Court. The District Court, which deals with adults, permits the administration of proceedings in public.

Section 71 states:

> The District Court, when hearing charges against children or when hearing applications for orders relating to a child at which the attendance of the child is required . . . shall be known as the Children Court.

There are restrictions on the reporting of proceedings in the Children Court in that nothing shall be published which is likely to lead to the identification of a child concerned in the proceedings (s 93 of the 2001 Act as amended by s 139 Criminal Justice Act 2006).

The jurisdiction of the Children Court extends to all criminal offences except manslaughter or an offence which must be tried by the Central Criminal Court (s 75 of the 2001 Act). A young person, however, may be dealt with in relation to indictable offences in the adult system of jury trial in three situations:

(a)   where a young person elects for trial by jury;

(b)   where the Director of Public Prosecutions so directs; and

(c)   Where the Judge of the Children Court so directs having heard an outline of the alleged facts of an offence.

13.5   Sentencing

The Children Act 1908 is still the primary legislation governing the sentencing of juveniles. Part 5 of the 1908 Act contains the options open to the court following conviction.

Non-custodial options include:

(a)   Charge being dismissed.

(b)   Imposition of a fine or payment of damages.

(c)   Period of supervision by the Probation Service.

Custodial options open to the court are specifically age-related and allow for an order:

(a)   Sending an offender to an Industrial or Reformatory School.

(b)   Of detention in a place of detention.

(c)   Of imprisonment where a court has certified that an offender is 'of so unruly a character that he cannot be detained in a place of detention . . . or that he is so depraved of character that he is not a fit person to be so detained' (s 102(3)). In *The State (Holland) v Kennedy* [1977] IR 193 the Supreme Court set out guidelines for the process of certification.

JUVENILES IN THE CRIMINAL PROCESS

Industrial Schools (Residential Schools)

St Joseph's School in Clonmel and Finglas Child and Adolescent Centre Dublin are the two main certified Industrial Schools. The emphasis is on education, care, and rehabilitation as opposed to punishment. These schools cater for boys under the age of 15 years. No Industrial Schools exist for girls though Oberstown Girl's Centre has some places certified for such use. While the statutory title remains Industrial Schools, they are now referred to as Residential Schools.

Reformatory Schools (Special Schools)

The emphasis here is also on education rather than punishment. There are three certified Reformatory Schools at the moment:

1. Oberstown Boys Centre Lusk.

2. Oberstown Girls Centre Lusk.

3. Trinity House Lusk. As well as being a Reformatory School this is also a designated place of detention under the Act. It is a secure unit where children are locked in their rooms at nighttimes and access in and out of Trinity House is securely monitored. It caters for boys between the ages of nine and 17. This is for offenders charged or remanded in relation to the more serious offences of rape, murder, and manslaughter or those unsuitable for a more open regime. While the statutory title remains Reformatory Schools, they are now referred to as Special Schools.

St Patrick's Institution attached to Mountjoy Prison is a certified place of detention for boys from the ages of 16 upwards. While it is more similar in its regime to Mountjoy Prison than it is to Reformatory or Industrial Schools, its aim is to assist in rehabilitation of offenders through education and training.

The 2001 Children Act at Part 9 sets out the powers of the court at sentencing stage. Section 96 of the Act as amended by s 136 Criminal Justice Act 2006 sets out the principles relating to the exercise of criminal jurisdiction over children. It declares a preference for utilizing non-custodial sanctions rather than custodial sanctions:

> ... any penalty imposed on a child for an offence should cause as little interference as possible with the child's legitimate activities and pursuits, should take the form most likely to maintain and promote the development of the child and should take the least restrictive form that is appropriate in the circumstances; in particular, a period of detention should be imposed only as a measure of last resort.

Section 115 of the 2001 Act sets out ten non-custodial options available to the court and the community-based options listed have greatly increased the options available to the court. However, only the subsection allowing the court to make a restriction on movement order has been implemented. Further discussion on sentencing of juveniles may be accessed in Professor Dermot Walsh's book entitled *Juvenile Justice* (Thompson Roundhall, Dublin 2005)—Chapters 7 and 8.

Part 8 of the Act as amended enables a court to make an order directing the Probation Service to convene a family conference, in order to formulate an action plan for a child who has admitted responsibility for his or her criminal behaviour where the child and the child's parent, guardian, or family member agree to participate in such conference. This is the first time that we see legislation providing for family participation in seeking a solution to a juvenile involved in the criminal justice system.

Another of the most significant sections of the Children Act 2001 is s 258, which provides for the removal of a record of conviction after a three-year period has elapsed, where a person under 18 years was convicted of an offence and has not re-offended during that period. This section does not apply to offences which must be tried by the Central Criminal Court.

156

The full implementation and proper resourcing of the Children Act 2001 as amended has the potential to dramatically advance the state of juvenile justice in Ireland. It declares a preference for utilizing non-custodial sanctions rather than custodial sanctions and offers the courts a range of community-based options. It has established a Diversion Programme thus placing the Garda Juvenile Liaison Scheme on a statutory basis. New features of this programme include restorative cautioning and case conferences. Provision has been made for Family Welfare Conferences, which may be convened at the direction of the Children's Court. Family involvement in this manner represents a radical departure from the previous norm in juvenile justice practice.

Children's Detention Schools (Part 10 of the Children Act 2001 (as amended)) are to replace Industrial and Reformatory schools and are to be used as a place of last resort by the courts. The 2001 Act also includes a provision whereby a person does not have to disclose a conviction recorded against him or her as a child in certain circumstances.

The enormous number of amendments in the CJA 2006, particularly with regard to Anti-Social Behaviour Orders, increases the complexity of this sensitive area of practice.

CHAPTER 14

SENTENCING

14.1   Proportionality in sentencing

It is a long-established common law principle that punishment must be proportionate to the gravity of the offence. In *People (AG) v O'Driscoll* (1972) 1 Frewen 351 at p 359, Walsh J stated:

> 'The objects of passing sentence are not merely to deter the particular criminal from committing a crime again, but to induce him in so far as possible to turn from a criminal to an honest life and indeed the public interest would best be served if the criminal could be induced to take the latter course. It is therefore the duty of the courts to pass what are the appropriate sentences in each case having regard to the particular circumstances of that case—not only in regard to the particular crime but in regard to the particular criminal.'

It is clear from this passage that there are two aspects to the principle—the sentence must be proportionate both to the culpability of the offender and to any relevant personal circumstances. That the principle of proportionality has the status of a constitutional principle may be gleaned from the Supreme Court decision of *State (Healy) v Donoghue* [1976] IR 325. Speaking in the context of a constitutional guarantee to due process, personal rights and the right to personal liberty, Henchy J stated at p 353 that these rights imply 'a guarantee that a citizen . . . where guilt has been established or admitted, of receiving a sentence appropriate to his degree of guilt and his relevant personal circumstances'.

In *People v WC* [1994] 1 ILRM 321 at p 325, Flood J clearly identified the principle of proportionality as being based on a constitutional principle:

> 'In my view the selection of the particular punishment to be imposed on an individual offender is subject to the constitutional principle of proportionality. By this I mean that the imposition of a particular sentence must strike a balance between the particular circumstances of the commission of the relevant offence and the relevant personal circumstances of the person sentenced.'

In *People v M* [1994] 3 IR 306 at p 316, per Denham J, reference was made by the Supreme Court to proportionality being a 'constitutional protection'.

14.2   The plea in mitigation

Before passing sentence, the solicitor for the defendant (or counsel in a trial on indictment) will make a plea in mitigation of sentence, so as to cast the defendant in the most favourable light possible to the court. Such a plea will point to the circumstances of the defendant and the circumstances in which the offence was committed. Other factors useful to a plea of mitigation may be: the age of the defendant; their family circumstances and the effect which a custodial sentence will have on the defendant's family; any addiction problems; efforts at rehabilitation since the commission of the offence; remorse shown; reparation to the victim; cooperation with the police; and, where applicable, a plea of guilty. However, even serious illness may not prove sufficient to satisfy the court that leniency is justified. For example, in *People (DPP) v Connington* (unreported) 17 December 1990, CCA, the fact that the applicant suffered from AIDS was not a ground on which the Court of Criminal Appeal was prepared to reduce an eight-year sentence for robbery offences.

It would appear from the following statement by Egan J in *People v M* [1994] 3 IR 306; [1994] 2 ILRM 541, at p 315 that mitigating circumstances should be considered after the trial judge has given consideration to the possible sentence which should be imposed having regard to the gravity of the offence:

> '. . . a reduction in mitigation is not always to be calculated in direct regard to the maximum sentence applicable. One should look first to the range of penalties applicable to the offence and then decide whereabouts on the range the particular case should lie. The mitigating circumstances should then be looked at and an appropriate reduction made.'

In the same case at p 317, Denham J considered that while the impact of a crime on the victim is a factor to be considered in sentencing, the nature of the offence and the offender's personal circumstances are the key factors: '. . . having assessed what is the appropriate sentence for a particular crime it is the duty of the court to consider then the particular circumstances of the convicted person. It is within this ambit that mitigating factors fall to be considered.'

For a comprehensive list of mitigating factors which might arise, see the Law Reform Commission Report on Sentencing 1996.

The judge will seek to discover whether there are aggravating factors which need to be taken into consideration. These include: whether the offence was committed in circumstances of violence; whether the offence involved damage; the circumstances of the victim; whether a relationship which encompassed trust in or authority of the offender was present when the offence was committed; where there are a number of offenders to the offence, the prominence of the role played by the defendant.

The judge will also look for evidence of previous convictions. In *State (Stanbridge) v Mahon* [1979] IR 214, Gannon J cited Hewart LCJ in *R v Turner* (1924) 18 Cr App R 161 in the following statement: 'it cannot be too clearly understood that, where previous convictions are relied on for any purpose in a trial, they must either (a) be proved by lawful evidence, or (b) be expressly admitted by the accused person.' A member of the Garda Síochána reading from a police record usually presents evidence of previous convictions. If the defendant disputes any previous conviction, proper evidence, for example production of a court order, will be required. In certain cases, for example, offences under the Misuse of Drugs Act, a previous conviction for the same type of offence will result in a higher maximum penalty than that where an offender commits the offence for the first time.

Some comprehensive amendments to sentencing jurisdiction and powers have been introduced by the Criminal Justice Act 2006, most particularly at Part 10 (ss 98–112) of that Act.

14.3   Reports furnished to court

14.3.1   PROBATION REPORT

Prior to imposing sentence, it is usual for the court to adjourn sentencing so as to allow time for the probation and welfare service to prepare a report on the offender. The purpose of this report, known as a social inquiry report, is to present to the court a fuller picture of the offender including his social, educational, and family circumstances. It will also include an indication of the offender's attitude to crime and the prospects of rehabilitation of the offender in the community. In addition to this report, other reports may be made available to the court such as medical and psychiatric reports. Any report which is made available to the court must be made available to both defence and prosecution counsel (*People v McGinley* (1989) 3 Frewen 251).

14.3.2 VICTIM IMPACT REPORT

The Criminal Justice Act 1993 provides that evidence of the effect of the crime on the victim shall be taken into account in determining sentence where the offence relates to a sexual offence or involves personal violence or the threat of violence. The evidence may be given by way of a victim impact report, and submissions may be made to the court where necessary. The Act also gives the victim the right to have evidence of the effect of the crime heard by the court. Section 5 provides:

> (1) *In determining the sentence to be imposed on a person for an offence to which this section applies, a court shall take into account, and may, where necessary, receive evidence or submissions concerning, any effect (whether long-term or otherwise) of the offence on the person in respect of whom the offence was committed.*
>
> (2) *This section applies to:*
>   (a) *a sexual offence within the meaning of the Criminal Evidence Act 1992,*
>   (b) *an offence involving violence or the threat of violence to a person, and*
>   (c) *an offence consisting of attempting or conspiring to commit, or aiding, abetting, counselling, procuring or inciting the commission of, an offence mentioned in paragraph (a) or (b).*
>
> (3) *Where a court is determining the sentence to be imposed on a person for an offence to which this section applies, the court shall, upon application by the person in respect of whom such offence was committed, hear the evidence of the person in respect of whom the offence was committed as to the effect of the offence on such person upon being requested to do so.*

In *People v MC* (see O'Malley, *Sentencing Law and Practice*, Round Hall S & M (2000 p 357), Flood J said that the right conferred by s 5 must include the right to give evidence with the assistance of a solicitor or barrister by way of evidence-in-chief for the purpose of s 5, that the prosecution and defence have the right to cross-examine the victim on the evidence given, and that in the context of s 5, the victim is not a prosecution witness. The victim's legal representatives (or the unrepresented victim) may not make submissions as to the sentence which they consider ought to be imposed by the court.

In the *People v M* [1994] 3 IR 306, Blaney and Denham JJ pointed out that the general impact of a crime on a victim is a factor in sentencing, but the nature of the offence and the offender's personal circumstances are the key issues, as criminal law is an action between the State and the offender, rather than between the offender and the victim.

14.4 Maximum sentence

Section 29 of the Criminal Justice Act 1999 provides that a guilty plea does not preclude the imposition of a maximum sentence if the court is satisfied that exceptional circumstances relating to the offence so warrant. This provision clarifies the law which, since the Supreme Court decision in *People v G* [1994] 1 IR 587, had suggested that the imposition of the maximum sentence 'in a case where the trial judge unequivocally accepted the importance and genuineness of the admissions and plea of guilty (which could not be described as inevitable)' was an error of principle. In a number of cases subsequent to *G*, the early guilty plea was considered to preclude imposition of the maximum sentence. (See, eg, *People v D* 27 April 1995; *People v Duff* [1995] 3 IR 296; *People v Bambrick (Michael)* [1996] 1 IR 265; *People v FB* 24 January 1997 (see 1997 Annual Review of Irish Law 331).)

14.5   Minimum sentence

The Criminal Justice Act 1990, which abolished the death penalty, substituting life imprisonment in its place, provides that in the case of treason, murder, or attempts to murder persons to whom s 3 of that Act relates, ie members of the Garda Síochána, prison officers, head of a foreign State, members of government and diplomatic officers of a foreign State, or murder done in the course of an offence under s 6 of the Offences Against the State Act 1939, the minimum period of imprisonment to be served must be specified when passing sentence. In the case of treason or murder, the minimum period to be served is 40 years, and in the case of attempts to murder, the minimum period of imprisonment is 20 years, with a minimum period to be served also set at 20 years. Section 5 of the Criminal Justice Act 1999, which amends s 27 of the Misuse of Drugs Act 1977, provides that where a person is convicted of an offence under s 15A of the Misuse of Drugs Act 1977 (as amended), ie possession of drugs for the purpose of sale or supply, where the market value of the drugs amounts to £10,000 (or its euro equivalent) or more, 'the court shall, in imposing sentence, specify as the minimum period of imprisonment to be served by that person a period of not less than 10 years imprisonment' (see the Euro Changeover (Amounts) Act 2001 for amounts in euro). The court, however, has discretion where it is satisfied that there are 'exceptional and specific circumstances relating to the offence, or the person convicted of the offence, which would make a sentence of not less than 10 years unjust in all the circumstances'. Factors which may be considered by the court in the exercise of such discretion include: whether a person has pleaded guilty; the stage at which and the circumstances in which an indication to plead guilty was given; whether the person materially assisted in the investigation of the offence. In determining the sentence to be imposed the court may have regard to the minimum sentence in so far as it serves to underscore the gravity of the offence and so acts as an aid in determining the appropriate punishment: *People (DPP) v Renald* (unreported) CCA 23 Nov 2001.

14.6   Concurrent and consecutive sentences

In most cases judges have discretion as to whether to make a sentence concurrent or consecutive. Two general principles should inform the judge in the exercise of this discretion: (1) concurrent sentences should ordinarily be imposed when the offences arise from the same incident, referred to as the 'one transaction rule'; (2) when consecutive sentences are imposed, the totality of the resulting punishment should be adjusted to reflect the overall gravity of the offending behaviour. Cases may arise where the defendant is already serving a sentence for a separate offence; the judge still has discretion to impose a sentence to run concurrently, but it would appear that the Court of Criminal Appeal approves of consecutive sentences in such cases (see T O'Malley, *Sentencing Law and Practice* (Dublin: Round Hall S&M, 2000) pp 171 et seq).

Section 11 of the Criminal Justice Act 1984 provides that where an offence is committed while on bail, the trial judge has no discretion and must impose a sentence 'consecutive on any sentence passed on him for a previous offence, or, if he is sentenced in respect of two or more previous offences, on the sentence last due to expire'. The section further provides that where two or more consecutive sentences are passed in the District Court, the aggregate term of imprisonment in respect of those consecutive sentences shall not exceed two years. It would appear that s 11 does not preclude the courts from suspending a consecutive sentence: *People (DPP) v Dennigan* (1989) 3 Frewen 253. Where a consecutive sentence is imposed, the court must clearly indicate the date on which such sentence is to begin. Section 106 of the Criminal Justice Act 2006 amends s 5 of the Criminal Justice Act 1951, where one of the sentences running consecutively is a restriction on movement order.

14.7 Guilty pleas

It is common practice for a trial judge to pass a lesser sentence where a defendant pleads guilty to the offence with which he is charged. A plea of guilty indicates to the court that the offender accepts responsibility for his crime, may be indicative of remorse, saves the State the cost of a trial and, if indicated at the investigative stage, police resources. Furthermore, the guilty plea means that the victim of the offence will not be required to give evidence at trial. The degree to which a guilty plea will affect the measure of sentence will depend on the stage at which it is made. It may happen that an accused person will plead not guilty to an indictable offence at the preliminary stages in the District Court, and then plead guilty at arraignment in the trial court. Furthermore, it may happen that a trial will commence on a plea of not guilty but at some point into the trial the accused may change his plea to guilty, for example if an application to have evidence ruled inadmissible proved unsuccessful. In these situations, the accused should not expect such a substantial reduction in sentence as a consequence of the guilty plea as might be expected where the guilty plea is indicated at the investigative or District Court stages. A person who has pleaded guilty is not precluded from changing that plea to one of not guilty at any stage 'before the case is finally disposed of by sentence or otherwise': *Byrne v McDonnell* [1997] 1 IR 392 at 402. Section 29 of the Criminal Justice Act 1999 provides that in determining what sentence to pass, a court 'if it considers it appropriate to do so' shall take into account the stage in the proceedings at which the indication of a guilty plea was given and the circumstances in which such indication was given. The Act at s 29(2) clearly states that even where a guilty plea is given, the court will not be precluded from passing the maximum sentence prescribed for the offence where the court is satisfied that 'there are exceptional circumstances relating to the offence which warrant the maximum sentences'.

14.8 Forms of sentencing

14.8.1 PROBATION

Section 1(1) of the Probation of Offenders Act 1907 provides that a judge may dispose of a summary offence through the application of the Act. The section provides:

> *Where any person is charged before a Court of summary jurisdiction with an offence punishable by such Court, and the Court thinks that the charge is proved, but is of opinion that, having regard to the character, antecedents, age, health, or mental condition of the person charged, or to the trivial nature of the offence, or to the extenuating circumstances under which the offence was committed, it is inexpedient to inflict any punishment or any other than a nominal punishment, or that it is expedient to release the offender on probation, the Court may, without proceeding to conviction, make an order either:*
>
> *(i) Dismissing the information or charge; or*
>
> *(ii) Discharging the offender conditionally on his entering into a recognisance, with or without sureties, to be of good behaviour and to appear for conviction and sentence when called on at any time during such period, not exceeding three years, as may be specified in the order.*

The Act may be applied where the court is satisfied that any one of three alternative justifications warrant the application of the Act: (1) the character, antecedents, age, health, or mental condition of the person charged; (2) the trivial nature of the offence; (3) the extenuating circumstances under which the offence was committed (*McClelland v Brady* [1918] 2 IR 63). The court, however, must be satisfied that the charge has been proved, so a dismissal under s 1(1) does not amount to a dismissal on the merits. Because the court may apply the Act 'before proceeding to conviction', it follows that no conviction is recorded against the defendant (for a discussion of this point see M Wasik,

'Discharge Provisions and the Restricted Meaning of "Conviction" ' (1997) 13 LQR 637). Nonetheless, where the defendant is convicted at a later stage of another offence, the fact that the Probation Act was previously applied may be given in evidence of character and antecedents at the sentencing stage for that offence. Furthermore, the Criminal Justice Act 1993 s 6(12)(b) provides that 'references to the conviction of a person include references to dealing with a person under s 1(1) of the Probation of Offenders Act 1907', thereby enabling the court to make a compensation order for the benefit of the victim.

A dismissal under s 1(1)(i) is an unconditional discharge. A discharge under s 1(1)(ii) is conditional on the offender entering into a recognisance.

It is a well-established principle that 'the Act is not to be too strictly or narrowly construed': *Dunning v Trainer* [1909] 73 JP 400. The application of the Act is not precluded where an offender has previous convictions, but conversely, it should not automatically be applied where the defendant is a first-time offender (see O'Malley, *Sentencing Law and Practice*, p 304.) Previous application of the Act does not preclude further application on the same grounds: *Venters v Freedman* [1902] 66 JP 135. There are certain offences for which the Act cannot be applied. These include drunk driving offences under the Road Traffic Act 1961 (as amended), failure to cooperate in providing specimens etc under the Road Traffic Act 1994, ss 13–15; a number of fisheries offences (Fisheries (Amendment) Act 1962, s 16, and Foyle Fisheries (Amendment) Act 1961, s 3); revenue offences and excise offences under Finance Act 1983, s 94 and Finance Act 1984, s 78 respectively and offences of aiding and abetting any of the above offences (see J Woods, *District Court Practice and Procedure in Criminal Cases*, Limerick 1994, p 406. Section 1(1) of the Probation Act may only be applied in respect of offences under the Social Welfare (Consolidation) Act 1996 where the court is satisfied that arrears or repayments have been made (Social Welfare (Consolidation) Act 1996, s 217).

The Probation Act may be applied in the case of indictable offences punishable by imprisonment under s 1(2). The criteria for the application of the Act are the same as those contained in relation to summary offences. The important difference is that the offender must have been convicted of the offence, and the offender must enter a recognisance—there is no provision for an unconditional discharge.

The recognisance (whether under s 1(1) or (2)) where the court so orders shall contain a condition that the offender be placed under the supervision of a probation officer, and conditions for securing such supervision of the offender. The order is known as the probation order (s 2(1)). The recognisance may contain additional conditions 'with respect to residence, abstention from intoxicating liquor, and any other matters, as the Court may, having regard to the particular circumstances of the case, consider necessary for preventing a repetition of the same offence or the commission of other offences': Probation of Offenders Act 1907, s 2(2), as amended by Criminal Justice Administration Act 1914, s 8(2).

The probation officer is given the following duties under s 4 of the Act:

(a)   to visit or receive reports from the person under supervision at such reasonable intervals as may be specified in the probation order or, subject thereto, as the probation officer may think fit;

(b)   to see that he observes the conditions of his recognisance;

(c)   to report to the court as to his behaviour; and

(d)   to advise, assist, and befriend him, and, when necessary, to endeavour to find him suitable employment.

Under s 5 of the Act the court may, on the application of the probation officer, vary the terms or conditions of the recognisance if it considers it expedient to do so. The court may extend or decrease the duration of the recognisance, provided any extension does not exceed three years, and it may insert additional conditions. The recognisance may be varied where the person bound by it fails to show cause why such variation should not be made. The court may also discharge the recognisance under s 5.

An order under the Act may be the subject of a judicial review (*Mulhall v O'Donnell* [1989] ILRM 367) and may be appealed from the District Court to the Circuit Court despite the absence of a formal conviction (Courts of Justice Act 1953, s 33).

14.8.2 BINDOVER

The power to bind an offender to the peace is contained in the Courts (Supplemental Provisions) Act 1961, s 54, which provides that the power to bind a person to the peace or to good behaviour or both and to enter into a recognisance may be exercised by a judge of the Supreme Court, High Court, Circuit Court, and District Court. The power may be used on conviction of the defendant in addition to any other punishment imposed (*ex parte Harken* [1889] 24 LRI 427), and it may also be used in relation to a defendant whose case has been dismissed on the merits (*ex parte Davis* [1871] 35 JP 551). The Criminal Law Act 1997, s 10(4) provides that the power to bind the offender over to keep the peace or to be of good behaviour may be exercised without sentencing the offender to a fine or to imprisonment. Under the Courts of Justice Act 1928, s 18(1), the Circuit Court may release a person from an order made by the District Court binding a person to the peace. The person who has been bound over may apply to the Circuit Court to be released from the obligations and the recognisance imposed by the order within one month of order being made, having given seven days' notice to the officer in charge of the district in which the person resides. The Circuit Court may release the person bound from the obligations and recognisance or modify some or all of the obligations with or without conditions, and may require the person to enter into a new recognisance in the District Court.

14.8.3 COMMUNITY SERVICE ORDERS

The Criminal Justice (Community Service) Act 1983 provides for the making of community service orders in respect of persons aged over 16 years who have been convicted of an offence for which the appropriate sentence would be one of imprisonment or detention. Community service orders may not be made in respect of offences for which the sentence is fixed by law. The order shall require an offender to perform unpaid work for a period of not less than 40 hours and not more than 240 hours.

The court may make community service orders in respect of two or more offences, either concurrent or consecutive, or may make an order where the offender is already subject to an existing order, again either concurrent or consecutive, but in both instances the total number of hours may not exceed 240 (s 5).

The making of a community service order does not preclude the court from making other orders relating to revocation of any licence, the imposition of any disqualification or endorsement, orders of forfeiture, confiscation, seizure, restitution or disposal of any property or the payment of compensation, costs, or expenses (s 3).

The court may make a community service order only where it is satisfied that the offender is a suitable person to perform such work and that arrangements can be made for its performance by the offender. This assessment will be made on the basis of a report from a probation officer. The court must also obtain the consent of the offender before making the order, and must explain the effect of the order and the requirements under s 7(1) of reporting to a probation officer periodically and of performing satisfactorily the number of hours specified in the order. The offender is also required to notify the probation officer of a change of address (s 4).

The work must be performed within one year (s 7(2)), but this period may be extended on application to the court by the offender or the probation officer where it appears to the court that *'it would be in the interests of justice, having regard to the circumstances which have arisen since the order was made'* to extend that period (s 9). The work should not interfere, *'as far as practicable'*, with the offender's normal working or educational periods (s 7(3)).

Failure to comply with the requirements of s 7(1) is an offence punishable by a maximum fine of £300 (its euro equivalent), without prejudice to the continuance in force of the order (s 7(4)). Where such an offence is committed, the court may, in lieu of imposing a fine, revoke the order, or revoke the order and deal with the offender *'for the offence in respect of which the order was made in any manner in which he could have been dealt with for that offence if the order had not been made'* (s 8). Where the offender is convicted of a breach of s 7(1) by a District Court other than that which originally imposed the order, the offender may be remanded to appear before the court which originally imposed the order, which may deal with the offender in the same manner as set out in s 8(1)(a).

Where an offender proposes to change his or her residence to another District Court district or has done so, if arrangements can be made for the work to be performed in that district, the court may amend the community service order by substituting that district for the district of residence.

14.8.4   FINES

Under the District Court Rules 1997, ord 23 r 4 provides that the court shall 'take into consideration, amongst other things, the means of the accused, so far as they are known to it at the time' (see also Criminal Justice Administration Act 1914, s 43(2)). If the defendant does not object, or if he is of no fixed abode, or has sufficient means, the court may order the payment of a fine forthwith. The reason for ordering payment forthwith must be stated on the committal record if issued (see Criminal Justice Administration Act 1914, s 1(1)(4); r 6 District Court Rules 1997). The court shall order that the fine be paid within a period of not less than 14 days if there is no order to pay it forthwith.

The maximum fine, which may be imposed for a summary offence, is generally stated in the relevant statute. The maximum fine that may be imposed by the District Court is £1,000 or its euro equivalent (Criminal Justice Act 1984, s 17, as amended by the Criminal Justice Act 2006).

Section 10(3) of the Criminal Law Act 1997 provides that where a person is convicted on indictment of any offence other than any offence for which the sentence is fixed by law, the court has a general power to impose a fine. The amount of fine that may be imposed is unlimited unless a limit is imposed by statute. The fine may be in addition to or in lieu of another sanction, subject to any enactment requiring the offender to be dealt with in a particular way. The principle of proportionality is applicable, and so the fine imposed must be proportionate to the gravity of the crime and to the means of the particular offender.

A person in default of payment of a fine following summary conviction shall be imprisoned for a period not exceeding that set out in the Courts (No 2) Act 1986 and the District Court Rules 1997 as amended by s 195 of the Criminal Justice Act 2006. Where the fine imposed does not exceed £50, the maximum period of imprisonment, which may be imposed in default, is five days. For a fine exceeding £50 but not exceeding £250, the maximum period is 15 days; for a fine exceeding £250 but not exceeding £500, the maximum period is 45 days; for a fine which exceeds £500, the maximum period is 90 days: Courts (No 2) Act 1986, s 2(1) as amended by the Criminal Justice Act 2006. A fine for this purpose includes any compensation, costs or expenses in addition to a fine ordered to be paid. A summary conviction includes a conviction imposed on foot of a trial of a summary offence, and of a trial of an indictable offence tried summarily: Courts (No 2) Act 1986, s 2(4).

Section 100 of the Criminal Justice Act 2006 sets out procedures where the court makes an order for both a term of imprisonment and a fine.

14.8.5 COMPENSATION ORDERS

The Criminal Justice Act 1993 provides that a compensation order may be made by the court in respect of any person convicted of an offence instead of or in addition to dealing with him in any other way: Criminal Justice Act 1993, s 6(1). Such an order is in respect of any personal injury or loss resulting from the offence for which the offender has been convicted or any other offence that is taken into consideration by the court in determining sentence. The compensation is for the benefit of any person who has suffered such loss or injury. This differs from a fine, the latter being payable to the State. Despite the reference to a person convicted of an offence, a person who has been dealt with under s 1(1) of the Probation of Offenders Act 1907 is included in the description 'convicted person' for the purposes of the 1993 Act and a compensation order may thus be made in respect of such a person.

The compensation payable shall be of such amount as the court considers appropriate, but shall not exceed the amount of damages that, in the opinion of the court, the injured party would be entitled to recover in a civil action. If the order is made by the District Court, the amount shall not exceed the limit of that court's jurisdiction in tort, which currently stands at £5,000. In fixing the amount of compensation payable the court must have regard to any evidence and any representations that are made by or on behalf of the convicted person, the injured party or the prosecutor: Criminal Justice Act 1993, s 6(2). Where the offence related to property having been taken out of the possession of the injured party and the property has been recovered, any loss occurring to the injured party by reason of the property being damaged while out of his possession shall be treated as having resulted from the offence, irrespective of how the damage was caused or who caused it: s 6(3). A compensation order shall not be made in respect of injury or loss that results from using a vehicle in a public place unless the offender was driving the vehicle without insurance or the vehicle was taken out of the possession of the owner and damaged before recovery, irrespective of how the damage was caused or who caused it: s 6(4).

The court shall have regard to the means of the offender in determining whether to make a compensation order, or in determining the amount payable, and where the case involves payment to be made by a parent or guardian of the offender, the court shall have regard to the means of the parent or guardian: s 6(5). Evidence of means and financial commitments of the offender (or of the parent or guardian if applicable) may be sought by the court for the purpose of such determination. The order may provide for payment by instalments. Section 6(7) provides that where the court considers that it would be appropriate to impose both a fine and an order for compensation but the offender has insufficient means to pay both, then the court may make a compensation order and, if satisfied that the offender would have sufficient means after payment of such compensation, may impose a fine. The compensation order thus takes precedence over the fine.

The court which made the compensation order may, on the application of the convicted person, reduce the amount payable under the compensation order if the court is satisfied that there has been a substantial reduction in the means of the convicted person, and that the means are insufficient to satisfy the order in full. Conversely, if on the application of the injured party the court is satisfied that the means of the convicted person have substantially increased, the court may increase the amount of compensation payable, the amount of any instalment or the number of instalments, provided that the increased amount would not exceed the amount of damages that the injured party would be entitled to recover in a civil action, or the amount which is within the court's jurisdiction to impose, whichever is the lesser: s 6(8).

A compensation order may be the subject of an appeal. The operation of the compensation order must be suspended until the time for giving notice of appeal or of an application for leave to appeal has expired. Such an appeal may be in respect of the conviction, sentence or the compensation order, or in respect of all three. Where notice of appeal has been given, the operation of the compensation order must be suspended until the appeal is finally determined (this includes determination of the appeal through abandoning it). The compensation order shall not take effect if the conviction is reversed on appeal. The court hearing the appeal may annul or vary the compensation order. Where a compensation order has been made in respect of an offence taken into consideration, the order shall cease to have effect if the offender successfully appeals against the conviction of the offence or all the offences of which he was convicted.

The above forms of sentencing have been augmented by the Criminal Justice Act 2006 by the addition of restriction on movement orders (s 101) and their electronic monitoring (s 102).

14.8.6 DEFERRAL OF SENTENCE

It is a practice of the Irish courts to defer the imposition of sentence or the commencement of the sentence. Section 100 of the Criminal Justice Act 2006 outlines pertinent procedures. A deferral will often be made in order to give the offender an opportunity to undergo treatment for a drug/alcohol/aggression problem which may have been a factor in the commission of the offence; to give time to the offender to pay compensation; to see, especially in the case of a first-time offender, how the offender behaves during the deferment period. There is no limit to the length of a deferment; however, it was stated in *R v Spratling* [1911] 1 KB 77, giving recognition to the practice: 'We must not, however, be taken to decide that the Court can postpone sentence *sine die* against the will of the prisoner.'

In the case of *R v George* [1984] 1 WLR 1082, it was stated that the court should make clear to the offender the purposes for which the sentence is being deferred so that a later court will be able to assess if that purpose has been fulfilled. If the offender has 'substantially conformed or attempted to conform with the proper expectations of the deferring court, the offender may legitimately expect that an immediate custodial sentence will not be imposed' (T O'Malley, p 318). The Probation Service often combines this bind over with supervision, and progress reports may be sought periodically from the latter. The courts frequently adopt this practice (see Law Reform Commission, Report on Sentencing 1996). It is quite common for the courts to defer imposition of sentence so that reports may be obtained in relation to the offender, and for the preparation of victim impact statements. Section 100 of the Criminal Justice Act 2006 grants powers to notice parties who have received a copy of the order to have the matter re-entered before the court in circumstances where breaches of the terms of the order occur.

14.8.7 SUSPENDED SENTENCE

The practice of suspending sentences has no statutory basis but 'has long been recognized in the Courts in Ireland as a valid and proper form of sentence' *State (McIlhagga) v Governor of Portlaoise Prison* (unreported) S Ct 29 July 1971.

Where the trial judge decides to suspend a sentence, the usual practice is to impose the sentence and then to suspend its operation upon the offender entering into a recognisance, with or without sureties, to keep the peace and to be of good behaviour for a specified period, and to impose any further conditions as the judge considers appropriate in the circumstances. If the offender is in breach of his recognisance or commits a further offence, the sentence may be activated. The application should be made to the court of trial which imposed the sentence, even in circumstances where a sentence has been suspended by the Court of Criminal Appeal (see T O'Malley, p 291). The court has discretion as to whether to activate the sentence, and as to whether the full term or a shorter term should be served.

A further practice by the Irish courts has been to impose a sentence but to suspend part of the sentence, for example, imposing a five-year sentence with the final two years suspended. In *O'Brien v Governor of Limerick Prison* [1997] 2 ILRM 349, due to the difficulties which arise in relation to calculating remission periods following these types of sentence, the Supreme Court held that, because such a sentence cannot be reconciled with the Prisons Act 1907, they should not be imposed.

Another method of sentencing increasingly employed by the Irish courts is a system of imposing sentence, for example, for five years, but making provision for the sentence to be reviewed after two years. By this method, the trial judge retains seisin of the case and the prisoner may not be released before the review date. A recent decision by the Supreme Court has cast doubt over the validity of this practice (*People (DPP) v Padraig Finn* [2001] 2 ILRM 211).

14.8.8 IMPRISONMENT

Prior to 1997, a person found guilty of an offence could be deprived of his liberty by imprisonment or penal servitude. Other punishments included corporal punishment (whipping) and hard labour. Penal servitude was a distinct punishment, and was created as a substitution for deportation (see EF Ryan, and P Magee, *The Irish Criminal Process* (Cork: Mercier 1983), 396). Penal servitude was abolished by the Criminal Law Act 1997, which provides that no person shall be sentenced to penal servitude, any enactment empowering a court to impose penal servitude shall be treated as authorizing imprisonment up to the same maximum period, and any person who, immediately before the commencement of the Act, was subject to a sentence of penal servitude shall be treated as if undergoing a sentence of imprisonment: s 11(2). Section 11(3) provides for the abolition of hard labour, and s 12 abolishes corporal punishment.

The imposition of a sentence of imprisonment disqualifies that person from serving on a jury where that person has been sentenced to imprisonment for life or for a term of five years or more, or to detention under s 103 of the Children Act 1908. In such cases it is irrelevant if the sentence or part of the sentence was not served.

14.8.9 TEMPORARY RELEASE

The Criminal Justice Act 1960 provides for the temporary release of persons from prison and from St Patrick's Institution. Section 2 provides that the Minister for Justice 'may make rules providing for the temporary release, subject to such conditions (if any) as may be imposed in each particular case'. Under s 5 of the Act, the Minister is empowered to suspend the sentence, in whole or in part, at the time of the temporary release or at any time during or after the period of release. The rules governing temporary release are contained in the Prisoners (Temporary Release) Rules 1960 (SI 1960/167). These rules confer the decision-making power as to whether temporary release is appropriate on the prison Governor concerned 'subject to the directions of the Minister and subject to any exceptions which may be specified in the directions of the Minister': r 3. Temporary release may be in relation to day-to-day release, one-day periods (eg for a specific purpose such as a family occasion, job interview, etc) overnight periods (eg weekends or Christmas leave) or for a lengthy period. Every person released is subject to the following conditions: to keep the peace and be of good behaviour during the release period; to be of sober habits; not to communicate with or publish or cause to be published any matter by means of newspapers or any other publishing medium or to engage in public controversy. Section 108 of the Criminal Justice Act 2006 empowers the Minister to add restriction on movement orders and electronic monitoring of the person who has been granted temporary release.

Under s 6 of the Act a person who has been granted temporary release will be deemed to be unlawfully at large if (a) the period for which he was temporarily released has expired, or (b) a condition to which the release was made subject has been broken. Being unlawfully at large is an offence punishable by a maximum sentence of six months: Criminal Justice Act 1960, s 6(2). A further consequence of being unlawfully at large is, in the case of a person who is deemed to be unlawfully at large by reason of a breach of a condition of temporary release, that the period of temporary release which was granted shall be deemed to have expired: s 6(3). Where a person is deemed to be unlawfully at large, the currency of the sentence of such person must be suspended for all of that period in which the person was unlawfully at large: s 6(4). A member of the Garda Síochána may arrest without warrant a person whom he suspects to be unlawfully at large and may bring that person to the place in which he is required to be detained: s 7. It was stated in *State (Murphy) v Kielt* [1984] IR 458, at p 478; [1985] ILRM 141, per Griffin J, that before a person's release may be revoked, 'the question whether or not he has acted in breach of any of the conditions of such release must be asked and answered. It is only when a decision has been reached that he has broken one or more of the conditions that such person's right to be at liberty may be terminated.' Griffin J also considered that it is not necessary that the decision to revoke the temporary release should be judicially determined: 'the grant and determination of a temporary release are clearly acts which are administrative in nature. An informal procedure is all that is required, provided that such procedure is conducted fairly.' Temporary release may not be granted to a person serving a sentence imposed under s 27(3A) of the Misuse of Drugs Act 1977 (as inserted by the Criminal Justice Act 1999, s 5) during the minimum period of imprisonment specified by the court to be served under subsection (3B), that is, 10 years. Nonetheless, temporary release may be granted before that 10-year period because the rules whereby the prisoner may earn remission of sentence by industry and good conduct apply. Provision for remission is contained in r 38 of the Rules for the Government of Prisons 1947, which provides:

> A convicted prisoner sentenced to imprisonment, whether by one sentence or cumulative sentences, for a period exceeding one calendar month, shall be eligible, by industry and good conduct, to earn a remission of a portion of his imprisonment, not exceeding one-fourth of the whole sentence, provided that the remission so granted does not result in the prisoner being discharged before he has served one month.

Where such remission has been earned, the minimum period specified by the court to be served must be reduced by the amount of remission earned. Temporary release may not be granted before the prisoner has served the minimum period less the remission as applicable. A person therefore convicted and sentenced to the 10-year period who has earned the maximum remission permitted by the rule could not be granted temporary release before a period of seven and a half years has expired. Nor may temporary release be granted to a person serving a sentence for a murder or attempted murder to which s 3 of the 1990 Criminal Justice Act applies until the minimum statutory periods have expired, that is, 40 years in the case of murder and 20 years for an attempt to murder. The rule in relation to remission also applies to these offences.

14.9 Offences taken into consideration

The common law practice of taking offences into consideration was given statutory footing under s 8 of the Criminal Justice Act 1951. The section (as amended by the Criminal Justice (Miscellaneous Provisions) Act 1997) provides:

> *(1) Where a person, on being convicted of an offence, admits himself guilty of any other offence and asks to have it taken into consideration in awarding punishment, the court may, if the Director of Public Prosecutions consents, take it into consideration.*
>
> *(2) If the court takes an offence into consideration, a note of that fact shall be made and filed with the record of the sentence, and the accused shall not be prosecuted for that offence, unless his conviction is reversed.*

The section was examined by the Supreme Court in *DPP v Grey* [1987] ILRM 4. The case concerned 18 breaches of the Betting Duty (Certified Returns) Regulations 1934. The offences each carried a mandatory excise penalty of £800. The respondent submitted in the hearing at the District Court that it was open to the court to convict him of one offence and to take into consideration his admissions of guilt to the other charges in imposing a penalty. The District Court held that the Act of 1951 was applicable to the proceedings and accordingly fined the respondent £800 in respect of the charge to which he had pleaded guilty and took the other offences into consideration. The District Court then stated a case for the opinion of the High Court as to whether it had been correct in its finding. The High Court ruling, which found that the District Court had been correct, was appealed to the Supreme Court. The Supreme Court held that the section is only applicable to an award of punishment in respect of an offence where the court can genuinely and bona fide take into consideration an admission of guilt to other offences in deciding what level of punishment to award. Where a court has no discretion with regard to the imposition of a mandatory penalty, an admission of guilt to other offences could not be taken into consideration. If the court has no jurisdiction to try a particular offence, it cannot take that offence into consideration when determining the sentence for the offence for which it has jurisdiction to try. The court further held that if the offence is one for which the Legislature has provided that on conviction of such an offence, certain consequential orders must follow, that offence cannot be taken into consideration because the statutory consequential orders cannot be made. The court's reasoning for this finding was that an offence taken into consideration does not amount to a conviction. The Court of Criminal Appeal gave further consideration to s 8 in *People (DPP) v McCauley & Walsh* (unreported) CCA 25 Oct 2001.

14.10   Orders consequent on conviction

A number of statutes confer a power of disqualification, endorsement, forfeiture, and confiscation. See the Road Traffic Act 1961, ss 49 and 50 (as substituted by ss 10 and 11 of the Road Traffic Act 1994) as amended (see **Chapter 16**) for the law relating to disqualification for drunk driving offences.

The Criminal Justice Act 1994 (as amended by the Criminal Justice Act 1999) provides for the confiscation of benefits of drug trafficking (s 4), and confiscation of benefits derived from other offences (s 9), following conviction on indictment. Section 4 provides that 'where a person has been sentenced or otherwise dealt with by a court in respect of one or more drug trafficking offences . . . the court shall determine whether the person has benefited from drug trafficking'. The section further provides that such a determination may be dispensed with where the court is satisfied, having regard to the means of the offender and all the other circumstances of the case, the amount which might be recovered would not be sufficient to justify the making of the confiscation order.

Where the court does proceed with making a determination under the 1994 Act, the standard of proof which is applied is the civil standard of proof, ie on the balance of probabilities. Furthermore, three assumptions operate which are contained in s 5(4):

(a)   that any property appearing to the court—

   (i)   to have been held by the defendant at any time since his conviction, or

   (ii)   to have been transferred to him at any time since the beginning of the period of six years ending when the proceedings were instituted against him,

   was received by him, at the earliest time at which he appears to the court to have held it, as a payment or reward in connection with drug trafficking carried on by him,

(b)   that any expenditure of his since the beginning of that period was met out of payments received by him in connection with drug trafficking carried on by him, and

(c)   that, for the purpose of valuing any property received or assumed to have been received by him at any time as such a reward, he received the property free of any other interests in it.

None of the above assumptions shall be made by the court if '(a) the assumption is shown to be incorrect in the case of the defendant, or (b), it is satisfied that there would be a serious risk of injustice in his case if the assumption were to be made': Criminal Justice Act 1994 (as amended by the Criminal Justice Act 1999), s 5(2).

Where a person has died or absconded following conviction for a drug trafficking or other indictable offence, a confiscation order may be made only by the High Court, which upon application to it by the DPP may make the order if satisfied that he has died or absconded. In making the confiscation order, the High court may not make any of the assumptions set out above. In the case of a person who has absconded, the court, before making such a confiscation order, must be satisfied that the DPP has taken reasonable steps to contact him. Any person appearing to the court to be likely to be affected by the confiscation order shall be entitled to appear before the court and make representations: s 13.

CHAPTER 15

APPEALS AND JUDICIAL REVIEW

15.1 Introduction

Should a defendant disagree with the verdict or sentence of a criminal court then the possibility of appeal is available, as discussed in this chapter. Where it is contended, however, that a court or prosecuting authority or detaining authority has acted in excess or breach of its jurisdiction, or fails to observe constitutional or natural justice or has failed to act according to its legal duty then an appeal by way of judicial review in the High Court may be the appropriate course of action.

Since the enactment of the European Convention on Human Rights Act 2003, any alleged breaches of Convention rights can be pleaded in judicial review cases.

15.2 Remedies

15.2.1 CERTIORARI

An order of certiorari quashes the decision of a court. Such an order may be applied for if, for example, a court has acted in excess of its jurisdiction by imposing a sentence for an offence which is greater than the sentence provided by statute or breaches constitutional rights by failing to inform a defendant of his/her right to legal aid when a sentence of imprisonment is likely to be imposed: *State (Healy) v Donoghue* [1976] IR 325.

15.2.2 PROHIBITION

An order of prohibition prevents a body making a decision. Such orders are often sought where it is contended that there is such a delay in a prosecution that is has prejudiced an applicant's chance of a fair trial. Decisions of the High Court in such cases will be based on the circumstances of each individual case (the complexity of the offence alleged, the number of witnesses and so on). Offences involving the abuse of children and young people constitute a special category in relation to the issue of delay: *G v DPP* [1994] 1 IR 374. Factors to be taken into account include the interpersonal relationship between the parties; the extent of control exerted by the alleged abuser and the availability of alibis and witnesses: *B v DPP* [1997] 2 ILRM 118.

15.2.3 MANDAMUS

An order of mandamus compels a relevant body to perform a legal duty. A prisoner for example may take judicial review proceedings against prison authorities where it is contended that appropriate medical treatment has been requested and not provided.

15.2.4 DECLARATION AND INJUNCTION

The High Court can declare an action or omission to be in excess or breach of jurisdiction. It can also grant injunctions in the usual manner during the course of proceedings.

15.2.5 DAMAGES

Damages may be awarded where the court is satisfied that if the applicant had proceeded by way of civil claim s/he would had been awarded damages and if the claim has been included in the statement to ground the application (Order 84, r 24 of Rules of the Superior Courts 1986).

15.3 Bail pending judicial review

If the applicant is in custody by virtue of the order which is being reviewed, an application for bail can be made to the High Court judge before whom the application for leave to apply is being made.

15.4 Time limits

Order 84, rule 21 provides:

An application for judicial review shall be made promptly and in any event within three months from the date when grounds for the application first arose, or six months where the relief sought is certiorari, unless the Court considers that there is good reason for extending the period within which the application is made.

Even if time is extended where leave to apply is granted relief may ultimately be refused on the grounds of delay.

15.5 Procedures

15.5.1 LEAVE TO APPLY

The application is founded on two documents, a statement which states the legal grounds on which the application is being sought and an affidavit which verifies the facts in that statement. Rule 20 of Order 84 sets out the format these documents should take.

These documents are filed in the Central Office of the High Court beforehand and certified copies are handed in to the court when the application is actually made. The application is *ex parte*, therefore the respondents are not present and not on notice. At this stage the High

Court must only be satisfied that the applicant has an 'arguable case' on the documents before it and the fact that leave is granted is no indication as to the ultimate outcome of the case. It is open to the High Court to grant leave to apply on only some of the grounds stated and not on others. A refusal to grant leave can be appealed to the Supreme Court. Procedure generally is dictated by the Rules of the Superior Courts 1986 at Order 84, by direction of the court in individual cases and by practice directions, which appear from time to time in the Legal Diary.

15.5.2 NOTICE OF MOTION/SERVICE ON THE RESPONDENTS

When the court grants leave it will direct that the respondents be served with a notice of motion and copies of the statement grounding the application and the affidavit and a copy of the High Court order granting the leave. Unless the court directs otherwise this service must take place within 14 days after the grant of leave.

The court will fix the first motion date. The notice of motion is filed in the Central Office of the High Court. They will require sight of a certified copy of the High Court order so that they can confirm that the notice of motion corresponds to it. Service must be effected personally and an affidavit of service must be filed subsequently. If for some reason the notice of motion is not filed and/or all the documents are not served within time then the order granting leave will lapse and a further application would have to be made to the High Court to grant an extension of time for service.

15.5.3 NOTICE OF OPPOSITION AND REPLYING AFFIDAVITS

If the respondent intends to oppose the application a statement of opposition outlining their grounds and a verifying affidavit (if required) must be filed and served not later than seven days from the date of service of the notice of motion, or within a time specified by the court.

15.6 The list to fix dates

By virtue of a practice direction published in February 2001 the parties to the proceedings should be in a position to appraise the judge of the main issues in the case on the first motion date and give realistic time limits for the exchange of documents.

The case will then be adjourned from motion day to motion day to allow applicant and respondents to reply to each other's documents and when the case is ready to be heard it will be listed in a list specially designated to fix dates for hearing. At this point the court will require to know how long the case is estimated to take and distributes dates according to the case's position on the list. It frequently happens that all the available dates in the following term have been used up before the end of the list is reached. If a case is not reached it will go back to the next list to fix dates. In certain cases where delay in hearing the case would prejudice the parties in some way an application may be made to give the case a date in priority over other cases.

15.7 Notice to cross-examine

Although the Judicial Review procedure is essentially based on the filed documents either party may require any party who has sworn an affidavit in the proceeding to attend at the hearing of the case in order to cross-examine them on the contents of their affidavit. Order 40 Rule 31 allows notices to be served at any time before the expiration of 14 days after the end of time allowed for the filing of affidavits in reply.

15.8   Preparing a brief

A bound book containing all the documentation previously referred to must be lodged with the Central Office prior to the hearing. They should be presented in the following order:

1.   Notice of motion.

2.   Order of the High Court.

3.   Statement to ground the application.

4.   Verifying affidavit and exhibits.

5.   Notice of opposition.

6.   Verifying affidavits.

7.   Replying affidavits.

8.   Notice to cross-examine.

9.   Affidavit of service.

Legal submissions which it is proposed to make on the hearing date should be filed and served on the other side before the hearing date also.

15.9   The hearing

There may be a few cases listed for hearing on the same day. A call over will ascertain which cases can actually go on and which judges are available to hear them. The applicant opens the case to the judge and matters proceed from there. No other grounds apart from those set out in the statement to ground the application can be relied upon; however, the court may allow either party to amend the statement during the hearing if it thinks it is appropriate. Judgment may be given on the day or can be reserved.

15.10   Costs and the Attorney General's Scheme

The award of costs is at the discretion of the Court. Even if the applicant is unsuccessful the court may be prepared to make an order in the applicant's favour if the point raised were deemed to be of importance. The Attorney General's Scheme can be applied for in applications relating to criminal matters if the applicant is of insufficient means to fund the case. The application must be made at the *ex parte* stage and mentioned again at the close of the hearing. If a recommendation has been made at the outset it generally will not matter whether the applicant is successful or not, as fees under the scheme will still be paid, though it should be noted that the fees paid are considerably less than one might get if costs are granted.

15.11   Habeas corpus

15.11.1   INTRODUCTION

An application under Article 40.4.2 may be taken whenever it is alleged that a person is illegally detained in a prison, Garda station, mental hospital, etc. Practitioners refer to this application, a remedy available in Ireland since the seventeenth century, as a habeas corpus application, meaning 'you have the body'.

It is also known as 'an application under Article 40 of the Constitution'. The Constitution outlines the procedure, which takes the form of an *ex parte* application by way of affidavit setting out the reasons why it is claimed that the person is illegally detained. The application is made before a High Court judge who, on having the affidavit opened to her/him and on hearing any submissions of counsel deems that there is a case to answer, will order the production of the prisoner. The respondents will then be served with a copy of the affidavit and a copy of the order of the High Court and at the hearing of the matter respond to the claim and certify the grounds of detention. Because the loss of liberty without due legal process is such a serious infringement of one's constitutional rights the prisoner will normally be brought to court within a day of the *ex parte* application and a full hearing will be commenced immediately.

Some of the more common examples encountered by the criminal practitioner where such an application may be considered are:

i   when the warrant is illegal on its face, eg the warrant does not disclose any offence known to law (however in a case where the warrant does not reflect the order of the court it is open to the authorities to substitute a correct warrant);

ii   the person named on the warrant is not the person detained;

iii   where illegalities have been adopted in the person's committal or procedures adopted while the person is in custody make a previously legal detention illegal, eg refusing access to a solicitor;

iv   a juvenile is being held in a place not certified as being suitable for the detention of a person of that age;

v   there has been a breach of rights guaranteed under the European Convention on Human Rights, sufficient to render the detention unlawful.

15.11.2   COSTS

All applicants can apply for costs at the end of the case or if it is a suitable case the Attorney General's Scheme may be applied for at the *ex parte* stage. Where the point at issue was validly raised, even if the case is not won, the judge may feel that costs should be granted or the Attorney General's Scheme recommended.

15.12   Appeals

15.12.1   APPEAL FROM THE DISTRICT COURT TO THE CIRCUIT COURT

A general right of appeal is contained in s 18(1) of the Courts of Justice Act 1928. An appeal may be made against conviction and severity of punishment or against severity alone but an appeal cannot be made against conviction only. Leave to apply for appeal is not necessary.

The hearing in the Circuit Court is a hearing held in front of a Circuit Court judge sitting alone and evidence not given at the District Court may be adduced. A defendant may change his/her plea in this court. The Circuit Court may decrease, vary, affirm, or increase a sentence but only within the jurisdiction of the District Court. For example, s 3 of the Non-Fatal Offences Against the Person Act 1997, assault causing harm, allows for a maximum sentence of imprisonment of 12 months when dealt with summarily and a maximum of five years when dealt with on indictment in the Circuit Court. In an appeal from the District Court to the Circuit Court for this offence, it may only apply the lower tariff. There is no further right of appeal from the Circuit Court decision to a higher court; however, the decisions of the court are of course reviewable by way of judicial review, where such grounds present themselves.

15.12.2   PROCEDURE

Procedures regarding the making of an appeal are listed at Rule 101 of the District Court Rules 1997. It is necessary for an appellant to enter recognisance in all cases. Following a decision of ó Caoimh J in *Michael Darby v Governor of Mountjoy Prison* (unreported), 16 December 2002, it was the common view that there was no need to enter a recognisance in order to prosecute a District Court Appeal unless the trial judge in the District Court required one. This view was remedied by the legislature in the District Courts (Appeals to the Circuit Court) Rules 2003 (SI 484/2003). Article 3(B) of the regulations amended Rule 101 of the District Court Rules by the insertion of a r 4, which reads:

> . . . where a person is desirous of appealing in criminal proceedings . . . a recognisance for the purpose of appeal shall be fixed by the Court. The amount of the recognisance in which the appellant and the surety or sureties, if any, are to be bound shall be fixed by the Court and shall be of such reasonable amount as the Court shall see fit . . . The recognisance . . . shall be entered into within the fourteen days fixed by rule 1 of this order.

This rule came into operation on 17 November 2003. Applications to have recognisances fixed for appeal should be made therefore in every case where the defendant is desirous of appealing.

A notice of appeal must be served on the respondent and a copy of it with a declaration of service and a copy of the recognisances must be filed with the District Court Clerk within 14 days of the decision. Note that the 14 days includes the day of the decision and weekends; however, if the 14th day falls on a Saturday or Sunday or any other day when the District Court office is closed then that day will be excluded and the papers should be filed on the following day.

Once an appeal is in being the original order of the District Court is suspended until the appeal is determined.

15.12.3   EXTENSION OF TIME TO APPEAL

Should the appeal not be lodged within 14 days an application to extend time to appeal may be made. The appellant has no automatic right to an extension and will have to explain why the application was not filed on time. If the extension is granted the appellant must serve and lodge papers in the time specified by the court, ie the time granted may be less than 14 days.

Road traffic offences are discussed in detail in **Chapter 16** and it should be noted that in the case of an appellant who is appealing a driving disqualification, such order will only be suspended pending the outcome of the appeal when the appeal has been lodged within 14 days. In other words, while an extension of time to appeal may be granted, it is not within the power of the court to suspend the operation of the disqualification. Consequently, given the delays experienced in certain parts of the country in the listing of appeal hearings, the suspension may have already been served by the time the appeal has been heard.

15.13   Notification and reinstatement of appeals

An appeal is heard in the Circuit Court area in which the original case was determined and the appellant will be notified personally of the date the appeal will be heard. It is the appellant's responsibility to notify the authorities of any change of address since the original conviction date in the lower court. Should the appeal be struck out due to the appellant's non-attendance, application can be made to reinstate the appeal in the Circuit Court subject to the appellant showing to the Court's satisfaction that there was a good reason for the non-attendance.

15.14   Appeal from the Circuit Court, Special Criminal Court, or Central Criminal Court to the Court of Criminal Appeal

15.14.1   GENERALLY

The Courts of Justice Act 1924 established the Court of Criminal Appeal. The sections establishing it were repealed and replaced by s 12 of the Courts (Supplemental Provisions) Act 1961 and the sections outlining its powers were re-enacted by s 48 of that 1961 Act. Appeals from the Special Criminal Court are made to the Court of Criminal Appeal by virtue of s 44 of the Offences Against the Person Act 1939. The court must consist of not less than three judges being the Chief Justice or another member of the Supreme Court and two High Court judges. Decisions of the District Court may not be appealed to this court.

The Attorney General or DPP may appeal an order for costs in favour of an acquitted person under s 24 of the Criminal Justice Act 2006.

15.14.2   PROCEDURE

The Courts Acts and the Rules of Superior Courts 1981 govern procedure for an appeal to the Court of Criminal Appeal. A defendant must apply for leave to appeal from the decisions of these higher courts at the conclusion of the case or within three days. An application for leave to appeal must be made to the trial judge. Applications to extend time for leave to appeal may be made.

The certificate granting leave must be lodged with the Court of Criminal Appeal office within 21 days. However, leave to appeal is seldom granted, and if refused, the applicant must lodge an appeal against the refusal within 21 days. Bail may be applied for in the Court of Criminal Appeal pending the hearing of the appeal. The court must be persuaded on affidavit that there are substantial grounds for appeal.

15.14.3   POINT OF LAW OR CONDUCT OF TRIAL

An appeal to the Court of Criminal Appeal can be made only on a point of law or a point concerning the conduct of the trial—such point having been raised with the judge during the course of the trial. If, for example, defence counsel believes that there has been some flaw in the judge's charge to the jury, this should be raised by way of 'requisition' after the judge's charge and before the jury begins to deliberate. If this requisition is not raised, the applicant may be stopped from relying on this point of law for the purposes of an appeal.

The appeal itself is based on the transcript of the trial and it would be unusual to have evidence heard by the Court of Criminal Appeal.

The applicant can appeal against severity and conviction, severity only and (in contrast to appeals from the District Court) conviction only.

Under s 34 of the Criminal Procedure Act 1967 as amended by s 21 of the Criminal Justice Act 2006 the DPP or Attorney General may, in a case where the accused is acquitted, refer a question of law to the Supreme Court, having consulted with the trial judge.

15.14.4 POWERS OF THE COURT OF CRIMINAL APPEAL

The Court of Criminal Appeal can:

(a) quash sentences and substitute them with others; and

(b) quash sentences and remit the matter for retrial where the appeals are against conviction.

15.14.4.1 DPP'S Right of appeal against leniency of sentence

Section 2 of the Criminal Justice Act 1993 as amended by s 23 of the Criminal Justice Act 2006 allows the DPP a right to appeal to the Court of Criminal Appeal on the grounds of the leniency of any sentence pursuant to the trial on indictment of any offence. The application by the DPP must be made on notice given to the defendant within 28 days, or such longer period not exceeding 56 days as the court may, on application to it in that behalf, determine, from the date of conviction. There is no provision for extending that time limit.

15.14.4.2 Appeal against the decision of the court

The convicted person may appeal the decision of the Court of Criminal Appeal once the court and the DPP or the Attorney General certify that the case involves a point of law of exceptional public importance and that it is desirable in the public interest that such an appeal should be taken, as outlined in s 29 of the Courts of Justice Act 1924 as substituted by s 22 of the Criminal Justice Act 2006. Under s 22(3) of the 2006 Act, the DPP or Attorney General may appeal on the same basis, without prejudice to any decision previously made in favour of the accused.

15.15 Miscarriage of justice

Where it is alleged that a new or newly discovered fact shows that there has been a miscarriage of justice in relation to a conviction or that the sentence was excessive, recourse may be had to s 2 of the Criminal Procedure Act 1993. Prior to the commencement of this Act, there was no procedure to appeal in such a situation, as the points at issue had not been raised at the trial. Now the appeal can be heard in the Court of Criminal Appeal where the court's powers include:

(a) quashing of convictions,

(b) affirming sentences,

(c)   varying sentences, or

(d)   substituting alternative verdicts,

(e)   substituting alternative sentences, and

(f)   remitting matters for re-trial, and

(g)   ordering the payment of compensation, where a miscarriage of justice is found.

15.16   Appeal by way of case stated

A case stated under the Summary Jurisdiction Act 1857 as extended by s 51 of the Courts (Supplemental Provisions) Act 1961 is an appeal to the High Court from a decision of the District Court where the proceedings have concluded. The purpose of the appeal is to ask the opinion of the High Court on a point of law or a mixture of law and fact but not fact alone. All summary matters and indictable matters dealt with summarily are capable of being appealed by way of case stated.

Any party to the proceedings who is dissatisfied with the decision of the court can apply within 14 days of the determination of proceedings to the District Court judge to sign and state a case. However, a judge is entitled to refuse to state a case where he is of the opinion that the application is frivolous or if it is on a point of well-settled law.

The case stated will outline the facts of the case, the submissions made by parties to the case, and the grounds upon which the District Court judge reached his decision. The High Court is thereby asked for its opinion as to whether the District Court decision was correct. Drafts of the case stated may be circulated to the parties to it, before transmission to the High Court in order to confirm that they are in agreement as to the facts of the case. If the facts are in dispute then the facts 'shall be found' by the District Court judge. The signed case stated should be transmitted to the High Court within six months of the determination. The decision of the District Court is suspended pending the outcome of the case stated.

The High Court on hearing the case can:

(a)   reverse,

(b)   affirm, or

(c)   amend

the decision of the District Court and can:

(d)   award costs, although in criminal cases the defendant may be covered by the Criminal Legal Aid Scheme.

A defendant cannot appeal to the Circuit Court from the determination of the District Court and appeal by way of case stated at the same time. It should be noted that s 16 of the Courts of Justice Act allows a Circuit Judge to refer a question of law to the Supreme Court by way of case stated.

15.17   Appeal by way of consultative case stated

A consultative case stated lies before the determination of proceedings pursuant to s 52 of the Courts (Supplemental Provisions) Act 1961. This procedure enables a District Court judge, before s/he gives her/his decision in a case, to refer a question of law to the High

Court. Any party to the proceedings may request that a case be stated or the judge himself may refer such a case. All summary matters and indictable matters dealt with summarily are capable of being the subject of a case stated.

The District Court case will be adjourned pending the outcome of the High Court case. The case is prepared in the same manner as the appeal by way of case stated outlined above and should be transmitted within six months of the matter arising to the High Court. The High Court will answer the questions posed and the case is remitted to the District Court for a determination in accordance with those answers.

A defendant has the normal right of appeal against the ultimate determination of the District Court to the Circuit Court.

PART V

AREAS OF SPECIALIZED PROCEDURE

CHAPTER 16

ROAD TRAFFIC OFFENCES

16.1   Introduction

The objective of this chapter is to introduce the reader to the law on road traffic within the jurisdiction of Ireland. At the time of writing there are presently 13 Acts and hundreds of statutory instruments made thereunder which provide the statutory law in this area. These are cumulatively known as the Road Traffic Acts 1961–2006. There is also a wealth of authorative common law which must be examined for further clarity. Road traffic law is a very specialized and technical area of law. A successful prosecution of an alleged road traffic offence will depend upon a full discharge of the legal burden of proof through clear and concise evidence that all of the constituent elements of the alleged offence are present. This chapter is written from a practice perspective. The essential proofs and definitions of the offences herein are fully examined to emphasize the manner in which a road traffic case should be approached. These offences include:

(a)   Driving without a licence.

(b)   Driving without insurance.

(c)   Dangerous parking.

(d)   Obstructive parking.

(e)   Driving a defective vehicle.

(f)   Driving while unfit.

(g)   Driving without reasonable consideration.

(h)   Careless driving.

(i)   Dangerous driving.

(j)   Manslaughter.

(k)   Intoxicant offences.

The application of generic evidential principles and rules will precede a brief discussion on appeals.

This chapter assumes that the reader will have a clear understanding of the principles of the law of evidence as discussed at **Chapter 4**, the law relating to arrest and detention as discussed at **Chapter 6** and in particular the rights of an accused, and finally the law relating to the summons procedure as discussed at **Chapter 7**.

16.2 Driving without a licence

16.2.1 PROHIBITION

Section 38 of the Road Traffic Act 1961 (hereinafter called the 'Principal Act') states that a *person* cannot *drive* or allow another to drive his *vehicle* in a public place without a valid driving licence.

A 'person' includes a driver, owner, manager and registered owner. In *Briggs v Gibson's Bakery Ltd* [1948] NI 165, it was stated that 'person' includes a limited liability company.

'Drive' is statutorily defined in s 3 of the Principal Act as including managing or controlling and driving. In the case of *R v MacDonagh* [1974] RTR 372, it was held that the essential ingredient of driving is that the driver must have control of the movement of the vehicle. It also held that movement was produced by two factors. First the driver must be in the actual driver's seat and in control of the steering wheel, and second the action cannot be said to consist of driving unless it comes within the ordinary meaning of that word. In this case the action of pushing a vehicle while steering it with one hand was held not to amount to driving.

'Vehicle' is not defined legislatively; however, s 3 (1) of the Principal Act defines a 'mechanically propelled vehicle' as a vehicle intended or adapted for propulsion by mechanical (including electrical or partly electrical) means, including a bicycle or tricycle with an attachment for propelling it by mechanical power whether or not the attachment is being used. Section 3(2) of the Principal Act exempts a vehicle substantially disabled (by accident, breakdown, engine, or vital part removal) so that it is no longer capable of being mechanically propelled from being a mechanically propelled vehicle for the purpose of the Act.

'Public place' is defined by s 3 of the Principal Act, as substituted by s 49(1)(a)(iv) of the Road Traffic Act 1994 as:

(a)   *any public road, and*

(b)   *any street, road or other place to which the public have access with vehicles whether as of right or by permission and whether subject to or free of charge.*

There is considerable case law on the definition of a public place; however, one of the more instructive cases is *R v Waters* [1963] 47 Cr App Rep 149, wherein Lord Parker CJ stated that it is a question of degree and fact whether a place is public or private. Therein, it was held that even where a restricted class is excluded, the place would be public. The onus is stated to rest with the prosecution to prove that a place is public. A piece of ground can be public at a certain time and not at other times.

16.2.2 DEFENCES

Section 35(3)(a) of the Principal Act states that it is a good defence to show that the driver had an effective provisional licence for the particular class of vehicle which he was driving. Section 35(3)(b) of the Principal Act states that it is a defence for an employer who is prosecuted under s 38 for employing a person without a licence to show that the employee had an effective provisional licence.

16.2.3 EXEMPTIONS

There are a number of exemptions to the requirement to hold a valid driving licence. Section 38(6) of the Principal Act exempts members of the Gardaí driving in the course of their duty; s 38(7) exempts persons using such specified pedestrian controlled vehicles as are exempted by ministerial regulation. Regulation 7 of the Road Traffic (Licensing of

Drivers) Regulations 1989 (SI 285/1989) defines such vehicles as those neither constructed or adapted for use for carrying a driver or passenger and which do not exceed 407 kg unladen weight; s 33(7) of the Principal Act exempts persons undergoing a driving test, although regulation 28 of the said 1989 Regulations provides that such a person must hold a provisional licence; s 113 of the Defence Forces Act 1954 exempts members of the defence forces driving State-owned or controlled mechanically propelled vehicles during a period of duty or emergency.

16.2.4   PENALTIES

In the case of breach of s 38 of the Principal Act, both the driver and owner of the vehicle can be liable to the general penalty as provided under s 102 of the Principal Act as amended by s 2 of the Road Traffic (Amendment) Acts 1984 as amended by ss 2 and 23 of the Road Traffic Act 2002. Section 102 as amended provides that where a person is convicted of an offence under the Acts and no particular penalty is provided for in the section, then on summary conviction the following are the maximum penalties:

- On a first offence under the section or subsection—a fine of €800.

- On a second offence under the section or subsection—a fine of €1,500 and/or three months' imprisonment.

- On a third or subsequent offence under the section or subsection within any period of 12 months—a fine of €1,500 and/or three months' imprisonment.

- Otherwise (ie not within 12 months) a fine of €800.

It should be noted that this section does not include reference to the disqualification and endorsements provisions of the Act, which are additional to a penalty subject to the discretion of the judge or where mandatory provided by statute. Furthermore, when the relevant commencement order is in force, s 102 will be effected by the Road Traffic Act 2006.

16.2.5   DISQUALIFICATION

There are three types of disqualification from driving:

(1)   Special disqualification: Under the provisions of s 28 of the Road Traffic Act 1961 as amended by s 49(1)(c) of the Road Traffic Act 1994, the court has the discretion to disqualify a driver as a consequence of an application to it by a member of the Gardaí or appropriate licensing authority, that a person is unfit to drive a motor vehicle by reason of a physical disease, or physical or mental disability or evidence of incompetence to drive any vehicle or any class of vehicle.

(2)   Consequential disqualification: Under the provisions of s 26 of the Road Traffic Act 1961 and the Second Schedule to the 1961 Act as substituted and amended by s 26 of the Road Traffic Act 1994 and s 2 of the Road Traffic Act 1995, the court is obliged to impose an order of consequential disqualification where stated offences have been committed. This will arise where a person has been convicted of a drink driving offence, a driving without insurance offence and other offences specifically stated in the Acts.

(3)   Ancillary disqualification: Section 27(1)(a) of the Road Traffic Act 1961 provides a judge with the discretion to impose a period of disqualification for the commission of any offence under the 1961 Act, not being an offence which attracts a consequential disqualification order.

A person who is disqualified from driving may not drive any motor vehicle during the disqualification period unless they lodge an appeal against their conviction within 14 days of the date of their conviction. If a person does not appeal their disqualification they will receive a notice from the Fines Office of the District Court in the area in which they were convicted, requiring the defendant to hand in their driving licence forthwith in addition to the Court Order. Disqualification from driving for any reason carries an automatic three-year endorsement on the defendant's licence, which commences when the disqualification period ends. The Motor Taxation Office in the area in which the accused is resident will hold the licence for collection until the period of disqualification ends.

16.2.6   ENDORSEMENT

Section 36 of the Road Traffic Act 1961 as amended by ss 2, 8, and 25 of the Road Traffic Act 2002 establishes the law relating to the endorsement of a driving licence. An endorsement is a stamp placed on a licence by the Motor Taxation Office in the area in which the defendant lives. An endorsement will remain on a licence for three years. The endorsement period will begin on the date on which the licence is stamped. In accordance with s 36 of the 1961 Act the court may endorse a license where a person is convicted of any offence under the 1961 Act, where it does not make an ancillary or consequential disqualification order; the court shall endorse a licence where it has made an ancillary or consequential disqualification order. Second or subsequent endorsements very frequently result in mandatory disqualification from driving. It may also lead to an increase in insurance premium.

16.3   Driving without insurance

16.3.1   PROHIBITION

Section 56 of the Road Traffic Act 1961 as substituted by s 34 of the Road Traffic Act 2004 (operative from 24/01/2005, SI No 26/2005):

> *(1)   A person (in this subsection referred to as the user) shall not use in a public place a mechanically propelled vehicle unless—*
> *(a)   either a vehicle insurer or an exempted person would be liable for injury caused by the negligent use of the vehicle by him at that time or*
> *(b)   there is in force at that time either an approved policy of insurance whereby the user or some other person who would be liable for injury caused by the negligent use of the vehicle at that time by the user, is insured against all sums, subject to subsection (2) of this section, without limit, which the user or his personal representative or such other person or his personal representative becomes liable to pay to any person (exclusive of the excepted persons) by way of damages or costs on account of injury to person or property caused by the negligent use of the vehicle at that time by the user.*

Paragraph 56(1)(b) ceased to have effect by virtue of s 53 of the Road Traffic Act 1968.

Accordingly, pursuant to s 56 of the Principal Act, an insurer's obligations in respect of motor insurance can be summarized as follows:

> 'A person (user of a mechanically propelled vehicle) shall ensure that a vehicle insurer or exempted person is liable for the negligent use of a vehicle by him or her, with the exception of a pedestrian controlled vehicle and/or a State owned or driven vehicle.
>
>   A person/user must ensure that an approved policy of insurance issued by a vehicle insurer or a certificate of exemption from an exempt person shall cover any negligence on the part of the user, which includes such agents, servants or personal representatives, for injury without limitation, subject to the EU and international limits.'

'Person', *'public place'* and *'Mechanically propelled vehicle'* are defined in the preceding discussion regarding driving without a licence.

'Use' in relation to a mechanically propelled vehicle is defined by s 3(1) of the Principal Act as including parking. In the case of *Williams v Jones* [1972] Crim LR 50, a vehicle with its wheels off and battery removed was said to be in use. Section 3(5) of the Principal Act includes in the construction of 'consent to use', the use of a vehicle with the implied consent of a person.

'Use' should not be confused with 'driving', which is defined by s 3 of the Principal Act as including the managing and controlling of a motor vehicle. In *Samuelson v National Insurance* [1984] 3 All ER 107, the plaintiff's insurance policy covered the 'use' of the vehicle. It was not covered, therefore, where the car was stolen while a motor trade repairer was driving it.

A 'vehicle insurer' is an undertaking within the meaning of Regulation 2(1) of the EC (Non-life Insurance) Regulations 1976 (SI 115/1976) as amended by the EC (Non-Life Assurance) Regulations 1976 (SI 142/1991), as being a class 10 (mechanically propelled vehicle insurance) business in the State, who complies with the provisions of s 58 of the Principal Act as substituted by regulation 6 of the EC (Compulsory Insurance) (Amendment) Regulations 1992 (SI 347/1992) and who further complies with the provisions of s 78 of the Principal Act as substituted by regulation 9 of the 1992 Regulations.

Regulation 6 provides as follows:

The following section is hereby substituted for s 58 of the Act—

(1)   In this Act, 'vehicle insurer' means, subject to subsection (1) of section 78 of this Act,-

    (a)   an undertaking within the meaning of Article 2 (1) of the EC (Non-Life Insurance) Regulations 1976 (SI No 115 of 1976) as amended By Article 4 of the European Communities (Non-Life Insurance) (Amendment) (No 2) Regulations 1991 (SI No 142 of 1991) which carries on a class 10 mechanically propelled vehicle insurance business in the State, or a syndicate, within the meaning of s 3 of the Act of 1936, carrying on that business in the State, or

    (b)   A syndicate, within the meaning of section 3 of the Act of 1936, carrying on that business in the state.

(1)   For the purpose of this section and s 78

    —   'class 10 mechanically propelled vehicle insurance business' means a mechanically propelled vehicle insurance business within the meaning of s 3 of the Act of 1936 in relation to a risk classified under class 10 of Schedule 1 of the European Communities (Non-Life Insurance) Regulations 1976 (SI No 115 of 1976) but excluding Carrier's liability; 'the Act of 1936' means the Insurance Act 1936 (No 45 of 1936).

Regulation 9 of the 1992 Regulations provides:

The following section is hereby substituted for section 78 of the Act—

(1)   A person shall not carry on a class 10 mechanically propelled vehicle insurance business in the State unless he is a member of the Bureau.

(2)   A person shall not be an exempted person unless there is in force an undertaking by him in terms approved of by the Minister that he will deal with third-party claims in respect of mechanically propelled vehicles owned by him on terms similar to those standing agreed from time to time between the Minister and the Bureau in respect of the Bureau.

(3)   The provisions of this section shall have effect notwithstanding any other provision of this or any other Act.

(4)   In this section, 'the Bureau' means the Motor Insurers' Bureau of Ireland.

An 'approved policy of insurance' is a policy which complies with the provisions of s 62 of the Insurance Act 1961 as amended by regulation 5 of the EC (Road Traffic) (Compulsory Insurance) regulations 1975 (SI 178/1975), regulation 5 of the EC (Road Traffic) (Compulsory Insurance) (Amendment) Regulations 1987 (SI 322/1987), and regulation 4(1) of EC (Road Traffic) (Compulsory Insurance) (Amendment) Regulations 1992 (SI 347/1992). Section 56(2A) of the Principal Act, as substituted by regulation 4(1) of the 1992 Regulations, defines an approved policy as:

Section 56 of the Act is hereby amended by the substitution of the following subsection for subsection 2A (as inserted by the Regulations of 1975)—

> (2A) An approved policy of insurance referred to in paragraph (a) of subsection (1) of this section shall extend to damages or costs on account of injury to persons or property incurred by the negligent use of a mechanically propelled vehicle by the user in any of the designated territories to the extent required by the law relating to compulsory insurance against civil liability in respect of the use of mechanically propelled vehicles of the territory where the damages or costs may be incurred, or to the extent required by this Part of this Act, whichever is the greater.

16.3.2 DEFENCES

Sections 56(5) and 56(6) of the Principal Act provide:

> (5) Where a person charged with an offence under this section is the owner of the vehicle, it shall be a good defence to the charge for the person to show that the vehicle was being used without his consent and either that he had taken all reasonable precautions to prevent its being used or that it was being used by his servant acting in contravention of his orders.
>
> (6) Where a person charged with an offence under this section was the servant of the owner of the vehicle, it shall be a good defence to the charge for the person to show that he was using the vehicle in obedience to the express orders of the owner.

In *Singh v Rathour* [1988] 2 All ER 16, it was held that where the owner gives restricted consent and then the user goes beyond that consent, the vehicle use is outside the scope of the insurance cover.

It is an absolute defence if the defendant can show that there was insurance on the vehicle. It is also a defence if it can be proven that the owner or driver was an exempted person or that the vehicle was an excepted vehicle.

An 'exempted person' is defined under s 65(1) of the Principal Act as:

> (a) any person claiming in respect of injury to himself sustained while he was in or on a mechanically propelled vehicle (or a vehicle drawn thereby) to which the relevant document relates other than a mechanically propelled vehicle or vehicles forming a combination of vehicles of a class specified for the purposes of this paragraph by regulations made by the Minister provided that such regulation shall not extend compulsory insurance for civil liability to passengers:
>
> any part of a mechanically propelled vehicle, other than a large public service vehicle, unless that part of the vehicle is designed and constructed with seating accommodation for passengers; or
>
> a passenger seated in a caravan attached to a mechanically propelled vehicle while such a combination of vehicles is moving in a public place.

Section 4(2) of the Principal Act also provides three other exceptions to the general application of s 56. These are:

(a) State-owned vehicles used by a person in the course of employment;

(b) vehicles seized by a State employee in the course of his duty or a person using such vehicles in the course of his employment; and

(c) members of the Gardaí or ministerial officials using vehicles for the purpose of a test, its removal, or disposition under the Act or regulations thereunder.

It should be noted that these exceptions do not confer an exemption on the State in respect of the negligence of its servants or agents. Under s 59 of the Civil Liability Act 1961, the State is liable in tort for the negligence of the driver of a State vehicle. The relevant notice party herein is the Minister for Finance.

16.3.3 PENALTIES

Section 56(3) of the Principal Act, as amended by s 3(1) of the Road Traffic (Amendment) Act 1984 and ss 2 and 23 of the Road Traffic Act 2002, provides that the penalties for breach of a person's obligation to insure are a maximum fine of €3,000 and/or six months' imprisonment. The disqualification provisions also apply in respect of a breach of the obligation to insure. This arises by virtue of the provisions of s 27(1)(a) of the Principal Act, which gives the court jurisdiction to impose an ancillary disqualification order where a person is convicted of an offence under the Act, other than an offence to which s 26 applies or other than a crime or offence in the commission of which a mechanically propelled vehicle is use. Item 11 of the Second Schedule to the Principal Act, as substituted by s 49(1)(i) of the Road Traffic Act 1994, established the provisions in relation to the mandatory disqualification provisions. These can be summarized as follows:

- On a first offence a court may disqualify for less than one year.

- Each conviction must be endorsed on the driver's licence.

- On a second or subsequent conviction a court must disqualify.

- Where the court decides not to impose a disqualification for drivers convicted of a first offence of driving without insurance the court shall endorse five penalty points on the defendant's licence.

16.3.4 PENALTY POINTS

The Road Traffic Act 2002 as amended by the Road Traffic Act 2004 introduced the legislative framework for the penalty point system in Ireland. Initially motorists guilty of speeding, driving without insurance, careless driving and seat belt offences were awarded penalty points. Under the Road Traffic Acts 2002–4 any driver who receives 12 penalty points in any three-year period will incur a six-month disqualification from driving and a subsequent endorsement on their licence. On 26 January 2006, the Minister for Transport announced a further proposed 31 driving offences that will incur penalty points. These were introduced on 3 April by the Road Traffic Acts 1961–2005 (Fixed Charge Offences) Regulations 2006.

16.3.5 COMPENSATION ORDER

Section 6 of the Criminal Justice Act 1993 provides for compensation orders in respect of road traffic cases. Section 6(4) provides:

A compensation order shall not be made in respect of an injury or loss that results from the use of a mechanically propelled vehicle (within the meaning of the Road Traffic Act 1961) in a public place unless it appears to the court that:
(a)   It is in respect of an injury or loss as respects which the use of the vehicle by the convicted person was in breach of their obligation to insure, or
(b)   It is in respect of a loss, which is treated by subsection (3) as having resulted from the offence.

Section 6(3) provides:

Where the commission of the offence by the convicted person involved the taking of property out of the possession of the injured party and the property has been recovered, any loss occurring to the injured party by reason of the property being damaged while out of his possession shall be treated for the purposes of subsection (1) as having resulted from the offence, irrespective of how the damage was caused or who caused it.

Accordingly, a compensation order can only be made where:

(a)   there is no insurance cover as provided for under s 56 of the Principal Act; or

(b)   the offence involved the taking of property which was later recovered, but loss arose to the injured party by reason of the property being stolen and subsequently damaged.

This compensation order may be made in addition to or instead of a prison sentence, but cannot exceed the jurisdiction of the court hearing the matter.

16.3.6 BURDEN OF PROOF

In a prosecution under s 56 of the Principal Act, a presumption of non-insurance against the defendant exists where a member of the Gardaí had demanded the production of a certificate of insurance in accordance with s 69 of the Principal Act and the party had failed, refused, or neglected to produce same, or alternatively did produce the certificate but refused to allow the Garda member to examine it.

In the case of *Lyons v Cooney* [1978] IR 41 at 48, the law with regard to the production of a certificate of insurance in accordance with section 69 of the Principal Act was summarized as follows:

> 'The fact the vehicle was uninsured can be proved by the prosecution in either of two ways. They could adduce evidence of a positive nature probative of the fact that the vehicle was uninsured. For example, they could put in evidence a statement by the defendant admitting that the vehicle was uninsured. Alternatively, they could rely on the provisions of s 56, sub-section 4, which cast on the defendant the onus of showing that the vehicle was not used in contravention of the section when "the person on whom the demand was made" (not, be it noted, "the defendant") refused or failed to produce the necessary certificate.'

It should be noted that this presumption does not shift the legal burden of proof, but rather the evidential burden of proof. In *Cranny v Kelly*, 5 April 1996, High Court (unreported), Lavan J held that the test to be applied in determining whether knowledge of insurance existed is a subjective test.

16.4 Dangerous parking

16.4.1 PROHIBITION

Section 55(1) of the Principal Act as amended by section 52 of the Road Traffic Act 1968, s 3 Road Traffic (Amendment) Act 1984 and s 23 of the Road Traffic Act 2002 provides that:

> *A person shall not park a vehicle in a public place, if, when so parked, the vehicle would be likely to cause danger to other persons using the place.*

'Person', 'vehicles' and 'public place' are defined in the preceding discussion regarding driving without a licence.

'Park' is defined pursuant to s 3 of the Principal Act as keeping or leaving a vehicle stationary. It should be noted that an original parking may be safe but may be rendered dangerous by nightfall.

There is no statutory definition to instruct with regard to 'cause or likely to cause danger' however, case law can assist with what is likely to be held as dangerous in this regard. In the case of *Parish v Judd* (1961) 95 ILT & SJ 38, the defendant's vehicle's lights had broken and he towed the vehicle as close as he could get to street lighting. The plaintiff crashed into the unlit car and sued for negligence and nuisance, alleging that the defendant had dangerously parked the vehicle. In dismissing the plaintiff's claim the court held that in order to establish his case the plaintiff would have to prove the following evidential facts:

(a) that the vehicle was an obstruction;

(b) that it was a danger (the judge held that this element was not present due to the fact that the defendant had towed the vehicle near to street lighting); and

(c) that the defendant's vehicle became unlighted as a result of some fault on the part of the defendant or, if not due to his fault initially, then subsequently it became his fault by non repair or removing it.

Accordingly, it is this writer's opinion that in order to establish dangerous parking the proofs similar to those listed in the *Parish* case above would need to be established by the prosecution.

16.4.2   PENALTIES

If it is a first offence (except a first offence regarding lighting-up hours), there is a maximum fine of €800 and/or one month's imprisonment. Where it is a first offence of dangerous parking during lighting up hours, or a second offence or subsequent offences, a fine of up to €1,500 and/or 3 months' imprisonment is allowed for.

Disqualification is optional for a first offence under s 27 of the Principal Act. However, where a second or subsequent offence is committed within three years of a similar offence then, under s 26 and the Second Schedule item 10 of the Principal Act as re-enacted in the Road Traffic Act 1994, disqualification is mandatory if the offence involves a mechanically propelled vehicle which did not fulfil the requirements imposed by law with respect to lighting and reflectors as provided under the Road Traffic (Lighting of Vehicles) Regulations 1963.

Where the court decides not to impose a disqualification for drivers convicted of a first offence of dangerous driving the court shall impose five penalty points on the defendant's licence.

16.5   Obstructive parking

16.5.1   PROHIBITION

Section 98(1) of the Principal Act provides that:

> *A person shall not do any act (whether commission or omission), which causes or is likely to cause traffic through any public place to be obstructed.*

'Person' and 'public place' are defined in the preceding discussion regarding driving without a licence.

'Cause or is likely to cause' is defined in the preceding discussion regarding dangerous parking.

Traffic is not statutorily defined; however, it should be noted that certain provisions of the road traffic legislation expressly exclude pedestrians as traffic, whereas certain provisions expressly include pedestrians as traffic. As a general rule, pedestrians are included unless expressly excluded.

16.5.2   DEFENCES

Section 98(3) of the Principal Act provides that it is a good defence to show that either:

(a)   there was lawful authority for the act complained of; or

(b)   that it was due to an unavoidable accident.

'Obstruction' is not statutorily defined; however, the case of *O'Connor v Leonard* 103 ILTR 43 is instructive in this regard. It dealt with an unsuccessful prosecution under s 98 of the Principal Act, where it was held that the prohibition contained therein was not absolute and that the test of reasonableness must be applied. In the circumstances of this case, the defendant had parked his vehicle to unload goods for delivery to a shop. Parking was not permitted on the side on which he parked; however, it was permitted on the other side of the street. The court held that there was no obstruction by virtue of the fact that there was a free lane on the side on which the defendant had parked, thereby permitting traffic to flow without obstruction.

Accordingly, a successful prosecution will only arise where it can be shown that the defendant acted unreasonably.

16.5.3 PENALTIES

A person in breach of s 98 is guilty of an offence in accordance with the general penalty provisions more particularly set out at paragraph **16.1.4.** above.

16.6 Driving a dangerously defective vehicle

16.6.1 PROHIBITION

Section 54(2) of the Principal Act, as amended by s 6 and the schedule to the Road Traffic Act 1968 and s 23 of the Road Traffic Act 2002 provides:

> (2) *Where a mechanically propelled vehicle is driven in a public place while there is a defect affecting the vehicle which the owner thereof knows of or could have discovered by the exercise of ordinary care and which is such that the vehicle is, when in motion, a danger to the public, such owner shall be guilty of an offence.*

'Mechanically propelled vehicle', 'drive', 'public place', and 'owner' are defined in the preceding discussion regarding driving without a licence.

'Defect affecting the vehicle'—it would seem evident from reading s 54 (2) that this defect must be patent, and one which the owner had knowledge of and which affected the vehicle while it was being driven. In a prosecution under s 54 the vehicle must be inspected by the prosecution and the defect proven. The defendant will of course insist that his own expert independently assesses the car.

'Owner's knowledge'—this must be actual knowledge or knowledge which could be inferred in the circumstances in that the defendant failed to take reasonable care to find the defect (eg failed to have the vehicle serviced regularly). 'Owner' in the context need not be the registered owner, but may be the lessee or hirer under a hire purchase agreement.

'Danger to the public'—this must be within the knowledge of the defendant, hence the owner must be aware of the defect yet continue to drive the vehicle with such knowledge.

16.6.2 DEFENCE

Section 54(3) of the Principal Act provides that it is a defence for the owner to show that the vehicle was driven without his or her authority.

16.6.3 PENALTIES

Under s 3 of the Road Traffic (Amendment) Act 1984 as amended by s 23 of the Road Traffic Act 2002, the fines are as follows:

- a maximum fine of €1,500; and/or

- a maximum of three months' imprisonment;

- disqualification.

An ancillary disqualification order can be made under s 27 of the Principal Act as amended. This is mandatory under s 26 as amended on a second or subsequent offence within three years of the offence for which he was convicted. Under s 36 of the Principal Act as amended, an endorsement on the defendant's licence is mandatory, on conviction.

16.7 Driving while unfit

16.7.1 PROHIBITION

Section 48(1) of the Principal Act as amended by s 3 Road Traffic (Amendment) Act 1984 provides:

> *A person shall not drive or attempt to drive a mechanically propelled vehicle in a public place when he is, to his knowledge, suffering from any disease or physical or mental disability which would be likely to cause the driving of the vehicle by him in a public place to be a source of danger to the public.*

'Person', 'drive', 'mechanically propelled vehicle' and 'public place' are defined in the preceding discussion regarding driving without a licence.

'Attempt' is not statutorily defined; however, in the instructive case of *Haughton v Smith* [1975] AC 476, it was stated by the learned judge that:

> 'the act relied on as constituting the attempt must not be an act merely preparatory to commit the completed offence, but must bear a relationship to the completed offence referred to as proximate to the completion of the offence and as being immediately not merely remotely connected with the completed offence. Obviously whenever the test of proximity becomes crucial in a particular case, difficult questions of fact and degree will arise.'

Accordingly, the determination of whether an 'attempt' arises will depend upon the facts of each individual case.

The expression 'to his knowledge' gives rise to a subjective test as to whether the defendant had the requisite mental intention or *mens rea* for this offence.

The expression 'danger to the public' gives rise to an objective test in determining whether or not the illness or incapacity which the defendant suffered was of danger to the public. Medical evidence would be of considerable significance in determining whether the illness or incapacity would be regarded by the reasonable man as a danger to the public. The prosecution must prove this fact before an offence can be shown to have been committed.

16.7.2 PENALTIES

Under s 48(2) of the Principal Act, as re-enacted by s 3(5) of the Road Traffic (Amendment) Act 1984 as amended by s 23 of the Road Traffic Act 2002 and the Road Traffic Acts 1961–2005 (Fixed Charge Offences) Regulations 2006, the penalties are as follows:

- for a first offence a maximum fine of €800 and/or one month's imprisonment;

- for a second or subsequent offence a maximum fine of €1,500 and/or three months' imprisonment;

- Disqualification—mandatory under the Second Schedule, item 3, of the Principal Act on a second offence within three years of a first conviction.

As in the case with other offences under the Act an ancillary disqualification order can be made under s 27 of the Principal Act as amended, at the discretion of the court. Endorsement is mandatory under s 36 of the Principal Act as amended.

Where the court decides not to impose a disqualification for drivers convicted of a first offence of driving while unfit, the court shall endorse three penalty points on the defendant's licence.

16.8 Driving without reasonable consideration

16.8.1 PROHIBITION

Section 51A(1) of the Principal Act as inserted by s 49 of the Road Traffic Act 1968 provides:

> a person shall not drive a vehicle in a public place without reasonable consideration for other persons using the place.

'Person', 'drive', 'vehicle', and 'public place' are defined in the preceding discussion regarding driving without a licence.

'Without reasonable consideration'—there is no statutory definition as to what constitutes reasonable consideration and there is little authority to rely upon; however, this offence has always been regarded as a lesser offence than careless driving. Robert Pierse, in his text *Road Traffic Law, Volume 1. Commentary (First Law)* at p 480 states:

> 'The standard appears to be "reasonable" linked to "consideration to the public". It possibly involves *mens rea* as "consideration" involves an activity the human mind. It relates to "nuisance" to others rather than bad driving.'

This would appear to be the correct interpretation of the ingredients of this ambiguous offence.

'Other persons using the place'—in *Dilkes v Bowman Shaw* [1981] RTR 4, it was held that an actual road user must be inconvenienced before a person may be convicted of this offence.

16.8.2 DEFENCES

The defences of automatism and ambiguous evidence, as they apply to dangerous and careless driving, also apply to a lesser extent to this offence.

16.8.3 PENALTIES

The Road Traffic Acts 1961–2005 (Fixed Charge Offences) Regulations 2006 apply to this offence. There is an on the spot fine of €80 and two penalty points endorsed on the driver's licence where s/he admits to the offence in accordance with the practice and procedure set forth in the 2006 Regulations. On conviction the defendant shall be liable to a fine of €120 and four penalty points endorsed on their licence. No consequential disqualification provisions apply to offences under this section. However, the court does have the discretion to impose an ancillary disqualification order pursuant to s 27 of the Principal Act as amended.

16.9   Careless driving

16.9.1   PROHIBITION

Section 52 of the Principal Act, as replaced by s 50 of the Road Traffic Act 1968, as amended by s 23 of the Road Traffic Act 2002 provides:

> *A person shall not drive a vehicle in a public place without due care and attention.*

'Person', 'drive', 'vehicle', and 'public place' are defined in the preceding discussion regarding driving without a licence.

'Due care and attention'—there is no statutory definition of due care and attention, and there is also little precedent in this jurisdiction to define this term. In England, however, it has been held, in the case of *Wilson v McPhail* [1991] SCCR 170, that the standard required is that of:

> 'whether the driver was exercising the standard of care, skill and attention which a competent and reasonably prudent driver is expected to show in the circumstances.'

In the case of *Trentham v Rowlands* [1974] RTR 164, it was held that if there is evidence of several breaches of the highway code, this will be strong evidence of falling below the standard of ordinary and prudent driving.

Accordingly, in this jurisdiction where a driver has failed to comply with the rules of the road, it would be reasonable to presume that he or she has failed to exercise due care and attention.

In *Crispin v Rhodes* (1986) 40 SASR 202, it was held that 'due care' means adequate caution in the circumstances; watchfulness, caution, and vigilance are required.

16.9.2   DEFENCES

16.9.2.1   Automatism

The defence of automatism has succeeded in numerous English cases where certain personal conditions such as an epileptic fit, unconsciousness, or a sudden illness have all provided defences to cases of careless and dangerous driving.

In *A-G's Reference (No 2 of 1992)*, *The Times* of 31 May 1993, it was held by the Court of Appeal that the defence of automatism required the total destruction of voluntary control. Impaired or reduced control was not enough. There is no reported Irish case on this point.

16.9.2.2   Duress

A defence of driving in terror when the defendant and his friends were being pursued by a mob was accepted in the case of *DPP v Bell* [1992] RTR 335.

16.9.2.3   Emergency

A public emergency is not a defence even for a member of the Gardaí or emergency services.

16.9.2.4   Mechanical defect

In *R v Spurge* [1961] 2 QB 205, a sudden mechanical defect, due to no fault of the driver, causing loss of control, was held to be a good defence.

16.9.3   PENALTIES

Section 52 (2) of the Principal Act as amended by s 3 of the Road Traffic (Amendment) Act 1984 as amended by ss 2 and 23 of the Road Traffic Act 2002 provides the penalties for a s 52(1) offence.

These can be summarized as:

- €1,500 fine and/or three months' imprisonment.

Section 22 of the Road Traffic Act 2004 amended the First Schedule, Part 1 of the Road Traffic Act 2002 to include careless driving as a penalty points offence. Accordingly, where the court does not disqualify the defendant, it shall endorse five penalty points on the licence.

A discretionary ancillary disqualification order can be made pursuant to s 27 of the Principal Act as amended.

A mandatory disqualification order can be made under s 26 and the schedule to the Principal Act (as inserted by the Road Traffic Act 1994), where the contravention involves the commission of a second of subsequent offence under s 50 as amended within a period of three years.

Section 36 of the Principal Act provides that a person convicted of a s 50 offence for the second time in three years must have his or her licence endorsed. In *DPP v O'Brien* [1989] IR 260, the Supreme Court held that endorsement is mandatory in all instances where a defendant is convicted of a s 50 offence, including a first offence.

16.10   Dangerous driving

16.10.1   PROHIBITION

Section 53(1) of the Principal Act, as amended by s 51 of the Road Traffic Act 1968, s 3 Road Traffic (Amendment) Act 1984, s 49 Road Traffic Act 1994, s 23 Road Traffic Act 2003, and s 13 Road Traffic Act 2004 provides:

> *A person shall not drive a vehicle in a public place in a manner (including speed) which, having regard to all the circumstances of the case (including the condition of the vehicle, the nature, condition and use of the place and the amount of traffic which then actually is or might reasonably be expected then to be therein) is dangerous to the public.*

'Person', 'drive', 'vehicle', and 'public place' are defined in the preceding discussion regarding driving without a licence.

'Traffic' is defined in the preceding discussion regarding obstructive parking.

'Manner' shall be examined in the context of 'in a manner which is dangerous' as discussed below.

'Speed' is a consideration in determining whether the driving is dangerous in the context of this offence. In *Welton v Toreborne* (1908) 72 JP 419, it was held that where speed is taken into account in a conviction for dangerous driving this shall be a bar to any subsequent conviction for speed.

'Circumstance' is defined as including various factors which the court can consider; however, it is not necessary for the court to state the circumstances or factors it relied upon when making a conviction. These circumstances include 'condition of the vehicle', 'nature of the place', 'condition of the place', 'use of the place', 'amount of traffic', and other circumstances.

'Condition of vehicle'—in *R v Strong* [1995] Crim LR 428, the defendant's brakes and steering were defective; however, he had only bought the car a few days before the fatal accident. On examination, the examiner stated that it was necessary to go under the car to discover the defects. Relying on the words 'obvious to a careful and competent driver' in s 2A(2) of the English Road Traffic Act 1988, the court held that there was not sufficient evidence to convict of dangerous driving.

'Nature of place' includes the width of the road, where it is situate, and traffic signals in its vicinity.

'Condition of place' would include the state of the road due to weather and other factors also relating to its state of maintenance.

'Use of place' would include whether it was a busy town street or a country road, whether it was a primary road, secondary road or a motorway.

'Amount of traffic' would include the volume of traffic reasonably expected.

'Other circumstances' which the court could take into consideration would include whether the defendant had consumed alcohol or drugs and how long he or she had driven without a rest.

'Dangerous to the public' is not statutorily defined; however, Pierse in *Road Traffic Law, Volume 1 Commentary* (First Law) p 430, cites from the judgment of Barra O'Briain J in the case of *People v Quinlan* [1962] ILT & SJ 123. In defining this term, Pierse states:

> 'Judge Barra O'Briain's (then president of the Circuit Court) standard charge to a jury is a good guide on the nature or the kernel of the offence, ie:—"driving in a manner (including speed) which a reasonable prudent man having knowledge of all the circumstances proved in court would clearly recognise as involving unjustifiably definite risk of harm to the public."'

The case of *AG v McGrath* [1965] Ir Jur Rep 57 is also instructive in regard to this expression. In that case, Deale J in the Circuit Court held that the dangerous driving of the accused must be the sole cause of the death or serious bodily harm. This case has now been overruled by the Court of Criminal Appeal in *People v Gallagher* [1972] IR 365, where it was held by Kenny J as follows:

> 'Problems of causation have been the subject of arguments in universities and in law courts for centuries and it is important that the jury should not be confused by refined distinctions between material, effective, substantial or predominant cause. If they are told that they must be satisfied beyond reasonable doubt that the dangerous driving was one of the causes which contributed in a real way to the death or serious bodily harm and that they must decide this by applying principles of common sense, they will understand the issue which they have to try.'

In accordance with this judgment, it should be noted that even where the dead or injured person may have contributed in some way to the accident, this is not a matter which can be put to the jury as a mitigating ground on which they are entitled to acquit the accused.

16.10.2 DEFENCE

The defences available in a dangerous driving situation are the same as those which apply to careless driving. It should be noted, however, that s 53(3) of the Road Traffic Act 1961 as substituted by s 13 of the Road Traffic Act 2004 expressly excludes as a defence evidence of the fact that the alleged offender was not in excess of the speed limit applying in relation to the vehicle or the road.

16.10.3 PENALTIES

16.10.3.1 Mode of trial

This is dependent upon the mode of trial. If death or serious bodily harm is the result of the dangerous driving then the trial is by way of indictment; otherwise it is a summary trial.

If the driving does not cause death or serious bodily harm, or the charge does not so allege, the offence is a summary one wherein there is no right to a jury trial.

16.10.3.2 Fines

Summarily, the accused can be fined £2,500 (or its euro equivalent) maximum. On indictment (ie in death or serious bodily harm cases) the accused can be fined £15,000 (or its euro equivalent) maximum.

16.10.3.3 Imprisonment

Summarily, the maximum term of imprisonment is six months. On indictment (ie in death or serious bodily harm cases) the maximum term is 10 years.

16.10.3.4 Endorsement

A summary or indictable conviction for dangerous driving carries a compulsory endorsement on the defendant's licence.

16.10.3.5 Disqualification

Under s 26(5)(b)(i), where a person is convicted summarily under s 53, the court may, in the case of a first offence where it is satisfied that a special reason (which it specifies in its order) has been proved by the convicted person to exist in his or her particular case to justify such a course, decline to make a consequential disqualification order, or may specify a disqualification of less than one year. Otherwise, the penalty that applies is one year's disqualification in the case of first offence; and not less than two years in the case of a second or subsequent offence within three years from the date of the previous (or last) offence. On indictment (ie in death or serious bodily harm cases), the period of disqualification is two years on the first offence and on a second offence or subsequent offence four years.

16.10.3.6 Certificate of competency

Section 26(3) of the Principal Act as re-enacted by s 3(a) of the Road Traffic (Amendment) Act 1995 provides that where the dangerous driving charge is successfully prosecuted on indictment, the consequential disqualification order shall operate also to disqualify the guilty driver from holding a driving licence during a specified period. Further, until he or she has produced to the appropriate licensing authority (as may be specified in the order) a certificate of competency or both a certificate of competency and a certificate of fitness, he or she shall not be entitled to a licence.

Both the Road Traffic Act 1994 and Road Traffic (Amendment) Act 1995 refer to 'special reasons' in relation to a disqualification order. Under s 26(5) of the Principal Act for first offences in summary trials for charges under s 53 (dangerous driving) or s 56 (driving without insurance) of the Principal Act, a court may decline to make a consequential order where it is satisfied a special reason has been proven to exist. Alternatively, for such special reason, on conviction under either of the aforementioned sections, the court may specify that disqualification for a period of less than one year may be imposed.

Further, a special reason similarly proven under s 26 (3) of the Principal Act, as substituted by s 2 of the 1995 Act, can obviate the necessity of an otherwise automatic order requiring a certificate of competency and/or fitness being incorporated with the consequential disqualification order following convictions on ss 53 and 106(i)(a) or (b) of the Principal Act. It should further be noted that s 30 of the Principal Act allows for postponement of disqualification for a special reason.

Special reasons which have been accepted by the courts include mitigating or extenuating circumstances which the court should take into account when considering sentence. These include circumstances which relate to the nature of the offence, do not affect public safety and must not relate to the driver's personal circumstances. In *Reynolds v Roche* [1972] RTR 282, the fact that a disqualification would cause serious hardship to the defendant's family was not accepted as a special reason. It must be noted that in all instances where a special reason is accepted by the courts, this special reason must be specified in the court order of conviction and sentence.

16.10.3.7 Sentencing criterion

There are no formal criteria in respect of sentencing in dangerous driving cases; however, where such driving causes death or serious bodily harm, the courts have enunciated factors which should be taken into account. In *R v Boswell* [1984] RTR 315, the factors which will go to severity of sentence are listed as including intoxicants; excessive speed; racing; competitive driving; disregarding warnings by passengers and others; prolonged, persistent bad driving; several people killed or injured; the offence being committed while on bail. Factors which will go to mitigate against a long sentence or a custodial sentence at all are stated to include: one-off mistake; plea of guilty; good character; remorse; the deceased is a friend; monetary recompense re culpability; injury to the defendant themselves; stopping at scene; and driving due to an emergency.

16.11 Manslaughter

The principles of this offence are to be found in any authoritative criminal law text. Indictments for manslaughter in dangerous driving cases resulting in death are rare nowadays, in view of s 53 of the Principal Act, which provides for the crime of dangerous driving causing death, often referred to as 'motor manslaughter'. For further examination of the offence of manslaughter see the recommended reading list for this course as set out in the Criminal Litigation module introductory booklet.

16.12 Intoxicant offences

16.12.1 PROHIBITION

Section 49 of the Principal Act, as re-enacted by s 10 of the Road Traffic Act 1994, provides as follows:

> *(1)   (a) A person shall not drive or attempt to drive a mechanically propelled vehicle in a public place while he is under the influence of an intoxicant to such an extent as to be incapable of having proper control of the vehicle.*
> *(b) In this subsection 'intoxicant' includes alcohol and drugs and any combination of drugs or of drugs and alcohol.*
> *(2)   A person shall not drive or attempt to drive a mechanically propelled vehicle in a public place while there is present in his body a quantity of alcohol such that, within 3 hours after so driving or attempting to drive, the concentration of alcohol in his blood will exceed a concentration of 80 milligrams of alcohol per 100 millilitres of blood.*
> *(3)   A person shall not drive or attempt to drive a mechanically propelled vehicle in a public place while there is present in his body a quantity of alcohol such that, within 3 hours after so driving or attempting to drive, the concentration of alcohol in his urine will exceed a concentration of 107 milligrams of alcohol per 100 millilitres of urine.*
> *(4)   A person shall not drive or attempt to drive a mechanically propelled vehicle in a public place while there is present in his body a quantity of alcohol such that, within 3 hours after so driving or*

attempting to drive, the concentration of alcohol in his breath will exceed a concentration of 35 micrograms of alcohol per 100 millilitres of breath.

(5)   (a) *The Minister may, by regulations made by him, vary the concentration of alcohol for the time being standing specified in sub-section (2), (3) or (4) of this section, whether generally or in respect of a particular class of person, and the said subsection shall have effect in accordance with any such regulations for the time being in force.*

      (b) *A draft of every regulation proposed to be made under this subsection shall be laid before each House of the Oireachtas and the regulation shall not be made until a resolution approving of the draft has been passed by each such House and section 5(2) of this Act shall not apply to a regulation made under this subsection.*

(6)   (a) *A person who contravenes subsections (1), (2), (3) or (4) of this section shall be guilty of an offence and shall be liable on summary conviction to a fine not exceeding €2,500 or to imprisonment for a term not exceeding 6 months or to both.*

      (b) *A person charged with an offence under this section may, in lieu of being found guilty of that offence, be found guilty of an offence under section 50 of this Act.*

(7) *Section 1(1) of the Probation of Offenders Act, 1907, shall not apply to an offence under this section.*

(8) *A member of the Gardaí may arrest without warrant a person who in the member's opinion is committing or has committed an offence under this section.*

'Drive', 'mechanically propelled vehicle', 'person' and 'public place' are defined in the preceding discussion regarding driving without a licence.

'Attempt' is previously defined in relation to the discussion of s 49 of the Principal Act as amended.

'Arrest'—many sections of the Road Traffic Acts authorize the Gardaí to arrest an alleged offender without a warrant where the member is of the opinion that an offence has been committed on the basis of his or her observation of the offence or where the condition of a driver leads him or her to believe that an offence has been committed. These provisions include:

- in the 1961 Act—ss 19, 40, 49, 50, 51, 53, 55, 69, 82, 107, 112, and 113.

- in the 1968 Act—ss 16, 28, 56, and 59.

- in the 1994 Act—ss 10, 11, 12, 14, and 25.

A Garda member is, however, obliged to comply with the Criminal Justice Act 1984 (Treatment of Persons in Custody in Garda Stations) Regulations 1987 (SI 119/ 1987), which provide that a detainee be informed of their rights under the said regulations.

In *DPP v Spratt* [1995] 2 ILRM 117, the defendant was arrested pursuant to s 49 of the Principal Act, as amended. In the District Court, it was not established that the Criminal Justice Act 1984 (Treatment of Persons in Custody in Garda Stations) Regulations 1987 had been adhered to. The District Court stated a case for the opinion of the High Court as to the effect, if any, resulting from the non-compliance with the regulations. The High Court stated that while it must be proven that the 1987 Regulations have been complied with, it is a matter for the court of trial to adjudicate in every case as to the impact of the non-compliance. Failure to comply does not necessarily lead to a dismissal of the charge against the accused.

Section 50 of the Principal Act, as re-enacted by s 11 of the Road Traffic Act 1994 as amended by s 23 of the Road Traffic Act 2002, provides as follows:

(1)   (a) *A person shall be guilty of an offence if, when in charge of a mechanically propelled vehicle in a public place with intent to drive or attempt to drive the vehicle (but not driving or attempting to drive it), he is under the influence of an intoxicant to such an extent as to be incapable of having proper control of the vehicle.*

      (b) *In this subsection 'intoxicant' includes alcohol, drugs and any combination of drugs and alcohol.*

(2) *A person shall be guilty of an offence if, when in charge of a mechanically propelled vehicle in a public place with intent to drive it, or attempt to drive the vehicle (but not driving or attempting to drive it), there is present in his body a quantity of alcohol such that, within 3 hours after so being in charge,*

the concentration of alcohol in his blood will exceed a concentration of 80 milligrams of alcohol per 100 millilitres of blood.

(3)   *A person shall be guilty of an offence if, when in charge of a mechanically propelled vehicle in a public place with intent to drive or attempt to drive the vehicle (but not driving or attempting to drive it), there is present in his body a quantity of alcohol such that, within 3 hours after having been so in charge of the vehicle, the concentration of alcohol in his urine will exceed a concentration of 107 milligrams of alcohol per 100 millilitres of urine.*

(4)   *A person shall be guilty of an offence if, when in charge of a mechanically propelled vehicle in a public place with intent to drive or attempt to drive the vehicle (but not driving or attempting to drive it) there is present in his body a quantity of alcohol such that, within 3 hours after so being in charge, the concentration of alcohol in his breath will exceed a concentration of 35 micrograms of alcohol per 100 millilitres of breath.*

(5)   (a)   *The Minister may, by regulations made by him, vary the concentration of alcohol for the time being standing specified in subsections (2), (3) or (4) of this section, whether generally or in respect of a particular class of person, and the said subsection shall have effect in accordance with any such regulations for the time being in force.*

       (b)   *A draft of every regulation proposed to be made under this subsection shall be laid before each House of the Oireachtas and the regulation shall not be made until a resolution approving of the draft has been passed by each such House and s 5(2) of this Act shall not apply to a regulation made under this subsection.*

(6)   (a)   *A person guilty of an offence under this section shall be liable on summary conviction to a fine not exceeding €2,500 or to imprisonment for a term not exceeding 6 months or to both.*

       (b)   *A person charged with an offence under this section may, in lieu of being found guilty of that offence, be found guilty of an offence under s 49 of this Act.*

(7)   *Section 1(1) of the Probation of Offenders Act, 1907, shall not apply to an offence under this section.*

(8)   *In a prosecution for an offence under this section it shall be presumed that the defendant intended to drive or attempt to drive the vehicle concerned until he shows the contrary.*

A person liable to be charged with an offence under this section shall not, by reference to the same occurrence, be liable to be charged under s 12 of the Licensing Act, 1872, with the offence of being drunk while in charge, on a highway or other public place, of a carriage.

A member of the Gardaí may arrest without warrant a person who in the member's opinion is committing or has committed an offence under this section;

'Mechanically propelled vehicle', 'person' and 'public place' are defined in the preceding discussion regarding driving without a licence.

'Arrest' is discussed previously in relation to s 49 of the Principal Act as amended.

There is no statutory definition of 'in charge'; however, numerous cases have developed criteria. In particular, *DPP v Watkins* [1989] 1 All ER 1126 is most instructive. In this case, the court held that there were generally two classes of case:

(a)   Where the defendant is the owner or in lawful possession of the vehicle or can be shown to have recently driven the vehicle, he will be held to be in charge of it, unless he can prove that he has given over charge of the vehicle to someone else; and

(b)   Where the facts do not come within (a) above, but the defendant is sitting in the vehicle or is otherwise involved in it having regard to certain circumstances. Examples of such circumstances would be that he has been given the keys; he is in or near the vehicle so as to suggest that he is in charge of it; he has a key which fits the ignition; he is the only person near the vehicle who by his actions suggests that he is in charge of it, and by his actions he suggests that he has the intention to take control of it.

In the case of *DPP v Byrne* (unreported, 6 December 2001) (Sup Ct (Irl)), a driver asleep in his car was said to be in charge with intent to drive for the purposes of an offence contrary to s 50(3) of the Road Traffic Act 1961. The circumstances which led the court to this opinion included the fact that the driver was in the driver's seat, the keys were in the ignition and had been turned two clicks and the car was parked on the hard shoulder of the road.

Section 51 of the Principal Act, as amended by s 3 (6) of the Road Traffic (Amendment) Act, 1984, as amended by section 23 of the Road Traffic Act 2002 provides:

(1)   A person shall not in a public place—

(a)   Drive or attempt to drive or be in charge of an animal drawn vehicle; or

(b)   Drive or attempt to drive a pedal cycle,

while he is under the influence of intoxicating liquor or a drug to such an extent as to be incapable to having proper control of the vehicle or cycle.

(2)   A person who contravenes sub-section (1) of this section shall be guilty of an Offence and: If the offence relates to an animal drawn vehicle he shall be liable on summary conviction in the case of a first offence to a fine not exceeding €800 or, at the discretion of the court to imprisonment for any term not exceeding one month or to both such fine and such imprisonment and in the case of a second or any subsequent offence, to a fine not exceeding €1,500 or, at the discretion of the court, to an imprisonment for any term not exceeding three months or to both such fine and such imprisonment, and

If such offence relates to a pedal cycle, he shall be liable on a summary conviction to a fine not exceeding €1,500 or, at the discretion of the court to imprisonment for any term not exceeding three months or both such fine and such imprisonment.

(3)   A person liable to be charged with an offence under this section shall not by reference to the same occurrence be liable to be charged under section 12 of the Licensing Act 1872, with an offence of being drunk while in charge, on the highway or other public place, or a carriage.

Where a member of the Gardaí is of the opinion that a person is committing or has committed an offence under this section he may arrest the person without warrant.

'Person' and 'public place' are defined in the preceding discussion in relation to driving without a licence.

'Attempt' is defined in the preceding discussion regarding driving while unfit.

'Arrest' and 'in charge' have been examined in the discussion of s 49 of the Principal Act as amended.

Section 59 of the Road Traffic Act 1968 provides:

(1)   A person who is found in a public place in such a condition because he is under the influence of intoxicating liquor or a drug as to be a source of danger to the traffic or himself shall be guilty of an offence.

(2)   A person charged with an offence under this section shall not in respect of the facts alleged to constitute such offence be charged under section 12 of the Licensing Act 1836, section 12 of the Licensing Act 1872, section 25 of the Licensing (Ireland) Act 1874 or section 9 of the Summary Jurisdiction Act 1908.

(3)   Where a member of the Gardaí is of the opinion that a person is committing an offence under this section he may arrest the person without warrant.

'Arrest', 'person' and 'public place' are defined in the preceding discussion regarding driving without a licence.

The following section is substituted for s 12 of the Act, 1994:

(1)   This section applies to a person in charge of a vehicle in a public place:

(a)   at a time when the vehicle is involved in an accident, or

(b)   who, in the opinion of a member of the Garda Síochána, has consumed intoxicating liquor, or

(c)   who, in the opinion of a member of the Garda Síochána, is committing or has committed an offence under the Road Traffic Acts 1961 to 2002 (other than s 49, 50 and 51 of the Principal Act, and s 12 to 15).

(2)   A member of the Garda Síochána may require a person to whom this section applies:

(a) *to provide, by exhaling into an apparatus for indicating the presence of alcohol in breath, a specimen of his or her breath and may indicate the manner in which he or she is to comply with the requirement.*

(b) *to accompany him or her to a place (including a vehicle) at or in the vicinity of the public place concerned and they require the person to provide, by exhaling into such an apparatus, a specimen of his or her breath and may indicate the manner in which the person is to comply with the requirement, or*

(c) *where the member does not have such an apparatus with him or her, to remain at the place in his or her presence or in the presence of another member of the Garda Síochána until such an apparatus become available to him or her (but the member shall not require the person to so remain for more than one hour) and the member may then require the person to provide, by exhaling into such an apparatus, a specimen of his or her breath and may indicate the manner in which he or she is to comply with the requirement.*

(3) *A person who refuses or fails to comply forthwith with a requirement under this section, or to comply forthwith with such a requirement in a manner indicated by a member of the Garda Síochána, shall be guilty of an offence and shall be liable on summary conviction to a fine not exceeding €2,500 or imprisonment for a term not exceeding six months or both.*

(4) *A member of the Garda Síochána may arrest without warrant a person who in the member's opinion is committing or has committed an offence under this section.*

(5) *In a prosecution for an offence under this Part or under s 49 or 50 of the Principal Act, it shall be presumed, until the contrary is shown, that the apparatus provided by a member of the Garda Síochána for the purpose of enabling a person to provide a specimen or breath pursuant to this section is an apparatus for indicating the presence of alcohol in breath.*

16.12.2   OBLIGATION TO PROVIDE PRELIMINARY BREATH SPECIMEN

Section 12 of the Road Traffic Act 1994, as substituted by s 10 of the Road Traffic Act 2003 provides:

12.—(1) *This section applies to a person in charge of a mechanically propelled vehicle in a public place who, in the opinion of a member of the Garda Síochána—*

    (a) *has consumed intoxicating liquor,*

    (b) *is or has, with the vehicle, been involved in a collision, or*

    (c) *is committing or has committed an offence under the Road Traffic Acts 1961–2003.*

(2) *A member of the Garda Síochána may require a person to whom this section applies—*

    (a) *to provide, by exhaling into an apparatus for indicating the presence of alcohol in the breath, a specimen of his or her breath,*

    (b) *to accompany him or her to a place (including a vehicle) at or in the vicinity of the public place concerned and there require the person to provide, by exhaling into such an apparatus, a specimen of his or her breath, or*

    (c) *where the member does not have such an apparatus with him or her, to remain at that place in his or her presence or in the presence of another member of the Garda Síochána until such an apparatus becomes available to him or her (but the member shall not require the person to so remain for more than one hour) and the member may then require the person to provide, by exhaling into such an apparatus, a specimen of his or her breath, and the member may indicate the manner in which the person is to comply with the requirement.*

(3) *A person who refuses or fails to comply immediately with—*

    (a) *a requirement under this section, or*

    (b) *such a requirement in a manner indicated by a member of the Garda Síochána, is guilty of an*

> offence and is liable on summary conviction to a fine not exceeding €2,500 or imprisonment for a term not exceeding 6 months or both.
>
> (4) A member of the Garda Síochána may arrest without warrant a person who in the member's opinion is committing or has committed an offence under this section.
>
> (5) In a prosecution for an offence under this Part or under ss 49 or 50 of the Principal Act, it shall be presumed, until the contrary is shown, that an apparatus provided by a member of the Garda Síochána for the purpose of enabling a person to provide a specimen of breath pursuant to this section is an apparatus for indicating the presence of alcohol in the breath.

In *DPP v Joyce* [1985] ILRM 206, the court held that in order to comply with the provisions of s 12, a Garda member is obliged to request the specimen of breath from a *person in charge of a mechanically propelled vehicle in a public place*.

'Person', 'public place', and 'mechanically propelled vehicle' are defined in the preceding discussion regarding driving without a licence.

'In charge' is discussed above regarding s 49 of the Principal Act as amended.

In *DPP v Gilmore* [1981] ILRM 102, the court held that a positive Breathalyser result would be sufficient to substantiate the evidence of a Garda member that a s 49(2) or a s 49(3) offence had been committed. Section 4 of the Road Traffic Act 2006 has extended the obligation to provide a specimen to mandatory breath testing, without prejudice to the powers under s 12.

16.12.3   OBLIGATION TO PROVIDE SPECIMEN FOLLOWING ARREST

Section 13 of the Road Traffic Act 1994, as amended by s 3 of the Road Traffic Act 2003 provides:

> (1) Where a person is arrested under section 49(8) or 50(10) of the Principal Act or section 12(3), or where a person is arrested under section 53(6), 106(3A) or 112(6) of the Principal Act and a member of the Gardaí is of opinion that the person has consumed an intoxicant, a member of the Gardaí may, at a Garda station, at his discretion, do either or both of the following—
>
> require the person to provide, by exhaling into an apparatus for determining the concentration of alcohol in the breath, 2 specimens of his breath and may indicate the manner in which he is to comply with the requirement,
>   require the person either—
>   to permit a designated doctor to take from the person a specimen of his blood, or at the option of the person, to provide for the designated doctor a specimen of his urine, and if the doctor states in writing that he is unwilling, on medical grounds, to take from the person or be provided by him with the specimen to which the requirement in either of the foregoing subparagraphs related, the member may make a requirement of the person under this paragraph in relation to the specimen other than that to which the first requirement related.
>
> (2) Subject to section 23, a person who refuses or fails to comply forthwith with a requirement under subsection (1)(a) shall be guilty of an offence and shall be liable on summary conviction to a fine not exceeding €2,500 or to imprisonment for a term not exceeding 6 months or to both.
>
> (3) Subject to section 23, a person who, following a requirement under subsection (1)(b)—
>
> refuses or fails to comply with the requirement, or
> refuses or fails to comply with a requirement of a designated doctor in relation to the taking under that subsection of a specimen of blood or the provision under that subsection of a specimen of urine, shall be guilty of an offence and shall be liable on summary conviction to a fine not exceeding €2,500 or to imprisonment for a term not exceeding 6 months or to both.
>
> (4) In a prosecution for an offence under this Part or under ss 49 or 50 of the Principal Act it shall be presumed, until the contrary is shown, that an apparatus provided by a member of the Gardaí for the purpose of enabling a person to provide 2 specimens of breath pursuant to this section is an apparatus for determining the concentration of alcohol in the breath.
>
> (5) Section 1(1) of the Probation of Offenders Act, 1907, shall not apply to an offence under this section.

In order to invoke the jurisdiction under s 13, the defendant must be arrested and brought to a Garda station for driving and being in charge of a mechanically propelled vehicle while under the influence of an intoxicant.

'Arrested' and 'in charge' are previously discussed in relation to s 49 of the Principal Act as amended.

'Driving' and 'mechanically propelled vehicle' are defined in the preceding discussion regarding driving without a licence.

'Intoxicant' for the purposes of this section includes alcohol and/or drugs.

In the case of *DPP v O'Connor* (unreported, 9 March 1999) (Sup Ct (Irl)), it was held that in order to escape the obligation to permit a blood specimen to be taken, the defendant must actually provide a specimen of urine and not merely agree to provide one within a reasonable time.

In the case of *DPP v Cabot* (unreported, 20 April 2004) (High Court, O'Caoimh J) it was held that there is no legal requirement or obligation on the Gardaí to advise an arrested person in relation to the defences which apply in the event of a subsequent prosecution for drunk driving or to advise him that failure to comply with the requirements under the aforementioned s 13(1) might constitute an offence punishable at law.

16.12.4   PROCEDURE FOLLOWING PROVISION OF BREATH SPECIMEN

Section 17 of the 1994 Act sets out the procedure in respect of the procedure following provision of a breath specimen. It provides as follows:

(1)   *Where, consequent on a requirement under s 13(1)(a) of him, a person provides two specimens of his breath and the apparatus referred to in that section determines the concentration of alcohol in each specimen—in case the apparatus determines that each specimen has the same concentration of alcohol, either specimen, and in case the apparatus determines that each specimen has a different concentration of alcohol, the specimen with the lower concentration of alcohol, shall be taken into account for the purposes of ss 49(4) or 50(4) of the Principal Act and the other specimen shall be disregarded.*

(2)   *Where the apparatus referred to in s 13(1) determines that in respect of the specimen of breath to be taken into account as aforesaid the person may have contravened s 49(4) or 50(4) of the Principal Act, he shall be supplied forthwith by a member of the Gardaí with two identical statements, automatically produced by the said apparatus in the prescribed form and duly completed by the member in the prescribed manner, stating the concentration of alcohol in the said specimen determined by the said apparatus—*

(3)   *On receipt of the statements aforesaid, the person shall on being requested so to do by the member aforesaid—forthwith acknowledge such receipt by placing his signature on each statement, and thereupon return either of the statements to the member.*

(4)   *A person who refuses or fails to comply with subsection (3) shall be guilty of an offence and shall be liable on summary conviction to a fine not exceeding £500 or to imprisonment for a term not exceeding 3 months or to both.*

(5)   *Section 21(1) shall apply to a statement under this section as respects which there has been a failure to comply with subsection (3)(a) as it applies to a duly completed statement under this section. In order to comply with the procedure herein, the Garda must obtain two specimens from the alleged offender and two identical analysis statements from the Bureau. The alleged offender is obliged to sign both of these statements one of which must be returned to the Garda in charge of the investigation of the offence.*

In the case of *DPP v Syron* (unreported, 7 March 2001) (High Court, O'Higgins J) it was held that the absence of a regulation which laid down the procedure for the scientific calculation of the quantity of alcohol to breath did not preclude the certificate from being prima facie evidence of the facts of quantity it purported to exhibit. In this case the intoxyliser presented a reading of 89 microgrammes of alcohol per 100 millilitres of breath, while the summons showed a figure of 73 microgrammes of alcohol. The high court refused to dismiss the summons on the basis that the defendant had not been deprived of his right to challenge the certificate in whatever manner he saw fit; in addition, he had not been deprived of fair procedures or natural justice.

16.12.5 PROCEDURE REGARDING TAKING OF BLOOD SPECIMENS AND PROVISION OF URINE SPECIMENS

Section 18 of the 1994 Act provides:

(1) *Where under this Part a designated doctor has taken a specimen of blood from a person or has been provided by the person with a specimen of his urine, the doctor shall divide the specimen into two parts, place each part in a container which he shall forthwith seal and complete the form prescribed for the purposes of this section.*

(2) *Where a specimen of blood or urine of a person has been divided into two parts pursuant to subsection (1), a member of the Gardaí shall offer to the person one of the sealed containers together with a statement in writing indicating that he may retain either or the containers.*

(3) *As soon as practicable after subsection (2) has been complied with, a member of the Gardaí shall cause to be forwarded to the Bureau the completed form referred to in subsection (1), together with the relevant sealed container or, where the person has declined to retain one of the sealed containers, both relevant sealed containers.*

(4) *In a prosecution for an offence under this Part or under s 49 or 50 of the Principal Act, it shall be presumed until the contrary is shown that subsection (1) to (3) have been complied with.*

This section gives rise to a presumption that the Garda member and doctor have complied with its provisions unless the contrary can be proved. Accordingly, it is imperative for a defence solicitor to ask his client whether he or she asked to be tested by his or her own doctor, and if so whether this request was complied with.

Further, the doctor should be questioned in regard to the equipment he used and whether it was sealed pre- and post-testing. Nothing should be taken for granted. The Garda member should be questioned in regard to the time lapse from receipt of sample by doctor to sending it to the Bureau, as this must be done as soon as is practicable.

In *Dean v DPP* [1988] RR 148, the specimen was held to be inadmissible by virtue of the fact that the doctor did not use the accepted procedures when taking the sample.

16.12.6 PROCEDURE AT BUREAU REGARDING SPECIMENS

Section 19 of the 1994 Act provides:

(1) *As soon as practicable after it has received a specimen forwarded to it under s 18, the Bureau shall analyse the specimen and determine the concentration of alcohol or (as may be appropriate) the presence of a drug or drugs in the specimen.*

(2) *Where the Bureau receives two specimens of blood so forwarded together in relation to the same person or two specimens of urine so forwarded together in relation to the same person, it shall be sufficient compliance with subsection (1) for the Bureau to make an analysis of and determination in relation to one of the two specimens of blood or (as may be appropriate) one of the two specimens of urine.*

(3) *As soon as practicable after compliance with subsection (1), the Bureau shall forward to the Gardaí station from which the specimen analysed was forwarded a completed certificate in the form prescribed for the purpose of this section and shall forward a copy of the completed certificate to the person who is named on the relevant form under s 18 as the person from whom the specimen was taken or who provided it.*

(4) *In a prosecution for an offence under this Part or under s 49 or 50 of the Principal Act, it shall be presumed until the contrary is shown that subsections (1) to (3) have been complied with.*

The Bureau is a corporate body and therefore acts in the same manner as any corporate body through its authorised agents or analysts. Accordingly, the Bureau and not the analyst certifies the accuracy of a tested specimen.

The phrase '*As soon as practicable*' gives rise to two very serious obligations on the part of the Bureau:

(a) The Bureau must forward as soon as practicable a completed certificate in the prescribed form to the Garda station from whom the specimen was received.

(b) The Bureau must forward a copy of the certificate to the person from whom the specimen was taken.

In *Hobbs v Hurley* (unreported) 10 June 1980, High Court, a specimen taken at 12.55 am on 19 September received by the Bureau on 20 and 21 September, signed by the analyst on 10 October and sealed by the Bureau on 11 October was deemed to comply with the 'as soon as practicable' obligations on the part of the Bureau.

In *DPP v McPartland* [1983] ILRM 411, a Bureau certificate with the same address as the summons, which in both instances was incorrect, was held admissible by virtue of the fact that the defence had raised no objections to the inaccuracy on the summons nor had it sought to have it amended.

In *DPP v Flahive* [1988] ILRM 133, a typographical error on the Bureau's certificate was deemed as not affecting the admissibility of the certificate.

'Analyse' is defined by s 9 of the Road Traffic Act 1994 as including any operation used in determining the concentration of alcohol in a specimen of breath, blood, or urine, and any operation used in determining the presence (if any) of a drug or drugs in a specimen of blood or urine.

In *R v Coomaraswamy* [1976] Crom LR 260, the court held that the duty of the prosecution was limited to proving that the alcohol limit was exceeded.

16.12.7 OBLIGATION TO ACCOMPANY MEMBER TO GARDA STATION TO PROVIDE BLOOD OR URINE SPECIMEN

Section 14 of the 1994 Act provides:

(1) Whenever a member of the Gardaí is of opinion that a person in charge of a mechanically propelled vehicle in a public place is under the influence of a drug or drugs to such an extent as to be incapable of having proper control of the vehicle, he may require the person to accompany him to a Gardaí station.

(2) A person who refuses or fails to comply with a requirement under subsection (1) shall be guilty of an offence and shall be liable on summary conviction to a fine not exceeding €2,500 or to imprisonment for a term not exceeding 6 months or to both.

(3) A member of the Gardaí may arrest without warrant a person who in the member's opinion is committing or has committed an offence under subsection (2).

(4) Where a person is at a Gardaí station either pursuant to subsection (1) or having been arrested under subsection (3), a member of the Gardaí may there require the person either—to permit a designated doctor to take from the person a specimen of his blood, or at the option of the person, to provide for the designated doctor a specimen of his urine, and if the doctor states in writing that he is unwilling, on medical grounds, to take from the person or be provided by him with the specimen to which the requirement in either of the foregoing paragraphs related, the member may make a requirement of the person under this subsection in relation to the specimen other than that to which the first requirement related.

(5) Subject to s 23, a person who, following a requirement under subsection (4)—

refuses or fails to comply with the requirement, or

refuses or fails to comply with a requirement of a designated doctor in relation to the taking under that subsection of a specimen of blood or the provision under that subsection of a specimen of urine, shall be guilty of an offence and shall be liable on summary conviction to a fine not exceeding €2,500 or to imprisonment for a term not exceeding 6 months or to both.

(6) Section 1(1) of the Probation of Offenders Act, 1907, shall not apply to an offence under this section.

'Arrest' is defined in the preceding discussion regarding s 49 of the Principal Act as amended.

A person arrested under this section must be informed that he is being arrested and the reason for the arrest.

In *Alderson v Boothe* [1969] 2 All ER 271, it was held that an arrest under a similar provision of the English legislation was unlawful, as the arresting officer merely stated his wish to bring the arrestee to the police station for further tests. He did not explain that he was in fact arresting the arrestee, or the reason for same.

16.12.8 OBLIGATION TO PROVIDE BLOOD OR URINE SPECIMEN WHILE IN HOSPITAL

Section 15 of the 1994 Act provides:

(1) *Where, in a public place, an event occurs in relation to a mechanically propelled vehicle in consequence of which a person is injured, or claims or appears to have been injured, and is admitted to, or attends at, a hospital and a member of the Gardaí is of opinion that, at the time of the event—the person was driving or attempting to drive, or in charge of with intent to drive or attempt to drive (but not driving or attempting to drive), the mechanically propelled vehicle, and the person had consumed an intoxicant, then such member may, in the hospital, require the person either—to permit a designated doctor to take from the person a specimen of his blood, or at the option of the person, to provide for the designated doctor a specimen of his urine, and if the doctor states in writing that he is unwilling, on medical grounds, to take from the person or be provided by him with the specimen to which the requirement in either of the foregoing subparagraphs related, the member may make a requirement of the person under this subsection in relation to the specimen other than that to which the first requirement related.*

(2) *Subject to s 23, a person who, following a requirement under subsection (1) refuses or fails to comply with the requirement, or refuses or fails to comply with a requirement of a designated doctor in relation to the taking under that subsection of a specimen of blood or the provision under that subsection of a specimen of urine, shall be guilty of an offence and shall be liable on summary conviction to a fine not exceeding £1,000 or to imprisonment for a term not exceeding 6 months or to both.*

(3) *Notwithstanding subsection (2), it shall be an offence for a person to refuse or fail to comply with a requirement under subsection (1) where, following his admission to, or attendance at, a hospital, the person comes under the care of a doctor and the doctor refuses, on medical grounds, to permit the taking or provision of the specimen concerned.*

(4) *Section 1(1) of the Probation of Offenders Act 1907 shall not apply to an offence under this section.*

This section created a new power on the part of Gardaí, in that it authorizes both a Garda member with a designated doctor to enter a hospital where an injured person, or a person who claims or appears to have been injured, is suspected of having consumed an intoxicant, to take a blood or urine sample from the injured person. It should be noted that the injured person's doctor may refuse to permit the taking of the said sample for medical reasons only.

16.12.9 DETENTION OF INTOXICATED DRIVERS WHERE A DANGER TO SELVES OR OTHERS

Section 16 of the 1994 Act provides:

(1) *Where a person is at a Garda station having been arrested under s 49(8) or 50(10) of the Principal Act or s 12(3) or 14(3) or required under s 14(1) to accompany a member of the Gardaí to a Garda station and complies with the requirement he may, at the Garda station, if the member of the Gardaí for the time being in charge of the station is of opinion that the person is under the influence of an intoxicant to such an extent as to be a threat to the safety of himself or others, be detained in custody for such period (not exceeding 6 hours from the time of his arrest or, as the case may be, from the time he was required to accompany a member to the station) as the member of the Gardaí so in charge considers necessary.*

(2) *Where a person is detained under subsection (1), the member of the Gardaí for the time being in charge of the Garda Station shall—in case the person detained is or the said member is of opinion that he is 18 years of age or more, as soon as is practicable if it is reasonably possible to do so, inform a relative of the person or such other person as the person so detained may specify of the detention, unless the person so detained does not wish any person to be so informed, and in case the person detained is or the said member is of opinion that he is under the age of 18 years, as soon as is practicable, if it is reasonably possible to do so, inform a relative of the person or such other person as the person so detained may specify of the detention.*

(3)   A person detained under subsection (1) shall—in case he is or the member of the Gardaí for the time being in charge of the Garda station is of opinion that he is 18 years of age or more, upon the attendance at the station of a person being either a relative of, or a person specified pursuant to subsection (2) by, the person so detained, be released by the said member into the custody of that person, unless—the later person is or the said member is of opinion that he is under the age of 18 years, the person so detained does not wish to be released into the custody of the latter person, or the member aforesaid is of opinion that the person so detained continues to be under the influence of an intoxicant to such an extent that, if he is then released into the custody of the latter person, he will continue to be a threat to the safety of himself or others, and shall, if not so released, be released at the expiration of the period of detention authorized by subsection (1), and (b) in case he is or the member of the Gardaí for the time being in charge of the Garda station is of opinion that he is under the age of 18 years, upon the attendance at the station of a person being either a relative of, or a person specified pursuant to subsection (2) by, the person so detained, be released by the said member into the custody of that person, unless the latter person is or the said member is of opinion that he is under the age of 18 years, and shall, if not so released, be released at the expiration of the period of detention authorized by subsection (1).

The maximum period of detention under this section is six hours. The detainee is also entitled to have a relative or a person nominated by him or her informed of his detention as soon as practicable. It should be noted that the detainee is entitled to the same rights as any person in custody

16.12.10   GARDA POWERS OF ENTRY

Section 39 of the 1994 Act grants the Gardaí the following powers of entry:

(1)   A member of the Gardaí may for the purpose of arresting a person under s 106(3)(a) (inserted by this Act) of the Principal Act, enter without warrant (if need be by use of reasonable force) any place (including a dwelling) where the person is or where the member, with reasonable cause, suspects him to be and, in case the place is a dwelling, the member shall not so enter unless he or another such member has observed the person enter the dwelling concerned.

(2)   A member of the Gardaí may for the purpose of arresting a person under s 49(8) or 50(10) of the Principal Act, enter without warrant (if need be by use of reasonable force) any place (including the curtilage of a dwelling but not including a dwelling) where the person is or where the member, with reasonable cause, suspects him to be.

(3)   A member of the Gardaí may, for the purpose of making a requirement of a person under subsection (1) of s 15, enter without warrant any hospital where the person is or where the member, with reasonable cause, suspects him to be.

(4)   A designated doctor may, for the purposes of taking from a person a specimen of his blood or being provided by a person with a specimen of his urine under subsection (1) of s 15, enter any hospital where the person is or where the doctor is informed by a member of the Gardaí that the person is.

Dwelling is not defined under the Act; however, giving it its ordinary meaning it would include any property used for human habitation including a family home.

16.12.11   PROVISIONS REGARDING CERTAIN EVIDENCE IN PROSECUTIONS UNDER SECTIONS 49 AND 50 OF PRINCIPAL ACT

Section 20 of the 1994 Act provides:

(1)   On the hearing of a charge for an offence under ss 49 or 50 of the Principal Act, it shall not be necessary to show that the defendant had not consumed intoxicating liquor after the time when the offence is alleged to have been committed but before the taking or provision of a specimen under ss 13, 14, or 15.

(2)   Where, on the hearing of a charge for an offence under ss 49 or 50 of the Principal Act, evidence is given by or on behalf of the defendant that, after the time when the offence is alleged to have been committed but before the taking or provision of a specimen under ss 13, 14, or 15), he had consumed intoxicating liquor, the court shall disregard the evidence unless satisfied by or on behalf of the defendant—

211

that, but for that consumption, the concentration of alcohol in the defendant's blood (as specified in a certificate under s 19) would not have exceeded the concentration of alcohol for the time being standing specified in subsection (2) of the said ss 49 or 50, as may be appropriate, whether generally or in respect of the class of person of which the defendant is a member,

that, but for that consumption the concentration of alcohol in the defendant's urine (as specified in a certificate under s 19) would not have exceeded the concentration of alcohol for the time being standing specified in subsection (3) of the said ss 49 or 50, as may be appropriate, whether generally or in respect of the class of person of which the defendant is a member, or

that, but for that consumption, the concentration of alcohol in the defendant's breath (as specified in a statement under s 17) would not have exceeded the concentration of alcohol for the time being standing specified in subsection (4) of the said ss 49 or 50, as may be appropriate, whether generally or in respect of the class of person of which the defendant is a member.

(3) (a) A person shall not take or attempt to take any action (including consumption of alcohol but excluding a refusal or failure to provide a specimen of his breath or urine or to permit the taking of a specimen of his blood) with the intention of frustrating a prosecution under ss 49 or 50 or the Principal Act.

A person who contravenes this subsection shall be guilty of an offence and shall be liable on summary conviction to a fine not exceeding €2,500 or to imprisonment for a term not exceeding 6 months or to both.

(4) Where, on the hearing of a charge for an offence under ss 49 or 50 of the Principal Act, the court is satisfied that any action taken by the defendant (including consumption of alcohol but excluding a refusal or failure to provide a specimen of his breath or urine or to permit the taking of a specimen in his blood) was taken with the intention of frustrating a prosecution under either of those sections, the court may find him guilty of an offence under subsection (3).

It should be noted that offences committed under ss 49(1) and 50(1), as amended, are dependent from an evidential perspective on the opinion evidence of a witness, who is usually a Garda member. This opinion is normally based upon observations of the defendant at the time of the commission of the offence, as opposed to evidence of a scientific nature. Offences committed in breach of ss 49(2), (3), and (4), in contrast depend from an evidentiary perspective on proof of concentration of alcohol (ss 49(2) and 49(3) of the Act) and breath (s 49 (4) of the Act). A defendant may not be convicted of both classes of offence arising out of the same set of circumstances.

16.12.12 PROVISIONS REGARDING CERTAIN EVIDENCE IN PROCEEDINGS UNDER THE ROAD TRAFFIC ACTS, 1961 TO 1994

Section 21 of the 1994 Act provides:

(1) A duly completed statement purporting to have been supplied under s 17 shall, until the contrary is shown, be sufficient evidence in any proceedings under the Road Traffic Acts 1961 to 1994, of the facts stated therein, without proof of any signature on it or that the signatory was the proper person to sign it, and shall, until the contrary is shown, be sufficient evidence of compliance by the member of the Gardaí concerned with the requirements imposed on him by or under this Part prior to and in connection with the supply by him pursuant to s 17(2) of such statement.

(2) A duly completed form under s 18 shall, until the contrary is shown, be sufficient evidence in any proceedings under the Road Traffic Acts 1961 to 1994, of the facts stated therein, without proof of any signature on it or that the signatory was the proper person to sign it, and shall until the contrary is shown, be sufficient evidence of compliance by the designated doctor concerned with the requirement imposed on him by or under this Part.

(3) A certificate expressed to have been issued under s 19 shall until the contrary is shown, be sufficient evidence in any proceedings under the Road Traffic Acts 1961 to 1994, of the facts stated therein, without proof of any signature on it or that the signatory was the proper person to sign it, and shall, until the contrary is shown, be sufficient evidence of compliance by the Bureau with the requirements imposed on it by or under this Part or Part V of the Act of 1968.

(4) In a prosecution for an offence under ss 49 or 50 of the Principal Act or ss 13, 14, or 15 it shall be presumed until the contrary is shown that each of the following persons is a designated doctor—

A person who by virtue of powers conferred on him by this Part took from another person a specimen of that other person's blood or was provided by another person with a specimen of that other person's urine.

A person for whom, following a requirement under ss 13(1), 14(4), or 15(1) to permit the taking by him of a specimen of blood, there was a refusal or failure to give such permission or to comply with a requirement of his in relation to the taking of such a specimen.

A person for whom, following a requirement under ss 13(1), 14(4), or 15(1) to provide for him a specimen of urine, there was a refusal or failure to provide such a specimen or to comply with a requirement of his in relation to the provision of such a specimen.

(5) *Where, pursuant to ss 13, 14, or 15, a designated doctor states in writing that he is unwilling, on medical grounds, to take from a person a specimen of his blood or be provided by him with a specimen of his urine, the statement signed by the doctor shall, in any proceedings under the Road Traffic Acts 1961 to 1994, be sufficient evidence, until the contrary is shown, of the facts stated therein, without proof of any signature on it or that the signatory was the proper person to sign it.*

This section gives rise to a presumption of a designated doctor until the defendant proves the contrary.

16.12.13 DEFENCE TO REFUSAL TO PERMIT TAKING OF SPECIMEN OF BLOOD OR TO PROVIDE TWO SPECIMENS OF BREATH

Section 23 of the 1994 Act provides:

(1) *In a prosecution of a person for an offence under s 13 for refusing or failing to comply with a requirement to provide 2 specimens of his breath, it shall be a defence for the defendant to satisfy the court that there was a special and substantial reason for his refusal or failure and that, as soon as practicable after the refusal or failure concerned, he complied (or offered, but was not called upon, to comply) with a requirement under the section concerned in relation to the taking of a specimen of blood or the provisions of a specimen or urine.*

(2) *In a prosecution of a person for an offence under ss 13, 14, or 15 for refusing or failing to comply with a requirement to permit a designated doctor to take a specimen of blood or for refusing or failing to comply with a requirement of a designated doctor in relation to the taking of a specimen of blood, it shall be a defence for the defendant to satisfy the court that there was a special and substantial reason for his refusal or failure and that, as soon as practicable after the refusal or failure concerned, he complied (or offered, but was not called upon, to comply) with a requirement under the section concerned in relation to the provision of a specimen of urine.*

(3) *Notwithstanding subsection (1) and (2), evidence may be given at the hearing of a charge of an offence under ss 49 or 50 of the Principal Act that the defendant refused or failed to comply with a requirement to provide 2 specimens of his breath, or that the defendant refused or failed to comply with a requirement to permit the taking of a specimen of his blood or to comply with a requirement of a designated doctor in relation to the taking of a specimen of blood, as the case may be.*

'Special substantial reasons' are discussed above. It is difficult to say when a special substantial reason will be accepted. In *AG v Jordan* (1973) 107 ILTR 112, a failure to understand the prescribed caution then necessary under the old drunk driving regulations was held to be a 'special reason'.

16.12.14 BAR TO CERTAIN DEFENCE TO CHARGES UNDER SECTIONS 49 AND 50 OF THE PRINCIPAL ACT

Section 24 provides:

It shall not be a defence for a person charged with an offence under ss 49(1) or 50(1) of the Principal Act to show that, in relation to the facts alleged to constitute the offence, an analysis or determination under the Road Traffic Acts 1961 to 1994, has not been carried out or that he has not been requested under s 12 to provide a specimen of his breath.

Where a person is charged with driving while unfit on the basis of evidence of incapacity, the person is barred from relying upon the fact that the prosecution did not seek to obtain a breath, urine, or alcohol sample from him or her. This prohibition is recognised at common law in the case of *DPP v Lee* (unreported) 2 March 1988, High Court.

16.12.15 PENALTIES

(a) Disqualification.

(b) Fine and/or imprisonment.

(c) Costs.

Disqualification is mandatory where convicted of drunken driving. The period of disqualification is dependent upon the level of alcohol in the blood, breath or urine and is more particularly set forth in the preceding paragraphs where the relevant offences are cited.

The following table will assist in establishing the period for which a person can be disqualified:

Blood alcohol level	Breath alcohol level	Urine alcohol level	1st offence	2nd offence
81–100 mg alcohol per 100 ml of blood	36–44 mcg of alcohol per 100 ml of breath	108–135 mg of alcohol per 100 ml of urine	3 months	6 months
101–150mg of alcohol per 100 ml of blood	45–66 mcg of alcohol per 100 ml of breath	136–200 mg of alcohol per 100 ml of urine	1 year	2 years
Exceeding 150 mg of alcohol per 100 ml of blood	Exceeding 66 mcg of alcohol per 100 ml of breath	Exceeding 200 mg of alcohol per 100 ml of urine	2 years	4 years

A person may also be fined and/or imprisoned in accordance with the provisions of the relevant offence for which they have been convicted.

Section 22 of the Road Traffic Act 1994 provides that where a person is convicted of an offence under ss 49 or 50 of the Principal Act as amended by the 1994 Act, or ss 13, 14, or 15 of the 1994 Act, the court can make the convicted person pay a contribution of costs to the medical bureau, unless there are special and substantial reasons for not so doing.

16.12.16 APPEAL

Penalties and disqualifications come into effect 14 days from the date of conviction. This allows the defendant 14 days in which to appeal the conviction. In the event of an appeal, the conviction for motoring offences including drink-driving offences will be adjourned pending the outcome of the appeal. A defendant who appeals their case to the Circuit may receive a harsher sentence. However, in regard to drink driving offences where a defendant is disqualified for a period of in excess of one year, disqualification periods are frequently halved where special reasons are given and where the defendant can show that he has taken steps to deal with his irresponsible drinking behaviour. It should be noted that a disqualification for three or six months consequential to a conviction for drink driving cannot be appealed.

CHAPTER 17

THE PROCEEDS OF CRIME

17.1 Introduction

The traditional focus of criminal law enforcement has been arrest and prosecution. The work of the Gardaí consisted, in the main, of investigating the suspected crimes, gathering the necessary evidence, arresting the persons involved, and prosecuting them before the criminal courts with a view to securing imprisonment and/or fines. Financial information emerging in the course of such investigations was mostly used as proof to substantiate the alleged crimes.

Under the law and practice as it existed, a person who had profited from criminal activity could only be discommoded by the imposition of a fine or term of imprisonment subsequent to a conviction after trial, or on a plea of guilty. There was an inherent practice in the courts when suspending sentences to order compensation. In the case of felony, the courts appear to have had no power to impose a fine except in the case of manslaughter. A power existed to direct payment of compensation when applying the provisions of the Probation of Offenders Act 1907 and later the compensation provisions of the Criminal Law Act 1993. The court had a common law power to impose a fine on conviction for any misdemeanour, and there appears to be no limit in Ireland to the amount of the fine which might be imposed. However, numerous statutes provide for the imposition of fines, usually up to a maximum amount, for unclassified offences. The judges of the criminal courts have an inherent power to return stolen property to its rightful owner upon conviction of the accused, where the ownership of the property is established during the criminal trial or where the accused admits that it was stolen.

Historically, many items—mainly vehicles and cash—were declared to be forfeited under the section but this was always limited to personal property which came into the possession of the Gardaí as part of their investigation. There was no concept of an investigation or an attempt by the courts to evaluate the amount by which the person had profited from the criminal activity and to deprive him or her of that profit. The realization that in order to successfully combat organized crime, steps would have to be taken to deprive those involved of the benefit of their criminal activity, gained momentum in law enforcement agencies on an international scale in the late 1970s and early 1980s.

The enactment of legislation providing for the freezing, confiscation, forfeiture, and disposal of assets obtained as a benefit of, or in connection with, criminal activity has created a new area of law of which both criminal and civil practitioners need a working knowledge, as its effect is felt not simply in the operation of criminal prosecutions but also across the civil law spectrum. The two primary pieces of legislation, the Criminal Justice Act 1994 (as amended) and the Proceeds of Crime Act 1996, though they have similar characteristics, and possibly the same effect, are fundamentally different, as will be seen below.

17.2 Confiscation of criminal assets

17.2.1 HISTORY

The concept of confiscation or forfeiture is not an invention of modern legislation. For example, a convicted felon in times past forfeited his property to the Crown. More recently, s 30 of the Misuse of Drugs Act, 1977, provides: *'A Court by which a person is convicted of an offence under this Act may order anything shown to the satisfaction of that Court to relate to an offence to be forfeited and either destroyed or dealt with in such manner as the Court thinks fit.'* That section, however, deals with the physical objects relating to the offence, such as weighing scales and cash used in the commission of the offence rather than the profits or proceeds of the offence. A proviso was inserted for persons claiming to be owners or otherwise interested in the property to oppose the making of an order.

More recently, it has been accepted that some criminals have put themselves beyond the reaches of the ordinary criminal code, by not becoming directly involved in the commission of the offence and by the strict enforcement of codes of secrecy, and that in order to successfully combat such organized crime, steps would need to be taken to deprive those involved of the benefit of their criminal activity.

17.2.2 THE APPROACH IN THE UNITED STATES OF AMERICA

A brief summary of the approach taken by the United States is instructive. Congress enacted legislation in the 1970s which dealt with the following areas:

(a) the infiltration of organized crime and racketeering into legitimate organizations (anti-money laundering) (Organized Crime Control Act 1970);

(b) a new penalty of forfeiture, allowing the State to confiscate the property of those convicted of crimes under the Act, ie Title (IX), Racketeer Influenced and Corrupt Organizations ('RICO');

(c) the introduction of a regime that permitted the authorities to obtain forfeiture in a civil court without criminal conviction, facilitating the seizure of narcotics and all raw materials, products, or equipments used in the production of same and preventing their handling or transportation, ie seizure of the 'instruments' (Comprehensive Drug Abuse, Prevention and Control Act 1970);

(d) imprisonment, large fines and forfeiture of the profits of the criminal enterprise. It was, however, a pre-requisite under this legislation that a criminal conviction had been secured, prior to proceeding and assessing the profit (Continuing Criminal Enterprise Act 1970);

(e) civil forfeiture of all proprietary proceeds of illegal drug activity, including any type of monies and negotiable instruments used or usable for the purpose of illegal drugs or the commission of an act in violation of the anti-drugs laws. This procedure acted *'in rem'* against property, ignoring the guilt of the owners, and accordingly did not require any pre-trial conviction (Psychotropic Substances Act 1978).

These developments in this area of law therefore initially created an offence of money laundering, and then developed forfeiture procedures for the instruments used in the course of the offence. Thereafter, a procedure was introduced which, after conviction, provided for the assessment and confiscation of the profit made from that offence, and finally for a forfeiture procedure which acts *'in rem'* against property which was clearly the proceeds of criminal activity, without requiring a criminal conviction. More recently the United States have added a system of administrative forfeiture by a federal agency, which does not require judicial intervention. (There is no mirror of such an administrative system in Ireland, as all forfeiture requires same form of judicial intervention. Any attempt at this introduction would face difficulties due to our Constitutional policy of Separation of Powers.)

The system in the United States has been the subject of a number of criticisms including the following:

(a) Certain law enforcement officers acquired a reputation for selective, even racist, application of the civil forfeiture provisions.

(b) Many of the agencies vested with the responsibility for application of civil forfeiture provisions were required to be partly self-financing, leading to selectivity on the basis of profit motive.

(c) Settlements were forced on citizens who were in a position to prove proper title, simply because of their inability to afford the legal fees necessary to mount such a legal challenge.

17.3 International legislative initiatives

17.3.1 GENERALLY

In the early 1990s, a number of international initiatives were introduced. These included:

- the United Nations Convention against Illicit Traffic in Narcotic and Psychotropic Substances, 1988 (Vienna Convention);
- the Basle Statement of Principles 1988;
- the Financial Action Task Force on money laundering ('FATF') July 1989;
- the Council of Europe Convention on Laundering, Search, Seizure and Confiscation of the Proceeds of Crime, 1990 (Strasbourg Convention); and
- the European Community Directive on money laundering (91/308–EC).

These international conventions and treaties have relevance to the development of investigative strategies and practices which focus on the identification and confiscation of the proceeds of crime. The issues examined and addressed included the creation of an offence of money laundering, the use of procedures which would prevent the banking system being used as a money laundering vehicle, the relaxation of bankers' duty of secrecy to the customer, confiscation and forfeiture concepts, and enhanced international mutual cooperation in criminal matters.

17.3.2 THE UNITED NATIONS CONVENTION AGAINST ILLICIT TRAFFIC IN NARCOTIC DRUGS AND PSYCHOTROPIC SUBSTANCES 1988

The United Nations Convention was signed in Vienna, Austria on 20 December 1988. The primary aim of this Convention was to criminalize the laundering of the proceeds of drug trafficking and provide for confiscation of those monies. In addition, the Convention provided for:

(a) extradition between the countries party to the Convention in criminal proceedings for money laundering;

(b) mutual legal assistance;

(c)   the transfer of criminal prosecutions from one signatory State to another;

(d)   the traditional secrecy and confidentiality existing between a bank and its customer being disregarded during criminal investigations;

(e)   signatory States taking appropriate measures to facilitate the confiscation of assets representing the proceeds of money laundering.

17.3.3 BASLE STATEMENT OF PRINCIPLES 1988

This statement of principles emanated in 1988 from the 'Basle Committee', consisting of representatives of the Central Banks of the G-10 Nations, who meet at the Bank for International Settlements in Basle, Switzerland. The G-10 countries consist of the United States, United Kingdom, Belgium, Canada, France, Italy, Japan, the Netherlands, Sweden, Switzerland and Luxembourg. The Basle Committee adopted the Statement of Principles on the prevention of criminal use of the banking system for the purpose of money laundering, and formulated two measures to prevent banks from being used in money laundering schemes:

(a)   the requirement that customers be clearly identified; and

(b)   greater co-operation between banks and law enforcement authorities.

17.3.4 FINANCIAL ACTION TASK FORCE ('FATF')

Following the 15th Economic Summit of the G-7 countries in Paris in July 1989, the Financial Action Task Force on money laundering ('FATF') was established. The mandate of the FATF was to assess the results of the cooperation which had already commenced between the G-7 countries in order to prevent the banking systems of those countries from being used unwittingly or otherwise as part of money laundering operations. The first report of the FATF was published in June 1990, and has been regarded as being particularly influential since it contained no fewer than 40 recommendations for improvement in the laws designed to combat money laundering. Amongst the key recommendations were:

(a)   that the United Nations Convention of 1988 be adopted and ratified by all countries;

(b)   that bank secrecy should be curtailed;

(c)   that money laundering should be criminalized by means of national criminal laws extending not only to proceeds deriving from drug trafficking but also to proceeds from other crimes;

(d)   that all cash transactions over certain levels be registered and all suspicious transactions be reported;

(e)   that bank employees be specifically trained to recognize suspicious transactions; and

(f)   that international cooperation be strengthened, and extradition of persons suspected of involvement in money laundering schemes be facilitated.

17.4 European Union initiatives

17.4.1 THE COUNCIL OF EUROPE CONVENTION ON LAUNDERING, SEARCH, SEIZURE AND CONFISCATION OF THE PROCEEDS OF CRIME (STRASBOURG CONVENTION) 1990

The Council of Europe Convention on Laundering, Search, Seizure and Confiscation of the Proceeds of Crime (Strasbourg Convention) was signed in November 1990 by a number of European States. A number of countries that were not Member States of the Council of Europe, such as Australia, Canada, and the United States, participated in the deliberations leading up to the adoption of the Convention in 1990. The Convention requires the signatory states to:

(a) adopt legislative measures to establish intentional money laundering as a criminal offence under domestic law; and

(b) prevent bank secrecy being invoked by banks as a ground for refusing to cooperate with investigating authorities.

Much of the Convention concerns international cooperation, including the power to take provisional measures such as freezing or seizing of assets in one country in respect of criminal proceedings taken in another signatory country. It should be noted that the Council of Europe Convention is only one of a number of conventions emanating from the Council of Europe in Strasbourg on international cooperation in the investigation and prosecution of serious fraud offences. Part VII of the Criminal Justice Act 1994 (ss 46–56) makes provision for international cooperation in relation to criminal matters. The European Convention on Mutual Assistance provides for cooperation between the authorities in the obtaining of evidence in one signatory State for the purpose of criminal proceedings or investigations in another.

17.4.2 EUROPEAN COMMUNITY DIRECTIVE ON MONEY LAUNDERING (91/308 EC)

The primary legal obligation upon Member States of the European Union is imposed by Council Directive 91/308/EEC, dated 10 June 1991, on the prevention of the use of the financial system for the purpose of money laundering. The view expressed in the preamble is that if financial institutions were used for money laundering purposes, the soundness and stability of the institutions and the confidence in the financial markets as a whole would be seriously jeopardized, and the trust of the public would be lost. This is particularly important having regard to the provisions of Council Directive 89/646/EEC, known as the 'Second Banking Directive', which establishes the concept of a single banking licence which may be granted to a bank, and which would entitle the bank to operate throughout the European Union. Another justification for action on the part of the European Union in combating money laundering was that if the Union did not take action, then Member States might themselves be encouraged to take independent national initiatives which might be incompatible with the objectives inherent in the completion of the single market. Further, persons involved in money laundering might seek to avail themselves of the liberalized regime for movement of capital within the Union. Therefore, one of the fundamental objectives of the Directive in requiring coordinated action on the part of Member States was to prevent any Member State becoming a haven for the proceeds of money laundering operations.

The provisions of the Directive impose an obligation on Member States to ensure that credit and financial institutions carry on business in such a way as to facilitate investigations into money laundering operations by the relevant authorities, such as:

(a)   identifying their customers in certain circumstances; and

(b)   keeping adequate records of suspicious transactions, which would then be made available to the relevant authorities.

In this regard, materials used to identify customers and documents relating to relevant transactions must be retained for a period of at least five years. From the definition of money laundering contained in Article 1 of the Directive and set out above, it is clear that the scope of the Directive extends not only to the laundering of the proceeds of drug trafficking but also to the proceeds of other types of criminal activity which may be designated as such for the purpose of the Directive by each Member State. All Member States of the EU now have in place money laundering legislation.

17.5   Irish Strategy for the confiscation of criminal assets

17.5.1   GENERALLY

Ireland's response to International and European Conventions, Agreements and Directives, as appropriate, was to introduce a comprehensive series of legislative provisions, which include:

(a)   the Criminal Justice Act 1994;

(b)   the Criminal Assets Bureau Act 1996;

(b)   the Proceeds of Crime Act 1996;

(c)   the Disclosure of Certain Information for Taxation and Other Purposes Act 1996;

(c)   amendments to the Revenue Acts and to the Social Welfare Acts; and

(d)   the Proceeds of Crime Act 2005.

The overall effect of this legislation is to provide a statutory mechanism for identifying the proceeds of criminal activity and denying persons of its enjoyment.

17.5.2   THE CRIMINAL JUSTICE ACT 1994

Ireland's responsibilities under the Conventions and Directive 91/308 EC, outlined above, was the introduction of the Criminal Justice Act 1994 ('the 1994 Act'), which included the following provisions:

(a)   the introduction of the use of Restraint Orders against persons charged or about to be charged with drug trafficking and other serious crime;

(b)   the introduction of the use of Confiscation Orders against persons convicted of drug trafficking and other serious crime, to be obtained on a civil standard of proof;

(c)   the introduction of an offence of money laundering for the handling of the proceeds of drug trafficking and other criminal activity;

(d)   the imposition of duties of identification and record keeping on designated bodies, such as banks and insurance companies;

(e)   the imposition of an obligation on designated bodies to report suspicious transactions to An Garda Síochána;

(f)   mutual international cooperation.

17.5.2.1 Restraint orders

Where proceedings have been instituted for a drug trafficking offence or any other indictable offence, or the court is satisfied that such proceedings are to be instituted, and it appears to the court that a Confiscation Order may be made, the High Court may by order prohibit any person from dealing with any realisable property as empowered under ss 23 and 24 of the 1994 Act. A Restraint Order may be discharged or varied thereafter on an application made by any person affected by it (ss 24(5) and 24(6)). Furthermore, the High Court may at any time appoint a Receiver to take possession of the property and manage or otherwise deal with the property (s 24(7)).

17.5.2.2 Confiscation orders

Once a person has been convicted on indictment of a drug trafficking offence and sentenced, the court of trial must determine the following issues:

(a) whether that convicted person has benefited from the offence;

(b) the extent to which that person has benefited;

(c) the amount that is realisable, i.e. the total sum available to that convicted person to enable them to discharge a Confiscation Order.

The court then makes a Confiscation Order for the sum that is realizable.

A similar provision applies to all other offences prosecuted on indictment, save that the court makes a determination only where the Director of Public Prosecutions has made an application. The 1994 Act makes two distinctions between drug trafficking offences (dealt with under s 4) and offences which are not such (dealt with under s 9). In assessing the benefit for the former, any payments received by the defendant at any time in connection with drug trafficking carried out by him or her constitutes such a benefit; while in all other cases such assessment is limited to the particular offence for which that person has been convicted. Furthermore, there is a statutory rebuttable presumption that any property appearing to the court to have been received by the defendant for a period of up to six years prior to the proceedings being instituted against him or her constitutes a receipt in connection with drug trafficking. It is, effectively, a mandatory requirement for the court to conduct such an investigation following conviction for drug trafficking (see s 25 of the Criminal Justice Act 1999), while it is up to the Director of Public Prosecutions to institute such an application before the court in other offences.

It is interesting to note that the court at this stage has effectively determined the trial, in that the accused has been convicted and has been sentenced to the extent that the court believes is appropriate. It is only then that the court proceeds to assess the benefits or proceeds of the particular offence and thereafter makes a Confiscation Order. This would appear to support an argument that the legislation is designed to seek 'reparation' of the particular benefits or profits of the offence rather than to apply a further sanction. Furthermore, the standard of proof required to determine any question arising under the 1994 Act is that applicable to civil proceedings. It may be contended that a Confiscation Order actually constitutes a penalty, in light of the European Court of Human Rights judgment in *Welsh v United Kingdom* (20 EHRR 247), and the fact that the 1994 Act itself perceives this procedure as occurring within 'proceedings for an offence' (see s 3(16)(F)). This may have implications under Article 38 of the Constitution or Articles 6 and 7 of the European Convention on Human Rights. There is, however, support for the contrary argument. See decisions of the Privy Council in *McIntosh v Lord Advocate* (2001) 2 All ER 638 and of the European Court of Human Rights in *Phillips v United Kingdom* (5 July 2001).

17.5.2.3 Enforcement of Confiscation Order

Once a Confiscation Order has been made, it constitutes a judgment debt payable to the Director of Public Prosecutions by the accused, which can be enforced as if it constituted a High Court judgment debt (s 19). If it is not paid, the 1994 Act provides a schedule of penalties, relative to the amount remaining outstanding, which must be served consecutive to the sentence already imposed. It can be argued that such a penalty would constitute a type of contempt of court sanction for non-compliance with the Confiscation Order, rather than a further sanction for the original offence. The penalties range from 45 days for an amount not exceeding £500 to 10 years for an amount exceeding €2,500,000. Furthermore, the court is empowered to appoint a Receiver to take possession of property and if necessary sell it in satisfaction of this Confiscation Order (s 20).

17.5.2.4 Purpose of the Criminal Justice Act 1994

The purpose of the 1994 Act is to provide a mechanism whereby a court can assess the profit that has been made from a particular offence for which the accused has been convicted, and insist on reparation of that particular profit. The court therefore draws a distinction between that profit, which should be seen as reparation and paid to the State, and the sentence, which constitutes a sanction relating purely to the moral reprehensibility of the offence committed. It remains to be seen, however, whether the courts will accept such an interpretation.

There has been little judicial interpretation of these provisions to date, as there have been only a small number of cases processed by the courts. However, in *DPP v Gilligan*, it was submitted that as the word '*Court*' was not defined as including Special Criminal Court, the 1994 Act did not apply to that court. That court, however, in its judgment of 8 May 2001, was satisfied that it constituted a '*Court*' within the meaning of the Act. This ruling was overturned by McCracken J (October 2002), on application by Judicial Review in the course of which judgment he upheld the constitutional validity of the Act.

From an Irish standpoint the Act contained a number of novel provisions and constitutes quite a powerful tool in the deterrence of criminal activity.

17.5.3 PROCEEDS OF CRIME ACTS

Prior to the introduction of specific Proceeds of Crime legislation in the mid-1990s, limited powers vested in the Minister for Justice to freeze criminal assets. The Offences Against the State (Amendment) Act 1985 was enacted on 19 February 1985. This Act empowered the Minister for Justice, where he or she was of the opinion that certain monies held by a bank would, but for the operation of s 22 of the Offences Against the State Act of 1939 (which declared the property of an illegal organization forfeit to the Minister), be the property of an illegal organization, to freeze those monies and cause the bank to pay them to the High Court whence, after six months, they might be paid out to the Minister on the Minister's *ex parte* application and paid into the Exchequer. The constitutionality of the Act was upheld in the High Court shortly after its enactment (*Clancy and Anor v Ireland, Attorney General and Others* 1985 IR 326) whereupon the direction from the Minister for Justice to the Bank of Ireland to pay the sum of £1,750,816.27 held at that time in the joint account of two persons into the High Court was complied with.

Political pressure mounted during 1995 to enact radical measures to deal with drug trafficking and organized crime, following a number of high-profile murders.

The core legislation enacted in 1996 to give effect to the new strategy consisted of the Proceeds of Crime Act 1996 (as amended by the Proceeds of Crime Act 2005), which applies to property having a value of not less than €12,700 which directly or indirectly constitutes proceeds of crime. It constitutes a civil law remedy operating civil law procedures in the High Court with issues of evidence being determined 'on a balance of probabilities'. The Criminal Assets Bureau Act of 1996 created a statutory body, the Criminal Assets Bureau (CAB), which reflects the statutory remit of the Proceeds of Crime Acts and the Criminal Assets Bureau Act 1996, manifesting in civil litigation in Proceeds of Crime, Revenue, and Judicial Review cases.

17.5.4   PROCEEDS OF CRIME ACT 1996 (AS AMENDED)

The powers incorporated in the Proceeds of Crime Act 1996 (as amended by the Proceeds of Crime Act 2005) include:

(a) The High Court may grant an *ex parte* Interim Injunction, freezing such property on application to it by a member of An Garda Síochána not below the rank of Chief Superintendent, once it is *satisfied* that said property constitutes directly or indirectly the proceeds of crime (s 2).

(b) The court may also thereafter grant an Interlocutory Order over such property on application on notice within 21 days, if it *appears to the Court* that the said property constitutes directly or indirectly the proceeds of crime (s 3). Note there is a distinction between that standard of proof required when seeking a s 2 as distinct from a s 3 Order. This is because the latter is done on notice. Any person claiming to have a right to the property can make an application to the court to have this Injunction discharged (s 3(3)). At that stage the onus of proof as to the legitimate ownership of the property shifts to the applicant. Once the s 3 Interlocutory Order has been in place for seven years the court is empowered to make a Disposal Order transferring all such property to the benefit of the Central Exchequer (s 4). If consent is forthcoming, since the implementation of the Proceeds of Crime (Amendment) Act 2005 (the 2005 POC Act) a Disposal Order can be made prior to the seven-year limit.

(c) The court is further empowered to vary the Injunction for the purpose of releasing funds for essential legal, business and living expenses (s 6). Applications made under this section are difficult, as the applicant has to satisfy the court that such a variation was 'essential'. The Department of Justice put in place a Legal Aid Scheme especially for such cases, on an ad hoc basis, which ensures that all respondents, even if their assets are frozen, have access to legal aid. Effectively this means that s 6 applications for the release of funds for essential legal expenses would rarely be required.

(d) The Act also provides for the appointment of a Receiver to either manage the property or, as is more usual, to sell the property and lodge such proceeds to an interest-bearing bank account pending further Order of the court (s 7). This section thereby facilitates the disposal of wasting assets and the preservation of property value at any time after a 'section 2 order' as outlined at (i) above is made.

(e) The Act makes provision that the belief of a member of An Garda Síochána not below the rank of Chief Superintendent shall be 'evidence' (s 8). Some criticism has been made of the limited and hearsay nature of this evidence; however, it has always been accepted by a court that while such a belief may constitute 'evidence', it is still up to the court to decide the 'weight' to be attached to such evidence.

(f) The court can make an Order directing a Respondent to furnish details of his earnings over the previous six years and to outline his assets (s 9). A submission was made that such an Order could breach a respondent's right against self-incrimination. Mr Justice Moriarty in his judgment in *M v D* (February 1997) was loath to grant such an Order without an indemnity from the Director of Public Prosecutions that the affidavit pursuant to s 9 would not be used in the course of a criminal trial.

(g) The court is also empowered to make an Order compensating any respondent should any Order made under this Act be shown to have acted unjustly against such respondent (s 16). It is unnecessary for the applicant to give an undertaking as to damages as would ordinarily be required in the case of an application for Injunction.

(h) Sections 2.3 and 3.3 provide for third parties to make ownership claims or exclude their property from effect of Orders.

(i) Section 3.7 outlines that post conviction forfeiture under ss 4 and 24 of the Criminal Justice Act 1994 takes precedence. The Criminal Assets Bureau therefore refrains from progressing proceeds of crime confiscations while a prosecution is ongoing.

(j) Section 14 provides immunity for banking institutions when complying with the Act.

The 1996 Act (as amended) has been amended by s 189 of the Criminal Justice Act 2006 at s 168(7).

17.5.5 PROCEEDS OF CRIME ACT 2005

The Proceeds of Crime Amendment Act 2005 expands the objectives of the Criminal Assets Bureau (CAB) and addresses lack of CAB jurisdiction issues as identified by the Supreme Court.

(a) Section 3 broadens definitions of, *inter alia*, criminal conduct to include crime outside the State.

(b) Section 4 provides for an originating motion to ensure procedure by affidavit and not plenary proceedings. Also CAB can now recover taxes due from frozen assets.

(c) Section 5 provides for consent disposal at s 3 stage to avoid seven years' wait.

(d) Section 10 provides that s 11.7 Statute of Limitations Act does not apply in CAB cases, ie no two-year limit to disposal/forfeiture.

(e) Section 11 re-introduced a Statement of Means procedure but introduces protection against self-incrimination that cannot be used in any associated prosecutions.

(f) Section 12 introduces 'corrupt enrichment' powers arising from 'corrupt conduct' as offences against Prevention of Corruption Act 1889–2001, Official Secrets Act 1963, and Ethics in Public Office Act 1995.

(g) Section 20 amends s 38 of the Criminal Justice Act 1994 which applies to a specific and limited form of forfeiture. It empowers seizure and detention of a minimum €6,500 cash suspected of being derived from criminal conduct by An Gardaí and Revenue anywhere in the country and not just at ports and from drug activity as heretofore.

17.6 Distinctions between Criminal Justice Act 1994 and Proceeds of Crime Act 1996 (as amended)

(a) The former requires a conviction.

(b) The former acts *'in personam'* against a convicted person while the latter acts *'in rem'*, acting on property which constitutes the proceeds of crime.

(c) The former operates on benefit/profit while the latter operates on property.

(d) The remedy granted to the former constitutes a judgment debt in favour of the Director of Public Prosecutions, which can be executed 'immediately', while the latter only grants an injunction, which must remain in place for seven years prior to the grant of a Disposal Order. However, consent Disposal Orders may arise under s 4(A).

(e) The former arises from criminal proceedings while the latter operates completely independently of such proceedings.

Finally the issue arises as to what happens when one respondent is subject an application under both Acts. It was submitted before Judge Dunne in the course of a s 4 application made in the case of *DPP v Karl Dempsey* that such application constituted an abuse of process in the light of existing proceedings under the Proceeds of Crime Act for what, counsel submitted, was effectively the same property. The question is to some extent answered by virtue of s 3(7) of the Proceeds of Crime Act, which provides that where a Confiscation Order relates to property frozen under that Act such injunction shall stand lapsed. This effectively gives precedence to the 1994 Act. Judge Dunne was not prepared to hold that the s 4 inquiry, being as it was a statutory direction to the court, did constitute an abuse of process.

17.7 The Criminal Assets Bureau

17.7.1 INTRODUCTION

The Criminal Assets Bureau (CAB) is a statutory, multi-agency body consisting of members of An Garda Síochána (police), officials of the Revenue Commissioners (both Taxes and Customs Authority officials), officials of the Department of Social, Community and Family Affairs (hereafter called Social Welfare), and a Bureau Legal Officer together with administrative and technical staff. Its head is the Chief Bureau Officer, who must be a member of the Gardaí holding at least the rank of Chief Superintendent.

The primary function of the Bureau is to utilize all legal remedies available to the State in pursuance of targeted serious criminals. While its primary weapon is the Proceeds of Crime Act 1996 it also makes use of the criminal law, the Taxes Code, and the Social Welfare Code. It should also be noted that while the Criminal Assets Bureau generally operates the Proceeds of Crime Act, prosecution under this Act is also available to any member of An Garda Síochána not below the rank of Chief Superintendent.

The main focus of the Bureau has been on the proceeds of drug trafficking. However, the statutory remit of the Bureau covers all forms of criminal activity, and a number of actions have been taken against the other proceeds of criminal activity. Property targeted has included cash, various financial instruments, vehicles, real and personal property, and recently unjust enrichment resulting from corrupt payment to obtain rezoning of property under planning law.

CAB is answerable to the Commissioner of An Garda Síochána. The Chief Bureau Officer (CBO) must be not below the rank of Chief Superintendent. It can recover assets through civil or criminal litigation, although the Proceeds of Crime (PoC) Act provides for civil means only with its lower standard of proof, ie on balance of probabilities. Recovery can be either through PoC or Revenue legislation and summary recovery of overpayments in Social Welfare.

The Bureau has close links with the ARA (Assets Recovery Agency) in the UK and NI and other EU and international bodies and was one of the founder members of CARIN, the aim of which is international cooperation.

Since its formation, the Criminal Assets Bureau has fully implemented a multi-agency approach to deny persons engaged in criminal activity of the proceeds of their crimes in pursuance of its statutory remit. The powers and functions of all the agencies which comprise CAB are used to ensure that the full force of the State, and the totality of legislation enacted by the State under which these agencies act, is brought to bear on persons who engage in drug trafficking and other criminal activity.

There are statutory provisions allowing the free flow and disclosure of information and material, not only between Bureau officers but also by the Bureau to other members of An Garda Síochána, Revenue Commissioners and other government agencies in pursuance of its statutory objectives. It is this ability of all government agencies to exchange information and cooperate, and accordingly circumvent the usual bureaucratic difficulties, which affect most large government agencies.

Bureau officers are usually seconded from existing government agencies for the period of their service as officers within the Bureau, and retain their original powers and ability to exercise and perform duties, as members of such agencies (s 8(2), CAB Act). An example of the operation of this provision is the Judicial Review case of *Criminal Assets Bureau v James Gantley* (O'Sullivan J, 25 February 2000). The applicant sought to quash a determination by a Bureau officer of the Department of Social Welfare, to stop social welfare payments, on the basis that no evidence had been presented as to his criminality. The court, in upholding the refusal, held that the Bureau officer's powers, which he held with the Department of Social Welfare as a social welfare officer, were still exercisable by him on his assignment to the Bureau.

All staff, which includes lawyers and accountants, are located under the one roof ensuring not only cooperation at all levels but also in-house legal and forensic accountancy advice. The breakdown of staff in the Criminal Assets Bureau is shown in the diagram below.

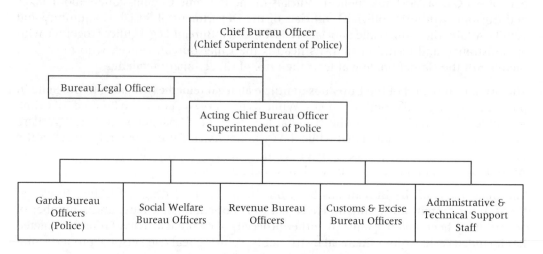

The objectives, functions and powers of the Criminal Assets Bureau, together with provision for administrative and operational matters and ancillary provisions, are contained in the CAB Act.

17.7.2 STATUTORY STRUCTURE OF THE CRIMINAL ASSETS BUREAU

The Bureau is a statutory body and the structure of the Criminal Assets Bureau (CAB) is set out in the CAB Act. CAB must submit an annual report to the Minister for Justice of its activities during the year, and the Minister presents that report before each House of the Oireachtas (Parliament). The Bureau is funded exclusively by the exchequer, has no preconceived financial targets to meet and returns all funds generated to the exchequer.

CAB is a body corporate with perpetual succession, an official seal, the power to sue and be sued in its corporate name and to acquire, hold, and dispose of land or an interest in land, or any other property. The powers and functions of the Chief Bureau Officer, the Acting Chief Bureau Officer, the Bureau Legal Officer, Bureau Officers and, where appropriate, members of the staff of the Criminal Assets Bureau are fully set out at ss 7, 8, and 9 of the CAB Act.

Under the CAB Act, officers and staff of the Bureau are appointed as follows:

(a) The Chief Bureau Officer ('CBO') is appointed by the Commissioner of the Gardaí and must be a person who is a member of the Gardaí holding at least the rank of Chief Superintendent (s 7).

(b) The Bureau Legal Officer (the 'BLO') is appointed by the Minister for Justice, with the consent of the Attorney General and the Minister for Finance. The BLO reports directly to the Chief Bureau Officer, and his or her role is to assist the CBO in the pursuit of his or her objectives and functions (s 9).

(c) Bureau Officers are appointed by the Minister for Justice, with the consent of the Minister for Finance, and are (i) members of the Gardaí nominated by the Commissioner of the Gardaí, (ii) officers of the Revenue Commissioners nominated by the Revenue Commissioners, and (iii) Officers of the Minister for Social Welfare nominated by the Minister for Social, Community and Family Affairs (s 8).

(d) Administrative, professional and technical members of staff of the Bureau are appointed by the Minister for Justice, with the consent of the Minister for Finance, after consultation with the Commissioner of the Gardaí.

Bureau Officers, when exercising and performing powers, do so under the direction and control of the Chief Bureau Officer. Bureau Officers retain their original powers and the ability to exercise and perform duties as members of the Gardaí, officers of the Revenue Commissioners or officers of the Minister for Social, Community and Family Affairs, as the case may be (s 8(2)). However, it should be noted that the powers and duties vested in the Bureau Officers by virtue of being a member of An Gardaí, or under the Revenue Acts or Social Welfare Acts, and the exercise or performance of such powers or duties shall be in the name of the Criminal Assets Bureau (s 8(2)).

The Chief Prosecution Solicitor's Office provides the legal services required by the Criminal Assets Bureau.

17.7.3 USE AND ADMISSIBILITY OF EVIDENCE, INFORMATION AND MATERIALS BY BUREAU OFFICERS

The CAB Act provides that Bureau Officers can be assisted by other Bureau Officers and by persons who are members of the staff of the Criminal Assets Bureau in carrying out their duties. It also provides that evidence obtained by Bureau Officers may be admitted in any subsequent proceedings (s 8(6)(a)) once this evidence complies with standard court rules as to admissibility. Further, the Act provides that any information and material obtained by any Bureau Officer pursuant to that Officer's statutory powers may be disclosed to other Bureau Officers. Also, any information and material in the possession of the Criminal Assets Bureau may be disclosed by it to An Gardaí, the Revenue Commissioners and other government agencies for the purpose of those bodies exercising or performing their powers or duties.

17.7.3.1 CAB warrant for the Search of Evidence

Section 14 of the CAB Act provides for a search warrant, which is vitally important for the work of the Criminal Assets Bureau. It provides that:

14.—(1) A judge of the District Court, on hearing evidence on oath given by a bureau officer who is a member of the Gardaí, may, if he or she is satisfied that there are reasonable grounds for suspecting that evidence of or relating to assets or proceeds deriving from criminal activities, or to their identity or whereabouts, is to be found in any place, issue a warrant for the search of that place and any person found at that place.

Section 14 also provides that, in situations of emergency, a Bureau Officer, being a member of the Gardaí not below the rank of Superintendent, may issue a search warrant where he or she is satisfied that the circumstances give rise to the need for the immediate issue of a search warrant which circumstances render it impractical to apply to a judge of the District Court under this section for a search warrant. The section provides that the warrant issued by a District Judge is valid for seven days and the warrant issued by a Superintendent is valid for 24 hours. The section also contains sub-sections that aid the efficiency and effectiveness of a search.

It is noteworthy that the search warrant provided for in s 14 of the CAB Act is a search warrant to search for assets (with, it should be noted, an ancillary power to search persons in the course of the search). Having regard to the nature of the evidence sought, it is possible, and indeed usual, that the proceeds of criminal activity, or evidence as to its identity or whereabouts, is to be found in places where the owner or occupier might have no knowledge whatsoever as to the nefarious source or significance of the evidence.

The provisions of s 14, in addition to providing a valuable tool in their own right for gathering evidence and materials relevant to the work of the Criminal Assets Bureau, are used in conjunction with the provisions of s 63 of the Criminal Justice Act 1994, which deals with an order to make materials available.

17.7.3.2   Power of arrest under the CAB Act

Section 16 of the CAB Act contains the power of arrest without warrant of a person suspected of committing or having committed an offence under ss 12, 13, or 15 of the CAB Act or under s 94 of the Finance Act 1983, but it provides that other than arrest and charge, no further action is to be taken except by or with the consent of the Director of Public Prosecutions.

17.8   Powers, objectives, and functions of the Criminal Assets Bureau

The powers, objectives and functions of the Criminal Assets Bureau are contained in ss 4 and 5 of the CAB Act. Section 4 of the Act sets out the objectives of the Bureau. Section 5 of the Act sets out its functions. These provisions read as follows:

4.—   Subject to the provisions of this Act, the objectives of the Bureau shall be—

(a)   the identification of the assets, wherever situated, of persons which derive or are suspected to derive, directly or indirectly, from criminal activity,

(b)   the taking of appropriate action under the law to deprive or to deny those persons of the assets or the benefit of such assets, in whole or in part, as may be appropriate, and

(c)   the pursuit of any investigation or the doing of any other preparatory work in relation to any proceedings arising from the objectives mentioned in paragraphs (a) and (b).

5.—(1)   Without prejudice to the generality of s 4, the functions of the Bureau, operating through its bureau officers, shall be the taking of all necessary actions—

(a)   in accordance with Garda functions, for the purposes of the confiscation, restraint of use, freezing, preservation or seizure of assets identified as deriving, or suspected to derive, directly or indirectly, from criminal activity,

(b)   under the Revenue Acts or any provision of any other enactment, whether passed before or after the passing of this Act, which relates to revenue, to ensure that the proceeds of criminal activity or suspected criminal activity are subjected to tax and that the Revenue Acts, where appropriate, are fully applied in relation to such proceeds or activities, as the case may be,

(c) *under the Social Welfare Acts for the investigation and determination, as appropriate, of any claim for or in respect of benefit (within the meaning of s 204 of the Social Welfare (Consolidation) Act, 1993) by any person engaged in criminal activity, and*

(d) *at the request of the Minister for Social Welfare, to investigate and determine, as appropriate, any claim for or in respect of a benefit, within the meaning of s 204 of the Social Welfare (Consolidation) Act, 1993, where the Minister for Social Welfare certifies that there are reasonable grounds for believing that, in the case of a particular investigation, officers of the Minister for Social Welfare may be subject to threats or other forms of intimidation, and such actions include, where appropriate, subject to any international agreement, cooperation with any police force, or any authority, being a tax authority or social security authority, of a territory or state other than the State.*

(2) *In relation to the matters referred to in subsection (1), nothing in this Act shall be construed as affecting or restricting in any way—*

  (a) *the powers or duties of the Gardai, the Revenue Commissioners or the Minister for Social Welfare, or*

  (b) *the functions of the Attorney General, the Director of Public Prosecutions or the Chief State Solicitor.*

While these provisions set out the objectives and functions of the Bureau, these provisions do not specifically limit its officers, as they retain their powers as officers of their parent agencies. Members of An Garda Síochána who are Bureau officers continue to investigate, give evidence, and where necessary prosecute criminal offences.

17.9 Disclosure of certain revenue and social welfare information

17.9.1 INTRODUCTION

Under s 5(1) of the Criminal Assets Bureau Act 1996, the revenue functions of the Criminal Assets Bureau are described as follows:

(b) under the Revenue Acts or any provision of any other enactment, whether passed before or after the passing of this Act, which relates to revenue, to ensure that the proceeds of criminal activity or suspected criminal activity are subjected to tax and that the Revenue Acts, where appropriate, are fully applied in relation to such proceeds or activities, as the case may be.

Section 1(1) of the CAB Act defines the Revenue Acts as:

- the Customs Acts;

- the statutes relating to the duties of excise and to the management of those duties;

- the Tax Acts;

- the Capital Gains Tax Acts;

- the Value-added Tax Act 1972;

- the Capital Acquisitions Tax Act 1976;

- the statutes relating to stamp duty and to the management of that duty;

- Part VI of the Finance Act 1983;

- Chapter IV of Part 11 of the Finance Act 1992; and

- any instruments made under any of these Acts, and any instruments made under any other enactment and relating to tax.

'Tax' means any tax, duty, levy, or charge under the care and management of the Revenue Commissioners.

THE PROCEEDS OF CRIME

Section 19 of the Finance Act 1983, now s 58 of the Taxes Consolidation Act 1997, permits and obliges the Revenue Commissioners to assess and collect tax on profits or gains from an unknown or unlawful source. Section 58(2) was originally introduced by s 11 of the Disclosure of Certain Information for Taxation and other Purposes Act 1996. The totality of s 58 now permits and obliges the Criminal Assets Bureau to charge profits or gains to tax under s 58(1), and also permits the Criminal Assets Bureau to deal with the assessment and collection of any tax as defined by virtue of and following an investigation by it.

The Disclosure of Certain Information for Taxation and Other Purposes Act 1996 also contained other ancillary amendments to facilitate the assessment and collection of taxes by a body such as the Criminal Assets Bureau. One of the most important sections of that Act was the amendment of the Criminal Justice Act 1994, by the insertion of a new s 63(A). That section permitted an exchange of information from the Revenue Commissioners to the Gardaí and vice versa, in appropriate circumstances.

Section 12 of the Disclosure of Certain Information for Taxation and Other Purposes Act 1996 sets out very detailed anonymity provisions in relation to the exercise of powers and functions of authorized officers as provided for by that Act. However, where the Criminal Assets Bureau is concerned, provisions more specific to the workings of the Criminal Assets Bureau were enacted (s 10 of the Criminal Assets Bureau Act 1996).

The Criminal Assets Bureau, in pursuing its statutory remit to collect taxes, can utilize all available legal remedies in the collection of taxes through the courts and by virtue of statutory remedies available under the Tax Acts that are available to the Revenue Commissioners. In fully applying the Revenue Acts to the proceeds of criminal activity or suspected criminal activity, the Revenue Bureau Officers of the Criminal Assets Bureau raise assessments to tax and, where appropriate, issue demands for tax and institute a variety of enforcement proceedings to recover the taxes due. On the enforcement side, the Criminal Assets Bureau can make use of s 962 of the Taxes Consolidation Act Certificates (formerly s 485 of the Income Tax Act 1967—Sheriff's Certificate), s 102 of the Taxes Consolidation Act 1997, attachments (formerly s 73 of the Finance Act 1988), High Court summary judgment proceedings, and judgment mortgages.

In applying the Revenue Acts generally, the Criminal Assets Bureau has collected Income Tax, Capital Gains Tax where CG50 Clearance Certificates could not be obtained, VAT, and PAYE/PRSI collected and not returned.

In the challenging of assessments raised by the Criminal Assets Bureau by statute, it has to be disregarded whether or not the profits or gains are the result of criminal activity. Therefore, unless the person assessed can show that the money or property has been obtained from a lawful source, there is no answer to the tax assessment. In these circumstances, the assessments become final and conclusive and the Bureau uses the enforcement procedures available.

The various appeal mechanisms in relation to assessments raised by the Criminal Assets Bureau are also available to persons in receipt of such assessments.

In a number of cases, defendants have sought to challenge the tax code, which operates not only for the work of the Criminal Assets Bureau but generally for the collection of taxes from all citizens. To date, the statutory provisions and the procedures already in place for the implementation of those provisions have withstood challenge except in a minority of cases.

17.9.2   SOCIAL WELFARE LEGISLATION IMPLICATIONS

17.9.2.1   General powers

As already stated, the Criminal Assets Bureau is a multi-agency body consisting of members of An Garda Síochána, officials of the Revenue Commissioners (both Taxes and Customs), officials of the department of Social, Community, and Family Affairs together with a Bureau Legal Officer and administrative and technical staff. The Criminal Assets Bureau's functions in relation to the Social Welfare code of legislation are to be found in s 5 of the CAB Act as delineated above.

Pursuant to the above statutory remit of the Criminal Assets Bureau under s 5, Social Welfare Officers who are also Bureau Officers of the Criminal Assets Bureau (Social Welfare Bureau Officers) conduct investigations and make decisions and determinations in relevant cases in respect of various social welfare benefits, in accordance with the statutory provisions of the Social Welfare legislation.

17.9.2.2   Legislative provisions utilized by Social Welfare Bureau Officers

The legislation operated by Social Welfare Bureau Officers consists of the following:

1.   the Social Welfare (Consolidation) Act 1993, as amended;

2.   the Social Welfare Act 1997; and

3.   the Social Welfare Act 1999.

In relation to the Social Welfare (Consolidation) Act 1993, as amended, the most relevant Parts are Part VI, which deals with the general provisions relating to social insurance, social assistance, and insurability (ss 204 to 245 inclusive), Part VII, which deals with decisions, appeals and the Social Welfare Tribunal (ss 246–76 inclusive), and Part VIII, which deals with overpayments, repayments, suspension of payments etc (ss 277–83 inclusive).

In relation to the Social Welfare Act 1997, s 34 of the Act inserts s 253(A)(1) into the Social Welfare (Consolidation) Act 1993. It provides that where the Chief Appeals Officer is of the view that the ordinary appeals procedures are inadequate to secure the effective process-ing of the appeals, he or she can invoke the provisions of s 253(A)(1) of the Social Welfare (Consolidation) Act 1993, certify that the ordinary appeals procedures are inadequate to secure the effective processing of the appeals, and direct the appellant to submit their appeal to the Circuit Court.

In relation to the Social Welfare Act 1999, this contains a number of amendments to the Social Welfare (Consolidation) Act 1993, as amended, relevant to the statutory remit of the Criminal Assets Bureau. These amendments are contained in ss 28–30 of the Social Welfare Act 1999. Section 28 inserts a new s 224A into the Social Welfare (Consolidation) Act 1993, and provides, *inter alia*, that civil proceedings arising out of the exercise of a Social Welfare Bureau Officer of his or her powers or duties may be brought by or against the Criminal Assets Bureau. The Criminal Assets Bureau is thereby empowered to sue for social welfare benefits deemed to have been wrongfully obtained.

Section 29 of the 1999 Act provides that where the Chief Appeals Officer invokes the provisions of s 253(A) of the Social Welfare (Consolidation) Act 1993, and directs a person to submit his or her appeal to the Circuit Court, such appeal should be so submitted within 21 days. Section 30 provides that Social Welfare Bureau Officers are empowered to investigate and decide claims to the supplementary welfare allowance.

17.9.2.3   Focus of Social Welfare Bureau Officers' investigations, decisions, and determinations

To date, investigations, decisions, and determinations have been made by Social Bureau Officers in respect of overpayments of various benefits such as unemployment assistance, lone parent's allowance, and disability allowance. A number of social welfare payments (unemployment assistance, lone parent allowance, child benefit, disability allowance, and fuel allowance) may be terminated as a consequence of decisions and determinations made by Social Welfare Bureau Officers.

The termination of improper social welfare payments and the recovery of social welfare overpayments by the Criminal Assets Bureau accords with the principles set out in the Department of Social, Community and Family Affairs Code of Practice. Under this Code of Practice, the Department of Social, Community and Family Affairs is obliged to make every effort to terminate any improper social welfare payments and to recover any overpayments of benefits, assistance, pensions, allowances, or other payments by the Department.

17.9.2.4 Procedures adopted by Social Welfare Bureau Officers in carrying out their statutory remit

Social Welfare Bureau Officers exercise the same powers and carry out the same procedures as Deciding Officers in the Department of Social, Community, and Family Affairs. Therefore, if, after carrying out an investigation, a Social Welfare Bureau Officer is of the view that there has been an overpayment to a person, the officer notifies that person the finding, outlining the reasons for the overpayment, the amount involved and how it is proposed to recover the money overpaid. If the person is having a social welfare payment refused or terminated, the Social Welfare Bureau Officer also notifies the person of the finding in this regard, outlining the reasons for the refusal or termination and of the fact of either the refusal or termination of the payment. In relation to an overpayment, the person will have an opportunity to comment on both the Social Welfare Bureau Officer's finding and the proposed method of repayment, and bring to the officer's attention any facts or circumstances which the person considers relevant to both the finding and the repayment of the overpayment. Likewise, in relation to the refusal or termination of a social welfare payment, the person concerned is afforded an opportunity to comment on the Social Welfare Bureau Officer's finding and bring to the officer's attention any facts or circumstances which the person considers relevant to the finding.

Consideration will be given to the circumstances in which the overpayment arose, and to the person's ability to repay it. The amount of the repayment should not reduce the person's income below the weekly rate of supplementary welfare allowance appropriate to the person's circumstances. If this happens, the person's repayments may be reduced, deferred, or suspended until he or she is able to repay the overpayment at a rate that he or she can afford.

The Department of Social, Community, and Family Affairs has set out full details of the process of recovery of social welfare overpayments in their information leaflet 'SW 2 Appeal Procedure Available to a Person Affected by a Determination of a Social Welfare Bureau Officer'. As with all social welfare decisions and determinations, all cases decided and determined by a Social Welfare Bureau Officer can be appealed to the Social Welfare Appeals Office.

If a person has claimed a social welfare payment or has had a social welfare payment revoked, and that person is unhappy with the decision, he or she has the right to appeal, which involves having the matter referred to an Appeals Officer of the Social Welfare Appeals Office for determination. The Social Welfare Appeals Office operates independently of the Department of Social, Community and Family Affairs, the Social Welfare Services Office and the Criminal Assets Bureau. The Chief Appeals Officer heads the Social Welfare Appeals Office. That Officer is also Director of the Appeals Office.

17.9.2.5 Procedures for appeals against decisions or determinations of Social Welfare Bureau Officers

A person wishing to appeal a decision of a Social Welfare Bureau Officer must do so within 21 days of the decision on their claim being sent to them. In exceptional cases, appeals received outside this period may be accepted.

Appeals against decisions made by Social Welfare Bureau Officers can be given by the appellant to their local Social Welfare Office, or can be sent directly by them to the Social Welfare Appeals Office (D'Olier House, D'Olier Street, Dublin 2).

A person seeking to make such an appeal can either complete a form (form SWAO 1, which can be obtained at any local Social Welfare Office of the Department of Social, Community, and Family Affairs) or set out the grounds to their appeal fully in a letter.

When a person appeals a decision of a Social Welfare Bureau Officer, the Chief Appeals Officer may do one of two things:

(a) arrange to have that person's case placed before an Appeals Officer, who may revise the decision if he or she considers it warranted. The Appeals Officer may decide to hold an oral hearing of the person's case, which the person would be invited to attend.

(b) Deal with the person's appeal on the basis of the written evidence that the person has received.

Alternatively, the Chief Appeals Officer can invoke the provisions of s 253(A)(1) of the Social Welfare (Consolidation) Act 1993 (inserted by s 34 of the Social Welfare Act 1997), and certify that the ordinary appeals procedures are inadequate to secure the effective processing of the appeals and direct the appellant to submit their appeal to the Circuit Court. It should be noted that all appeals against the decisions of Social Welfare Bureau Officers have so far resulted in the Chief Appeals Officer invoking the provisions of s 253(A)(1) of the Social Welfare (Consolidation) Act 1993 as described above.

Section 253(A)(2) of the Social Welfare (Consolidation) Act 1993 provides that notice of an appeal as submitted to the Circuit Court pursuant to a direction as described above be given to the Deciding Officer. This would also include giving notice of such an appeal to the Social Welfare Bureau Officer.

Such appeals dealt with by the Circuit Court may be conducted in any manner determined by the presiding judge, subject to the constitutional requirements of fair procedure being adopted.

More information on the Social Welfare Appeals Office is contained in information leaflet SW 56.

A good example of where information gathered in investigations by the Criminal Assets Bureau has been used to cut off social welfare allowances and to seek repayment of any overpayments made is the case of *Martin Hyland* heard before Dunne J in the Circuit Civil Court on 11 May 1999. In those proceedings the judge upheld the decision of a Social Welfare Deciding Officer to cut off unemployment assistance to Mr Hyland (*The Irish Times*, 12 May 1999). An article in the *Sunday World* newspaper had alleged that Mr Hyland was involved in drug dealing. This article had come to the attention of the Department of Social, Community, and Family Affairs and CAB were directed to carry out an investigation. This investigation led to a recommendation that Mr Hyland's unemployment assistance be terminated. Dunne J upheld this decision and stated that Mr Hyland's evidence as to his place of residence had been evasive, inconsistent and, at times, contradictory.

17.9.3 THE FINANCING OF THE CAB

Section 19 of the CAB Act sets out the financial arrangements for the funding of the Criminal Assets Bureau. It provides that the Minister for Justice, Equality and Law Reform, with the consent of the Minister for Finance, may make advances to the Criminal Assets Bureau from time to time out of monies provided by the Oireachtas for the purpose of expenditure by the Bureau in the performance of its functions.

17.9.4 OTHER RELEVANT PROVISIONS OF THE CAB ACT

Section 18 sets out the relationship of the Bureau Officers, members of staff of the Criminal Assets Bureau from their original civil service positions with their positions within the Criminal Assets Bureau from a salary perspective and as members of the Gardaí where relevant. It also extends the scope of the provisions of the Garda Compensation Scheme to Bureau Officers, members of staff of the Criminal Assets Bureau and the solicitors of the Chief State Solicitor's Office engaged in Criminal Assets Bureau work.

Section 20 of the Act sets out the arrangements whereby tax collected by the Criminal Assets Bureau is to be accounted and remitted to the central fund. Section 21 of the CAB Act provides that yearly, but not later than six months after the end of each year, the Criminal Assets Bureau is obliged to submit an Annual Report to the Minister for Justice of its activities during the year, and the Minister is to lay that report before each House of the Oireachtas. Sections 23, 24, and 25 of the Act make minor changes to various Tax Acts, including the Disclosure of Certain Information for Taxation and Other Purposes Act 1996 (now incorporated into the Taxes Consolidation Act 1997, as amended).

17.9.5 ANONYMITY PROVISIONS IN THE CAB ACT

Due to the anticipated security aspect of the Bureau's functions, the Act contains provisions designed to protect the anonymity of bureau officers. Section 10 of the CAB Act is an all-encompassing provision which dictates that *'all reasonable care must be taken to ensure that the identity of a bureau officer who is an officer of the revenue commissioners, or an officer of the minister for social, community and family affairs, or a member of the staff of the bureau, shall not be revealed'*. This provision only applies to certain bureau officers and staff. It does not apply to the Chief Bureau Officer, the Bureau Legal Officer, any member of An Garda Síochána or the Solicitor to the Bureau.

The Act further provides that where such Bureau Officers are exercising powers or duties they shall be accompanied by a Bureau Officer who is a member of An Garda Síochána, and shall not be required to identify themselves. Furthermore when exercising any power or duty in writing, such exercise shall be in the name of the Bureau. In court proceedings the identity of such Bureau Officers shall not be revealed and where they may be required to give evidence the judge may, on application by the Chief Bureau Officer, give directions as to the preservation of anonymity. While there may be provision for the taking of evidence behind screens this has never been sought or granted. Generally such evidence is given in open court, only the name and address of such Bureau Officer being preserved.

Where a Bureau Officer is an Officer of the Revenue Commissioners or an Officer for the Minister for Social Community and Family Affairs, when exercising powers or duties, he or she shall be accompanied by a Bureau Officer who is a member of the Gardaí, and shall not be required to identify himself or herself (s 10(2)(a) and (b) and s 10(3)). When exercising any power or duty in writing, the officer shall exercise same in the name of the Criminal Assets Bureau (ss 10(4) and 10(5)).

In court proceedings, the identity of a Bureau Officer who is an officer of the Revenue Commissioners, an Officer of the Minister for Social, Community and Family Affairs, or a member of staff of the Criminal Assets Bureau shall not be revealed. Where in any proceedings a Bureau Officer or a member of staff of the Bureau may be required to give evidence, whether by affidavit, certificate, or oral evidence, the judge or person in charge of the proceedings may, on the application of the Chief Bureau Officer, if satisfied that there are reasonable grounds in the public interest to do so, give such directions for the preservation of the anonymity of the Bureau Officer or member of staff of the Criminal Assets Bureau as he or she thinks fit (s 10(7)).

There are prohibitions contained in the CAB Act with regard to identifying Bureau Officers who are officers of the Revenue Commissioners, Officers of the Minister for Social, Community and Family Affairs, or members of staff of the Bureau, and the families of all such officers and staff, including their addresses, which makes it an offence to do so. There are also offences for assault, obstruction and intimidation of these persons.

17.9.6 CHALLENGES OF THE IRISH CIVIL FORFEITURE MODEL

17.9.6.1 Constitutional challenges (linked to ECHR Articles)

In the course of applications made under the Proceeds of Crime Act 1996, a number of respondents have challenged its constitutional validity. Almost all points have been canvassed in the two lengthy and comprehensive judgments of McGuinness J and O'Higgins J respectively in *Gilligan v Ireland, Attorney General, Criminal Assets Bureau and Others:* and *Murphy v GM, PB and Others*. Both of these cases were appealed to the Supreme Court, heard together and judgment delivered on 18 October 2001.

While the courts have yet to determine any Proceeds of Crime issues on the basis of the European Convention on Human Rights (ECHR), it should be noted that many of the constitutional arguments presented reflect Convention arguments (see **Chapter 2**). The following are some of the arguments which have been advanced and the court's determination on same. (Relevant Articles of the Convention are delineated in brackets, to facilitate distinguishing them.)

- The Act is in breach of Article 38, as it constitutes a criminal procedure by another name (ERSATZ civil law); a civil procedure, which does not ensure the protections, required 'in due course of law'. (A right to a fair trial under Article 6 of the Convention: Such protections would include the presumption of innocence, the criminal standard of proof 'beyond reasonable doubt' rather than the civil standard of 'on the balance of possibilities', a right to a trial by jury, which are clearly not contained in the Act.)

  Held: (a) These forfeiture proceedings are civil, not criminal in nature. 'There is no provision for the arrest or detention of any person, the admission of persons to bail, for the imprisonment of a person for the non payment of a penalty, for a form of Criminal Trial initiated by summons or indictment, for the recording of a conviction of any form or the entering of a *nolle prosequi* at any stage, all elements which would indicate that the Act creates a criminal offence'. 'In general such a forfeiture is not a punishment and its operation does not require criminal procedures'. (b) There is no bar in the determination, in the course of civil or other proceedings, of matters which may constitute elements of a criminal offence, and accordingly protections under Article 38(1) are not applicable.

- The Act constitutes a reversal of the (standard) onus of proof.

  Held: The reversal only operates after the establishment to the court's satisfaction of certain issues. Furthermore, there is a right to cross-examine. Finally, there is no constitutional infirmity in the procedure whereby the onus is placed on a person seeking property to negative the inference from evidence adduced that a criminal offence has been committed.

- The Act infringes a right against self-incrimination—Article 38 Constitution—Fair procedures (Art 6 of the ECHR; *Saunders v United Kingdom* chapter 2).

  Held: The court agreed with Moriarty J in *M v D* (February 1997). The State's sophisticated version of 'the innocent have nothing to fear' is not necessarily their whole answer. Before an order is made under s 9 of the Act, there should be a requirement of an indemnity from use by the DPP of any evidence given pursuant to such an order.

- The Act, by the operation of s 6, restricts a defendant's right of access to the court. (Article 6 (4) of the Convention, Right to Free Legal Aid or Article 13, Right to an Effective Remedy.)

  Held: The structure of s 6 is no different from any application for legal aid. Even under the judgment of Gannon J in *State (Healy) v Donoghue* [1976 IR 325], no one is automatically entitled to legal aid, as they have to show both necessity and lack of means.

- The Act in its operation breaches rights to private property. (Article 1 of Protocol 1 of the Convention.)

  Held: The Proceeds of Crime Act 1996 does provide onerous and far-reaching penalties and forfeitures, but these are directly connected with the establishment to the satisfaction of the court that the property concerned is either directly or indirectly the proceeds of crime. The State has a legitimate interest in the forfeiture of the proceeds of crime. The right to private ownership cannot hold a place so high in the hierarchy of rights that it protects the position of assets illegally acquired or held.

- The Act is in breach of Article 15(5) in that it is retrospective in its effect. (Article 7 of the Convention.)

  Held: The acquisition of assets which derive from crime was not an illegal activity before the passing of the 1996 Act, and did not become an illegal activity because of the 1996 Act.

- Extra-territoriality

  Held: There does exist between sovereign States a recognized 'comity of esteem', that one State will not act in a manner clearly in violation of the sovereignty of another. However, this is not a matter for constitutional limitations. There is no breach of the concept of comity of esteem by the issue of a worldwide injunction, which operates '*in personam*' (*Darby v Weldon No 2* [1989] All ER 1002 at 1011).

The High Court (McGuinness J) concluded in these cases that the Act constitutes a proportional and legitimate delimitation on rights in the interests of the common good, considering the extent of the particular malaise it is designed to remedy. However, the court did express reservations, especially with regard to the operation of s 9, stating that particular care would have to be taken, whether by limiting the purpose for which the information disclosed may be used, or otherwise, to protect the privilege of a respondent against the revealing of information which could later be used in a criminal prosecution. The court also stated that it should be slow to make an order under s 3 on the basis of s 8 evidence alone, ie without any corroborative evidence.

17.9.6.2   Manifestation of CAB procedures in practice

The format of Proceeds of Crime litigation envisaged by the Proceeds of Crime Act 1996 was as follows:

(a)   An interim Order under s 2 to immediately freeze assets in danger of being lost, which expires after 21 days unless extended.

(b)   An interlocutory Order, s 3, based on affidavit which if granted freezes assets for seven years allowing time for claimants if any to bring applications to recover.

(c)   A final disposal Order under s 4 after a plenary hearing, whereby assets are finally forfeited to the state.

(d)   Any third party affected can bring applications under 2.3 and 3.3 to recoup monies legally owed/owned.

(e)   The respondent can bring applications under s 6.3 for business living or other expenses.

(f)   An undertaking as to damages, normal in ordinary injunctive applications, is not required here due to s 16, which provides for compensation.

Procedural process has changed due to the impact of Supreme Court case law. The Proceeds of Crime Act 1996 envisaged that originating ss 2 and 3 motions would be injunctive and therefore on affidavit, with the final s 4 application being the plenary hearing. A judgment in a case of Farrell deemed s 3 a plenary stage, and therefore the final section 4 stage was relegated to a motion. The Proceeds of Crime Amendment Act 2005 provides for originating motions to bring back procedures on affidavit unless application is made for a plenary hearing.

Most actual litigation is on procedural points and not on substantive issues, eg must a s 3 motion be issued, served and decided on within 21 days to preserve the initial s 2 freezing order; it need not be so issued, etc. One respondent might have multiple litigation, eg a Proceeds of Crime case, summary recovery procedures, appeal Commissioner and consequential JR proceedings, eg Hunt.

The Criminal Assets Bureau (CAB) has its own panel of counsel who act on both sides approved by the Attorney General. The litigation engaged by CAB occurs in the following jurisdictions:

● High Court: Proceeds of Crime litigation; Judicial Review Revenue; Summons for unpaid taxes (income, VAT, etc); Summary procedures to recoup Social Welfare overpayments.

● Circuit Court: Appeal from Appeal Commissioners decision on tax due; Appeal from Social Welfare Office decision.

● Appeal Commissioner: Appeal under ss 933 and 957 (miscellaneous income) Taxes Consolidation Act 1997 (TCA) as amended.

17.9.6.3   CAB case law

● *Cahill:* Settlement of Proceeds of Crime at s 3 stage. No legal (save lapse of time issues), just historical issues.

● *Creaven:* District Court jurisdiction (no issue warrants) does not extend beyond district granting them. Issuing of warrants is an administrative not a judicial function.

● *Keogh:* Tax payer can rely on non-statutory taxpayers' charter as defence.

● *Donovan:* Proceeds of Crime applies only to assets derived from crimes committed within the State.

● *Hanratty/Farrell:* Statute of limitations does not apply to ss 2 and 3 (as amended). Do not have to specify activity from which assets derive.

● *Griffin:* Query: Can contemporaneous Revenue prosecution and appeal procedure breach right of non self-incrimination? Reply: Not necessarily, but Appeal Commissioner must bear this in mind when hearing appeal.

17.9.6.4   Civil Libertarian challenges

Civil Libertarian critique of the Irish Proceeds of Crime civil forfeiture model tends to be met with the following:

(a)   There is no evidence of selectivity.

(b)   As its operation is funded by the central fund there is no 'agency profit motive' and accordingly operates as an effective deterrent.

(c)   All proceeds go to the central fund.

(d)   Legal aid is available, where appropriate.

(e) No order can be made if the court 'is satisfied that there would be a serious injustice'.

(f) Compensation is available if court orders are proved to be incorrect in the granting of initial freezing orders.

(g) It does not impinge on valid existing property rights.

(h) It constitutes a proportional response to a serious social malaise.

APPENDICES AND PRECEDENTS

Acknowledgement

It would not have been possible to compile this book of precedent applications but for the generosity of certain criminal lawyers who share the editor's view that trainee solicitors should benefit from their experience.

Many of the documents in this booklet represent the facts of actual cases. The identification of the parties, the dates and record numbers of the actual cases have been omitted to protect identity.

CONTENTS

CONTENTS

APPENDIX 1

PRE-COURT DOCUMENTATION

1.1 Custody Record

C.84.

GARDA SÍOCHÁNA CUSTODY RECORD Garda Station _____ **District** _____ **No** _____

A. Details Concerning Person in Custody

1. Name_____
2. Address_____
   Home Circumstance Code_____
3. Alias_____
4. Date of Birth_____ 5. Sex_____
6. Marital Status____ 7. Nationality_____
8. Height___ 9. Hair Colour___
10. Eye colour____
11. Complexion____ 12. Facial hair_____
13. Eye type_____
14. Any distinguishing marks/ deformities/amputations / scars/ facial oddities / alerts (personality and possible tendencies).

Signature of Member _____

B. Details of Arrest

15. Arrest time_____ Date_____
16. Name of arresting member_____
17 Place of arrest_____
18. Arrival at Station Time ___ Date___
19. Offence(s) or other matter in respect of which arrest was made

_____

20. Signature of member _____

DETENTION

21. To be completed in respect of a person detained under section 4 of the Criminal Justice Act 1984:
I have reasonable grounds for believing that the detention of

_____

is necessary for the proper investigation of the offence(s) in respect of which the said person has been arrested.

_____

Signature of Member in charge Time & date

C. Initial Action Taken

22. Information given to arrested person in accordance with Regulation 8(1)
Time_____
Signature of member_____
23. Notice of rights
Time_____
Signature of member _____

24. I acknowledge receipt of notice of

_____

Signature of person in custody

Remarks:

Persons under 17 or mentally handicapped persons

25. Parent, guardian or spouse (as case may be) informed of arrest
Time:___ Signature of member_____
26. Where not possible to contact a parent, information given to arrested person in accordance with regulation (b)
Time____ Signature of member_____
27. To be completed where notification of solicitor or other person requested by person in custody or, where any person under 17 or mentally handicapped, on person's behalf.

Time request made	Name & status to be notified	Time request complied with	Initials

Remarks:

Time Initials
28. District headquarters notified
Home District Headquarters Notification

_____

D. Details of Any Action Occurrence Involving the Person in Custody
Instructions:
1. All other matters required by the records on the treatment of persons in custody should be recorded in this section.
2. Entries need not be restricted to one occurrence.
3. All entries should be signed or initialled by the member making them.
4. Where the authority of a member of a rank is required for any action the name and rank of the member given authority is to be recorded.
5. Where the consent of the person in custody is required for any action, that consent should be acknowledged in writing by the person on this record or a separate document, as the case may be.

Date	Time of Action/ occurrence	Details of action / occurrence	Member's signature/ initials

(If necessary additional pages with it (section D) headings may be attached

1.2   Information for persons in custody (Form c.72(s))

GARDA SÍOCHÁNA

(Information for persons in custody)

Reason for arrest

You will have been informed of the offence or offences for which you have been arrested.

Notification to other persons

If you are seventeen or over, you may, on request, have a solicitor or other person named by you notified that you are in custody in a particular station. If the person first nominated cannot be contacted, you may nominate another person.

If you are under seventeen, your parent or guardian (or, if you are married, your spouse) will be notified and asked to attend at the station without delay.

Non-Irish Nationals

If you are a foreign national you may communicate with a diplomatic or consular representative of your own country who is either in the State or accredited to the State on a non-residential basis, or a diplomatic or consular representative of a third country which may formally or informally offer consular assistance if your country has no resident representative in the State.

Your consul will be notified of your arrest if you so wish.

If you are a national of the United States of America your consular representative will be notified of your arrest unless you otherwise request.

Legal Advice

You may communicate privately with a solicitor either in writing or by telephone, or consult with the solicitor in the station.

Visits, telephone calls, etc.

You may, if you wish, (a) receive a visit from a relative, friend, or other person with an interest in your welfare and (b) make a telephone call or send a letter, provided that (i) the member in charge is satisfied that it will not hinder or delay the investigation of crime and (ii) in the case of a visit, it is practicable for the visit to be adequately supervised.

Searches

If you are to be searched, the reason for the research will be explained to you.

Fingerprints, palm prints, photographs, and tests

If you have been arrested under section 30 of the Offences Against the State Act 1939 or detained under section 4 of the Criminal Justice Act 1984, or section 2 of the Criminal Justice (Drug Trafficking) Act 1996, a member of the Garda Síochána, when authorized by an officer not below the rank of Superintendent, may take your fingerprints, palm prints, or photograph. A member may also make tests to see if you have been in contact with a firearm or explosive substance and for that purpose may take swabs from your skin or samples of your hair.

In any other case, a member may take your fingerprints, etc with your written consent and, if you are under seventeen, the written consent of an appropriate adult.

Taking of bodily samples

If you have been arrested under section 30 of the Offences Against the State Act, 1939, or detained under section 4 of the Criminal Justice Act, 1984, or under section 2 of the Criminal Justice (Drug Trafficking) Act, 1996, a member of the Garda Síochána when authorized by an officer not below the rank of Superintendent, may take or cause to be taken (eg by a doctor) from you bodily samples for forensic testing. In these cases certain types of sample may not be taken without written consent. If you are seventeen or over your written consent will be required and if you are under fourteen the sample(s) in question may be taken with the written consent of your parent or guardian. If you are fourteen or over but under seventeen your written consent and that of your parent or guardian will be required. Failure to provide written consent may have certain legal consequences, which will be explained to you.

In any other case a member may take bodily samples with your written consent.

Meals

There is no charge for meals supplied. However, it you wish to have a meal of your own choice it will be supplied, if practicable, but at your own expense.

Member in charge

The member in charge of the station is responsible for overseeing the application of the statutory regulations for the treatment of persons in custody and for that purpose will visit you from time to time. Any matters relating to your treatment should be brought to the attention of the member in charge.

Identification parades

If you take part in an identification parade—

(a) you will be placed among a number of other persons who are, as far as practicable, of similar height, age, general appearance, dress, etc.;

(b) you may have a solicitor or friend present at the parade;

(c) you may take up any position you wish in the parade and, after a witness has left, change your position in the parade, if you wish, before the next witness is called;

(d) you may object to the member conducting the parade regarding any of the persons on the parade or the arrangements for it.

Bail

You may be released on bail if the member in charge considers it prudent to do so and no warrant directing your detention is in force. If you are not given bail, you may apply for it when you come before the Court.

Legal Aid

This is dealt with on application to the Court and may be granted in certain circumstances.

Examination by a doctor

You have the right to request a medical examination by a doctor, including one of your own choice.

1.3 Notice to persons whose interview is being electronically recorded

1. This notice explains the use which will be made of the electronic recording of the interview.

2. The interview will be recorded on ( ) videotapes.

3. One of the videotapes will be sealed in your presence and will be kept securely and treated as an exhibit for the purpose of any criminal proceedings.

4. The other tape will be kept by the Garda Síochána. The Director of Public Prosecutions and the Chief State Solicitor's Office may have access to them.

5. If you are legally represented you should bring this notice to the attention of your solicitor.

6. A copy of the video tape recorded interview can be obtained by your solicitor, or if you are represented by yourself, by writing, quoting your name and the date of your interview to the address below:

Address: Superintendent_____(Name of Garda Station)

1.4   Warrant to search

Chuirt Duiche   **The District Court**

WARRANT TO SEARCH
Court District_____

(Pursuant to Section 26 Misuse of Drugs Acts, 1977 and 1984)

WHEREAS I, THE UNDERSIGNED * Justice of the District Court/Peace Commissioner, am satisfied by the information on oath of:

That there is reasonable ground for suspecting that a person is in possession in contravention of the Misuse of Drugs Acts, 1977 and 1984 of a controlled drug namely:

_____

*/forged prescription */duly issued prescription which has been wrongfully altered and such */drug */prescription is on the premises */other land at:

_____

You_____

Are hereby authorized, accompanied by such other members of the Garda Síochána and such other persons as may be necessary, at any time or times within one month of the date of issue of this warrant, to enter (if need by force) the premises */other land at:

_____

_____

to search */ such premises */other land and any persons found there to examine */any substance */article */other thing found there, to inspect */any book */record */other document */found there and, if there is reasonable ground for suspecting that an offence is being */has been committed under the Misuse of Drugs Acts, 1977 and 1984 in relation to */a substance */article */other thing */found on such premises */other land */that a document so found is a document mentioned in subsection (1)(b) of section 26 of the Misuse of Drugs Acts, 1977 and 1984 */is a record */other document */which you have reasonable cause to believe to be a document which may be required as evidence in proceedings for an offence under the Misuse of Drugs Acts 1977 and 1984, to seize and detain the substance */article */document */other thing as the case may be.

Dated:_____

Signed:_____

District Justice of the District Court assigned to the said District.
*Peace Commissioner assigned to the said county,
*and surrounding counties
*Delete whichever does not apply

1.5 Outline of Standard Criminal Litigation Documentation (most exhibited in this Booklet)

Standard Criminal Litigation Documentation

This list itemizes documentation, which the Criminal Practitioner will encounter in practice. The documents exhibited herein are first those in the District Court and then the Higher Courts. Judicial Review applications, which originate in the High Court have been itemised separately.

District Court
1. Charge Sheet
2. Summons
3. Bail Bond
4. Statement of Means
5. Book of Evidence
6. Bond on Sending Accused Forward
7. Notice of Appeal
8. Recognisance of Appeal
9. Committal Warrant

Circuit Criminal Court
1. Return for Trial
2. Indictment

High Court
1. Copy Order 84 Rule 13 Notice
2. Notice of Motion
3. Grounding Affidavit
4. Application to Revoke Bail
5. Personal Applicant Documentation
6. Committal Warrant

Judicial Review
1. Form 13
2. Notice of Motion
3. Grounding Affidavit
4. Submissions (a) Applicant and (b) Respondent
5. Statement of Grounds of Opposition

Central Criminal Court
1. Return for Trial
2. Bill of Indictment
3. Issue Paper

Court of Criminal Appeal
1. Notice of Application for Leave to Appeal
2. Grounds of Appeal
3. Submissions (a) Applicant and (b) Respondents
4. Appeal Against Undue Leniency

APPENDIX 2

DISTRICT COURT

2.1 District Court—Charge Sheet

_____Garda Station

Charge sheet no ....of 200____

*Prosecutor

_____

*Complainant

*Accused

_____

*Defendant_____

_____

_____

OFFENCE(S) CHARGED:

L2248

For that you the said accused on the _____ 20____ at _____

In the Dublin Metropolitan District, did dishonestly appropriate property to wit _____ without the consent of_____ the owner thereof.

Contrary to Section 4 of the Criminal Justice (Theft and Fraud Offences) Act 2001

L3648

For that you the said accused on the _____ 20____ at _____

In the Dublin Metropolitan District, handled stolen property to wit _____
knowing that the said property was stolen or being reckless as to whether the said property was stolen

Contrary to Section 17 of the Criminal Justice (Theft and Fraud Offences) Act 2001.

*Delete where inapplicable

DISTRICT COURT

2.2   District Court—Summons

AN CHÚIRT DÚICHE   THE DISTRICT COURT

DUBLIN METROPOLITAN DISTRICT
COURTS (NO 3) ACT, 1936. SECTION 1.
SUMMONS

PROSECUTOR: DIRECTOR OF PUBLIC PROSECUTIONS

ACCUSED:

                                        CASE NUMBER:
                                        SUMMONS DATE:

APPLICANT:

TO THE ABOVE NAMED ACCUSED

WHEREAS ON THE _____—AN APPLICATION WAS MADE TO THIS
OFFICE BY THE ABOVE-NAMED APPLICANT ON BEHALF OF THE ABOVE-NAMED
PROSECUTOR FOR THE ISSUE OF A SUMMONS TO YOU, THE ABOVE-NAMED
ACCUSED, ALLEGING THE OFFENCE, THE PARTICULARS OF WHICH ARE SET OUT
HEREUNDER.

THIS IS TO NOTIFY YOU THAT YOU WILL BE ACCUSED OF THIS OFFENCE AT A
SITTING OF THE DUBLIN METROPOLITAN DISTRICT COURT TO BE HELD

....

*AT: COURT NO   ,   FOUR COURTS DUBLIN 7 * ON: DAY OF
          2006 AT: 1400 HOURS

....

AND TO REQUIRE YOU TO APPEAR AT THE SAID SITTING TO ANSWER THE SAID
ACCUSATION.

OFFENCE ALLEGED: THAT YOU, THE SAID ACCUSED DID ON OR ABOUT
          AND   SEND BY MEANS OF THE TELECOMMUNICATIONS SYSTEM
OPERATED BY BOARD TELECOM EIREANN A MESSAGE OF AN INDECENT
CHARACTER ADDRESSED TO_____CONTRARY TO SECTION 13(1)
(A) OF THE POST OFFICE AMENDMENT ACT 1951 AS AMENDED BY THE POSTAL AND
TELECOMMUNICATIONS SERVICES ACT 1983.

APPROPRIATE DISTRICT COURT CLERK
ÁRAS UÍ DHALÁIGH,
INNS QUAY
DUBLIN 7

31-   -1400-1870H-NEWTOWN GDA. STN.—1

2.3   **Money recognisance (own bond—remand)**

Charge Sheet_____   Case No_____

AN CHÚIRT DÚICHE   THE DISTRICT COURT

Form 43-Rule 31

DUBLIN METROPOLITAN DISTRICT

CRIMINAL PROCEDURE ACT 1967
Section 26
MONEY RECOGNISANCE
(Remand)

Prosecutor: The Director of Public Prosecution at the suit of_____

Accused:_____

I,_____

of_____a Principal Party

acknowledge myself to owe to the State the sum of _____
euro to the use of the Minister for Finance AND in lieu of surety/sureties I have, pursuant
to the direction of the Judge, lodged the sum of _____ euro;

AND I further acknowledge that both of the said sums are liable to be forfeit to the said
Minister if I fail in the condition hereunder.

Signed:_____

Acknowledged before me this   day of   200

_____
Judge of the District Court

The condition of this recognisance is that the above-named accused will appear before the
District Court at Court No   , Chancery Street, Dublin 7 _____
on the   day of   200   at   m. and any adjournment thereof until
his presence is no longer required.

Conditioned that he/she sign on daily at _____ Garda Station between the

hours of _____ am and _____ pm.

Further conditions as follows:_____

(CASH LODGED)

2.4 **Money recognisance (own bond plus surety—remand)**

Charge Sheet_____ Case No_____

DUBLIN METROPOLITAN DISTRICT

CRIMINAL PROCEDURE ACT 1967
Section 22
RECOGNISANCE
(Remand)

PROSECUTOR: The Director of Public Prosecution at the suit of_____

Accused:_____

We,_____ the accused

of _____ a Principal Party

and _____

of_____a Surety

and_____

of_____a Surety

severally acknowledged ourselves to owe to the State the several sums following, that is to say, the said accused the sum of € _____ and the said surety/sureties the sum of €_____each to the use of the Minister for Finance if the above-named accused fail in the condition hereunder.

_____ACCUSED

_____SURETY

_____SURETY

Acknowledged before me this   day of   200

_____
Judge of the District Court for the time
Being assigned to the said District.

The condition of this recognisance is that the above-named will appear before the District Court at Court No.   Chancery St., Dublin 7 on the   day of 200   at   m. and any adjournment thereof until his presence is no longer required. Further conditioned as follows: That he/she sign on daily at   Garda Station between   a.m.   and p.m.

2.5   Money recognisance (sending forward for trial or sentence)

Charge Sheet_____   Case No_____

AN CHÚIRT DÚICHE   THE DISTRICT COURT

DUBLIN METROPOLITAN DISTRICT
CRIMINAL PROCEDURE ACT 1967, SECTION 22

RECOGNISANCE ON SENDING FORWARD FOR TRIAL OR SENTENCE

PROSECUTOR: The Director of Public Prosecutions

ACCUSED:_____

I/we_____of_____

A Principal Party and_____of_____

a_____and_____of_____

_____a_____

severally acknowledged myself/ourselves to owe to the state the several sums following, that is to say, the said principal part the sum of € _____ and the said surety/sureties the sum of € _____ each to the use of the Minister for Finance if the above-named accused fail in the condition hereunder.

_____Accused

_____Surety

_____Surety

Acknowledged before me this   day of   200

Signed _____

Judge of the District Court

The condition of this recognisance is that the above-named accused will appear before the present/next sitting of the Circuit Court for Dublin City and County for the disposal of criminal business and will not depart from the said Court without leave and will attend there in person from day to day during the time the said Court shall be held or any adjournment thereof for the purposes of his/her *trial/* sentence and also attend any other Court to which his/her trial may be transferred until the charge against him/her shall be duly disposed of according to law.

Further conditioned that:_____

_____

_____

2.6 **Money recognisance (own bond) (sending forward for trial or sentence)**

Charge Sheet_____ Case No._____

AN CHÚIRT DÚICHE   THE DISTRICT COURT

Form 42   Rule 31

DUBLIN METROPOLITAN DISTRICT
CRIMINAL PROCEDURE ACT 1967

Section 26

MONEY RECOGNISANCE

(Sending forward for trial or sentence)

PROSECUTOR: The Director of Public Prosecutions

ACCUSED:_____

I,_____

of_____a Principal Party

acknowledged myself to owe to the State the sum of €_____
to the use of the Minister for Finance AND in lieu of surety/sureties I have, pursuant to
the direction of the Judge sending me forward for *trial/* sentence lodged the sum of
€_____ ;

AND I further acknowledge that both the said sums are liable to be forfeit to the said
Minister if I fail in the condition hereunder.

Signed: _____

Acknowledged before me this   day of   200

_____
Judge of the District Court

The condition of this recognisance is that the above-named will appear before the present/
next sitting of the Circuit Court for Dublin City and County for the disposal of Criminal
Business, and will not depart from the said Court without leave and will attend there in
person from day to day during the time the said Court shall be so held or any adjournment
thereof for the purposes of his/her *trial/*sentence and also attend any other Court to
which his/her trial may be transferred until the charge against him/her shall be duly
disposed of according to law.

Conditioned that he/she sign on daily at_____Garda Station between the

hours of_____am and_____pm.

Further conditions as follows:_____

(CASH LODGED)

2.7   District court (LEGAL AID FORM L.A. 1)

REF NO:_____

Form L.A. 1

CRIMINAL JUSTICE (LEGAL AID) ACT 1962

CRIMINAL JUSTICE (LEGAL AID) REGULATIONS 1965–1978

CLAIM FOR FEES (SOLICITOR ONLY, DISTRICT COURT OR AN APPEAL TO THE CIRCUIT COURT) AND SOLICITOR'S TRAVELLING AND SUBSISTENCE EXPENSES.

Part I (*The declaration hereunder is to be completed by the person in respect of whom a certificate for free legal aid was granted. If two or more persons whose cases where heard together were granted free legal aid certificates, a separate declaration should be furnished by each such person.*)

I declare that I have not made or agreed to make and will not make or agree to make a payment towards the costs or expenses of the case(s) in relation to which the certificate(s) for free legal aid was/ were granted on

........................*day of* ...., 20 ....*on my behalf.*

I further declare that I am not aware of a payment or intention to make a payment by any other person (other than under the Act) towards such costs or expenses.

Signed:_____

Date:..

Part II (to be completed by the Solicitor assigned)

1. State name(s) and address(es) or person(s)   ....
   in respect of whom legal aid certificate(s)   ....
   was/were granted   ....
                                                     ....
                                                     ....

2. State type of certificate (eg Form E (ii) see   ....
   First Schedule to the 1965 Regulation).   ....

3. State in general terms the change(s)   ....
   involved.   ....

4. State name and location of Court which   ....
   granted certificate(s) and date granted   Dates(s) ....

5. State name and location of Court which   ....
   heard case and date(s) of hearing(s)   Dates(s) ....

DISTRICT COURT

6. If the hearing on any of the duties mentioned
at No 5 consisted only of an application for an
adjournment, was the application by you or
on your behalf, or the prosecution, made in
the opinion of the Court, for the purpose of
your convenience (Regulation 3 (2) (b) of the
Criminal Justice (Legal Aid) (Amendment)
Regulations 1978))?

....
....
....
....
....
....
....

7. Were Counsel assigned?

....

8. If two or more certificates for free legal aid
were granted in respect of the person/a person
named at No 1 and the cases in respect of
which they were granted were heard together
or in immediate succession, state whether the
Court gave a direction as to whether more
than one certificate for free legal aid should be
deemed to have been granted and, if so, give
particulars of the Court's direction
(Regulation 7(4)).

....
....
....
....
....
....
....
....
....

9. If two or more persons are named at No 1 and
their cases were heard together, state (a)
whether the Court gave a direction regarding
fees and, (b) if so, give particulars of the
Court's direction (Regulation 10(7)).

....
....
....
....
....

10. Amounts Claimed
   (a) Fees:
   in respect of attendance at hearing on

Date	Solicitor's fee

"   "   "   "   "   "
"   "   "   "   "   "
"   "   "   "   "   "
"   "   "   "   "   "

   (b) Solicitor's travelling and subsistence expenses:—

Date	Depart	Return				Travel	Subsistence

* Time of departure form and return to residence or office should be given.

** A return journey not made on the same day as an outward journey should be shown under its proper date. If Public Transport is used, cheap or short-term return tickets should, where practicable, be availed of. In the case of a journey made to visit a place for the purpose of the case Regulation 11 (3) a statement explaining the necessity for the journey and signed by the Solicitor should be furnished on a separate sheet.

*** Vouchers should accompany claims for taxi or car hire expenses in excess of 50p for a single hiring.

   (c) Total of amounts claimed at (a) and (b).   € [   ]

I declare that—

(i) the particulars given by me in this Part of this Form are correct;

(ii) in my claim for travelling and subsistence expenses set out above I have made no claim either for travelling expenses or for subsistence allowances in connection with a Court hearing at any place on a day where in that place on that day I was engaged on court business other than business in connection with the case(s) in relation to which I had been assigned pursuant to the certificate(s) for free legal aid to which this claim relates (Regulation 11 (5)).

(iii) to the best of my knowledge and belief no payment has been made by or on behalf of the persons(s) named at No 1 towards the costs or expenses of the case(s) to which this claim relates and no agreement has been entered into by or on behalf of such person(s) to make any such payment (Regulation 12 (1)).

(iv) no fees have been claimed by me in respect of any day on which the hearing consisted only of application for an adjournment by me or on my behalf or the persecution, made in the opinion of the Court, for the purpose of my convenience (Regulation 3 (2) (b) of the Criminal Justice (Legal Aid) (Amendment Regulations 1978); and

I hereby apply for payment of the sum of €   being the amount shown at No 10 (c) above.

Signed_____

(Solicitor assigned)

Name in capitals ....

Name of Solicitor's firm (in caps)...

Address of Solicitor's Office ....

Date:.................................Solicitor's ref. no.......................................

II. I certify that I am liable for VAT and I hereby claim VAT at the appropriate rate in respect of taxable services completed by me under the Criminal Legal Aid Scheme, as set out in this claim form.

SIGNED_____

_____

Part III (to be completed by the District Court Clerk, County Registrar, or Registrar, as the case may be of the Court which heard the case).

I certify that the information given in reply at Nos 1 to 9 PART II of this Form is correct and the solicitor who has assigned PART II of this Form is the Solicitor who was assigned pursuant to the certificate(s) for free legal aid to which this Form relates.

I further certify that the said solicitor whose name appears on this Form attached at the ....Court sitting at ....on each of the dates for which fees are claimed at No 10 of PART II of this Form in connection with the case(s) in relation to which a certificate/certificates for free legal aid was/were granted on behalf of the person(s) named at No 1 of PART II of this Form.

DISTRICT COURT

I further certify that the following is the reason given by the Court for deeming that more than one certificate has been granted (see No 8 of PART II of Form and Regulation 7(4) of 1965).

....

....

....

....

....

Signed_____

Office held by person signing..

Date ....

PART IV (for use in the Department of Justice)

NAME	AMOUNT
....	€ ....
....	€ ....
....	€ ....

Approved for payment in the sum of € ....

(Signature of approving office)

Date...

NOTES

(a) Where one Court grants the certificate(s) for free legal aid in respect of which a claim is made on this form and the case(s) is/are heard in a different Court, the solicitor concerned should lodge the claim with the Officer of the Court which heard the case(s).

(b) A claim form should be completed in respect of each certificate for free legal aid granted, except

    (i)   where two or more certificates are granted to a person and the cases in relation to which they are granted are heard together or in immediate succession and, in the absence of a direction otherwise by the Court, one certificate is deemed, in accordance with the provisions of Regulations 7(4), to have granted, one claim only should be completed;

    (ii)   where certificates for free legal aid have been granted on behalf of two or more persons whose cases have been together, one claim form only should be completed in respect of such certificates.

(c) Details as to the scale on which subsistence allowance is payable to solicitors under the Regulations may be obtained form court Officers.

(d) This form, when PARTS I, II and III have been completed should be sent to the Accountant, Department of Justice.

(e) Claims for the payment of allowances to witnesses under the Act should not be made on this form. Such claim should be made on the relevant forms and should accompany this form for payment.

258

2.7   DISTRICT COURT—LEGAL AID FORM L.A. 5

CRIMINAL JUSTICE (LEGAL AID) ACT 1962

CRIMINAL JUSTICE (LEGAL AID) REGULATIONS 1965

**CLAIM FOR FEE FOR MEDICAL OR TECHNICAL REPORT
NECESSARILY REQUIRED FOR USE BY THE DEFENCE
IN A CASE IN RELATION TO WHICH A CERTIFICATE
FOR FREE LEGAL AID HAS BEEN GRANTED**

PART I (to be completed by the person who prepared the report)

1. Name:..

2. Address: ....

3. Professional or technical qualifications:

   ....

4. Subject matter of Report:.......................................

5. Outline of work involved in preparing Report:........................

6. Length of Report (approx. number or words): ....

7. Date of which Report submitted:..

8. Fee claimed:...

   Signed:..

   Date:..

Part II. (to be completed by the Solicitor assigned
    the certificate for free legal aid)

    The certificate for free legal aid relation
    to the case in which the Report referred to
    the Part I was prepared, was granted by
    the (a) ... . Court at (b) ... .
    .... on 20

The Report was required for use by the defence
because (c).................... ....
-

....

I certify that the information given at items 1 to 4
and at items 6 and 7 of PART I is correct

SIGNED:..

NAME OF SOLICITOR'S FIRM: ....

ADDRESS OF SOLICITOR'S OFFICE ....

PART III   (to be completed by the District Court Clerk, county Registrar, or Registrar as
the case may be of the Court which heard the case) transmitted. I certify that a certificate
for free legal aid was granted, as set out in PART II.

Signed: ....

Office held by person signing:..

Date:...

DISTRICT COURT

PART IV (for use in Department of Justice)

         Approved for payment in the sum of € ....

                                      (Signature of approving officer)

                                      Date: ....

(a)   Name of Court.

(b)   Location of Court.

(c)   Give full explanation as to why it was necessary to obtain Report.

CHÚIRT DÚICHE   THE DISTRICT COURT

DUBLIN METROPOLITAN DISTRICT

NOTICE OF APPEAL

COMPLAINT _____ v _____ DEFENDANT

CASE NO(S). FINE NO(S). _____

DATE(S) OF COURT _____ COURT NO(S). _____

TAKE NOTICE THE DEFENDANT HEREBY APPEALS TO THE JUDGE OF THE CIRCUIT COURT AT THE NEXT SITTING OF THE CIRCUIT COURT FOR THE COUNTY AND CITY OF DUBLIN AGAINST THE ORDER(S) MADE BY THE JUDGE OF THE DISTRICT COURT IN THE ABOVE-MENTIONED PROCEEDINGS.

DATE _____ SIGNED _____

(Defendant or his Solicitor)

THIS NOTICE MUST BE SERVED ON:

THE CHIEF CLERK, DUBLIN DISTRICT COURT, ÁRAS UÍ DHÁLAIGH, INNS QUAY, DUBLIN 7.

STATUTORY DECLARATION AS TO SERVICE OF THE NOTICE OF APPEAL ON THE COMPLAINT

I _____ of _____

Do solemnly and sincerely declare that I duly served a copy of the above NOTICE OF APPEAL on the _____ day of _____ 20 _____ , by handing a true copy thereof believing the same to be true and by virtue of the Statutory Declarations Act 1938

SIGNED _____

(Defendant or his Solicitor)

Declared before me by _____ who is personally

Known to me or who is identified to me by _____

Who is personally known to me in District Court No _____ in said District on

the _____ day of _____ 20 _____ .

SIGNED _____

(One of the Judges of the District Court assigned to the said District)

DISTRICT COURT

AN CHÚIRT DÚICHE   THE DISTRICT COURT
DUBLIN METROPOLITAN DISTRICT
NOTICE OF APPEAL

COMPLAINT _____ v _____ DEFENDANT

CASE NO(S) FINE NO(S) _____

DATE(S) OF COURT_____ COURT NO(S) _____

TAKE NOTICE THE DEFENDANT HEREBY APPEALS TO THE JUDGE OF THE CIRCUIT COURT AT THE NEXT SITTING OF THE CIRCUIT COURT FOR THE COUNTY AND CITY OF DUBLIN AGAINST THE ORDER(S) MADE BY THE JUDGE OF THE DISTRICT COURT IN THE ABOVE-MENTIONED PROCEEDINGS.

DATE _____ SIGNED _____

(Defendant or his Solicitor)

THIS NOTICE MUST BE SERVED ON:

THE COMPLAINT AT: _____

- - - - - - - - **DETACH HERE AND KEEP FOR FURTHER REFERENCE** - - - - - - - -
BRIEF INSTRUCTION FOR COMPLETING APPEALS FORMS

1. An appeal should be lodged within 14 days of the Court Order. If you are outside this time limit you must first apply for an extension of Time To Appeal.

2. Complete 2 Notices of Appeal.

3. The Notice of Appeal must be dated and signed by the Defendant or his/her Solicitor and copy served on both the Complainant and The Chief Clerk, Dublin District Court, Áras Uí Dhálaigh, Inns Quay, Dublin 7.

4. You serve the Notice of Appeal on the Complainant first and then you serve the Notice of Appeal on the Chief Clerk.

5. The Notice of Appeal served on the Chief Clerk must be accompanied by:

    • A Statutory Declaration of Service signed by the Defendant or his/her Solicitor stating when the Notice of Appeal was served on the Complainant. This Declaration must be acknowledged by a District Court Judge, a Peace Commissioner or a Commissioner for Oaths.

    • A Recognisance For Appeal signed by the Defendant, surety (if any) and a District Court Judge.

    • If you are making a late Appeal the Court Order extending the time for the lodgement of the Appeal.

    • £10.00 (or euro equivalent) Stamp Duty is payable on some Appeal, eg £10.00 (or euro equivalent) Stamp Duty is payable on Appeals against some cases brought by Dublin Corporation, Dublin Co. Council (arrears of rent/rates).

AN CHÚIRT DÚICHE   THE DISTRICT COURT

COMPLAINT ....

DEFENDANT..

Date of Conviction (or Order) ....

BE IT REMEMBERED that the above-named DEFENDANT

of ....Principal Party

and (name of surety(ies))..

of ....

personally came before me, the undersigned, a Justice of the District Court assigned to said

District and severally acknowledged themselves to owe the State the several sums

following, that is to say, the said Principal Party the sum of.............................euro

and the said Surety(ies) the sum of................................euro (each) to be made

and levied off their several goods and chattels, lands and tenements respectively to the

use of the Minister for Finance if the said Principal Party fail in the condition hereunder.

Signature of Principal party _____

Signature(s) of Surety(ies) _____

TAKEN AND ACKNOWLEDGED this.........day of.........200.........at the Metropolitan

District Courthouse, ..., Dublin in said District before me.

Signed:_____

Justice of the District Court.

THE CONDITION of the above written Recognisance is such that if the said Principal
Party prosecute his/her appeal in these proceedings to the Circuit Court to be held at
Chancery Place, and attend personally at the next sitting of the Circuit Court and from
day to day until such appeal shall have been determined, and abide and perform the
judgment and order of the said Circuit Court thereon and pay such costs as may be
awarded by the said Circuit Court and not to abscond pending the execution of the
original Order or Order of the Circuit Court thereon; then the said Recognisance to be
void; otherwise to remain in full force and effect.

AN CHÚIRT DÚICHE   THE DISTRICT COURT

DUBLIN METROPOLITAN DISTRICT

NOTICE OF INTENTION TO APPLY FOR AN EXTENSION OF TIME TO APPEAL

TO: (1) THE CHIEF CLERK, DUBLIN DISTRICT COURT ÁRAS UÍ DHÁLAIGH, INNS QUAY, DUBLIN 7.

and

TO: (2) THE COMPLAINANT _____

_____

Case/Fine No. _____

TAKE NOTICE that the Defendant _____

of _____

will apply on the (a) _____ 20 _____ at 10:30 am/2:00 pm to the District
court Judge *see below*

sitting at Court No. (b) _____ for an extension of Time to Appeal and/or to fix
Recognisance of Appeal *see below*

in the above case which was heard in Court No. _____ on _____

Signed: _____

Solicitor/Defendant

Date: _____

JUDGE'S ORDER

Time for appeal refused/extended to/for (c) _____
see below

Recognisance for Appeal Self € _____ Surety € _____

Signed: _____

Judge of the District Court

Date: _____

Notes for Completion of Form

(a) You can pick your own date to go to Court, but you **MUST SERVE** a copy of this notice on the Complainant and The Chief Clerk, Dublin District Court, at least **48 hours** before your chosen Court date.

(b) Your application should be made to the Court in which the original penalty was imposed.

(c) THIS IS NOT THE DATE OF YOUR APPEAL but the date by which you MUST HAVE SERVED COMPLETED NOTICE OF APPEAL FORMS ON BOTH THE COMPLAINANT AND THE CHIEF CLERK, DUBLIN DISTRICT COURT. When your application has been heard you should bring this form to the Appeals Office, Áras Uí Dhálaigh, IMMEDIATELY in order that the Appeal Papers can be completed. If the Appeals Papers are not completed the penalty imposed will be enforced.

APPENDIX 3

CIRCUIT COURT

3.1 Indictment

The PEOPLE at the suit of the DIRECTOR OF PUBLIC PROSECUTIONS.

-V-

_____

_____

DUBLIN CIRCUIT CRIMINAL COURT.

BILL NO. _____ / _____

CHARGE PREFERRED TO THE JURY.

STATEMENT OF OFFENCE

Count No 1. Unlawful possession of a controlled drug for the purpose of supply, in contravention of the Misuse of Drugs Regulations 1988 and 1993 made under section 5 of the Misuse of Drugs Acts, 1977 and contrary to section 15 and section 27 (as amended by section 6 of the Misuse of Drugs Acts 1984) of the Misuse of Drugs Acts 1977, as amended by the Criminal Justice Act 2006.

PARTICULARS OF OFFENCE

_____ _____ had on the _____ day of November, _____ in the County of the City of Dublin unlawfully in your possession a controlled drug, to wit Diamorphine, for the purpose of selling or otherwise supplying it to another.

STATEMENT OF OFFENCE

Count No 2. Unlawful possession of a controlled drug, contrary to section 3 and section 27 (as amended by section 6 of the Misuse of Drugs Act 1984) of the Misuse of Drugs Act 1977, as amended by the Criminal Justice Act 2006.

PARTICULARS OF OFFENCE

_____ had on the _____ day of _____ , _____ in the County of the City of Dublin unlawfully in your possession a controlled drug, to wit Diamorphine.

CIRCUIT COURT

STATEMENT OF OFFENCE

Count No 3.   Unlawful possession of a controlled drug for the purpose of supply, in contravention of the Misuse of Drugs Regulations, 1988 and 1993 made under Section 5 of the Misuse of Drugs Acts, 1977 and contrary to Section 15 and Section 27 (as amended by Section 6 of the Misuse of Drugs Acts, 1984) of the Misuse of Drugs Acts, 1977, as amended by the Criminal Justice Act 2006.

PARTICULARS OF OFFENCE

_____ had on the _____ day of November, _____ in the County of the City of Dublin unlawfully in your possession a controlled drug, to wit Cocaine, for the purpose of selling or otherwise supplying it to another.

STATEMENT OF OFFENCE

Count No. 4.   Unlawful possession of a controlled drug, contrary to section 3 and section 27 (as amended by section 6 of the Misuse of Drugs Acts, 1984) of the Misuse of Drugs Act, 1977, as amended by the Criminal Justice Act 2006.

PARTICULARS OF OFFENCE

_____ had on the _____ Day of November, _____ in the County of the City of Dublin unlawfully in your possession a controlled drug, to wit, Cocaine.

APPENDIX 4

HIGH COURT

4.1 High Court—Copy Order 84 Rule 13 Notice

BAIL APPLICATIONS

The attention of practitioners is directed to Order 84 Rule 13 of the Rules of the Superior Courts which requires an application to be made to the Court for an Order to bring up a prisoner to give evidence. Such application should be made at least two clear days before the hearing; and the Notice of Motion (for bail) should have been filed beforehand in the Central Office.

Chief Registrar

High Court—S.I. 811 of 2004—Order 84 Rule15(1)—Rules of the Superior Courts (Bail Applications) 2004

This SI which came into force on 29 December 2004 and provides that the applicant's affidavit shall set forth fully the basis upon which the application is made to the High Court and in particular:

(a) shall give particulars of whether and, if so, in what other Court bail has been refused to the applicant;

(b) shall specify where the applicant is being detained;

(c) shall specify the usual place of abode or address where the applicant normally resides;

(d) shall specify the address at which it is proposed the applicant would reside if granted bail;

(e) shall provide full particulars of the offence or offences with which the applicant is charged;

(f) shall include the identity, address and occupation of any proposed independent surety and of the amount that such surety may offer;

(g) the terms of bail which were previously fixed in relation to the offences (if any);

(h) whether there had been any previous High Court applications for bail in respect of the offences;

(i) whether any warrants for failure to appear have been issued in relation to the applicant;

(j) what surety and/or other conditions relating to bail (if any) the applicant is proposing;

(k) the personal circumstances of the applicant and in particular whether the applicant was legally aided in relation to the charges in any other Court;

(l) any other relevant circumstances.

The affidavit should also set out when and where the applicant last appeared and was remanded to. Copies of all charge sheets, if available, and any other relevant documentation, should be exhibited. The SI should be consulted whenever an affidavit for High Court Bail is being drafted.

4.2   High Court—Notice of Motion Bail Application

THE HIGH COURT

IN THE MATTER OF BAIL APPLICATION

The People (at the suit of the Director of Public Prosecutions)

-v-

_____

AT PRESENT PENDING IN THE DUBLIN METROPOLITAN DISTRICT AT DISTRICT COURT NO 44 CHANCERY STREET IN THE CITY OF DUBLIN.

DRAFT/

NOTICE OF MOTION

TAKE NOTICE that on the_____ day of March_____ at the hour of eleven o'clock in the forenoon or as soon as possible thereafter, Counsel on behalf of the Applicant shall apply to this Honourable Court sitting at The Four Courts in the City of Dublin for:

1. An Order admitting the Applicant to bail on such terms as this Honourable Court shall deem meet.
2. An Order providing for the costs of this application.

AND FURTHER TAKE NOTICE that the said Application shall be grounded on the Affidavit of the applicant which sworn herein the day of_____ , a true copy of which is served herewith, this Notice of Application and Affidavit of Service thereof, the nature of the case and the reasons to be offered.

This_____ day of_____

Signed.

_____ & _____

Solicitors for the Applicant,

_____

_____

Send to: The Registrar   and to: The Chief Prosecuting Solicitor
High Court Central Office   Chapter House, Abbey Street,
Four Court, Dublin 7   Dublin 1

4.3   Grounding Affidavit

THE HIGH COURT

IN THE MATTER OF A BAIL APPLICATION

The People (at the suit of the Director of Public Prosecutions)

-v-

_____

AT PRESENT PENDING IN THE DUBLIN METROPOLITAN DISTRICT AT DISTRICT COURT NO. 44 CHANCERY STREET IN THE CITY OF DUBLIN.

DRAFT/

AFFIDAVIT OF _____

I,_____ Assistant Barman of_____ , _____ In the County of the City of Dublin, aged 18 years and upwards make oath and say as follows:

1. I am the Applicant herein and I make this affidavit from facts within my own knowledge save where it otherwise appears and wheresover appearing I believe the facts to be true.

2. I was arrested on the_____ of February_____ at Chancery Street in the City of Dublin and charged as set out on Fitzgibbon Street Charge Sheets 121/____ , 122/____ and 123/____ and I beg to refer to copies of said Charges upon which pinned together and marked with the letter 'A' I have endorsed my name prior to the swearing hereof.

3. The arresting officer, Detective Garda_____ opposed my application for bail on the said charges on the ground that I have previously failed to appear in Court. I say that I have never failed to turn up in the Court whenever required. On one occasion in or about October_____ a Bench Warrant was issued for my arrest because I was late arriving to Court due to a bus strike. I say that this explanation was given to the presiding District Judge on my arrival in Court and that the explanation was accepted and the said Bench Warrant cancelled.

4. My application for bail was further opposed by Detective Garda_____ on the ground that I would interfere with witnesses. I say that this allegation is untrue and that I do not know the identity of the witnesses. I have not spoken to any witness in this case nor have I made any threats to any witness. I say that I do not know of any other person who may have spoken to or threaten any witness.

5. I reside at_____ , in the County of the City of Dublin and I reside there with my wife and three children. I have lived there for the past seven years. The Gardaí know where I live and can contact me in respect to these charges at any time.

6. I am presently employed as an assistant Barman in [Agent please insert the address of the public house]. I have only recently obtained this employment and I am fearful of losing it if I stay in custody in respect of the said charges.

7. I am innocent of the charges which have been preferred against me and, if granted bail, I will attend Court on the_____ March_____ and on all subsequent remand dates.

8. I will not interfere with any witness or evidence if granted bail by this Honourable Court.

9. I say that if granted bail by this Honourable Court, I undertake to abide by all the terms of my Bail Bond including reporting to the Garda Station on whatever basis as to this Honourable Court may seem just.

HIGH COURT

10. I say that my proposed bails person is my brother_____, who resides at_____ _____ and that he is willing to offer himself as a Surety in the sum of €500.00.

11. I, therefore, pray this Honourable Court for an Order admitting me to bail.

SWORN by the said_____

This 1ˢᵗ day of March_____

At Mountjoy Prison in the County of the

City of Dublin, before me a commissioner for Oaths

And I know the deponent.

_____

COMMISSIONER FOR OATHS

This affidavit is filed by_____ &_____ Solicitors of Ormond Chambers, Ormond Quay in the City of Dublin on behalf of_____ the Applicant herein.

4.4   ## Application to Revoke Bail

THE HIGH COURT

RECORD NO_____

IN THE MATTER OF A BAIL APPLICATION

THE DIRECTOR OF PUBLIC PROSECUTIONS

-V-

_____

Applicant

NOTICE OF MOTION

TAKE NOTICE that on Monday the 27th of July at 11.00 in the forenoon, Counsel on Behalf of the Director of Public Prosecutions will apply to this Honourable Court sitting at the Four Courts in the City of Dublin for Orders in the following terms.

(1) An Order sitting aside the Bail fixed by the District Court sitting at_____ on the 26th day of June,_____

(2) An order refusing the Applicant's Bail.

(3) Such Order or any other such Order as to this Honourable Court shall seem meet and just.

WHICH Application will grounded on this Notice of Motion, the evidence of Garda _____ such oral and other evidence as may be adduced the nature of the case and reasons to be addressed.

Date this_____ **day of**_____

Signed:_____
Chief Prosecuting Solicitor

_____

_____

4.5   **Personal Application Documentation**

FORM A

AFFIDAVIT TO BE SWORN BY A PRISONER ON REMAND AWAITING TRIAL WHO WISHES TO APPLY FOR BAIL TO THE HIGH COURT.

THE DIRECTOR OF PUBLIC PROSECUTIONS

OR

_____ **Complainant.**

V

_____

I,_____ make oath and say as follows.

1.   I am at present in custody in_____ Prison.

2.   I was arrested on the_____ day of_____ and was charged at_____ District Court with the following Offence(s)

     _____

     _____

3.   I was remanded in the custody on the_____ day of_____ to the _____ day of_____ .

OR

I was returned for trial to the next Sittings of the Circuit at_____

4.   I was given liberty to obtain bail in my own surety of €_____ and one independent surety of €_____ or two independent sureties of €_____ each. I have been unable to obtain sufficient sureties.

OR

I was refused bail.

(Strike out whichever is inapplicable).

5.   I ordinarily live at_____

with the following members of my family and am employed at_____

(The general family circumstance of the applicant should be set out in this paragraph).

6.   I wish to apply for bail to the High Court.

OR

I wish to apply for a reduction of the bail which has already been granted to me.

(Strike out whichever is inapplicable).

7. (If applicable) the following person(s) is (are) prepared to go bail for me.

    _____

    _____

    In the sum of €_____ each.

    Name:_____

    Address:_____

    Occupation:_____

    Name:_____

    Address_____

    Occupation:_____

8. I am not in custody on remand awaiting any other charge nor am I serving my sentence on conviction.

9. My grounds for applying for bail are:

SWORN this_____ day of_____
by the above named_____
At_____
In the County of_____
before me a Commissioner for Oaths in
And for the said County and I know
the Deponent.

_____
Signature of Applicant

_____

Commissioner for Oaths

4.6   **Requisition for Copy Order**

Name of Applicant		Reason for Application
Address of Applicant		
Name of Prosecutor		
Name of Defendant		
Address of Defendant		
Charge Sheet Number		
Case number		
Date of Court Order		
Court number		
Result		
Offence details		
Number of orders		
Fee slip attached € per order		
Amount due		
Amount paid		

Date received	Remarks
Date issued	

4.7   Judicial Review—Form 13

THE HIGH COURT

JUDICIAL REVIEW NO_____

Between:

THE DIRECTOR OF PUBLIC PROSECUTIONS

<u>Applicant</u>

-AND-

HIS HONOUR JUDGE_____

<u>Respondent</u>

-AND-

_____

<u>Notice Party</u>

STATEMENT OF GROUNDS OF APPLICATION FOR

JUDICIAL REVIEW

(A) Applicant's name: The Director of Public Prosecutions

(B) Applicant's address:_____ Street, Dublin_____ .

(C) Applicant's description: Statutory Officer, pursuant to the Prosecution of the Offences Act 1974.

(D) Relief sought:

1.   Judicial Review in the form of an Order of Certiorari quashing the Order of the Respondent made herein on the_____ day of September _____ whereby he ruled that the above named Notice Party was unfit to plead, and declined to proceed further with the summonses against him.

2.   Judicial Review in the form of an Order of Mandamus directing the Respondent to proceed with the said summonses.

3.   An Order pursuant to Order 84 Rule 26(4) of the Superior Court Rules 1986, remitting the matter to the respondent to proceed in accordance with the law.

4.   Further or other relief.

5.   Costs.

(E) Grounds upon which relief is sought:

1.   The respondent acted in excess of jurisdiction in finding as a fact that the Notice Party was unfit to plead in the circumstances where there was no medical evidence to that effect before him.

2.   The Respondent acted in excess of jurisdiction in holding that evidence as to the effect of incarceration on the Notice Party was equivalent to evidence as to the Notice Party's fitness to plead.

3.   The Respondent acted in excess of jurisdiction and contrary to the principles of natural and constitutional justice in refusing to allow the Applicant an adjournment in circumstances where an issue arose as to the Notice Party's fitness to plead and the Applicant required time to consider the said issue and, if necessary, arrange for the Notice Party to be examined by an independent doctor.

HIGH COURT

   (F) Name and address of the business of the Solicitor for the Applicant:

_____ Chief_____ Solicitor,_____

Dated this_____ day of_____ _____

Signed:_____

        _____

TO:

The Registrar

Central Office

Four Courts

Dublin 7

And

The District Court Clerk

(on behalf of District Judge_____)

And

_____

_____

And

_____ and Associates,

Solicitors for the Notice Party

4.8   Notice of Motion

THE HIGH COURT
JUDICIAL REVIEW

BETWEEN

THE DIRECTOR OF PUBLIC PROSECUTIONS

APPLICANT

AND

DISTRICT JUDGE_____

RESPONDENT

AND

_____

NOTICE PARTY

DRAFT NOTICE OF MOTION

TAKE NOTICE that on the_____ day of_____ _____ , at the hour of _____ o'clock in the forenoon, or at the first available opportunity there-after, Counsel acting on behalf of the above named Applicant will apply to this Honourable Court, sitting at the Four Courts, Chancery Place, Dublin 7 for the following relief:

1.   An Order of Judicial Review in the form of an Order of Certiorari quashing the Order of the Respondent made herein on the_____ day of September_____ whereby he ruled that the above named Notice Party was unfit to plead, and declined to proceed further with summonses against him.

2.   An order of Judicial Review in the form of an Order of Mandamus directing the Respondent to proceed with the hearing of said summonses.

3.   An order pursuant to Order 84, Rule 26 (4) of the Rules of the Superior Courts 1986, remitting the matter to the Respondent with such direction as to this Honourable Court may deem fit.

4.   Further or other relief.

5.   Costs

     WHICH SAID APPLICATION will be grounded upon within Notice of the Motion, the order of this Honourable Court made on the_____ day of _____ _____ giving leave to apply for Judicial Review of the said Orders, the statement of grounds of Application for Judicial Review, the Affidavit of _____ _____ , Solicitor, together with the documents referred to exhibited therein, an Affidavit of Service of the foregoing documents, the nature of the case and the reasons to be offered.

Dated this_____ day of_____ _____ .

SIGNED_____

    Chief_____ Solicitor

    _____

HIGH COURT

To:

The District Court

(on behalf of the District Court Judge Windle)

(Agent please insert address)

and

_____

(Agent please insert address)

and

_____ and Associates,

Solicitors for the Notice Party

(Agent please insert address)

4.9   Grounding Affidavit

THE HIGH COURT
JUDICIAL REVIEW NO_____

BETWEEN

THE DIRECTOR OF PUBLIC PROSECUTIONS

APPLICANT

AND

JUDGE_____

RESPONDENT

AND

_____

NOTICE PARTY

AFFIDAVIT OF_____

I,_____ State Solicitor, of_____ County_____ aged 18 years and upwards, do Make Oath and say as follows:

1.   I am the State Solicitor for the County of_____ and I have been involved in the prosecution of the Notice Party before the Respondent in relation to the charge which is subject matter of the within proceedings. I make this affidavit from the facts within my own knowledge, save where otherwise appears, and whereso appearing I say and believe the same to be true and accurate.

2.   I say that the Notice Party herein was summonsed to appear before the District Court in relation to a charge of selling intoxicating liquor at_____ County_____ on the_____ of July_____ without taking out the proper licence required by the Finance (1909–10) Act 1910 for the sale of intoxicating liquor, contrary to Section 50 (3) of the Finance (1909–10) Act 1910, as amended by section 69 of the Finance Act 1983 and section 155 (5) of the Finance Act 1992.

I beg to refer to a true copy of the summons served on the Notice Party, upon which, marked with the letter 'A' I have signed my name prior to swearing proof.

3.   I say that under section 78 or the Excise Management Act 1827, as amended by section 70 of the Finance Act 1982, the District Judge is empowered to mitigate the penalty to not less than one half of the full penalty provided for the statue. Under section 78 of the Finance Act 1984, section 1 of the Probation of Offender Act 1907 does not apply.

4.   The matter was first listed for hearing before the Respondent on the_____ of June_____ . On that occasion it was adjourned to the_____ of July_____ as the defending solicitor wished to produce in court the licence, which he believed the Notice Party, has obtained. (If Mr_____ was not present on the_____ of June_____ he should preface the previous information by the words 'I am informed that. . . .'). I understand that the licence was actually taken out on the_____ of July_____ being the day before the resumption of hearing.

5. On the_____ July_____ I appeared on behalf of the Applicant, when the Notice Party pleaded guilty through his solicitor. On hearing that the Notice party had now taken out the relevant licence, the Respondent state that he was dismissing the summons again the Notice Party. I strenuously object to such a course being taken by the Respondent and pointed out that the Respondent could not dismiss the summons and that he should impose the penalty to reduce it to one heal thereof if he so wished. I reminded the Respondent of the Supreme Court decision in the case of Scott Gray. I say that the Respondent did not accept my submission and stated that he was dismissing the charge because if was unfair that the prosecution could fix the penalties in these cases.

6. The Respondent then proceeded to dismiss the said charge and in this regard I beg to refer to a certified copy of the Order made by the Respondent on the _____ of July _____ aforesaid, upon which, marked with the letter 'B' I have signed my name prior to swearing hereof.

7. I say that_____ (please insert name of prosecuting Garda) was present in court and ready to give evident to the Respondent as to the facts of the case, following the Notice Party's plea guilty, so as to enable the Respondent to impose the appropriate penalty, but he was not allowed to do so given the course of action adopted by the Respondent. In the circumstances I therefore pray this Honourable Court for relief in the terns of the Statement of Grounds herein.

SWORN etc.

4.10   **Statement of Grounds of Opposition**

THE HIGH COURT
RECORD NO_____

BETWEEN

_____

APPLICANT

AND

THE DIRECTOR OF PUBLIC PROSECUTIONS

RESPONDENT

STATEMENT GIVING GROUNDS OF OPPOSITION TO
APPLICATION FOR JUDICIAL REVIEW

A.   The Solicitor for the second named Respondent is the Chief_____ Solicitor, _____ ,_____ ,_____ .

B.   The application for Judicial Review is opposed on the following grounds:

(i)   There is no time bar to the prosecution of such offences are charged herein.

(ii)   There has not been alleged or any delay by the Respondent in prosecuting in the Applicant in respect of the charges laid against him.

(iii) If there were delay in making of a complaint against the Applicant, the Applicant has been responsible for the said delay. The complaints were at the time complained of, minors and the Applicant was a priest in a position of dominance and control over him.

(iv)   The lapse of time between the date of commission of the alleged offences and the date of trial is not so great as to give rise to an unavoidable or incurable presumption of prejudice against the Applicant.

(v)   The Applicant has not established that any alleged delay has caused or will cause him to suffer prejudice in the preparation or presentation of his defence to charges laid against him.

(vi)   Insofar as the length of time from the commission of each offence to the date of trial of the Applicant is concerned, same will not be so great as to render the trial unfair, particularly having regard to the capacity and duty of the Trial Judge, by appropriate directions to counter any, alleged prejudice and to secure that the trial the Applicant will be fair in all aspects.

(vii) The Applicant's entitlement to a trial in due course of law and to a trial with reasonable expedition have not been denied in the circumstances.

(viii) The Applicant's constitutional rights will not be denied by permitting the trial of the charges laid against him to proceed.

Dated this_____ day of_____ .

Signed_____
    Chief Prosecuting Solicitor
    Solicitor for the Respondents,

    _____

    _____

HIGH COURT

To:

The Registrar,
The High Court
Central Office,
Four Courts,
Dublin 7.

And

_____ and Co.,

Solicitors for the Applicant

_____

County_____

And

_____

CENTRAL CRIMINAL COURT

For further material and updates to *Criminal Litigation* please visit the Online Resource Centre at www.oxfordtextbooks.co.uk/orc/lsim/.

APPENDIX 6

COURT OF CRIMINAL APPEAL

6.1   **Court of Criminal Appeal—Notice of Application for Leave to Appeal**

Form 3.

Notice of Application for Leave to Appeal

_____

COURT OF CRIMINAL APPEAL

_____

The people at the suit of the Director of Public Prosecutions

V

_____

To the Registrar of the Court of Criminal Appeal.

I,_____

(a) State Offence   having been convicted of the offence of (a) **Murder**
Shortly   and thereupon sentenced to **Life Impt**.

And having applied to the judge who tried me for a certificate that my case was a fit case for appeal,

And having been refused such certificate and being now a prisoner in **Mountjoy Prison**.

[or now living at_____]

(b) Delete words   and being desirous of appealing against my (b) said conviction & _____
as   sentence, do hereby give you notice that I will apply to the Court of
Appropriate   Criminal Appeal for leave to appeal on the grounds hereinafter set
                   forth.

Dated this_____Day of _____ _____

(Signed)

(or Mark) . . . . . .

_____

Applicant

Signature and address of

Witness attesting mark:

_____

Particulars of trial and conviction

1. Date of Trial:_____
2. In what Court: **Central Criminal Court**
3. Sentence:**Life Impt**.

Grounds of application:

Solicitor to supply the grounds.

NOTE:

The applicant should answer the following questions:

(a) Does the applicant desire to be present at the hearing of his application for leave to appeal?. **Yes**.

(b) Does the applicant desire to be present at the hearing of interlocutory application in relation to his application for leave to appeal? . . . .

(935)127738. 10,000 7–80. F.P.–G20

6.2   **Grounds of Appeal**

THE COURT OF CRIMINAL APPEAL

BETWEEN/

THE DIRECTOR OF PUBLIC PROSECUTIONS RESPONDENT

AND/_____ APPELLANT

GROUNDS OF APPEAL

The trial was unsatisfactory on the following grounds:

1. The verdict was unsafe and against the weight of evidence.

2. The Jury attached undue weight to the evidence of the complaint.

3. The learned trial judge erred in law or, in the alternative, erred in a mixed question of law and fact whereby in charging the Jury, the learned Judge failed to direct the Jury adequately or at all as to the lack of corroboration of the Complainant's evidence.

4. The learned Trial Judge erred in law or, in the alternative, erred in a mixed question of law and fact in permitting the Prosecution to call evidence in rebuttal of a Defence witness whereby the character of the witness was put in issue.

5. The verdict of the Jury was unsafe in that the Jury attached undue weight to the evidence of recognition of the Complainant in all the circumstances.

DATED THIS_____DAY OF_____,_____.

SIGNED:_____

　　　　　_____

　　　　　SOLICITOR,

　　　　　_____

　　　　　_____

TO: THE REGISTRAR,
**　　　　 COURT OF CRIMINAL APPEAL,**
**　　　　 FOUR COURTS**
**　　　　 DUBLIN 7**

APPENDIX 7

MISCELLANEOUS DOCUMENTS

7.1   Police Property Documentation

Schedule B
O.31A,. r2(2)

POLICE (PROPERTY) ACT, 1897
Section 1(1)

NOTICE OF APPLICATON FOR AN ORDER FOR
THE DISPOSAL OF PROPERTY

District Court Area of *insert District Court Area*   District No *insert district Area number*

Applicant: insert applicant's name

of: *insert applicant's address*

Respondent: *insert respondent's name*

of: *insert respondent's address*

Whereas the following property has come into the possession of the Garda Síochána at *insert name of Garda station in the said District*

Insert details of property

TAKE NOTICE that the above named applicant, being

    * a superintendent of the Garda Síochána,

    * a claimant of the said property.

Will apply at a sitting of the District Court to be held at *insert district Court location or number* on the *insert date* day of *insert month* 20 *insert year* at *insert time* a.m. *or time* p.m. pursuant to Section 1(1) of the above mentioned Act for an Order for the delivery of the said property to the owner thereof or such Order with respect to the property as to the Court may seem meet

Dated this *insert date*

       Signed:

               Applicant/Solicitor for the Applicant

               To insert respondent's name and address

Note: Please contact the appropriate District Court Office to arrange a court date for the application

*Delete words inapplicable.

MISCELLANEOUS DOCUMENTS

Police Property Documentation

POLICE PROPERTY ACT 1897
Section 1(1)

NOTICE OF APPLICATION FOR AN ORDER FOR THE DISPOSAL OF PROPERTY

INDEX

INDEX

INDEX

INDEX